ON UNDERSTANDING WOMEN

ON UNDERSTANDING WOMEN

By MARY R. BEARD

Editor, *America Through Women's Eyes;*
Author, *Woman as Force in History;*
Co-author, *The Rise of American Civilization*

GREENWOOD PRESS, PUBLISHERS
NEW YORK   1968

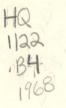

PREFATORY NOTE

THE RISE of modern feminism, the world-wide political up-heavals of the century with their efforts to enlist women as partisans of an old order or a revolution, the new individualist, socialist, fascist, communist and Hitlerite literature on the sub-ject of sex, the avalanche of fiction based on its motif, and the easy habit of generalisation indulged in by psychologists or special pleaders have lured me into an effort to sketch ways that must be traveled before the rôle of women in the civilis-ing process can be understood at all. My perspective is his-torical but historians of competence must lay the fundamental basis for a grasp of the subject merely challenged here. If this outline raises questions, starts disputes, and draws the kind of criticism which will lead to sounder views, I shall consider my daring justified.

Naturally, as a novel undertaking, the book may appear weird and unsymmetrical to the masters of system with a pro-founder knowledge of history. If the reader finds the threads difficult to follow, an examination of the Summary, printed at the end of the volume, may be consulted at any time; in-deed it might be wise to read that first. It contains in concise form the argument which I have tried to develop. There is sure to be an over-emphasis in places but my apology is that, when contentions have long been weighted too much on one side, it is necessary to bear down heavily on the other.

A few acknowledgments are given with full recognition of the writer's shortcomings. Mary A. Nourse, Mrs. Abby Scott Baker, and Mrs. Margaret Wadsworth Genzmer volunteered to spend in the Congressional Library at Washington, D. C., such leisure, as they could command, helping with researches.

MARY R. BEARD

New Milford, Connecticut
September 18, 1931

CONTENTS

PART I

PART II

PART III

PART IV

PART V

PART VI

ON UNDERSTANDING WOMEN

ON UNDERSTANDING WOMEN

PART I

THE SYMPHONY OF LIFE

All life is one
One life is here
One life is there
One life is everywhere

THUS the ancient East intoned its ritual of unity — under the spell of destiny. That was to say: Nature, Humanity, and the Gods are indistinguishable — aspects of the same phenomenon, itself eternal mystery. Out under the open sky in the calm of the desert or close to the heart of the jungle where all life surges ferociously, the simple truth could be apprehended with easy intuition, almost subconsciously. After four thousand years, the rising sun is still greeted in India with uplifted hands and voices chanting: "O blossom of eastern silence . . . bring thou the dawnward way, and be our advocate before the speechless God !" But the West has added verbal elaborations and reinforced the doctrine of unity by the metaphysics of the Greeks, the realism of the theologians, and the symbolism of the higher physics.

Indeed the concept of unity has engaged the minds of thinkers from Thales to Einstein, from Homer to Marx. From the East to the West flowed the idea, or what Croce would call a sense of the Prodigious. Its oldest form Lord Tennyson was continuing to express when he wrote poetically of

One far-off divine event
To which the whole creation moves.

I

Its latest form is written in the language of biology. Thus we are told that all life is one, bound together by the force which unites the population of the waters made up of creatures splendid and insignificant, simple and complex, analysed by scientists with extra eyes called microscopes. Whether they be rotifers or crustacea, hydromedusæ or brachiopodæ the daily life of them all is a battle for existence and the propagation of the species whatever form that contest assumes in any particular case. And to the same fundamental elements and principles the zoölogical orders that inhabit the jungles of the land are reduced by the studies of the scientists who track them to their lairs and examine their habits and anatomy.

When it comes to human beings, however, more complicated divining rods are necessary. Anthropological, archæological, literary and historical aids have to be utilised in the quest for an understanding of the male or the female, owing to the artificial collaterals with which mankind has surrounded its life. Not only extra eyes but an objective mind besides has to be brought into play. Even so, it seems to reinforce the ancient intuitive conviction, based on experience, that one life is here, one life is there, one life is everywhere.

Whether it is the plainsman forced up to mountain retreats by the inroad of enemies mightier than himself and compelled to discover the secrets of the hills or the mountaineer forced down to the valleys by the foes of cold and famine, like a hungry deer, and to adjustments with the strange folkways of another soil. Whether it is the people of the desert impelled cityward and later back to the sands or on to the wilderness as an answer to congestion and boredom. Whether it is the miner in the cavern or the pedant in his academic grove. The geisha in her tea house or the bacteriologist in his laboratory. The Harlem darky with his saxophone or the winner of the Prix de Rome. Each is blood brother or sister to every other human being, at least on the plane of physical want and the effort to gratify it. Viewed narrowly, all life is universal hunger and an expression of energy associated with it. Food in savagery. Food in civilisation. Clothing for æsthetes. Nudity for rebels. Sex in the raw. Sex under restraint. Shelter in caves, huts, and palaces.

Linked with unity there prevails everywhere, in forms high or low, the concept of destiny — an immense movement of forces overruling the little designs of men and women, nations, races, and empires. In part these forces are physical and have to do with physical needs and energies, but to all appearances they transcend material requirements, driving human puppets like leaves before a gale.

At one moment Napoleon could say to Goethe: "What have we to do with Destiny?" that favorite theme of the older poetry. But the very next instant he could cry out that he, with all his might, was but the child of Destiny. Certainly absorption in its tragic concept — that is, in the direction of energy which Spengler calls the "logic of time" — is a "fact which suffuses the whole of mythological, religious, and artistic thought and constitutes the essence and kernel of all history." Before the very altar to the Unknown God was pursued a search for light upon Fate, the Unknowable.

Everywhere this sense of destiny colors thought. Now it is the Japanese, enclosed by seas on a set of little islands topping volcanoes, who are curious about the significance of the "divine winds" which carry men and women and nations onward to their ends. Again it is the luxurious and relatively secure American, possessing half a continent, boasting like Napoleon about the manifestness of his destiny, who matures like Napoleon in questioning fate and the future, as the earth trembles beneath his feet. The yogi's mentality may be content with poverty, asceticism and Nirvana, as other minds at the opposite extreme are lulled by wealth, sensuousness and motion. But where thinking, rather than feeling, is found, all speculation on the nature of things, all effort to understand them involves reference to drift and potentialities, no less than to achievements, follies, and failures.

Among the ancients of Europe the conclusion was reached that the tendency of destiny was circular or perhaps represented only a drop from a golden age into turmoil and wickedness from which no earthly rescue was possible. In a rare summary, Marcus Aurelius drew the limits for meditation in his age: "The rational soul wanders round the whole world and through the encompassing void, and gazes into infinite time, and considers the periodic destructions and rebirths of the universe, and reflects that our posterity will see nothing new, and that our ancestors saw nothing greater than we have seen. A man of forty years, possessing the most moderate intelligence, may be said to have seen all that is past and all that is to come; so uniform is the world." Imperialism, Pax Romana, oligarchy, state religion, slavery and militarism were the staples of consciousness for mankind back through the centuries to Aurelius and beyond. In his time, philosophers still believed in a golden age in the dim and distant past which had been dissolved by the natural process of decay and death or by a cataclysmic blow delivered by revengeful gods to whom all mortals were mere clay. This ideology — the concept of a Garden of Eden and its closure — Europeans received as an Eastern legacy though they were prepared by their own myths to receive it cordially.

Such Greeks as Æschylus and Euripides realised that human beings had once inhabited dark caves and had lived the life of cave dwellers but they had an ingenious explanation for that state of affairs based on the traditional belief in the degeneration of man — the law of social cycles resembling birth and death for individuals. Even as late as the eighteenth century the French scientist, Buffon, was revamping this identical legend when he declared that the process of decay would speed up in the New World because it was divorced from the Old World culture and would drag down with it fauna and flora. So seriously was the idea taken that Thomas Jefferson in his study of plants and animals in Virginia undertook to overthrow the gloomy prophecy in part.

Nor did Christianity do much to offset the morbid philosophy of doom. Perhaps it helped to increase the pessimism which regarded the world as laboring heavily under its Day of Judgment for it dwelt upon the brevity and vanity of earthly concerns and sought to confine all hope to a new golden age — to come, after death, in heaven.

It was not until the modern age that the concept of destiny as human progression wilfully planned toward desirable ends on earth began to work a revolution in the ancient idea of doom for all, men and women, states and orders alike. To be sure, ships were slightly improved by the ancients, strides were made in mathematics, and amazing advances were achieved in the arts; but on the whole modes of living remained very much the same through the long centuries as Marcus Aurelius had known them, the dissolutions of war making the chief breaks in the treadmill. Among the ancients, Seneca was almost alone in suspecting that the idea of destiny as a vicious circle of things was not in keeping with the facts or the possibilities of the human scene. Nor did the mediæval theologians with all their speculating and delving go beyond him. Indeed the very system of thought within which they worked — the Garden of Eden, the fall of man, and redemption — was as rigid as the treadmill of fate on which Marcus Aurelius saw mankind forever laboring.

With the advent of modern science and invention, however,

the law of obedience to the iron rule of destiny was broken. Experimentation became the great privilege and pleasure. Then it was realised that at least certain elements of fate, such as epidemics, famines, and kindred calamities, could be overcome by the advance of understanding and by applications of positive knowledge. Yet when viewed in a larger setting the idea of freedom for mankind through knowledge and the conquest of fugitive forces still operates within the concept of unity and destiny. As science works outward in its searches and applications, it constantly comes upon the interrelations of energy and finds it impossible to draw sharp lines anywhere in the world of mind, matter, and force, to use traditional terms. Nor can those who seek to escape a tragic destiny through increasing knowledge avoid the thought that all their labors and achievements have grown and must continue to grow out of the nature of things; were implicit in the scheme of things in the beginning.

Such then seem to be the conclusions to which we are led in every effort to understand atoms, societies, states, men, or women. Of course any one may start in blithely at any particular point on any particular theme and, as long as he naïvely narrows his horizon, can proceed with artificial confidence. But those who seek to get their bearings before they set sail on an intellectual expedition must take a look at the Scylla and Charybdis of unity and destiny.

THE WORLD AS APPEARANCE OF DIVERSITY

OTHERWISE this world of human beings, conceived by philosophers as a unity evolving under destiny, is simply a world of scattered things, bewildering in its forms of diversity. Thus we may say, by way of illustration, that the "man's world" is made up of:

mountaineers carving homes and communities out of stony crags or shaping them from logs and boughs within the timber line

lumber-jacks trekking over the globe in the wake of receding forests to hunt more trees for buildings and ships, for furniture and bric-à-brac

woodmen following fuel to cities where they prepare it for urban fires, sawing, sawing, sawing until they can earn enough to return to deforested fields and learn to till them

muleteers tramping weary miles beside beasts sometimes laden only with tiny sticks for the market — all that is available in an arid region

shepherds yodelling to fugitive lambs on wide-reaching plains or hillsides

coolies crawling in the muck of rice fields or contesting for places on the Bunds with the guards of alien masters

miners digging in the caverns for coal or precious ores

peasants bent and grubbing over crops or plodding to consumers with their produce, to Belgrade, Canton, numerous towns in Europe and Asia, now fairly prosperous, now starving and re-lapsing into banditry

terrace-makers, plotting napkin-sized farms in the midst of lava and rock occasionally ruined by the invasion of a telegraph pole

engineers making dykes and dams, bridges and aqueducts, trans-porting humanity and freight from place to place over land and sea, over lofty peak and open vale, puffing, running, oiling, loading, dumping, reloading on and on and on interminably

farmers driving tractors over vast level spaces

fishermen, seamen, and other amphibious beings, pals of danger and conquerors of the deep

burden-bearers with their Atlas loads of boxes and bales, sewing-machines and cupboards, pianos and pigs, in lieu of railways carrying the world's goods on their backs

human horses trotting, panting, coughing, between shafts, through rain and sleet and sun often with no shelter by day or by night

traders selling everything from worn rubber tires for the soles of Balkan shoes to the intestines of Chinese pigs for European sausage skins

manufacturers producing Fords for Thibet, Birmingham gods for Oriental heathen, silk hats for African chiefs, comforts, baubles, luxuries and trinkets

chauffeurs showing would-be Hannibals the vistas from the Alps

airmen rushing from Berlin to Moscow to Tokyo to London to

New York to Mexico City to Saigon, spanning continents and seas, testing wings and weights

builders of empire surveying the fringes of industrialised areas for chances to expand their enterprise

cookie-pushers distributing diplomatic confections to ladies at tea in the interims of more martial excitements

guides circulating misinformation to innocents abroad demanding sensations

telegraphers flashing messages over the wires concerning births and deaths, marriages and divorces, hotel reservations, business deals, greetings, felicitations, appointments, disasters

station-masters directing the movements of trains and passengers in the magnificent metropolis and on the lonely trails

policemen watching the wayward and protecting property and life

clerks in offices and warehouses sorting and recording decisions, transactions, shipments, losses and profits

lawyers arguing, reviewing, defending, prosecuting, denying, judging, liberating, or condemning their fellow creatures to imprisonment and death

doctors patching up nerves, bones and brains

priests and preachers working with souls — at sunset for Allah, at sunrise for Fundamentalists, at midnight on Russian festivals, and every day, every hour for special purposes

waiters, tailors, shoeshiners, porters, doormen, and lackeys in hostelries, feeding and furbishing the guests however querulous, dirty, hungry, insolent or ill

missionaries trying to standardise the wages of sin and virtue

scientists in laboratories brewing in test tubes, examining through lenses the composition of the universe, combining elements, announcing theories

writers transferring to paper their emotions, their inherited beliefs, their hopes, their fears, their dreams

artists and architects working for patrons private and confident of taste or public, fickle and diffident

officials perfunctory, aggressive, genial, wise and foolish, ruling, supervising, intervening in the manners of men and women

orators swaying those who can be affected by rhetoric to accept their leadership in war and peace

magicians whirling themselves or their toys in popular entertainment for the effects of motion on the retina of the eye, on the breathing of the heart, on the action of the mind

diplomats juggling words for courts, republican and monarchical athletes racing, jumping, pounding, pushing, throwing, clutching, rowing, riding, driving, yelling and expiring

politicians playing the classical yet self-renewing game, perilous or futile, grave or gay, for stakes great or small

radio operators broadcasting rhythms for twentieth century youth to dance by, news that shakes the world, speeches, concerts, weather warnings, market prices, news of goods that are ready to be bought and sold

inventors applying the learning of the laboratory to the making of new tools with a view to saving labor, providing pleasure, eliminating waste

scholars scanning the ideas and events of the past, assembling and classifying data, repeating and expounding, directing neophytes

collectors of fauna, flora, art and implements, costumes and the records of people dead and gone

conspirators planning what and whom they may devour

organisers and executives forcing their contemporaries into molds conformable with strange designs

persecutors still looking for witches to hang or burn and finding them of course

criminals

kings trying to stem the tide of democratic revolution which tends to engulf them all

courtiers and sycophants heralding and lauding their overlords

jesters evoking laughter subtle or ribald

boulevardiers parading the Corsos in proud remembrance of the days when men were the cocks of the walk

creators and distributors of women's wear, cosmetics, and perfumes determining the tastes and modes of females

workers in woods and metals, in stone and leather, in kingfisher feathers and ivory, in chemicals and abstractions

makers of opiates counting that day lost whose slow-descending sun finds no new body drugged, no feeble resistance overcome

soldiers drilling and fighting, protecting and defiling, obeying orders, mutinying, singing pæans, cursing, dying boldly, hobbling on crutches, begging in the streets, strutting, supplying the raw material of legend, poetry and song, of religion, art and social organisation, their banners flying, bands playing, leaders shouting, victorious in battle, haggard in defeat, vain of glory, cruel of lust, impatient for sons to maintain the traditions of conquest or revenge

lovers, free and bound.

Or we may say that the "woman's world" consists of:

urban market women shifting wares, exhibiting and selling cattle, fruit, cakes, vegetables and flowers, beribboned, bebustled, becapped, proud and lusty competitors with one another in quality and style

country producers, all working still at the home, garnering harvests, cooking meals, minding offspring, caring for the sick beside their own hearths and answering calls from afar, watching sheep on lofty sky lines, carding, dyeing, shaping clothes, blankets, rugs, transforming flax and wool into sheets, towels, garments, household decorations and comforts, spinning as they guard the flocks by day, knitting as they lead them to shelter by night, conceiving designs for textile ornamentation, embroidering, comparing work with neighbors, judging art, training maidens in domestic crafts, tramping and climbing, carrying water, sometimes riding the donkey, washing in the holes and streams, endlessly washing, supplying clean apparel whatever the physical cost, mending, combining and recombining old clothes into new with fancy stitching, sending men folks to town resplendent in rosebud sox and bright bread-bags, milking goats and cows, feeding poultry and pigs, gathering up the eggs, washing the pots and pans, making and nursing the fires, wielding brooms and brushes, weaving baskets and mats, devising presents for celebrations, toiling for daughters and weddings

cooks, priestesses of the holy stove, peeling, chopping, mixing, roasting, garnishing, pushing into the oven and pulling forth life-giving food for the hungry, studying dietetics for infants, for the invalid, for the hale and the hearty, for the dependent poor, in bondage, free and humanistic

nurses slaving for the injured and the invalid in orphanages and asylums, in hospitals and on the battlefields, publicly, privately, by district visitation in town or village, in leper colonies, on request, for pay, filially, socially, religiously emigrating from Occident to Orient at the urging of the Church, repeating ancient practices and instigating reforms

schoolmistresses disciplining infancy and youth in ways of virtue and paths to learning, over-righteous and stolid, original and imaginative, holding back and leading on the interminable procession of the fresh-born

veiled women peering through artificial obstructions on the ways of gods and men, eluding parents to let their faces shine before

all people at hours of the promenade, daring to cast off traditions on their own initiative when nationalism is involved or
to obey behests of the State

seamstresses in cities modelling custom-mades for the meticulous
and the opulent

operators with machines turning out the ready-mades for the poor
or hurried multitudes

shoppers window-gazing, longing, spending, spending, spending,
making the industrial wheels go round and determining their
output, fingering, sorting, bargain-hunting armed with elbows,
stacking high the lingerie and trinkets

sales-girls waiting on the ladies and plotting to be ladies in their
turn, rubbing nails and powdering their noses

secretaries managing offices while their chiefs strut and stride, faithful, competent, successful, ambitious, pantherine, crafty, long-
suffering, confidential, and loyal

modern karyatids with baskets of fruit and flowers on their heads
or jugs on their shoulders making offerings in temples and
marts

beasts of burden lugging bags at railway stations, running uphill
with heavy packs on their backs, walking upright freighted
between home and shop, between field and field, now laden
with a wee cargo of sticks discovered by hard exploration, now
with injured lambs or goats from the pasture, again with coal
or greater treasure for a client, at least with babies and then
not so straight of spine what with the clumsy tots plunging or
sleeping, often bent nearly double with objects to tote upstairs
and down, water for bathers, fuel for grates, meals and parcels,
luggage and bedding

charwomen down on their knees scrubbing business blocks, kitchens,
stoops, black of gown, red of hands, rheumatic in bones, dreaming asleep and awake of mops and rags and suds

domestic servants and factory employees and flappers struggling to
swim through the breakers of economic tides

exotic entertainers firing young blood, circus performers, swan and
nose divers, rodeo strategists, parachutists, and high kickers

domestic amusers with babies, one baby this year, another next,
possibly one free year, then twins, one's own, one's employer's,
pushing carts, scolding, chattering, spanking, laughing, wheedling, nursing, bottling, with nice babies, lovely babies, cross
babies, sick babies, babies learning to walk and babies that won't
walk, anyway babies

dog fanciers and tenders

actresses putting new wine into old bottles to tempt the uninitiated
and excite the jaded

hostesses promoting trade, letters and philosophy, marrying off their
sons and daughters, allaying tedium

innovators, in the prize ring, at Olympic games, in parliaments, in
the air, in forum and college, in law and religion, in science
and letters, in business and the arts, exploring, rushing, spying,
Amazonic, shy, resourceful, sensational, important, unimportant

gamblers counting on gaming to escape the pains of labor and
thought

street walkers prowling for prey

slaves toiling in brothels, little girl brides, chattels

evangelists with wiles and warnings inflaming the hearts of the
simple and piling up for themselves treasures upon earth

social workers doing unto the least of His brethren that which the
Christ asked in tribute to Himself

fighters and fans and freelovers

warblers and painters and sculptors and poets

novelists absorbed in the mating and forsaking of the sexes

psychics, astrologers, clairvoyants, mediums, telling fortunes and
linking the ages of fear and the fates

gold star mothers offering sons to Mars and patriotism.

Across the diversities presented in the life of men and women
cut the lines of human categories — racial, class, intellectual,
and occupational:

Britons, Scotch, Nordics, Latins, Irish, Welsh, Germans, French,
Americans, Turks, Orientals, Japanese, or Chinese

water gypsies dwelling ever on the waves, courting, marrying, re-
producing, trading, loading and hauling, fighting for business,
struggling to make headway against "love, law and chance"

pygmies of the African interior living close to nature, remote from
seas and commerce

Indians trying to wrest an existence from the cacti of the desert

Bushmen providing favorite data for anthropology

the precious and dilettante classes of the cities

dwellers on the Main Streets of the world

intelligentsia

sects

reformers
performers
tourists
Negroes aping the manners of the whites
Whites emulating the tastes and conduct of the blacks
Yellows modernising their races
Occidentals turning to Mohammed or Buddha for adventurous relief
   from monotony or responsibility
Orientals seeking in Christianity a rejuvenation from apathy
labor organisations and federations, farmers and peasants
Fascists knitting an international alliance with the threads of armed
   dictatorships
the powerful and the weak, the inarticulate and the verbose
individualists, socialists, communists, anarchists, Ku Kluxers and
   Nazis
the sheep and the goats
activists and passivists.

WRITTEN HISTORY AS ASPECTS AND FRAGMENTS

THOUGH more or less aware of the overshadowing concepts
of unity, destiny and progress, the writers of history, even the
widest in outlook, seize upon mere aspects of the whole, fragments of the diversity, incidents in the drama. Thus the well
of information upon which the human mind must draw for an
understanding of men or women is clogged with wrecks,
débris, and accidental accumulations. Over written history the
gods of chance and chaos have evidently presided. Everything
seems to depend upon the historian — his locus in time and
space, the mere detail of birth, affiliations of class, and the
predilections of sheer uncritical emotions.

One thing is certain. Few of the writers of history have
played any large part in its making. It is true that Cæsar
wrote a political tract on the Gallic war which is cherished as
history and that many of the great of old have arrayed themselves for posterity in memoirs. But in the main the compila-
tion, arrangement, and interpretation of facts called written

history have been committed to clerks on the side lines. And nowhere has the hypnotic element of patronage, royal, class or popular, been wanting. Histories have been written to please monarchs, flatter castes, landed and capitalist and laboring, and to beguile multitudes. For centuries historians were concerned principally with war and politics — the prime preoccupations of ruling aristocracies founded on land. With the rise of manhood suffrage, political parties were drawn into the historical record. Finally in our own time when economic democracy thrusts itself into the world forum in thunderous tones, history widens a little to include "social movements," reluctantly, stubbornly yielding ground to the inevitable. As the advent of modern institutionalised education opened the way for women to study with the high priests in Clio's temple, they easily slid into the grooves worn smooth by tradition, assuming with humility and without thought the garb of the disciple.

When the roll of the fragmentists who have written history is called, the inner sources of their intellectual partiality become apparent. Herodotus, "the Father of History," entertained his public with travelogues, gleaning his materials in Egypt largely from holy men. Thucydides tells us that "before his time no events of importance had occurred in the world," and as a military man and administrator, he made war and politics the chief concern of his own time. Polybius and Tacitus treated history largely as a contemporary political contest, interspersed with colorful details respecting the populations involved, geographical surroundings, and origins of Roman power. As a modern critic remarks, in reviewing a new biography of Tiberius, "Tacitus wrote so well and had such genius in character drawing that he formed the reputation of Tiberius for nineteen hundred years; and in consequence modern critical historians have to begin the life of Tiberius with a biography and psychological analysis of his historians. Add that one of

the chief sources for the life of Tiberius, after Tacitus, is Sue-
tonius, who had the mind of the city editor of a tabloid, and
you can hardly wonder that so many modern historians have
had to labor for the rehabilitation of Tiberius."

After the ancients had passed and Christian historians came
upon the scene, other great interests were dominant in historical
writing. The least among the scribes were monkish chron-
iclers making "pitiful compendiums" out of such things as
crossed their cloistral horizon: "This year was the great wind
on Thomas'-mass-night, this year died the great . . . in this
year the tribute was delivered, in this year appeared comet and
archbishop . . . died . . . in this year was Bamborough entered by storm and much booty taken . . . this year the army
went . . . this year the army stole away . . . this year the army
made peace . . . this year wondrous adders were seen in the
land of the South-Saxons. . ."

The greatest of the mediæval historians, besides using the
chronicle method, bent their energies to justifying the Christian
faith, showing why so many dreadful events were let loose by
the devil, immortalising the founders of the Church, working
over for Christian purposes the pagan legends of European
peoples, and explaining the dualism of good and evil by reference to the wickedness of sex, guided by women vamping under
the direction of the serpent.

While the mediæval historians were still busy building up
their epics, the period in which they worked was closed in a
terrific battle between State and Church, known as the "Reformation," and this was followed shortly by a mighty contest
between the new divine-right monarchs and the rising bourgeoisie enriched by the profits of world exploration and trade
and prepared to wage wars over the wealth of empires. Until
our own time this struggle had raged. Naturally the historians
of the bourgeois epoch dedicated themselves to politics and

war, attacking and defending the course of events by reference
to the past.   Constitutional battles, Cromwell, the Great Frederick, Napoleon the First, revolution and nationalism occupied
their attention and from their respective canvases all was excluded that did not suit the drama dictated by their major
interests.

Gibbon was popular because he was a free-thinker in the
age of reason, even though his particular free-thinking and
reason consisted of rebellion against a domineering ecclesiastical
institution.   Ranke waded in laboriously for data on war and
politics and as Spengler says "is a good example of the historian
who frankly excluded all material not germane, fitting into his
scheme of life."   Macaulay was a Manchester Whig, concerned
with defending the particular excellence of his party and promoting commercial expansion.   John Richard Green took
pains to rewrite the pageantry of England in terms pleasing
to his middle-class constituents, having an eye to the tenderness
of the non-conformist conscience.   Treitschke told a long tale
in an effort to swell the dignity of Prussia under the indomitable
Hohenzollerns.   And so one might proceed in an analysis of
historical biases.

Only at the dawn of the twentieth century did it occur to
the historians to look at themselves, inquire into the causes of
their emphases and fragmentism.   As James T. Shotwell points
out in his *Introduction to the History of History,* "Until recently, history itself has lacked historians. . . The history of
history had to await the rise of scientific historical criticism before it attracted the attention even of historians. . . And yet
the history of history demands rather than invites attention. . .
For the history of history is the story of that deepening memory
and scientific curiosity which is the measure of our social consciousness and our intellectual life."   After dealing with various
interpretations as they finally appeared, he concludes that the

"historical interpretation of interpretations themselves" is the climax of the study and "less ambitious than theological, philosophical, or even economic theories, it views itself as part of the very process which it attempts to understand."

In these circumstances it is not surprising that written history — the chief source of knowledge about human affairs — has abandoned the unity of life and neglected one-half of the beings that have made up the human world. Insisting that "Woman is History," Spengler in the next strange breath declares that "Man makes History." He might well have put an addendum to the effect that man has composed most of the written history, giving to the normal accumulation of biases the bent of sex. H. G. Wells has provided numerous illustrations of the way it is done. For instance he says: "Of Amenophis IV we shall have more to tell later, but of one, the most extraordinary and able of Egyptian monarchs, Queen Hatasu, the aunt and stepmother of Thotmes III, we have no space to tell. She is represented on her monuments in masculine garb, and with a long beard as the symbol of wisdom." Queen Hatasu, on Wells' confession, was "the most extraordinary and able of Egyptian monarchs" but while he has space for the less significant, he has none for her.

Throughout·his outline history of the world, Wells keeps the single-mindedness of the man. When he digresses from the story of his kind and refers to women, he finds space to comment on the extreme corpulence of fat females — among primitive peoples whose "women were probably squaws . . . grossly fat, almost as the Bushmen women are often fat today." Accidentally he encounters women as household servants among the Aryans. Incidentally he discovers that the Sumerians had priestess-queens and indeed a goddess, Ishtar. He believes that Ikhnaton was weakened by domesticity. He inclines to Aristotle's view of the Greek times, as that view has been commonly reported, that women were unfit for freedom. He notes that "most women were married" in early America. Of such dominant women in history as Olympias of Macedon he cannot be ignorant but his preference is decidedly for Philip and he lays Alexander's general insanity on the heritage from his mother, overlooking qualities of the father which Bercovici brings into the horrible family picture.

According to Wells, man even raised the curtain on culture as the farmer, cook and artisan. Speaking of primitive beginnings, he says: "Neolithic men cultivated and ate wheat, barley and millet. . . Their grain they roasted, ground between stones and stored in pots, to be eaten when needed. . . In the ancestral lands of the Southeast men had already been sowing wheat perhaps for thousands of years. . . Probably he prepared the ground for his sowing with a pole. . . Fire was too troublesome to make for men to be willing to let it out readily. . . Man storing graminiferous grasses for his cattle might easily come to beat out the grain for himself." Perhaps Wells means Man-woman by the term Man but in that case the word is peculiarly unsuitable because the female of the species in the very infancy of the race initiated the industrial arts and, according to the best if still tentative findings of present-day anthropology, probably agriculture besides.

Critics less popular than Wells, more scientific in pretensions and more universal in their claims, are guilty of the same lapses in thinking. Take for example that compendium of history, the *Encyclopædia Britannica*. Men whose manuscripts are not extant and who are merely mentioned by the ancients in passing are admitted by its editors to the list of immortals whereas no such honor is paid Theano, Arete, or Leontium, among other women, about whom as much is actually known and who were deemed worthy of higher recognition by their contemporaries. According to this scheme of selection, the records of the varied activities of modern women might easily slip from the writings of future historians and biographers, the one-sided narrative of mortal aspiration, ambition, and achievement going on forever, an injustice in itself, and a hindrance to accurate sex judgments.

This is no idle speculation. If the historians of the twenty-fifth century, let us say, should have access to no other fragment of our time in the field of science than the introduction or advertisement of the *Biographical Dictionary of American Men of Science,* they would naturally come to the conclusion that women of this century could not enter laboratories, were not interested in science, and had no deeds, large or small, to their credit, in that realm.

That interesting prelude runs as follows: "It is hoped that the publication will be a contribution to the organisation of science in America. There is here given for the first time a fairly complete survey of the scientific activity of a *country* * at a given period. As a reference book for the field it covers, it may be even more useful in academic circles than *Minerva* or *Who's Who in America.* But the chief service it should render is to make *men* of science acquainted with one another and with one another's work. There scarcely exists among scientific *men* the recognition of common interest and the spirit of coöperation which would help to give science the place it should have in the community. It is fully as important for the *nation* as for *men* of science that scientific work should be adequately recognised and supported. We are consequently in the fortunate position of knowing that whatever we do to promote our *own* interests is at the same time a service to the *community* and to the *world.*"

Now if the student of our age working in the twenty-fifth century had available only this fragment from the truly useful

* Italics mine.

Dictionary, he or she would never suspect that among the 13,500 *men* whose biographical sketches appear between the covers, at least 150 *women* of science are included among the ABCs alone. Assuming that such an average is sustained throughout the work, there are more than a thousand women deemed worthy of secret mention, if not publicity. The ratio may not be large but the proportion of one woman to twelve or thirteen men is significant, especially when the whole problem of access to laboratories, research funds, appointments, and training is considered. However of such fragmentism and accidents of record is written history made.

Naturally women would be less than human if they did not expect more than this at the hands of the noted psychologist, Professor Cattell, who has edited the collection of worthies. Though it may be a mere slip caused by masculine preoccupation, it cuts at the root of truth as fact and contributes to the prevalence of the opinion that the world of scientific thought is a shut-in academy or retreat for men only. Yet in justice it must be said that the selection of scientific women, whose biographies and achievements are chosen for inclusion in the *Dictionary,* is based on systematic criteria, while the inclusions in the *Encyclopædia Britannica* seem to be wholly fortuitous — mixers of love potions gaining admission while important writers, physicists, and mathematicians are denied entry.

While Professor Cattell is enough of a realist to admit women of science to the pages of his record, his European colleagues are often less generous. The French historian, M. Alphonse de Candolle, writing in the late nineteenth century, *Histoire des Sciences et des Savants depuis deux Siècles,* excluded women by fiat from the rational gild. He based an intelligence test on the roster of the Academy without examining, as a man of science should, the conditions surrounding the admission of members or the bestowal of public honors, and then proceeded to render a final verdict upon the capacity of women to climb his Olympus: "Le développement de la femme s'arrête plus vite que celui de l'homme et chacun sait que les études à l'âge de 16 à 18 ans comptent plus beaucoup dans la production d'un savant de distinction. En outre, l'esprit féminin est primesautier. Il se plaît aux idées qu'on saisit vite, par une sorte d'intuition. Les méthodes lentes d'observation ou de calcul, par lesquelles on arrive sûrement à des vérités, ne peuvent lui plaire. Les vérités elles-mêmes, abstraction faite de la nature et de leurs conséquences possibles, sont peu de chose pour la plupart des femmes — surtout les vérités générales, qui ne touchent à aucun individu en particulier. Ajoutez une faible indépendance d'opinion, une faculté de raisonnement moins intense que chez l'homme, et enfin l'horreur du doute, c'est-à-dire d'un état de l'esprit par lequel toute recherche dans les sciences d'observation doit commencer et souvent finir. En voilà plus qu'il ne faut pour expliquer la position des femmes dans les affaires scientifiques. Disons, pour les consoler, que

> Sur ce fait
> Bon nombre d'hommes sont femmes."

That is to say, in the words of M. de Candolle, women are insufficiently rational, independent and sceptical for the slow methods of observation and calculation by means of which scientific truths are reached. Yet Marie Curie had many predecessors whom the Frenchman might readily have known.

Even the "originator of The New History," Professor James Harvey Robinson, who can with justice claim to have widened the conception of historical construction, writes with a consciousness of kind akin to that displayed by his former collegiate associate, Professor Cattell: "In the formation of what

we may call our historical mind — namely, that modification
of our animal and primitive outlook which has been produced
by *men* [italics mine] of exceptional venturesomeness. . ."
After which, in dealing with the middle ages, he offers a
summary in a similar vein: "Schools were closed, to be reopened later here and there, after Charlemagne's edict, in an
especially enterprising monastery or by some exceptional bishop
who did not spend his whole time in fighting." Apparently
the Abbess of Whitby and other Sisters who founded schools
and taught there were not there at all. Evidently the rôle of
women in the civilising process from primitive times has
escaped Robinson's observation.

Nor do writers on historical jurisprudence always avoid the
practice of treating their subject as a mere phase of the man's
world. Accustomed to dealing with the forms of the law
rather than the practices within its charmed circle and entirely
outside it, they display a tendency to emphasize, in the English-
speaking societies at least, the terms of the common law, as
expounded by Blackstone, which extinguished the personality
of the married woman, and to overlook the offsetting exceptions furnished by equity and by customs that never got within
reach of the ordinary law courts. Maitland, an unquestioned
authority on English Constitutional History, says that "Blackstone, like other common lawyers, was not very fond of the
chancery. The view of the thinking English lawyer of his
time seems to have been that the chancery was a necessary
evil, though they were unwilling to confess what may seem
to be the truth, namely, that trial by jury was becoming an
antiquated form of trial inadequate to meet the complicated
problems which arise under modern law. . . I believe that
we may think of equity as becoming a fixed and well ascertained body of law towards the end of the seventeenth century;
perhaps 1688, the year of the Revolution, would be as good

a year as any to name. . . Equity in the course of the eighteenth century became a great body of rules supplementing the common law, enforcing certain obligations which common law did not enforce, giving certain remedies which the courts of common law did not and could not give."

In fifteenth century England a great many women were active traders on their own account or equal partners with their husbands and so recognised at law. In *Liber Albus,* the White Book of the City of London, compiled in 1419 by the common clerk, John Carpenter, and the Mayor, Richard Whittington, decisions recognising their independent status are recorded.

One such, entitled "The case of a Wife trading alone," states that "Where a woman *coverte de baron* follows any craft within the said city by herself apart, with which the husband in no way intermeddles, such woman shall be bound as a single woman in all that concerns her said craft. And if the husband and wife are impleaded, in such case, the wife shall plead as a single woman in a Court of Record, and shall have her law and other advantages by way of plea just as a single woman. And if she is condemned, she shall be committed to prison until she shall have made satisfaction; and neither the husband nor his goods shall in such case be charged or interfered with." Students of Blackstone might suppose that every English husband was always liable for his wife's debts.

In another case, entitled "Of hiring House," the decision reads: "If a wife, as though a single woman, rents any house or shop within the said city, she shall be bound to pay the rent of the said house or shop, and shall be impleaded and sued as a single woman, by way of debt if necessary, notwithstanding that she was *coverte de baron,* at the time of such letting, supposing that the lessor did not know thereof."

A third case entitled "Of Debt" is also illuminating by reason of the decision that closed it: "Where plaint of debt is made against the husband, and the plaintiff declares that the husband made the contract with the plaintiff by the hand of the wife of such defendant, in such case, the said defendant shall have the aid of his wife, and shall have a day until the next Court, for taking counsel with his wife and 'Idem dies' (the same day of respite) shall be given to the plaintiff."

With the swift expansion of commerce which followed world exploration, women engaged in trade in increasing numbers and accumulated property on their own account so that the law, if conceived for men by men, was rendered elastic to cover their activities. Wherever property and substantial economic interests were involved, an inherited adroitness found ways of evading the rigor of the formal law, such as prenuptial settlements, private agreements, and appeals to courts of equity.

In the interest of establishing a just balance and restoring women to their place in the main body of jurisprudence — as distinguished from domestic relations — it seems fitting, therefore, to make an extended quotation from the history of English law: "The courts of equity greatly modified the rules of the common law by the introduction of the wife's separate estate. . . The principle seems to have been originally admitted in a case of actual separation when a fund was given for the maintenance of the wife while living apart from her husband. And the conditions under which separate estates might be enjoyed had taken the Court of Chancery many generations to develop . . . intervention of trustees, though common, was not necessary. A clear intention to deprive the husband of his common law rights was sufficient to do so. In such a case a married woman was entitled to deal with her property as if she was unmarried. . . Connected with the doctrine of separate use (which sometimes required written and specific bonds for her own administration) was the equitable contrivance of *restraint on anticipation* with which later legislation has not interfered, whereby property might be so settled to the separate use of a married woman that she could not, during coverture, alienate it or anticipate the income. No such restraint is recognised in the case of a man or of a feme sole and it depends entirely on the separate estate; and the separate estate has its existence only during coverture.

"In yet another way the Court of Chancery interfered to protect the interests of married women. When the husband sought the aid of that court to get possession of his wife's *choses* in action, he was required to make a provision for her and her children out of the fund sought to be recovered. This is called the wife's *equity to a settlement,* and is said to be based on the original maxim of Chancery jurisprudence, that 'he who seeks equity must do equity.'

"Two other property interests of minor importance are recognised. The wife's pin-money is a provision for the purchase of clothes and ornaments suitable to her husband's station, but it is not an absolute gift to the separate use of the wife; and a wife surviving her husband cannot claim for more than one year's arrears of pin-money. Paraphernalia are jewels and other ornaments given to the wife by her husband for the purpose of being worn by her but not as separate property. The husband may dispose of them by act inter vivos but not by will, unless the will confers other benefices on the wife, in which case she must elect between the will and the paraphernalia. She may also on the death of her husband claim paraphernalia provided all creditors have been satisfied, her right being superior to that of any legatee."

From an examination of the methods pursued by historians, it is evident that Emil Reich has ample warrant when he writes in the preface to his work on *Women through*

the Ages: "Women, or more than one-half of humanity, has
by nearly all 'serious' historians been neglected as a subject
unworthy of their meditations. In this respect Polybius or
Thucydides is in line with the mediæval woman-hating chron-
iclers. More especially in this country (England) there is no
easier way of making oneself looked down upon than by pay-
ing attention to the rôle of women in social and industrial life.
English history is the history of a people that has never taken
women *au serieux.*"

How this extraordinary state of affairs came about is explained, partially at least, by Robert Briffault in his monumental work on *The Mothers* — a chapter of history representing a wide emancipation from tradition and the full fruits of
scientific thinking. "When we speak of human nature," he
says, "we generally mean masculine human nature. We are in
the habit of regarding the evolution of humanity and of human
ideas and sentiments as, in the main, products of the masculine
mind. That assumption appears justified by a survey of human
societies during historical times. The older speculations on
social origins, such as the acute and learned discussions of Sir
Henry Maine, had no other inductive basis than that afforded
by classical history and the pictures of patriarchal society in the
Old Testament; they assumed not only the invariability of
human nature, but that human society itself had from its
origin to the present day been constituted in essentially the
same manner. It would indeed be difficult to conceive how
notions and sentiments originating in the instincts of women
could in those conditions have played any important part in
the development of traditional heredity. Our knowledge of
human origins, has, however, undergone a profound transformation within the last fifty years, and whatever the value
of our present conclusions, they have been removed from the
sphere of abstract speculation to that of inductive inference."

FRAGMENTISM IN PRACTICE AND CONFLICT

THE same partialiity of view which characterises historical writing is displayed in other judgments formed with reference to particular practices and above all in the heats of social conflicts. Each observer and participant is controlled by his little world of conceptual thought, created in time and place, under the influence of limited experience, meager historical understanding, and the mores of classes and orders. Much that passes for subtle reasoning is an elaboration of simple reactions. Thus two American motorists not long ago, encountering an old woman in the mountain fastnesses of Montenegro were unable to convince her that they were not Montenegrins. Her world was bounded by her mountains. She noticed that they dressed peculiarly and spoke a strange tongue but, dominated by the idea that Montenegro embraced the world, she persuaded herself that English was a curious version of her native tongue, that the Americans were just queer Montenegrins.

Again when the same travelers visited the aborigines of Formosa, carrying cameras and typewriters, they awakened no special curiosity among the natives. It happened however that the woman in the party wore around her shoulders a fur collar. That caught the primitive eye immediately. Here might be the sign of a wayfaring animal from a neighboring forest — an unusual kind of animal against which the savages must be on guard. Driven far into the interior by alien invaders, made brothers of four-footed creatures once more, they saw the whole world from the angle of their personal experiences, their practical necessities.

More sophisticated, but still fragmentary, are the treatises on women written by doctors who view the subject from the perspective of mental diseases and generalise from a few hundred or a few thousand cases of abnormality. Thus an author of a heavy volume lately issued in Vienna, *Wie Bist Du, Weib,* argues that woman is a mere biological machine quite distinct from man who enjoys the luxury of a mind. Another in *Feminismus und Kultur Untergang* maintains that the feminist movement, which after all is but a phase of natural history, really strikes the death knell of the social order. Undaunted by the contention of Herbert Spencer that the subjection of women marks a low state of civilisation, this learned author finds their emancipation from ancient legal and recent economic discriminations a sign of moral and intellectual dissolution.

This type of "medical" mind is constantly revealed in practical affairs. Recently three London hospitals — King's, Westminster, and Charing Cross — and one New York Hospital — the Infirmary for Women and Children — sought to restrict the training of women in medicine, alleging as reasons that they are prone to marry after they are trained, that the embarrassment of teaching mixed classes is almost insurmountable, and that the profession is already overcrowded. Nevertheless it would seem that their much lauded science must seek light on the causes and cure of disease from every quarter and that a spread of the knowledge of medicine among women is essential to its extirpation if that, rather than fees, is the goal of medical science.

Even when the horizon is stretched, a similar fractional view of woman's rôle in civilisation is displayed. Since the outbreak of the World War, social orders and political systems have been in dissolution or grave peril over the whole earth. Ruling classes have been unhorsed, revolutionary experiments have been attempted, and cherished traditions repudiated. Nothing is more natural than that those who have suffered from these transformations or are alarmed by dire prospects should seek for a cause or, to speak more accurately, a scapegoat; hence women, obviously involved in this turmoil, seeking rights beside submerged millions of men, come in for a full measure of criticism and abuse at the hands of the distressed. In Germany, fascism carries on an open campaign against ambitious women, lays a large part of the nation's ills to their quest for a place in the sun, and orders them back to the kitchen, the children and the church. In Italy, fascism calls for a monster population and bids women nurture and sacrifice for it. On this side of the ocean, a gentleman of wealth offers a large sum of money to four leading colleges, always in need of it, to be devoted to promoting a "sound" public opinion to the effect that feminism threatens the stability of the family and the nation — a fund rejected by the beneficiaries on various grounds. And American advocates of a bigger and better navy, such as Admiral Fiske, have implied that women who desire the end of warfare are simply engaged in "stabbing in the back" the valiant men-at-arms. Out of such a tangle of "ideas" born of particular conflicts, interests, and distresses is made the mosaic of conceptual thought or opinion respecting women and their place in the process of civilisation.

Inevitably also in their long struggle to release their energies, formulate their ideas, break down barriers of law and tradition, women themselves have contributed to a one-sided view of their work in the world. Vigilance and battle have been the necessities of their opportunity and growth. It took a genuine sex war long ago in Athens to maintain women's right to serve as doctors to members of their own sex who preferred their ministrations. The story goes that the death rate was menacing and yet women were reluctant to summon male physicians to whom the monopoly of healing had been

given. In the circumstances, Agnodice, grieved at their plight
and attitude, garbed herself as a man to study under Hier-
ophiles and discover any new learning on the subject of medicine, and then quietly passed the word along that she was
serving women in disguise. Evidently she did so with skill
as well as sympathy for when news reached the public of
men that she was not of them, "she was like to be condemned
to death for transgressing the law — which, coming to the
ears of the noble women, they ran before the Areopagites, and
the house, being encompassed by most women of the city, the
ladies entered before the judges and told them they would no
longer account them for husbands or friends, but for cruel
enemies, that condemned her to death who restored to them
their health, protesting that they would all die with her if she
were put to death. This caused the magistrates to annul the
law and make another, which gave gentlewomen leave to study
and practice all parts of physick to their own sex, giving large
stipends to those that did it well and carefully. And there
were many noble women who studied that practice and taught
it publicly in their schools as long as Athens flourished in
learning." This precedent encouraged Mrs. Celleor, a well-
known London midwife, who lived in the reign of James II
and heard of it through the Latin writing of Hyginus, to urge
steadfastness upon her sex when its privileges were again
jeopardised. With this idea in mind she wrote a treatise on
the skill, distinction, and medical manuscripts of the Greek
women as revealed in ancient Letters, indicating the extension
of their teaching and practice to Egypt, Italy and Asia Minor.

From that day to this, women have been engaged in a continuous contest to defend their arts and crafts, to win the right
to use their minds and to train them, to obtain openings for
their talents and to earn a livelihood, to break through legal
restraints on their unfolding powers. In their quest for rights

they have naturally placed emphasis on their wrongs, rather than their achievements and possessions, and have retold history as a story of their long Martyrdom. As Sièyés contended in the French Revolution that the middle class had been nothing but was destined to be everything, so feminists have treated the history of women as if it had been a blank or a record of defeat. Thus unwittingly they have contributed to the tradition that history has been made by men alone; that civilisation, at least the evils of it, is the fruit of masculine labors or will, and have demanded that those who have hitherto been nothing should become as near like the males as possible to be something. When democracy took over the trappings of monarchy, it substituted the sovereignty and majesty of the people for the sovereignty and majesty of the war lord. In a like manner, feminists have been prone to prize and assume the traditions of those with whom they had waged such a long, and in places bitter, conflict. In doing so, they have participated in a distortion of history and a disturbance of the balanced conceptual thought which gives harmony and power to life.

Nor has this distortion of vision been corrected to any appreciable degree by the women scholars who have been admitted to the schools and libraries for research. Too often they have approached the institutions of church and state in the spirit of receptivity instead of inquiry. Broadly speaking, they have taken over the historical and social teachings of their masculine professors — man-made views of the universe — without critical examination, without applying the Socratic elenchus to the propositions they have studied. The mantle of discipleship rather than understanding has descended upon them and thus the female scholastic has joined the male in adherence to tradition, keeping aloof from the movement of investigation and innovation. The same loyalty of the disciple is likewise found in the typical woman who turns to political adventuring today, wondering how much of man's work she may assume and execute, never inquiring apparently whether there is a function she can perform of a better quality within the State.

THE SYNTHESIS OF UNITY

To THIS point then we are brought in the argument. The world has been conceived by philosophers, prophets, and scientists as unity, embracing all mankind working under a sense of destiny, with the possibility of a brighter future opened up by science and the new concept of progress. Judged narrowly by appearances, it seems to be broken into varieties of man's work and woman's work, slashed by varieties of race, class, nation, and interest. Written history, compiled mainly by men, though not always, has been fragmentary whether dealing with economics, politics or social development. And the pattern of conceptual thought about women has been derived from partial history and partial experience colored by the passions of conflict.

How can we attain the balance — the balance necessary for understanding women as well as any other living thing ? There appears to be only one answer: the narrative of history must be reopened, must be widened to take in the whole course of civilisation as well as war, politics, gossip and economics. Woman and her work in the world can best be understood in relation to the total process that has brought mankind from primitive barbarism to its present state. Her moods and aspirations have their roots in the very beginnings of society and they have been nourished through the centuries by opportunities of her own making as well as by those of man's contrivance. Seventeen centuries before Mary Wollstonecraft called for a vindication of the rights of women, viewed abstractly, Plato was sufficiently familiar with women and men devoid of sex complexes to provide that they should have equal guardianship in his ideal republic. Nor did the Stoics exclude women from their circle of grace, knowing full well that through the route of trial and error their wives, daughters and female friends had demonstrated their fitness for responsibility and philosophic communion.

It is only by attempting to comprehend the wide course of civilisation, therefore, that we can hope to understand women. In its evolution we see the interplay of government, politics, economics, modes of living and working, schools of thought, religion, power, class, society and family, the arts and ambition, and the biological and cultural aspects of sex. Everything is related to everything else: religion to philosophy, philosophy to commerce and war, war to politics, politics to religion, women to religion, philosophy, war, commerce and politics, and men to religion, philosophy, war, commerce and politics. Here are revealed the actions and reactions of social forces molding both the sexes. Here also it is made clear, as Briffault says, that "a natural disposition may be suppressed by educational influences acting positively or negatively, by not affording it the opportunity to develop, or by utterly repressing it; it may be reduced; it may be cultivated; or it may be stimulated to abnormal and excessive development. It may be, and in the vast majority of cases is, transformed by being deflected into quite different channels."

So there is another aspect to the search for more light upon women. Through a widening of historical narration and interpretation, there may accompany the better understanding a discovery of those modes of social arrangement and control likely to develop the highest powers of men as well as women.

Since all civilisation seems to be staked on knowledge and women are a part of history, if not all of it as Spengler alleges, the importance of such a widening operation is not to be denied. Indeed it marks a return to the problem posed by Thomas Henry Buckle, profound student of the history of civilisation, more than seventy years ago, in an address delivered at the Royal Institution in London on March 19, 1858. "The subject upon which I have undertaken to address you," he said, "is the influence of women on the progress of knowledge, undoubtedly one of the most interesting questions that could be submitted to any audience. Indeed, it is not only very interesting, it is also extremely important. When we see how knowledge has civilised mankind; when we see how every great step in the march and advance of nations has been invariably preceded by a corresponding step in their knowledge; when we moreover see, what is assuredly true, that women are constantly growing more influential, it becomes a matter of great moment that we should endeavor to ascertain the relation between their influence and our knowledge."

In one sense at least when this larger search is undertaken by minds competent in scholarship, it will raise anew the question put by Hegel: "What is the ultimate design of the world ?" Certainly it will broaden thought beyond the realms of law, politics and economics to a consideration of culture, its nature, its laws and its course. It is the fashion to elbow Hegel aside as befogged by metaphysics but it can scarcely be denied that his philosophy had a more profound influence, directly and indirectly, upon the fundamental thinking of the modern world than any other and wherever any unity is attempted in the multitudinous facts of life and history, his scheme of thought and his dialectics must be taken into consideration. Around the economic man and the economic woman, around the biologic man and the biologic woman, there is a still vaster complex of life, art, and aspiration which must be mirrored in our minds if either sex or both together are ever to be understood. Whether the ideal of true understanding can be attained or not, efforts in that direction should lead to firmer knowledge and truer efforts at coöperation.

PART II

THE ORIGIN OF OUR PHYSICAL COMFORTS

THE theory of biologic evolution set forth by Darwin some seventy-five years ago was justifiably a sensation at the time and its fruits in doctrines of social development have supplied nurture of vitamin strength. But no fruit can be eaten to excess. And some kinds must be eaten sparingly. Of such is that brand of modern psychology which professes to see "our animal nature" still dominant whatever the mutations of the body and society. We are told in *The Mind in the Making* that "We have no means of knowing when or where the first contribution to civilisation was made, and with it a start on the arduous building of the mind. There is some reason to think that the men who first transcended the animal mind were of inferior capacity to our own, but even if man, emerging from his animal state, had had on the average quite as good a brain as those with which we are now familiar, I suspect that the extraordinarily slow and hazardous process of accumulating modern civilisation would not have been greatly shortened. Mankind is lethargic, easily pledged to routine, timid, suspicious of innovation. That is his nature. He is only artificially, partially, and very recently 'progressive.' He has spent almost his whole existence as a savage hunter and in that state of ignorance he illustrated on a magnificent scale all the inherent weaknesses of the human mind."

But do we not in fact know something about first steps in the arduous building of the mind? And as it emerges from the animal state, does it not in truth "illustrate on a magnificent scale" the inherent *strength* of the human mind — at least as a creative and inventive force ?

The brute is about one hundred per cent obvious nature. Only within the narrowest limits can animals protect themselves from the elements. In no case are they nature's masters. The western plains of the United States were long strewn with the carcasses of cattle that dropped where they stood, helpless in the presence of a world they were unable to exploit. Only when they were fenced in by their human owners, scientifically fed and artificially guarded from burning sun and devastating thirst was life to any extent secure for them and even then the number of their days was tolled off by the will of man.

If the same dependence has characterised a large part of the human kind, it is not a universal rule among the higher animals, the story of whose mind-building is primarily a tale of the titanic struggle between mind and matter, with the mastery of mind over external nature assuming at last magnificent proportions. In the first steps in the rise of this mental architecture, the extension of the diet, the invention of the processes of cooking, the creation of the industrial arts, the guarding of the hearth, the modelling of family life about the fireplace, and the settlement on the land for purposes of tillage were unquestionable gains over our "animal nature" which the psychologists, concentrating on biological origins and infantilism, are apt to ignore.

"By the arts of life," declares an anthropological realist, Otis T. Mason, "are meant all those activities which are performed by means of that large body of objects usually called apparatus, implements, tools, utensils, machines or mechanical powers in the utilisation of force derived from the human body, from animals, and from natural agencies, such as gravity, wind, fire, steam, electricity, and the like." Then in studying the arts of life, Mason begins where they began — with the mind of woman.

When the forests began to recede, the water holes to dry up, the trees no longer to afford shelter, the elements to work greater havoc, the practical issues of survival were stupendous and neither lethargy nor timidity could cope with them. If primitive man was afraid of his own shadow and rigorous in adherence to tabus, the female of the species, of a practical bent, went to work with a will and demonstrated her rich constructive genius. Woman launched civilisation.

This is widely acknowledged today among anthropologists, one of the latest of whom, Robert Briffault, summarises in a succinct manner the research which led to this conviction: "The scattered facts of our reports of savage races have acquired the significance of broad generalizations which, whatever disputes there may be as to their interpretations, form the basis of our growing insight into the origins and development of our race and its mentality. Of those generalizations two have been particularly important in making that growth in our knowledge possible. One has reference to the form of primitive social organization, in which the most fundamental unit is not the state or the family, but a group of kinsmen having generally an animal or a plant for its badge. The other was the discovery that the part played in primitive society by women and their influence differed markedly from that which their place in civilised societies during historical times has assigned them."

As long as writers on social origins, such as Henry Sumner Maine, relied principally upon the Old Testament and similar predominantly patriarchal records, they easily fell into the habit of viewing the subject from the standpoint of masculine leadership, especially in war, politics, and religion. But when the veil was lifted on earlier stages of evolution, it was discovered that it was woman, principally responsible for the child she carried, who first turned external nature to the protection of human life, giving rise in the process to social groupings. Yet in spite of such revelations certain speculators on the beginnings of civilisation have continued to start with the war chief as the original organiser of society, apparently taking food, clothing and shelter as gifts from the gods. Thus they follow the path trod by Milton who, in *Paradise Lost,* represented man as made for meditation and valor and woman for mercy and grace. Evidently the basic arts of life counted for nothing.

But from modern researches we know that long before the valorous male organised political society on the basis of arms, social organisation had arisen on the basis of industry and the nurture of the species. As soon as fishing, hunting, building, weaving, and provisioning were undertaken with the interest of more than single individuals in view, a social organism of permanent and enduring form appeared, setting standards and establishing habits which served the processes of life as fundamentally as physical prowess, to put the case modestly. To the economists and theologians of the nineteenth century, John Ruskin flung out the challenge that whether there be one God or more, babies had to be washed and fed. So primitive women must have shouted their defiance to day-dreaming males when reveries got too much in the way of action imperative to the care of life.

As soon as human beings began their independent career, either by breaking with tree dwellers or by suffering exile from the Garden of Eden, the prime necessity was an intensely practical, creative intelligence — an intelligence uniting hand and brain, speculation and application, experiment and synthesis, desire and gratification. Eve was ready to taste the apple even if Adam crouched in terror, shivering before her culture from the start.   Whether it is now possible to enjoy creative thought unrelated to concrete materials and action, one might playfully debate.   But that time had certainly not arrived when the higher mammal, presumably faced with the thirst and famine induced by changes in nature, set forth on her quest for nutrition for herself and her offspring and by a slow, no doubt, yet steady research "reduced the determinism of natural heredity" by inventions of infinite variety.   "Were it not for its [creative intelligence's] slow, painful, and constantly discouraged operations through the ages, man would be no more than a species of primates living on seeds, fruit, roots and uncooked flesh and wandering naked through the woods and over the plains like a chimpanzee," remarks Robinson, and then immediately he himself lapses into traditional thinking by forsaking food, clothing and shelter — material, physical comforts — for descriptions of the hunter mind still operating subconsciously.

When Roger Bacon recommended that the mind of the thirteenth century turn from theological obsession to an interest in practical, common things, what is known as the "age of reason" was "dawning" and Bacon is still heralded as its prophet.   But as a matter of fact the age of theological obsession simply intervened between two ages of reason, the first of which was represented by the curiosity of women in matters related to living, and the second by men's realisation that the supreme task of civilisation is the conquest of external nature and its utilisation in promoting civilised living.   In the nineteenth century Carlyle dimly saw this transition when he declared that pure thinkers were finally passing into the twilight of history.

Even so, old men continued to see strange visions and speculators to dream fantastically while doers were transforming society by the wholesale manufacture of commodities which primitive women had made individually by hand. To this occupational divergence Robinson is clearly sensitive: "As one follows the deliberations of those bodies [academies], it is pathetic to observe how little the learning of previous centuries, in spite of its imposing claims, had to contribute to a fruitful knowledge of common things. It required a century of hard work to establish the elementary facts which could now be found in a child's book." And to what are these elementary facts related ? To the continuance and nurture of human life. Thus after centuries of speculation on mysteries, wars, and politics, the modern mind returned to the elements with which the mind of primitive woman wrestled.

First steps in civilisation were taken long before the makers of written history and philosophy entered the lists. And those steps were in truth such strides that the sophistication of the present age falters in the very effort to comprehend. It lacks even the imaginative naïveté of the primitive necessary to explain why we behave like human beings. While Adam studied the arts of killing and defending and contributed spears and axes adorned with interesting signs and symbols of his art as his addition to the lore of the jungle, Eve invented what no wisdom of the lair had suggested, namely cooking, spinning and weaving, sculpturing and pottery making and tailoring; she removed poisons from herbs, compounded remedies for sickness, prolonged infancy by various devices. Finally she crowned these achievements, many authorities believe, with discovering how to till the soil, thereby lifting human packs above the hardships and insecurity of hunters and nomads and, in the new treatment of the earth, our universal mother, instigating appropriate music, arts, poetics, religions, and moralities — or at least transforming old heritages into new images.

THE INVENTION OF COOKING AND RELATED ARTS

A CENTURY ago when American women were enlarging their interests, Margaret Fuller strongly objected to Richter's conception of woman as essentially a cook and also to Schiller's beatific vision, called *Dignity of Woman* — to the latter especially because in all its poetic beauty it contained "no grave and perfect man" but "only a great boy to be softened and restrained by the influence of girls. Poets, the elder brothers of their race," she protested, "have usually seen farther; but what can you expect of every-day men, if Schiller was not more prophetic as to what women must be ?"

If such dignities are no longer all that *must* be, at least mankind may be grateful that they *have been*. Because primitive woman made herself into a cook and guardian of the hearth, human beings no longer have to gnaw bones like dogs, or wait for sunshine to broil their meat. Though there were no scientific academies to which she could send reports of her researches and results, as Mason reminds us, the knowledge of her scientific advances spread from eye to eye, from palate to brain, and woman after woman improved on her neighbor's imitation until all the processes of cooking were devised. We are told that some primitive cooks had fifty ways of preparing corn alone for meal time. It may be that the primitive tortillas and other concoctions of the cuisine produced the jaundiced imagery with which the frightened male surveyed the universe, his nightmare lasting over into the day — dreams so enchanting in their vagaries to many writers on early society and to lovers of dreams in all times ! Nevertheless the basis was laid for an art capable of infinite improvement and refinement.

With the passing of the years the educable male took an

interest in the subject and did his own gorgeous bit for cookery. He prepared cook books galore and even resorted to Beautiful Letters in expressing his delight at the culinary performance. Thus Meredith sang:

> We may live without poetry, music, and art;
> We may live without conscience and live without heart;
> We may live without friends and live without books;
> But civilised man cannot live without cooks.

Primitive woman learned how to boil, bake and roast. She prowled around until she found the best sort of stones and then joined them into stoves and ovens. She made herself a fire-rake, the antecedent of the pitchfork, and a broom. She molded mortar and pestle implements for grinding seeds and grain. She made wonderful baskets for the harvesting of supplies, besides pots for the fire and for storage. She changed gourds into dippers and hewed bowls and spoons out of wood and bark.

From the red women of America, the white New England immigrants re-acquired many crafts of the forest and the soil, which had passed from memory in England, and were thus enabled to endure the rigors of pioneering and liberty. For one thing the natives taught the English newcomers to soak their shelled corn in wood ashes as a way of removing the woody hull and this "hulled corn," as it was known, became a staple colonial dish. The whites were also instructed in the original method of making "a stack o' wheats" by pounding corn in a hollow stone, mixing the flour with water, and baking the composition on a flat stone before the fire; in a little while an ingenious invader, whether of this sex or that we cannot say, seems to have set his cake to bake on the broad blade of his shovel or hoe producing the "hoe cake" of the Southern states. Even the beloved baked beans of Boston were the favorite food of red aborigines who cooked them in an earthen pot planted in hot ashes. So was the maple syrup an Indian condiment long before it became a democratic delicacy and commodity of trade. The Indian squaw even remembered the salt of which she was the manufacturer. Moreover she sometimes served sweet fruits with the meat or fish and occasionally wild spices and other dainties graced her feast. Centuries before lobster rose to the status of a Broadway luxury, the savage natives of America were finding it exceedingly toothsome.

By feminine means the diet was so enlarged that the primitive hunter ceased to be solely responsible for the larder. Reluctant as the male may have been to partake of the woman's experimental dishes when these were first placed before him, a shortage of meat or fish, coupled with pangs of hunger, probably made all food enticing and he might find himself none the worse for yielding to persuasion in the direction of his own experiment. And as the woman's persistent acquisition of nature lore progressed, a meal of considerable variety and elaboration of preparation took form, whether the vessels in which it was cooked were manufactured from clay or were the shells and leaves already available. Sometimes an object of barter was obtained by forest foraging. Vergil called woman the *oleæ inventrix,* inventor of the olive, and the olive in time became both nutrition and a source of profitable commerce along the entire Mediterranean.

Women were also the first brewers though we must not boast of this particular enterprise in a period of prohibitive zest, especially in view of the charge that liquor has been accountable for the extermination of entire races — an accusation brought against the Toltecs of Mexico, a highly cultured people, who drank a distillation from the aloe, apparently a deadly enemy of man. But there are those who say that without drink not only the perfect meal is impossible but the perfect conversation. Water, insists a leading French chef, ruins the digestion. Water, declares the bon vivant, leaves the brain too sluggish for delightful association. Although certain experts claim that water is the acme of hygiene and taste, the realist knows that water is rarely accessible in fine quality and that the quest for substitutes marked an inevitable stage of human evolution.

Until metals were exploited, women were masters of all the branches of the fire industry, utilising it for cooking, drying, smoking; preserving it; and causing it to be venerated. The Marquis of Worcester, who lived in the middle of the seventeenth century, is said to have been the first modern person to divert steam to any other purpose than the cooking of a good dinner but, if it had not been used first for the meals, the Marquis would hardly have employed it second for mechanics. The services fire could render were so numerous and its value therefore so great that the hearth where it burned became sacred and the oven, invented for its control, a holy monopoly of women for countless ages.

The origin of fire itself lies deep buried in mystery though the search for its secret is vigorous and ceaseless. Of this pursuit Frazer says: "It is an endless succession of systems, mythical, philosophical, scientific, confidently propounded, strenuously defended like fortresses built for eternity, glistening in rainbow radiance for a time, then bursting and vanishing like gossamer threads in the sunbeams or bubbles on a river. So it has been and so it will be. . ."

But at least he has assembled a great collection of fire myths and without taking them as other than fanciful tales like Prometheus or the *Origin of Roast Pig,* we find them dividing the honors, or the deceits, by which the wisdom was procured, about equally between the sexes. All such myths indicate secrecy about the discovery. Some range far beyond the strange explanations of animal or bird complicity, such as a tale of the Kakadu in northern Australia which relates how two men went hunting with two women; how the men caught ducks and spur-winged plovers and the women got lily-roots and seeds in the pools. While the men were fishing and expecting to cook their catch in the sun, the women built a fire and cooked their different food their own way. But the men saw the smoke, suspected magic, and accused the women of treachery. Unable to learn their fire secret, out of spite the men jumped into the river and became crocodiles.

Actual fear of cooked food appears in countless myths, some suggesting that only by an accidental interchange of sun- and fire-heated articles of diet was the general habit formed of eating from a pot or oven.

The subsidiary trades which they developed made women the early jacks of all. They were butchers, taking charge of the game when it was slain and conserving the hides and sinews, bones and fur for use in their industries. For manufacturing they devised their own tools. They were millers, making flour for gruel and cakes out of wild seeds until they learned to prepare it from corn and wheat. They were harvesters and bore the grasses, herbs and fruit home to the family storehouse. The carrying baskets made out of palm fibres by slave women in the southern part of the United States before the civil war displayed the same kind of coiled workmanship that their African kinswomen, from whom they had been torn, had long employed in their native land. Surplus supplies were stored much as squirrels store their nuts but women are thought to have tamed the wild cat to guard their food from vermin; certainly housewives in the country still cherish cats for their liveliness in killing rats. Little pools were dug for extra fish when the catch was large and it is possible that this bit of landscaping is the source of the attractive gold fish ponds of Japan.

Curiosity and confidence steadily expanded. Women fingered and rubbed and scraped and mixed and dyed and soaked and baked the natural fibres and grasses and pebbles and clay and skins and feathers with which they came into contact, thereby extending domestic economy. Fortunately the science of industrial management was accompanied by artistic feeling and the simple pots in which the herbs were boiled or seeds preserved often became objects of exceeding beauty. Decorations were gleaned from suggestions in the skins of snakes, in spider webs, the colors of birds, in natural forms as subtle sometimes as fleeting clouds. And this primitive affection for fine cooking utensils and objects of household use became so ingrained in women's hearts that, although they have now for generations been buying commodities made in men's factories, all of a kind and easy to procure, thousands of housewives are retracing their steps by the route of "modern art," back to the handmade pottery of their ancestors, in an effort to create and enjoy something as sincere and lovely again. While that instinct is generally deemed fruitless in these times, it is not without significance that our best thinkers in the realm of the arts are convinced that utility, sincerity, and beauty are strangely tied together.

CIVILISATION AND THE WATER HABIT

THE fact that civilisation always followed water routes is not entirely due to traders. An ethnologist has related the story of a family dispute among the Navajo Indians over the question whether the tribe should pitch its camp near building material or near a stream, a choice being imperative; of course he has the victory going to the women and the stream.

Indeed the water habit was one of the earliest civilised traits, with women as the chief guardians of wells and pools. Only a few years ago a white woman was appointed sheriff in a far western state because she knew best the water holes in the desert — a prime qualification for one who was set to capture horse thieves and other lawless characters. Not merely for laundry purposes have the women of the world knelt day by day beside the ponds and brooks and rivers, though that enterprise itself is one of the earth's most striking phenomena.

Their affinity for water led women to invent the suction pump. David Livingstone saw the Bakalahari women use "twenty or thirty ostrich eggshells and place them in a net. They tie a bunch of grass to one end of a short reed for a strainer and insert the apparatus in a hole as deep as the arm will reach, then ram down the wet sand firmly round it. Applying the mouth to the free end of the reed, they draw the water upward by sucking and discharge it into an ostrich shell, guiding the stream by means of a straw." The pump was the woman's mouth. For such purposes the bamboo furnished a fine pipe line and in the houses of the Dyaks in the Malays the bamboo stands ready for action to this day, being also used as a pipe to direct falling water. In early times springs were dug deeper and deeper until they became wells and an aqueduct or conduit was achieved by means of the reed or bamboo instrument.

THE OLD HERB WOMAN

If cooking had indigestion as a corollary, as of course it did, women piled up a long list of remedies. The mortar and pestle with which they ground their medical condiments is still the symbol of apothecaries though men have largely taken over that profession. For one specific ailment, a single herb might be deemed efficacious. Again assorted roots and herbs were blended in a brew.

Mason insists that "no one ever heard of a savage man having aught to do with the food-plant industry. The same is true of plant medicines. The first empirical physicians were not the sorcerers, but the herb women. They gathered the first materia medica." For men were continually coming home wounded and bleeding. Babies sickened and took on the pallor of death. And mothers also suffered from ills. Faced thus with the problem of sickness, woman created the office of doctor and elected herself to the position.

It was the primitive remedies of herb women which were still the basis of medicine among the fine Englishmen who sailed across the Atlantic to govern colonies in the seventeenth century. In concise form some of them are described in that fascinating vignette, *The Heart of a Puritan,* by Elizabeth Deering Hanscom made up of excerpts from letters and journals:

For paines in ye brest or Limmes: Weare a Wilde Catts skin on ye place grieved. . .

For a broken bone, or a Joynt dislocated, to knit them: take ye barke of Elme, or Witch-hazzle; cutt away the Outward part, & cutt ye Inward redd barke small, and boyle it in Water, till it be thick that it will rope; pound it very well, and lay of it hott, barke and all upon ye Bone or Joynt and tye it on: or with ye Mussilage of it, and bole Armeniack make a playster and lay it on.

My Black powder against ye plague, small pox: purples, all sorts of feavers; Poyson: either by Way of prevention, or after Infection. . . In the Moneth of March take Toades, as many as you will, alive; putt them into an Earthen pott, so yt be halfe full; Cover it with a broad tyle or Iron plate; then overwhelme the pott, so yt ye bottome may be uppermost; putt charcoales round about it and over it, and in the open ayre, not in an house, sett it on fire and lett it burne out and extinguish of it selfe: When it is cold, take out the toades; and inn an Ironmorter pound them very well, and searce them: then in a crucible calcine them so againe: pound and searce them again. The first time, they will be a browne powder, the next time black. Of this you may give a dragme in a Vehiculum (or drinke) Inwardly in any Infection taken; and let them sweat upon it in their bedds; but lett them not cover their heads; especially in the Small pox. . . The same powder is used playster wise with Vinegar for a gangrene, or bite of anie venemous beast, taking it likewise Inwardly: it is used like wise for all Cankers, Fistulas & old Ulcers and kings Evill, strewing it upon the sore, and keeping them cleane.

But magic early entered into the profession of healing as the woman acquired a rival in the medicine-man who sought to supersede her in tribal standing and influence and who won great success, especially by his assertion of control over pregnancy, which her wisdom did not as yet enable her to contest. By noise and incantation he undertook to deal with the "spirit" of life and death. Yet she rebelled now and then against the shaman and in fact never surrendered her connection with the *materia medica* of nature. In his book of travel, called *Under Turquoise Skies,* W. Robinson tells of a Navajo woman who in 1915 dared to weave into a blanket on her loom the sacred emblems used by medicine-men in their sand paintings. Naturally this agitated the magicians and they tried to wrest the blanket away from the covetous trader — in vain. The triumph of the merchant and his liking for the design only inspired other Navajo women to go and weave likewise. The result was that the use of the sacred emblem for earning pin-money became a flourishing industry among the Navajos.

In a recent account of a New Guinea community, the magazine, *Asia,* thus described the ruthless manner in which some of the medicine-men are known to assert their will:

The puri-puri men—medicine-men or sorcerers—are a striking exception. In the abuse of their power, they are the "gunmen" of the community. They seem to be free-lances, who do not answer to any superior authority except that conjured up by their own mysterious incantations and ingenuity. They are a curse, and the Australian government punishes severely their illicit practices. So great is the power of these men that by mental suggestion they frequently kill members of the tribe. In the social scheme of the village, they are the curers of ills. But if one of these hideous old men wants to work personal revenge, a favorite method is to flash upon his intended victim one of his magic instruments, merely a carved-wood crocodile head, about three inches long. He will dog the unlucky tribesman for several days, flashing his wand every now and then. The man will know that he is followed, he will have an unexpected stone thrown at him and in several days he will quite likely pine away and die.

However, Brinton declares that the Algonquins had "quite as famous medicine-women as medicine-men and the same was true generally."

If the League of Nations Commission, authorised to make a study of Chinese non-chemical medicine, goes deep enough into the subject, it may find that it has roots in the herb remedies of primitive woman. That is not to say that she was invariably a community blessing. The machinations of an aged dame in Hungary two years ago prove what could happen when skill was diverted to evil ends: she taught the wives of her village how to poison their husbands of whom they were anxious to divest themselves for one reason or another, chiefly, it seems, to get possession of their property. Indeed history is replete with the names and tales of famous women poisoners or mixers of love brews, dedicated to magic like the medicine-men. The old wise woman of the tribe readily descended into the witch. On the other hand she was the ancestress of the amazingly competent and unselfish woman country doctor who but yesterday in North America at any rate considered no distance too great and no disease too perilous for a call to be answered, summer or winter, in heat or cold, over mountain crag, on horseback, amid the attacks of wild animals, on foot, provided aid could be given to a sufferer.

These were precursors of that valiant army now serving as field nurses in the employ of the government of the United States.

THE FIRST CHIEF OF THE TEXTILE INDUSTRY

THE campaign against hunger and sickness was accompanied in early times by a battle against cold. Clothing undoubtedly resulted in part from discomfort, anxious as contemporary psychologists and nudists are to make it largely, if not completely, a matter of sex expression. The fire myths collected by Frazer show very clearly that early peoples in cold climates valued warmth and were conscious of the blessing that covering as well as fire conferred. Until women fashioned the dressmaking industry and the bootmaking art, humanity had gone naked and barefoot like the primates, and probably had a high death rate. But when women's minds attacked this phase of physical discomfort everything in nature that could be handled for weaving, blending or æsthetics was tried out and nothing conceived by the brain of an artist has ever been more wonderful than some of the antique costuming. Feather cloaks, for instance, unearthed in the old cliff dwellings of southwestern America and displayed again at the World's Fair at St. Louis, were the marvel of every observer. Rabbit cloth as fine as silk has been discovered in Mexico and this revived material now figures among the greatest luxuries on the market as moderns catch up with the ancients, the price unhappily being prohibitive for all but the very rich. The thread used by Eskimo women in some of their amazing sewing would fit only our finest needles, while modern spinners and weavers have never been able to manufacture as delicate a filament as that spun by the Egyptians.

Primitive women clothiers "used the sinews of deer and other animals, fibre of wild cotton, animal wool and hair sennit from the cocoa fibre, beaten tree bark sometimes decorated with shells, teeth, seeds and feathers, rushes. . . If aught in the heavens above or the earth beneath or in the waters wore a skin, savage women were found on examination to have had a name for it and to have used it in some way." There were certain garments for high ceremonial occasions — such as blankets for the rain prayer — which the men made for themselves after they learned the manufacturing art, lest they be contaminated by the touch of women, an idea bound up with the concept of the gods; but everything else in the way of clothing was made by the females for the family to wear.

If cold was not the sole motive for clothing, and no motive at all in the warmer climates, if sex consciousness was responsible for the fig leaves with which Adam and Eve departed from the Garden of Eden, if the Nudist cult now casts off even that modicum of wrapping, at least a contemporary archæologist believes that "a bit of cloth is one of the most interesting evidences of man's climb from days of savagery to the twentieth century civilisation." Women may accordingly plume themselves on having established all the branches of the textile industry—spinning and weaving, scraping and carding, dyeing and embroidering, tailoring and designing. They devised meshes and stitches, netting, looping, braiding, puckering, gathering, inserting of gores, and tucking, among other operations of the enterprise.

Admitting that it is the animal nature of birds to weave and braid, it was left to human nature to dye, fashion special tools for textile work, and incessantly modify patterns and methods in accordance with a changing and wilful taste. The first human implements were of stone. "The scraper is the oldest instrument of any craft in the world and it was the woman's," declares Mason. "One who goes to Southern California among the graves of extinct tribes of the Santa Barbara islands and its opposite mainland will get acquainted with a very dainty stone-working woman." An Inca historian, Garcilasso de la Vega, claims that "Mama Oclo, wife of Manco Capac, instructed the women of Peru in the manufacture of clothes for themselves, their husbands and children by weaving and sewing cotton and wool . . . with which she had been a successful experimenter." In Oriental tradition, silk was the discovery of Se-ling-she, an empress who lived some three thousand years B.C., and so important was the discovery to the economic life of the people that the name China, meaning goddess of silk worms, was bestowed upon the empress, while her subjects became known as Chinese. Moreover a Chinese princess is accredited with the diffusion of sericulture into India, having hidden in the lining of her headdress, when she changed her abode, the eggs of the silk moth and the seed of the mulberry tree for their nurture. An Indian princess, Nur Mahal, is thought to have created the cashmere shawl and that prized of perfumes, attar of roses. For her artistry as well as from love her husband called her: "The Light of the World."

In the museum at Kyoto, Japan, lies a manuscript written one thousand years ago telling how Korean women weavers brought their art to Nippon though there are those who believe that a native woman first unwound a cocoon and launched the silk industry of Japan. At any rate the countless cottages throughout the Island Empire, where women now spin and weave silk from the worms they carefully tend, are unbroken links in the industry probably started by their sex and now their chief source of wealth; for whatever ingredients the psychology of sex brought to the textile industry in its infancy, they were long ago submerged in the demands of trade.

Classical writings, about 2,500 years B.C., refer to the textile art and women's relation to it. Homer and Herodotus among the Greeks, Confucius among the Chinese, and Pliny among the Romans as the Christian era dawns, also take note of its existence. Herodotus says the Egyptian women shared in trades and handicrafts. In Homer the mother of Nausicaa is shown spinning purple fabrics at dawn by the hearth just as any virtuous woman would do, in the judgment of the Hebrew Book of Proverbs. Book Seven of the Odyssey gives us this picture of the home of Alcinous: "Within, thrones were firmly set here and there around the wall, throughout, from the threshold to the recess: there were thrown over them slender well-woven mantles, the works of women. Here the leaders of the Phæacians sat drinking and eating; for they held the feast all the year. . . . And there were fifty women servants in the house; some grind apple-colored corn in the mill, others weave the webs, and whirl the spindles as they sit, like the leaves of a tall poplar; and moist oil drips from the well-woven linen. And as the Phæacians are skilled above all men to guide a swift ship in the sea, so are the women practiced in weaving the web: for Minerva granted them exceeding skill in beautiful works and endowed them with a good understanding." Among the Hindus, Saraswatī, their Minerva, was revered as the divine protector of the fine arts.

Additional testimony on the creative intelligence of the early women is found in the first recorded history — namely picture-writing. Carved or painted on the walls of ancient cities such as Nineveh, Babylon, Thebes and in Assyria, Persia, Egypt, Peru and Mexico were the pictures of the textile industry covering in some cases the whole process from the raising of the hemp or flax to the spinning of yarn and the weaving of cloth. Since women are the actors in these scenes, some students have argued that they themselves must have been the artist-historians who left the record behind them. Indeed it is a strain for the imagination to believe that male artists would have portrayed themselves on such friezes as the Minoan in the sole capacity of cup-bearers, pages, musicians, bull-fighters, harvesters and sailors. Unless that was their idea of values.

And as we come down through the centuries, much of our knowledge of spinning and weaving continues to be secured from pictures. In the possession of rich burghers of Konstanz was a series, recently discovered, dating back to the early fourteenth century and showing for the European middle ages women still in charge of linen and silk spinning and children helping with the bobbins. Men and women both belonged to the Order of the Humiliaten, a great woolen weaving organisation that taught parts of Italy and northern Europe greater skill in the art. A century before, that is in the thirteenth, the Beghinen nuns were instructing the Germans and the people of the Netherlands in the art of fine spinning and embroidering, while the companion order of monks, the Begharden, had undertaken the heavier work of weaving involving operations such as treading.

THE EARLY PROVIDERS OF SHELTER

SPINNING and weaving have long been associated with women in the popular mind but shelter has been commonly attributed to the initiative of men. Here too however the natural propensity to easy generalisation must be checked by reference to ancient historical data. Students of natural history have often pointed out the zest of the female bird for building her own nest in cases where the male does not coöperate and of the female mammal or burrower in selecting her abode, her capriciousness, her ingenuity in protecting herself and her offspring from danger. But there is no need of resorting to animal analogies to prove the participation and possible leadership of human females in the development of shelter. The fact that American Indian women erected and dismantled the tribal tents led to the suspicion that they made the tent in the first place and the evidence is copious to that effect whether the shelter was devised of cloth or skin, adobe, mud, brush, or stone.

W. J. McGee who made studies for the Smithsonian Institute among the Seri Indians of the California Gulf, the most primitive type of the North American red people, observed that their brushwood dwellings were built by the women owners and that they sang as they worked, remarking on that aspect as follows: "The simple runes chanted in unison by Seri matrons engaged in building and lashing their okatilla house-bows apparently define a nascent stage in the development of the elaborate fiducial house-building ceremonies characteristic of various higher tribes." In the ancient New Mexican pueblos of the higher form imprints of women's hands as the plasterers may be seen, according to W. Robinson, though of course the men may have brought the cedar logs from the forests for the foundations, stones for the walls and clay for the cement. On the other hand there is a possibility that the Indian women carried some of this material, if not all, on their own backs. Legend at least says that, when the San Xavier mission was being built for Spanish masters, Indian women subjects actually carried the stones for many miles and that for the sake of "good medicine" they were careful not to let them touch the ground. Could the Spaniards suddenly have put this novel labor upon women and injected the tabu of good medicine? It scarcely seems plausible.

The strongest witness to women's original shelter-making perhaps lies in their early property rights over domiciles. Robinson insists that the squaw's ownership of the shelter among the Pueblos of New Mexico inhered in her work as mason. That the Zuñi women owned the "substantial houses they themselves built" is averred by Dr. A. L. Kroeber, an authority on the Pueblos, vouched for by Briffault. In North Queensland, "among the tribes of Princess Charlotte Bay, it is the regular usage for the husband to take up his residence with the family of his wife. . . His father takes the boy to his future mother-in-law and she builds a hut for him and her daughter next to her own." Far to the south in the desert, among the Arabs, A. P. Caussin de Perceval made note of the way in which the tent was always considered to be the possession of the woman who often used it as a "salon" where poets and musicians contested for her favor in ancient times. Robertson Smith interpreted the building by Mohammed of a separate house for each of his wives as a survival of the female proprietary right to the dwelling.

THE DISCOVERY OF AGRICULTURE

But the crowning primitive discovery was agriculture. The reason J. J. Hill states convincingly in *Highways of Progress:* "As far back as we know anything about civilisation, the cultivation of the soil has been the first and most important industry in any thriving state. It always will be. . . Not armies or navies or commerce or diversity of manufacture or anything other than the farm is the anchor which will hold through the storms of time that swept all else away. . . Civilisation is mostly the story of the triumph of the human stomach in its struggle for food sufficient for the work of physical and mental evolution. Events and epochs that puzzled the historians of the past are explained by a study of common human experience. An economic cycle runs through all the affairs of men from the earliest times. There is a period of foundation laying, in which agriculture is the accepted resource of the state and national strength is built upon it." Then quoting Dr. Johnson, who made the point in England, he adds: "Trade and manufactures must be confessed often to enrich countries . . . but trade and manufactures, however profitable, must yield to the cultivation of lands in usefulness and dignity. . . Mines are generally considered as the great source of wealth, and superficial observers have thought the provision of great quantities of precious metals the first national happiness. But Europe has long seen, with wonder and contempt, the poverty of Spain, who thought herself exempted from the labour of tilling the ground by the conquest of Peru, with its veins of silver. Time, however, has taught even this obstinate and haughty nation that, without agriculture, they may indeed be the transmitters of money, but can never be the possessors." After which borrowing of opinion, Hill again speaks his own mind: "It is not as in the old mythology Atlas whom we see groaning beneath the weight of the world upon his shoulders, but the homelier and humbler figure of the cultivator of the soil." Unhappily.

More passionately than Francis Bacon of Elizabeth's reign, John Ruskin of Victoria's felt the importance of "common things," partly as the result of machine production which had been allowed to run riot, obscuring the plainest needs — food, clothing and shelter for the masses — even more than the scholastics had done.

"The substantial wealth of man consists in the earth he cultivates," declared Ruskin, "with its pleasant or serviceable animals and plants, and in the rightly produced work of his own hands. . . The first beginnings of prosperity must be in getting food, clothes and fuel. These cannot be got either by the fine arts, or the military arts; neither painting nor fighting feeds men; nor can capital, in the form of money or machinery, feed them. All capital is imaginary or unimportant, except the quantity of food existing in the world at any given moment. . . And now examine the facts about England in this broad light. She has a vast quantity of ground still food-producing, in corn, grass, cattle, or game. With that territory she educates her squire, or typical gentleman, and his tenantry, to whom, together, she owes all her power in the world. With another large portion of territory — now continually on the increase — she educates a mercenary population, ready to produce any quantity of bad articles to anybody's orders; a population which every hour that passes over them makes acceleratingly avaricious, immoral, and insane. In the increase of that kind of territory and its people, her ruin is just as certain as if she were deliberately exchanging her corn-growing land, and her heaven above it, for a soil of arsenic, and rain of nitric acid. . .

"Now the peasants might still be able to supply this enormous town population with food (in the form of the squire's rent), but it cannot, without machinery, supply the flimsy dresses, toys, metal work, and other rubbish belonging to their accursed life. Hence over the whole country the sky is blackened and the air made pestilent, to supply London and other such towns with their iron railings, vulgar upholstery, jewels, toys, liveries, lace, and other means of dissipation and dishonour of life. Gradually the country people cannot even supply food to the voracity of the vicious centre; and it is necessary to import food from other countries, giving in exchange any kind of commodity we can attract their itching desires for, and produce by machinery. The tendency of the entire national energy is therefore to approximate more and more to the state of a squirrel in a cage, or a turnspit in a wheel, fed by foreign masters with nuts and dog's meat. And indeed when we rightly conceive the relation of London to the country, the sight of it becomes more fantastic and wonderful than any dream. . .

"I don't suppose any man, with a tongue in his head, and
zeal to use it, was ever left so entirely unattended to, as he grew
old, by his early friends; and it is doubly and trebly strange to
me, because I have lost none of my power of sympathy with
them. Some are chemists; and I am always glad to hear of
the last new thing in elements; some are palæontologists, and
I am no less happy to know of any lately unburied beast
peculiar in his bones; the lawyers and clergymen can always
interest me with any story out of their courts or parishes; but
not one of them ever asks what I am about myself. If they
chance to meet me in the streets of Oxford, they ask whether
I am staying there. When I say, yes, they ask how I like it;
and when I tell them I don't like it at all . . . they tell me I
ought to read the *Cours de Philosophie Positive*. As if a man
who had lived to be fifty-four, content with what philosophy
was needful to assure him that salt was savoury, and pepper
hot, could ever be made positive in his old age, in the imperti-
nent manner of these youngsters. But positive in a pertinent
and practical manner, I have been, and shall be; with such
stern and steady wedge of fact and act as time may let me
drive into the gnarled blockheadism of the British mob."

Must the civilisation which women launched all end in such
a tawdry and degrading expression? Ruskin feared it must.
Financial scheming, he insisted, was always "taking the peasant by the throat. He must pay — for he only *can*. Food
can only be got out of the ground, and all these devices of
soldiership, and law, and arithmetic, are but ways of getting
at last down to him, the furrow-driver, and snatching the roots
from him as he digs. . . 'Dust thou art, and unto dust shalt
thou return' is the first truth we have to learn of ourselves;
and to till the earth out of which we were taken, our first duty:
in that labour, and in the relations which it establishes between
us and the lower animals, are founded the conditions of our

highest faculties and felicities; and without that labour, neither reason, art, nor peace, are possible to man. . .

"But what I am, or what I fail to be, is of no moment to the cause. The two facts which I have to teach, or sign, though alone, as it seems, at present, in the signature, that food can only be got out of the ground, and happiness only out of honesty, are not altogether dependent on any one's championship, for recognition among mankind."

Research into the discovery of agriculture has not yet disclosed the decisive data for a confident statement of its beginnings. There are easy versions such as that offered by H. G. Wells, probably derived from Grant Allen, relative to the sprouting on graves of wild seeds borne there by mourners as food for their dead. There are also legends like that of Vergil in the *Georgics:* "Inventor, Pallas, of the fatt'ning oil, Thou founder of the plow and the plowman's toil." There are opinions of careful students such as Mason. By the avenues of archæology, art, linguistics, botany, history and tradition, clues appear from time to time. And three of these, presented in his compact treatise on *The Origins of Agriculture,* Harold Peake, M.A., F.S.A., believes to be the most fruitful as "possibilities, probabilities and well ascertained facts" up-to-date.

According to his survey, one line of investigation works for the sources of Bread Wheats which are thought to be the products of civilisation because no species has been found in a wild state; they are presumably the result of conscious crossing between something like Wild Emmer and one or more wild grasses, though there is as yet no agreement as to what grains were crossed or where and when the crossing was effected. The second line of investigation is that of the botanist, Professor Vavilov, who attempts to prove, by reference to centers where the greatest varieties of barley are grown today or where Wild Emmer was known to have once grown, the location of original agriculture, as a means of ascertaining how it started off.

The third research deals with traditions, and Peake indicates some of the material lying in that field: "About fifty years before the beginning of the Christian era, Diodorus Siculus was writing his history, in which he gave the story of Osiris and Isis, who were associated in Egypt with the cultivation of corn. In this account he states that Isis discovered wheat, or to be more exact Emmer, and barley growing promiscuously about the country along with other plants and unknown to mankind. In another passage he states that the country in which these plants were found by the goddess was Nysa."

This becomes intelligible if we accept the goddess as a sublimated primitive woman held in memory. In any case we are on as familiar ground as we were in 1928 when the American Grangers at a convention in Mt. Vernon indulged in rites of honor to the goddess Demeter "built on the agricultural mythology of the ancient Greeks" but "translated to meet the higher agricultural problems of the present day."

Like other leading investigators of scholarly disposition, Peake believes that women first learned how to till the soil and tempted the Adams not only to eat of apples but of vegetables as well. Admitting that his is only a more or less intelligent guess, he suggests substantiation: "We have seen that man in a hunting state was purely carnivorous and ate nothing but meat, and experience of primitive peoples has demonstrated that such folk are very conservative in their habits, and only with great difficulty are they persuaded to change them. . . We have already seen that, as time went on, the women were compelled to absent themselves from the hunting pack for longer and longer intervals as the demands of their infants increased, and we have suggested that during these periods, when food from the male group was delayed owing to lack of success in the chase, the women may have supplemented their fare with nuts and berries and perhaps with edible roots. It seems almost certain that it was the women who first introduced these new vegetarian elements into the primitive bill of fare. . . One day an accident happened and the store of grain became spilled and scattered on the bare hillside, or perhaps her husband, disapproving of the novel vegetarian fare collected by his wife, reproached her for her innovation, and threw down on the bare ground the store that she had collected with so much pains. We can imagine the poor woman's grief and disappointment at this loss; also her joy when, after many months, she found a rich crop of the desired grasses springing up at her door. We can well imagine that she repeated the process, which saved her from a laborious journey in search of food, and she would notice that the plants grew best where there were no weeds to interfere with their growth. It was a short step from this to take a stone hoe, such as had been used for the purpose of digging up edible roots, and to remove the weeds, thus turning over the soil and enabling the grain to germinate better and to grow a heavier crop. When this had been achieved, the first steps in agriculture had already been made."

That his guess is as intelligent as his discipline demands is shown by Peake's examination of it in the light of historical and geological data — such as the Ice Age accompanied by a recession in the supply of big game and the realisation that a diet of clams and limpets occasionally supplemented with an oyster feast was inadequate; a succeeding forest growth but smaller animal population soon disposed of; and next steps imperative. "Hungry and despondent, they were at times driven, like the inhabitants of Queensland or Kordofan, to collect the seeds of wild grasses, until there arose a woman who was to be their saviour and to lay the foundations of civilisation. It was, we may well believe, about 5000 B.C., or conceivably some centuries earlier, on the slopes of Mount Nysa, in Phœnicia, far away, that this woman collected the seeds of barley and of Emmer, which there grew wild, and scattered them upon a bare surface of the mountain side, where they were watered by the dew of Hermon that descended upon the mountains of Zion, so that the seed that she had cast upon the hillside she found increased a hundredfold after many days. This woman, one likes to think, was immortalised by the Egyptians as Isis [Egyptian women in the stone age having cultivated the ground for wheat, barley, and millet], as Cybele, Agdistis, and Dindymene by the people of Asia Minor, and later by the Greeks as Demeter and by the Romans as Ceres. Her memory has been preserved almost to our own time by our country folk as the Corn Goddess whose effigy was carried to the barn in the last harvest waggon."

When the first white immigrants landed in the New World, they found the native women planting, hoeing, and garnering corn, for which they exchanged iron kettles, shovels, and spades. They extended the barter unhappily to guns and whisky and thus contributed a black page to American relations as the "red fire" got into action. In his *Story of the American Indian,* Paul Radin emphasizes the rôle of maize in the native economy: "Here in this tropical forest where mountains alternate with the jungle [the seat of the splendid Maya civilisation] all that was basic in the culture of the aborigines of North America originated. This was, above all, the original home of maize, without which there could have been no agriculture, little stability of organisation, no concentration of population, no stone palaces, no complicated organisation in government and ritual, and no perfection in the arts. Though the original interest in maize was somewhat lost sight of as Maya civilisation became more and more complex, it regained its ascendancy as their culture spread to the north. Beyond the Rio Grande and the Gulf of Mexico, all social, economic, and religious activities were to center completely around it. Where agriculture stopped, civilisation stopped." Radin also states that in South America the indigenous potato was a rival of maize and "indeed had a much greater hold upon the life and imagination of these peoples than did maize." Perhaps when the history of the humble potato is traced far and wide it will provide another romance for the epic of civilisation.

Among all the American Indians that rose above the most primitive stage, agriculture and the agricultural woman were at the center of economy. The chief problem among them concerned the larder and, while the males helped to replenish it by means of hunting and fishing ventures, the timing of their expeditions was partly regulated by their women folk "who were to them a sort of calendar," as Mason expresses it. Dealing with *Omaha Sociology,* J. O. Dorsey writes that when the tribal council took up the question as to the start of the summer hunt, it was answered by the decision to proceed four days after the women had prepared their *caches* and had examined their cornstalks, after the pumpkins had been planted, the weeds cut and the beans harvested. Unless a squaw was ill, she assumed the responsibility for agriculture; if she was unable to manage this industry, it appears that her mate was genially ready to assist, taking upon himself the "double burden" of helping in an emergency and keeping fit for the chase. "The women buried in the *caches* whatever they wished to leave. Food, etc., was placed in a blanket, which was gathered up at the corners and tied with a thong; then the bundle was allowed to fall to the bottom of the *cache.* Then the women went over the cornfields to see that all the work had been finished. They prepared their pack-saddles and litters and mended moccasins and other clothing. The men spent part of the time in dancing. . . The day for the departure having arrived, the women loaded their horses and dogs and took as great weights on their own backs as they could conveniently transport." The return came with the ripening of the sunflower. The fall hunt began when the women wanted warm, thick fur for the clothing industry and the game had taken on coats of the right quality.

Everywhere in time and space women have shared the burdens of agriculture. For contemporary Persia, Clara Rice may serve as a witness: "Many country women work in the fields. For instance, in the province of Gholan, to the south of the Caspian, the planting out of the rice plants in the mud is done by the women where they often work in a foot of water or mud. They take their share, too, in weeding and in harvesting. The fields round the villages may produce wheat, barley, maize, millet, cucumbers, melons, tobacco and opium. A great deal of work falls to the women in the way of gleaning and grinding wheat and other grain. In most village houses, too, bread is made by the women. . . Most villages have a flour-mill worked by water within easy reach, but the women often find it easier to grind by the hand-mill in their own compounds than to carry heavy bags of grain and flour to and from the mill; expense too is saved, and there is not much current coin in a village . . . many of the little girls shepherd the flocks and herds in the fields or desert. . . Walnuts, almonds, and pistachios are abundant and provide a good deal of work for the women. . . Orange gardens are attended to largely by men. . . Butter and cheese are made by the women. . . Every house does not possess a well, so that the women's work is increased by drawing and fetching water from the village well, or from a stream. . . In many houses one or more hand-looms are found, the women and children weaving most of the material for the clothing." Any traveler in the Orient or in eastern Europe may easily find other illustrations of woman's persistent work on the soil.

Closely connected with agriculture in its later stages were the domestication and care of animals, but little can be said with certainty about the taming of wild creatures. Whatever may be written on the subject of the starting point, it is patent that some of the domestic animals, such as the cow, the goat, and the sheep, were intimately associated with women's work, furnishing food for the larder and materials for textiles and shoes; while the ass, the horse, and the camel, if they did, as claimed, facilitate the rise of slavery, also lightened many of the burdens which women carried. From authentic records we learn that women were often owners of cattle in pastoral societies. The ancient women of Arabia frequently possessed flocks and herds in their own right and, if they were busy at other tasks, were apt to send their husbands to act as shepherds on the plain — divorce, we are told, consisting simply of a refusal on the part of the male to act in this servile capacity. In an East Indian legend, the princess Sasīyasī, Mukerji relates, brought to her marriage as a dower droves of cows and horses together with a hundred chariots, and charmed him with her personality besides—so much indeed that he urged the Goddess of Night to report to her father his steadfast devotion to the daughter and his happiness of heart.

Whether women tamed the ass or not, they were quick to transfer to its back some of the packs they had long borne, though often they found the animal less competent than themselves. Referring to Kurdish women, Thomson says: "Soon we came to a place where the road was washed away and we were obliged to go around. We saw a woman there with a loaded donkey which could not pass with its load. The woman took the load on her back and carried it over and led the donkey over. She also carried a load of her own weighing at least one hundred pounds and she had a spindle in her hands. Thus she went spinning and singing over the rugged way which I had passed with tears and pain. In the evening they spin and make sandals; when they lie down they place under their heads the ropes used in binding the heavy loads of grass and wood which they bring down the mountains. After midnight they go up to get loads. In the early morning, I often saw women with great panniers on their backs and babies on top of these or in their arms, going four days over that fearful Ishtazin pass, carrying grapes for sale and bringing back grain." Atlas could have been a woman as easily as a man.

Whether on the journey or at home engaged in her unending solicitude for food, clothing and shelter, woman was early and long identified with the care and use of domestic animals.

THE DESIGNER OF LUXURIES

SOME of our modern critics contend that civilisation consists not in the accumulation of useful things but in the elaboration of the useless. If so, women still belong among the makers of civilisation. While the hunter carved idle fancies on the shaft of his arrows, women made designs of bewildering variety on their utensils and garments. From pottery to lace may have been quite an economic jump but figures on the former discovered in primitive graves linger in the patterns of the latter dainty product. Nothing is more conspicuous in the evolution of the priesthood than the way women employ their skill, derived from ages of discipline, for the adornment of clerical vestments.

It seems safe to say that most of the luxuries, no less than the comforts, of civilisation were born of the creative impulse of women. Perhaps three thousand years before the advent of Christ, caring little about clothing and not even knowing where they would sleep sometimes, the Egyptians wove the incredibly fine sheets lately unearthed from the tomb of a queen, calling to mind the women spinners and weavers depicted on Egyptian monuments. Indian blankets are akin in spirit if not in quality, while Anglo-Saxon grandmothers' quilts, treasured in garret chests, bear patterns often directly traceable to forms once familiar along the Nile. It would be interesting to know what was the character of the "comfy" bed-cover which Isabella d'Este, duchess of Mantua, gave to the Holy Father at Rome when she was wheedling him for favors.

In such commodities the oldest models, become classics, have "entered the great world-encompassing stream of art forms, pleasing to the entire human race." Jewelers repeat the designs used on ancient basketry and the ornaments loved of peoples at civilisation's dawn. The lamp which shed lustre in the Prytaneum at Athens or in the temple of Vesta at Rome was much of a piece with the Eskimo woman's lamp and in the Mediterranean countries that ancient product remains in evidence. As one watches the industrious fingers of homemakers in a machine-age department store being taught to fashion lamp shades in modes now popular, the mind travels back through all the ages to the time when their ancestors first began to decorate and illuminate their domiciles. So do knitting and embroidery classes signify the permanent itching of female hands for decorative labor.

These same bourgeois hands however would now find the making of carpets a less agreeable task. Yet from the straw *tatami* of the Japanese to the heavy and complicated floor coverings of India and Persia, this commodity has been intimately connected with women's toil. In Mexico, cotton mixed with feathers was once used for carpets, tapestries and bed coverings, the housewife apparently deciding to be warm by day and by night.

We owe to Clara C. Rice the following report from Persia: "Many very good carpets are made by the Qashgai women, under much the same conditions as in the Bakhtiari tribe. . . The young men of the tribe do little work; when away, they ride and hunt and rob — and when in the encampment they sit and smoke and give ear to the tellers of tales of romance and valour. The women lead hard and busy lives, but judging from their graceful appearance, their bright eyes and vigorous movements, such lives agree with them. . . Carpet-making is a great source of wealth to the bibis (chief wives). They employ women as weavers and have the looms near their own apartments so they can superintend the work. They feed the workers and when a large carpet which may have taken months to weave is finished, each weaver gets a present of a few shillings, but no regular wage."

While the article on Carpets in the New Standard Dictionary does not disclose how much of the early Western manufacture belonged to women, it throws a charming light on the phrase, "a carpet knight," now used in keen derision. "In medieval times knights who were created in the palace rather than on the battlefield became known as Knights of the Carpet, and it is in this sense that Shakespeare made use of 'carpet consideration.' On the day after her coronation Queen Mary made fourscore and ten Knights of the Carpet, so dubbed in her Presence Chamber at Westminster by the Earl of Arundel, who had previously knighted a number of the Knights of the Bath. A 'carpet knight' then became one who loved to be in attendance in women's chambers, but, according to some authorities, the term was applied to such knights as were created for their services in the cause of the arts and sciences. Dr. Brewer explained that 'carpet knights' were not military but strictly civil knights, such as mayors, lawyers, &c., precisely because they knelt on a carpet when the honor was conferred upon them, and not on the field of battle."

It seems that Western men had not taken kindly to carpets for a while. "A Bishop of Toledo, Sinchius, covered the floor of his palace with tapestry in 1255. This practice was followed by Eleanor, Queen of Edward I., during whose reign bedside carpets were introduced. At first they were not looked upon with favor, and when they were spread on the floors of the halls in the time of the Earl of Lancaster, who furnished his establishment with them in 1314, the nobility of the time looked upon them with disfavor."

Wall coverings were deemed equally effeminate in their day. "The workmanship of the famous Bayeux tapestry, a linen roll seventy-seven yards long, embroidered in colored worsteds, representing fifty-eight scenes in the life of William the Conqueror, is ascribed by tradition to his Queen Matilda. It is now preserved in the Hôtel de Ville at Bayeux in Normandy. This remarkable historic document is only twenty inches wide. Other famous tapestries, designed for ornamental hangings rather than for the floor, are those of Gilles and Jean Gobelin, two brothers, who were French dyers and flourished about the middle of the fifteenth century. They established a famous tapestry factory in Paris and later in Beauvais. So famous were the products of this factory that the property was taken over by the State in 1662, and from 1697 only the manufacture of tapestry was carried on." By this time woman's floor mats, made for comfort and adorned for beauty, had become the object of desire on the part of all who called themselves civilised, and tapestries evolved out of carpets were equally prized. From the squalor and incredible poverty of the cave age, mankind had advanced far on the road of civilisation — toward the day when the machine was to take over the fabrics made by the hands of women and often preserve the designs they borrowed from nature and elaborated by imagination, as capitalism scattered commodities throughout the earth to its toiling multitudes, some of whom had never reached a high degree of culture and some of whom had retrograded.

LIGHTENING LABOR WITH THE ARTS

DESPITE the heavy toil which marked the way up from primitive levels, it was lightened very soon in the human drama with joyful expressions of the woman's spirit: with songs for sowing and reaping, songs for spinning and weaving; chants for funerals and choruses for weddings, lullabies and feasts keeping pace with the war cries of the men. For a long time each sex had its special music, expressive of the division of labor and related to specific tasks. Some knowledge exists of the evolution of music from the stone age imitation of the noise of grinding mortar and pestle to the agricultural melodies connected with the planting of corn or beans or melons. It was felt that mysterious magic passed from the voices or the artificial sounds made with instruments to the earth, causing the seeds to sprout and the grain to grow.

The men's music generally centered about war and the chase; the women's about the home and its activities. Consequently the latter was gentler and more graceful in its rhythm. For example the Zuñi Indian sings to her little girl child:

> Little maid-child !
> Little sweet one !
> Little girl!
> Though a baby,
> Soon a-playing
> With a baby
> Will be going.
> Little maid-child !
> Little woman so delightful !

To her little boy she chants:

> Little man-child !
> Little man-child !
> Little boy !
> Though a baby,
> Soon a-hunting
> After rabbits
> Will be going.
> Little man-child so delightful !
> Little man !
> Oh, delightful !
> So delightful !

Out of the chants, lullabies and threnodies of women in the childhood of the race, kept alive in the field, at the distaff, and by the fireside, has been woven many a strain of pretentious music to soften and harmonise the crash of martial airs or the subtleties of great symphonies — reminding those who stop to consider origins that, from the beginning, life all one has dual aspects.

Other fine arts and rituals, adding to the charm and symbolism of existence, have sprung from the agriculture which women probably launched and the crafts they positively founded. "Agriculture and poetry," Radin remarks, "two traits that have always traveled together in America, these even the simplest peoples of eastern South America were never to lose. But they were never to elaborate them to any appreciable extent and agriculture was never to have those multitudinous cultural by-products, generally associated with them in North America, such as elaborate ceremonials and rituals and complex political and governmental units. In fact it can be said that in spite of the presence of agriculture, the autochthonous inhabitants of Brazil never really became sedentary. Beside the continuous and persistent pressure from the other side of the Andes, these barbarians always tended to relapse into their ancient ways. But we must make two exceptions. The Aruaks, called Taino, who overran the West Indies, were distinguished for wood-carving, stone work, pottery and an elaborate social organization. And these finally influenced the Indians of southeastern America. . . The other was a superior pottery development along the eastern Amazon."

All savages did not bury their dead but those who did developed ceremonial and religious music to accompany the act. Naturally the women were leaders in caring for the dead as they had been for the sick whose lives they struggled to preserve. In their mourning, they "threw in a prayer, a little hymn and some reference to the friendly totem, the god of the tribe" — precedents for male successors who devised chants celebrating the crucifix, the wings of angels and a star.

This stream of tendency is finely described by Mlle. Clarisse Bader in her study of India: "We have already mentioned that three goddesses presided over sacrifices: Ilā, the rite; Bhārati, the poetical union of gesture and voice, the mother of the Bhāratas, in whom a learned Indologist (M. Emile Burnouf) has recognized the originals of our Western bards. Lastly, the most august of all, Sarasvatī, 'the holy word, the word that conquers, the purifying virgin' as the Veda styles her who is also the inspirer of beauty.

"Sarasvatī was besides goddess of the waters. On this subject, M. Nève has pointed out the assimilation established by the primitive Aryan religions between speech and the liquid element. The three ancient Muses of Pieria, Memory, Meditation, and Song were originally Naiads, whose domain was transported from the world of matter to the world of intelligence.

"Pure and limpid like the streamlet following in its peaceful course the green slopes of the hills, impetuous like the torrent dashing in foam down the mountain side, rapid like the rivers

and streams hastening to reach their mouths, majestic and restless like the Ocean whose motions and sound are at the same
time all variety and all harmony — to all these was speech
compared by the genius alike of Greece, Rome, and India.

"Thus not only were the physical forces of nature deified,
but also pre-eminently the moral powers. Prayer and speech,
the sublime ideas of beauty and goodness, soared in the calm
regions of the understanding, and, what is worthy of remark,
all the pantheistical creeds symbolized such immaterial phenomena by feminine personifications."

PART III

THE RISE OF INTELLECTUALISM

FROM the creation of physical comforts to the creation of systems of rationalised philosophy was a mental stride not taken by all peoples and all races; not even by every people and every race that reached a high degree of physical comfort including the benefits derived from agriculture. Among those who did attempt an explanation of life, mind, and conduct in ancient times ideas were exchanged until the Greeks, creating the doctrine of ideas, set an intellectual pace which the later world has found it hard to excel.

The Greeks consciously framed social objectives and planned ways and means for their attainment. They discussed the nature of the universe and tried to discover its laws, convinced that it has a discernible principle. They were deeply concerned with material adjustments to the physical world and with spiritual relations to the gods. They debated the issues involved in the family organisation, offered new moral values, and pondered on destiny. They attacked the customary and suggested creeds with reference to the good life, the social order, the essence of power and virtue. They made a veritable cult of speculative intelligence while remaining unusually concrete. Because Greek intellectualism possessed activist enthusiasms, particularly for the State, in contrast with Oriental fatalism, reflecting satisfaction with the gods, it energized brains throughout its vast sphere of influence and fixed methods for rationalisation which no amount of mystical emotionalism flooding over the mind from other directions could completely and permanently annihilate.   It was upon the Greek basis that the makers of the modern age largely built their realistic edifice.

When the framers of the Constitution of the United States, for example, looked back to precedents for a guiding political philosophy and practice, they turned not to the Anglo-Saxon Witan for examination but to the Ecclesia of Athens, the Boulé, the Council of the Areopagus, the League of Delos and its mode of reducing seceders to subjection, the orations of Demosthenes, and to the Roman successors and imitators to see what they added of importance.   The American republic was grounded in part on Aristotelian reasoning.   Many of the French revolutionists of the eighteenth century likewise drank draughts of mental wine directly from that ancient fountain while today in the twentieth century the Bolshevik will-to-power may be traced back only a little more deviously through Karl Marx to Hegel and to Greek dialectics and the Platonist conception of the ideal State.   Thus for some two thousand years Hellenistic culture has been spreading in the Old World and the New, following its triumphal sweep through Asia Minor and Africa.   It is frequently remarked that every modern "intellectual" is still either a Platonist or an Aristotelian.

No doubt the Egyptologists are justified in calling attention to the popular neglect of their field and claiming for the culture of the Nile an earlier philosophic genius.   But it was limited mainly to a narrow political perspective to which other visions were minor.   Take Khufu as a type of the Egyptian mind lauded by Breasted, the ardent defender of Egypt: "In leaving the tomb of Khufu our admiration for the monument, whether stirred by its vast dimensions or by the fineness of its masonry should not obscure its real and final significance; for the great pyramid is the earliest and most impressive witness surviving from the ancient world to the final emergence of organised society from primitive chaos and local conflict, thus coming for the first time completely under the power of a far-reaching and comprehensive centralisation effected by one controlling mind. . . It will be evident that all the resources of the nation were completely at his disposal and under his control . . . and thus a great state was swayed at the monarch's slightest wish, and for many years held to the chief task, the creation of his tomb." Was not one controlling mind a restriction on the mental range of Egypt ?

On the other hand, in the old India, speculative thought, as its legends reveal, remained decidedly mystical.

Between these two moods stood Greece elbowing both ways and enlarging the middle ground. It produced a huge library of treatises on the physical universe, on politics and economics, on psychology, and on social philosophy. Whereas force was the emphasis in Egypt and religion in India, the Greeks aspired to a rationalist order.

In Athens diversity of opinion was the key to culture. This difference in motivation is evident in the arts of the Greeks and the Egyptians no less than in their politics and principles. Rigidity of muscle and pose characterised Egyptian sculpture; activity and elasticity gave grace and beauty to Greek modeling. Though fortunes of geography, war and language made the Greeks, instead of the Egyptians, the teachers of the West, they had a better outfit of concepts and logic with which to help untutored conquerors from Rome take up their cultural slack. Granted that the Greeks borrowed heavily from the Egyptians, they were apt pupils who far exceeded their masters in naturalistic and social explorations.

So overwhelming is the debt of the West to the Greeks that lovers of the classics usually find it hard to believe that the final word in literature and conceptual thought was not expressed within their pages. This is readily understood when one remembers the aspects of energy and life that were covered, such as the function of religion and the rôle of the gods; war and peace; scientific and religious bigotry; naturalism and humanism; the elevation of reason to supremacy in mind; intellectual snobbery; the theory that the psychology of emotion could explain mentality and conduct better than abstractions or ideology; the relativity of all concepts of right and wrong; the place of pleasure, virtue, righteousness, and politics with respect to destiny; cheap journalism and rhetorical speech versus permanent, national or cosmic perspectives; the laws of logic and their inadequacies; physics and its limitations; rules of oratory, drama, poetry; citizenship and free opinion; simple living as opposed to ostentatious display; sex and its ramifications; scepticism, pessimism, stoicism, sophistry; mechanism, dualism of mind and matter, pantheism; intuition; traditional as distinct from investigatory, factual and creative intelligence; the leadership of the intellectual in society; educational theory and practice involving such questions as whether virtue can be taught, whether inspiration can flow from ignorance, how aspiration can be achieved, what should go with it. The Greeks pushed scientific inquiry. They pursued Truth. They sought after culture or analysed and disowned it. They were extraordinarily articulate.

When their creative era closed, they had to their credit the collection, classification and analysis of all the learning that then existed upon which they could lay their hands; the framing of systems of education and text books for their manipulation; the invention of every kind of literature with stylistic devices for each magnificently worked out.

It is almost impossible to find an exception to the rule that every European thinker of the first rank down to the present generation was "illuminated" by classical studies whether he or she was a dramatist, novelist, poet, scientist, or philosopher.

Shakespeare, Corneille, Racine, and Schiller were students of Æschylus, Sophocles, and Euripides. A sense of prodigious destiny, over which the Greeks pondered, runs through the literature of their pupils everywhere; Goethe's *Faust* and Wagner's *Götterdämmerung* are among the best known examples in European discipleship.

Shelley exclaimed: "We are all Greeks; our laws, our literature, our art, our religion have their roots in Greece." From a sense of indebtedness to his teachers, Byron rushed to the aid of their feeble descendants when they were hard pressed by the Turks in 1823. Emil Reich declares that they shed light on all the contemporary problems of aristocracy and democracy, equity and the distribution of property, freedom and order, temperance and inebriety, man and woman, church and state, practice and ideals. To the Cyrenaic philosophy he attributes the "relief from the intellectual *cul de sac* in frankly æsthetic satisfaction" of Heine, Walter Pater, Omar Khayyam, among others. Langhorne, in his Introduction to an edition of *Plutarch's Lives,* says that, long before Bacon, Pythagoras had "led philosophy forth from the jargon of the schools and the fopperies of the sects. He made her what she was originally designed to be, the handmaid of Nature, friendly to her creatures and faithful to her laws."

Even the reputable expression of plastic form and beauty in the Far West still requires an interminable apprenticeship to the antique, that is Greek, models whether the artist is an emigré such as a Thomas Crawford carving Orpheus in his Roman garret near to the sources or the native struggling at home with clay and canvas. Poets in the wilderness of the United States long ago wrote *Orphics* or *Orphic Sayings* while in the vaunted creative "middle period" philosophic taste selected from the ancients the ideology best adapted to its mood. Thus William Cullen Bryant worked for years to put into English dress the "tragic sense of destiny" which Homer had helped him to feel. Those who followed Orpheus, the priest of Nature, sometimes had revolutionary inclinations. Unlike Ulysses who simply compelled his mariners to stop up their ears against the wiles of enchantresses and had himself bound to the mast, Puritan-style, Orpheus entrusted by the gods to make laws for mortals encouraged them to heed their own wishes; he sang rival hymns to the gods and in the manner of a god he obeyed his own spirit when the sirens attempted to dominate him. Obviously the ancient dispute over free will and destiny was grafted upon the philosophic trees of the New World.

Ideas themselves thus grew into creative forces — that is, general ideas about the operation of society and the natural world. In fact, ideas have surged to the front so tumultuously in crises that their devotees and manipulators have been inclined to make them of prime importance, even to argue that in the beginning was the word rather than the deed; hence to minimize the deed. But the two have really evolved together. They are parts of the same social ferment and the proof lies in the sources of Greek intellectualism — in ideas traced to their roots.

THE RÔLE OF THE PYTHONESS

As animistic in the beginning as any other primitives, the Greeks at the outset found it impossible to distinguish sharply between the seen and the unseen. Matter and mind, still so difficult to delineate that one hears leading scientists declare both are mere figments of the imagination, were so jumbled together among the early peoples that they all heard voices issuing from rocks, caves, trees, fire, water and the winds, bearing messages for good or ill — spirits living in a world shadowing the visible. And like little children crying in the night, usually they sought feminine guidance amid these portents. Thus the "voiceful trees," the speaking rocks, the sounds in the burning bush were generally to them great mothers counseling.

In the form of vapor rising from a cleft in the rocks of stony Pytho, the first known Greek oracle, Mother Earth, spoke prophetically to her people. But it was a visible priestess in a trance who gave the last pronunciamento at sacred Delphi after man through systematic experiments had learned to direct his communion with the unseen. Porphyry describes the last act in the drama of Delphian oracular wisdom — the reply to a question asked of the Pythoness by Amelius, friend of the philosopher, Plotinus. "Where is now the soul of Plotinus?" inquired the seeker after light. Then the woman in the case, as if speaking to Plotinus, made answer:

> Oft on thy struggle through the obscure unrest
> A revelation opened from the Blest —
> Showed close at hand the goal thy hope would win,
> Heaven's kingdom round thee and thy God within.

Thus she leaves "a train of light behind her as she departs on her unknown way," remarks Evelyn Abbott in an essay on *Hellenica*. From Fetichism, through Shamanism, to Nature-worship, Polytheism, Monotheism and on to Mysticism and Ecstasy ran the adjustments of mortals to the invisible and even to the inconceivable.

Especially before conversation — dialectics — undertook to deal with the emotions was this oracular approach to utterance effective. By prescription the medium was a virtuous, elderly woman of the lower class, elected by popular vote to sit on a tripod, shut herself in with the gods, and draw from that communion wisdom beyond the scope of one hundred per cent humanity. Visitors who brought her questions had them

transmitted to the Pythoness by representatives of the leading
Delphian families, accepting without hesitation the view that
a person so chosen to be the embodiment of sagacity and
prophecy would not be simply a self-seeker; that on the contrary she would be a trustworthy agent of divine will.

And the Delphian spokeswoman for the gods became the
"conscience of Greece" in more than a mystical sense. "It is
from Delphi that reverence for oaths, respect for the lives of
slaves, of women, of suppliants derive in great measure their
sanction and strength." Good and evil, rewards and penalties,
political and social action were regulated to an amazing degree
even in the most intellectual center of the ancient world during
its days of glory by the dicta of these temple women. Many
sorts of problems were carried to them for solution. They
encouraged colonisation. They selected the heroes to be
propitiated, venerated, or obeyed, as Jeanne d'Arc, their true
incarnation, divined in a later age the leader for the French.

Certainly all the great thinkers of Greece took oracular wisdom seriously. Pythagoras declared that he got many of his
precepts from a priestess at Delphi by the name of Aristocleia,
or Themistocleia, or Theiocleia, depending on the person who
quotes him. The great philosopher is also said to have written
a letter to her and to have been influenced by her answer in a
particular situation, as today mediums are consulted by Sir
Oliver Lodge.

Socrates, accredited author of the "first condition of all moral
progress," namely "Know Thyself," actually got the dictum
from the motto over the temple portal at Delphi. He was
frank enough about it himself, reporting not only that he derived inspiration from the Pythoness but his famous method of
reasoning, the elenchus, in addition. Should it not therefore
be called the Pythoness Elenchus in reality? Or just Great
Mother Perception of the Truth? Similarly when he refers

to Diotima as his teacher, the remark must be understood as a different thing from gallantry and conscience. Diotima was the priestess attached to a temple of Zeus on Mount Lykæon, a noted philosopher of the Pythagorean school, it is thought, who both gave verbal counsel and wrote out her wisdom. Sometimes she came to Athens where she was received with high honor and there she seems to have had a conversation with Socrates on the subject of love. Obviously the third sex was not born with modern feminism for Diotima regarded love as a terrible demon obnoxious to a person with intellectual tastes and in any event demanding the leash. "Who when he thinks of Homer and Hesiod and other great poets," she said, "would not rather have their children than ordinary ones? Who would not emulate them in the creation of children such as theirs which have preserved their memory and given them everlasting glory?" As a priestess naturally her interests lay outside the hearth. As a priestess she had the keys of the city at her disposal but her beauty was considered dedicated to the gods. Though one of the female oracles pronounced Socrates the wisest of mankind, delighting in his search for Truth, he himself reflected on the phenomenon of oracles, wondering how they could be rationally produced and what relation between man and the deities they actually signified. He belonged to a generation that had begun to struggle with the issue of matter and mind, trying to distinguish the visible from the invisible more precisely, the concrete from the abstract, the ideal from the material.

Æschylus believed in Delphic inspiration. Nor did Plato break with the faith in oracular wisdom. To the Delphic priestess for example he assigned the dictation of the code of Lycurgus. Still puzzled about such inspiration, Aristotle declared: "It is neither easy to despise such things, nor yet to believe them." The Epicureans and the Cynics denied and ridiculed. The Stoics and Academicians defended. And since the believers were in the large majority, Alexander struck Greece one of his hardest blows when he arrogated to himself the right to have the first consultation with the Delphic oracle. Owing to the practice of imputing to a pythoness the sentiment her questioner himself entertained, as parsons often derive their judgments today from the Almighty, Alexander's move was a fine piece of strategy. Not only were moralists and politicians affected by that form of divine communion and approval — the cult of the irrational — but the lyrics of Pindar, the drama of Æschylus and Sophocles, the plastic art of Pheidias, and the conduct of Epaminondas, Demosthenes, and Callicratides were profoundly influenced by that mystic operation.

The personality of a Greek Prophetess who could sway humanity from a tripod must have been richer than that of the diviner, Jeanne d'Arc, who had to resort to arms no less than dreams for her power. However the Delphi devotees who sought favor, together with those who received favor unsolicited, bestowed such lavish tribute on the temple in appreciation that by its very wealth and apparent supremacy its hold on faith was weakened. Efforts were made to bribe the oracle. Finally Delphi, a molder of the religion, the politics, and the arts of Greece, lost its unrivaled power in the Persian Wars and, with its passing, women encountered an increased competition of male prophets and seers. But the prophetess did not disappear. According to Tertullian there were any number in the first century A.D. still giving counsel to the worried. Roman emperors were among their patrons. And in the form of a voiceful stone, Mother Earth continued to speak to East and West until the Christians provided for her a different imagery while Mohammed attacked all images of god, natural or graven.

CONFLICT A KEY TO RATIONALITY AND RATIONALISATION

How THEN did it happen that the Greeks, harkening to the last to voices of mystery, advanced so far along the way to creative and rational thinking ? This too remains one of the Delphic curiosities debated by those seeking to understand the making of the human mind and no one who has thought long and hard about it feels sure of the answer. Certainly the Greeks were not endowed in the beginning with all the arts of sophistication; they acquired their talents only by tedious and painful struggles. It is not enough therefore to explore the literary fragments of a few outstanding philosophers and then declare the secret of the Greek mind in its highest ranges. As in primitive societies, women developed inventiveness while they wrestled with materials and experience — mind and utility constantly interwoven — so the later Greeks attained their intellectual achievements by working with the changeful concrete of their diversified world. In fact the peoples of the Hellenic world were torn with more kinds of conflict, realistic and fraught with poignancy, than any other races of antiquity. Their thinking, unusually critical in quality, reflected the multiform clashes through which they passed; outward struggles were mirrored in mind, providing food for thought, contingencies for debate and settlement, fateful events calling for adjustment, reconciliation, or acceptance.

First of all there was the racial contact — a constant stimulus to thought as well as to arms. The ruling Greeks were invaders who had to consider and dispose of difficult issues of occupation raised by the conquest of a native population long disciplined, at least over a considerable area, by the advanced Cretan culture — issues very different from those which the invaders of India encountered, for instance, in dealing with various Negroid races. This circumstance involved subtlety of mental adaptation together with physical prowess. New experiences also came to the Greeks through their relations to the neighboring Phœnicians with whom they traded and intermarried. Later the Greeks waged a hard battle against the Persians which deeply affected many of their thinkers, comparing the two civilisations, recording the events of the skirmishes, fearing or yearning after the luxury of their rivals. Moreover genuine and Hellenised Semites injected into the culture of the peninsula their angles on life and their currents of opinion. In addition the Greeks were great wanderers and observant travelers, voluntary and involuntary, free and exiled, the contact thus gained with Egyptians and other peoples setting fresh ideas in motion, religious, scientific and communal. Finally it seemed to a few leaders that only by a Macedonian dictatorship could their turbulent political manners be quelled; so they became defeatists for purposes of stability. It is fair to say however that by that date malaria had seriously decimated the ranks of Athenians and lowered the physical and mental energy of survivors, making them weary of strife and eloquence. Even the mighty Pericles dropped by the wayside a victim of the plague.

The second Greek conflict — marking a division in human experience between invaders such as the Hellenes and those known as Indians — was one involving agriculture and commercial enterprise. The Indians did not put to sea. They remained a landed people and their psychology reflected their economy. Nor did all the Greeks show much interest in the sea. Those along the coast, however, were adventurous and aggressive; they explored; they colonised; they gave the landed gentry no peace on account of their ambitions, their attendant religious heresies, and their proposals for the State. Against this menace to their culture the country gentlemen struggled valiantly and the heart of Athenian philosophy is red with resentment or scorn of mercantile pretensions and codes of honor. One has only to recall the history of politics in the United States to realise the import and the higher verbalism to which this conflict between agriculture and commerce inevitably gave rise.

India went through the racial conflict, spice of her legends, and Egypt the economic battle provocative of Ikhnaton's cosmic exploration. But Attica had a third and especially significant combat on which to meditate. That was over strident civil liberty. The issue between the individual and the State was joined along many lines. Great families such as the Alcmæonides and the Peistratides assumed the reins of government but no dictatorship withstood the buffets of rebellion for any length of time. The complete gamut was run from aristocracy to democracy and on to monarchy, followed by upheavals. Citizens were tenacious of their political rights, decisions were made by a show of hands, and through the drawing of lots rotation in office was practiced until Macedon won supremacy. The poor freeman had a voice in public affairs as well as the slave-owning gentleman, and when disfranchised alien merchants chafed under taxation without representation, they were apt to win the sympathies of the class with grievances of its own. Within and without their tribe, in dealing with members of their own caste or with dissident innovators from below, the strong and the powerful administrators of the body politic encountered a constant agitation for this reform and that expansion of interest, for this rigorous policy or that extension of privilege. Everybody had to have a political philosophy.

Greek individualism was unique and in part it may be explained by the unique topography of the country. No wide alluvial plains such as provided the arena for perpetual Egyptian autocracy made standardisation natural for the Hellenes. No broad level steppes, such as furnished the setting for the operations of the Russian Czarist soldiers and now present to Bolshevist governors the temptation to try a new species of uniformity, encouraged Greek nation-making on a stupendous scale. Greece was broken into patches between mountain barriers and, in the state of mechanical science during her proud career, economic unity was impossible. Tribes were laws unto themselves though Athens, when left to herself, found even law exceedingly hard to maintain.

Through all its course the demands of women kept feminine society wrought up and naturally everything that disturbed the hearth made an impression in the Agora. Pericles said that women should be seen and heard as little as possible but Aspasia and others managed to keep their sex in the limelight more than seems possible to us, looking backward. A newcomer from the commercial city of Miletus where she had been accustomed to intellectual companionship with men, for which her learned father had educated her, and counting on its enlargement, not its abolition in Athens of all places, she revolted against the inclination there to deny her equal opportunity and particularly to consign every foreign woman to the status of a concubine or slave if she had a love affair with a citizen.

If the hands actually raised when decisions were taken on the Acropolis were masculine, the women from time to time lifted their voices in protest against the ways of the tribal Elders. Thus Elpinice, daughter of Miltiades, instead of rushing to decorate Pericles on his return from the Samian War, stood still and confronted him with words rather than wreaths. Previously on more than one occasion she had brought her brother Cimon and Pericles together to settle grave disputes raging between them over Hellenic federalism versus Athenian imperialism and her independence was such that she had even contracted a romantic marriage in place of the "respectable" one. So she spoke with fervor about this aggressive military expedition of Pericles, sharing her brother's views that the wise course was to work for the union of all the Greeks against the outside world: "Are there actions, O Pericles, worthy of crowns and garlands, which have deprived us of so many brave citizens; not in a war with the Phœnicians and the Medes, such as my brother Cimon waged, but in destroying a city united to us both in blood and friendship?" But Plutarch reports that Pericles replied to the charge of fratricide simply with a line from Archilochus: "Why lavish sentiment on a head that's gray?" However that is not the whole import of the incident. In spite of his light consideration of the protest made by Elpinice, Pericles lost his office for four years on this very issue of imperialism. Furthermore his policy proved ruinous to Greece.

As a result of endless conflicts, racial, political, and social, the intellectual climate of Greece was too stimulating for mere dreaming and shadow-chasing to continue on primitive lines. Reasoned defences for caste and race and sex had to be concocted and because policies were determined in the open forum, eloquence as well as reason was imperative if anything new was to be accomplished or anything old perpetuated. Aggressors usually tried arguments before arms, thereby developing intellectual theses to justify their aims. By speech, by song, by written word, in the forum, on the stage, and at the school every experience was submitted to public review and criticism, whether it was a matter of taste, desire, observation, or vested interest. Greek intellectualism thus demonstrated the bold challenging of mind by mind in a tense public atmosphere. It was not cloister bred. Nor was it stifled by the hot atmosphere of courts. It seems that the very diversity of con-

flicts and experience furnished many facets for Greek thinking and gave it some appropriateness for the varied conflicts
and experience of the modern world — an appropriateness
which accounts in part for the sovereignty it enjoys in our own
time.

THE TOOTH AND CLAW PROCESS OF LEARNING

It is customary for writers who deal with the tooth and claw
struggle which attended the state-building process, or politics,
to assume with Edward Jenks and Franz Oppenheimer that
it sprang from masculine lust for dominance and the profits
of rule. However earnestly any one might prefer to believe
that the humanities have been the prerogative of women and
pugilism the prerogative of men, no such creed is historically
tenable when the details of fact are explored. The Greeks
knew well from long and intimate contact with reality that
lust was common to both and they grew to believe that love
was good for both.

   Their bible, Homer, assembled by Lycurgus from fragments
in Asia, offered them a dualism that could not be escaped, for
the highest symbolism in the sacred word represented the
patron saint of the Athenians, Athena, dressed in armor over
her handmade robes, protecting them with a spear no less than
the distaff, leading warriors to battle, determining its outcome,
wreaking havoc on foes, and promoting the interests of
favorites. One modern commentator sees a triumph for
feminism in the vote for Athena alone when a political faction
argued for the erection of a statue of Poseidon, god of sea and
commerce, beside her on the Acropolis. But in that action
there was little intrinsically feminist as the term is now interpreted. The vote was at bottom agrarian. St. Augustine got
the story somewhere and according to his version the issue was

submitted to the vote of all the citizens, men and women, "for it was the custom then for women to take part in public affairs." As it happened the women outnumbered the men by one and since they voted en bloc for Athena, she carried the day. But Poseidon was angry and to satisfy the offended god, the men soon disfranchised the women and began to reckon descent through fathers. The culture of the sea was advancing. A. Lang notes that "the whole domestic situation in the Homeric poems, the free equality of the women, the military condition, the life of the chiefs and retainers, closely resembles, allowing for differences of climate, that of the rich landowners of early Iceland as described in the sagas." And epic literature in general, codifying religious folklore, smacks of that same quality of archaic feudalism devoid of "purity, humanity, and mercy." If the goddesses of Olympus like the goddesses of Valhalla served their mates with food and drink, they were equally ready to seize an implement of war and rush into the trenches, so to speak, or shriek advice above the battle din.

This tradition of women as co-fighters and militarists was continued by post-Homeric poets. Pindar for example has Hephæstus splitting open the head of Zeus with his ax and Athena springing forth with a war cry. If Hesiod compelled Zeus to swallow Metis when she was about to give birth to Athena, his digression from the original myth was not due to a dislike of arms but to resentment at the growing reluctance of women to bring a dowry to their marriages and do all the home work besides — in the field as well as by the hearth. Hesiod went on celebrating belligerent heroes with all his mind and strength but he could no longer celebrate the female of the species so wholeheartedly. He was moved to say that the men of his day were rendered miserable because they could not farm without wives while marriageable girls were obsessed by other interests. Turning from Athena, protectress of weal, he therefore re-created Pandora, an old goddess, to make her the bearer of woe — a revelation of his own hunter-warrior psychology unprepared for the task of civilising himself or being civilised by woman. In poetic phraseology a sex war was announced.

The Greeks in fact had several female gods of war who still served the hearth, health, and industry but they had just one male god who was a regular worker, namely the lame Hephæstus, and he confined his labors to the production of fighting tools. Apollo's casual work was performed on special order. It was not the free choice of a superman.

Yet the Greeks did not have to view women and war entirely from the standpoint of mythology. Sparta was a living illustration of martial co-operation on a fifty-fifty sex basis. Though the Spartans lived by a landed economy, they made the conquered Helots till the soil for them while they trained themselves rigorously to rule parasitically over these servants, who outnumbered them ten to one. And because an enormous share of the landed wealth came into the possession of wives and daughters, the female of the species had to be as deadly as the male if the supremacy of her caste was to be maintained. She played her part in that scheme heartily for a long time, regarding it as her principal task to bear soldiers and in crises to be a doughty warrior or even a general herself.

For instance, when Pyrrhus threatened to conquer the state, Archidamia, the daughter of the Spartan king, entering the Senate, sword in hand, refused to permit the women to be dispatched to a safe retreat on the island of Crete, rallied the clan to redoubled effort, set the women to work on the trenches for trapping the elephants and saved Sparta from destruction. She had been disciplined for service to the State instead of to the hearth, the care of Spartan children (the weak ones were exposed until they died) being thrown on the community that

their mothers might so dedicate themselves. Propagation was
the sole purpose of marriage. "We are the only women who
bring forth soldiers," was their boast. And their men ran at
the heels of Acrotatus returning from the Pyrrhic War, Plutarch tells us, crying, "Go, Acrotatus, enjoy Chelonides and
beget valiant sons for Sparta." She was waiting with a rope
around her neck, ready for suicide in case of defeat. Women
hardened their bodies by wrestling naked with men, and great
amusement they found in muscular games, a pattern being
set by Cynisca, a king's daughter, who kept racing animals and
won an Olympian victory with her entry. Sparta never had
the harem like Ionia and Athens.

Spartan history runs from the ninth to the fourth centuries
and in the seventh and sixth there was a softening period following which the young king Agis and his mother Agesistrata,
"the richest woman in Sparta," attempted a return to rigor.
Luxury and the concentration of wealth had weakened the
thirst for political power and, although the proposal to restore
the old jurisprudence and rigid discipline of Lycurgus meant
personal sacrifice for these two rulers, they prepared themselves
for a simpler and hardier life and summoned their people to
the same. One of the provisions of the sumptuary laws had
commanded that no woman should drive to the Eleusinian
festival in a chariot with a pair of horses but even the wife of
Lycurgus, Callisto, it is said, dared to break the law and was
promptly fined, as she probably had expected. Naturally
then, the new reforming monarchs encountered a desperate
resistance and were paid for their temerity by the death penalty. Undaunted by this outcome the widow of the king and
her second husband, aided by the mother-in-law who brought
money and a powerful husband to the fray, sought to carry
out the drastic reform, and actually restored Spartan supremacy for a time. But the scheme was ultimately defeated

because, in spite of the martial tradition, the ruling class had been enervated by prosperity.

However, the Spartan tradition of military rigor affected all the Hellenes. In the regular course of reporting the Athenians learned also of other warlike women not far away, such as Tomyris, the war chief of the Massagetæ, described by Herodotus. When Cyrus the Great, coveting her realm, refused to settle the issue of ownership by a single battle three days within his territory or three days within hers, she decided to give him blood aplenty if that was what he had to have. Letting him advance therefore into her kingdom, her troops defeated him overwhelmingly and Herodotus then lowers the curtain on the scene as the queen fulfills her pledge to give Cyrus all the blood he wanted by plunging his body into a leather bag filled with the red gore of a life that was ended.

Miltiades was called by Pausanias the first great Greek and Philopomen was called the last of the Greeks by a Roman, each for his service in arousing a fierce military spirit and so unifying and defending the State. That there was a last powerful Greek, however, was due in part to the temper of the women in Macedonia who were still riding at the head of troops against the enemy, defending citadels, dying at the front, choosing mates with a view to the security of their estates or thrones, ridding themselves by means fair or foul of obstructors in their path, bestowing the hands of their daughters on suitors well placed for territorial advantage, and paving the way for the rise of their sons to tyranny. Thus they sought to maintain control over the land and the industries with which their sex had always been intimately identified or by aggressive warfare to acquire additional territory. Several women in the family of the all-conquering Alexander, destined to subdue the Greeks and hold the Persians in leash, raised and directed armies in the interests of the succession or aggrandisement. His half-sister Cyname knew just one kind of education to impart to her daughter, namely, military training. And Alexander himself, in the opinion of his latest biographer, Bercovici, as of the older writers, was compelled to become the master of the world by his militant Epirote mother behaving as the Homeric goddesses behaved. Half-wild ? So were they. When Alexander was in Asia, she joined the regent Antipater in making demands on the Athenians which caused the suicide of Demosthenes, their defender.

More light is shed on this tradition of sex equality in war by the story of Harpalcyus, king of the Amymnæans in Thrace. Because his wife died too soon to undertake their daughter's education, a military one, the king assumed the responsibility and Harpalcye repaid him well in after years by rescuing him from the Myrmidons. Then when her father also died, she turned to robbery, dwelling like Robin Hood in the forest, so fleet of foot that horses, strain as they might under the lashes of her victims, could not overtake her. Only a shepherd's snare finally brought the untamed creature to book.

When Laodice of Cappadocia put five of her own sons to death during her widowhood to prevent any interference with her whims and ambitions, she did but reveal a deep strain of the passion that produces all military struggle. These are mere illustrations of the part played by women in the interminable conflicts of the Hellenic peninsula which ran through so much of the warp and woof of life and thinking.

When in the midst of their pains and distresses, the Greeks began to ponder on war, they had to reckon with all its aspects, including the lusts at its source and the havoc it engendered. It was on the basis of personal experience as a soldier that Plato sought for other ways of settling disputes. Æschylus also considered the problem of the civilian, on his return from the front, and in his plays portrayed the sufferings inflicted on non-combatants particularly. Thus arose speculations concerning the elimination of profiteering, the restraint of commercial avarice, and education as a path to reason and restraint. In the welter of opinion, stock was taken of women's relation to the matter, evident in keen dramatic satires, Aristophanes for instance proposing to leave the whole issue of war in the hands of the ladies.

War acted as a mixer of races and mentalities, brought contacts with foreign civilisations, inflicted defeats and sufferings, enlarged Greek experience, widened the web of knowledge, and expanded social consciousness. This was a cruel process of learning, no doubt, dragging women into its brutalities as well as men. But in tracing the curious and devious course of mentality, its original function must be recognised.

THE CLASH OF CASTE AND CLASS

While wars, foreign and internecine, inflamed the desire of men and women for dominance, gave them triumphs to celebrate in gladness and defeats to grieve over in tragedy, and kept them in a ferment contrasting sharply with the solid despotism of Egypt, social divisions also brought clashes in reality and in thought. Nearly all the movements in politics and changes in forms of government recorded by Aristotle indicated these deep-seated antagonisms. Urban Athens no less than rural Sparta had caste lines separating the owners of servants or chattels from casual laborers and slaves, and from the beginning to the end of involuntary servitude, women were aggressive like men in promoting it.

The charge was made that his queen urged Darius to make war on the Greeks in order to get Athenian, Spartan, Argive, and Corinthian slaves. But the Greeks were equally zealous in the acquisition of such property. The grossest cruelty was

the meat and drink of Pheretina, wife of one and mother of
another king of Cyrene, "a Dorian woman transformed into
an Oriental Sultana." When the son she proposed to enthrone
was slain, Pheretina issued an order that the conspirators were
to be impaled, their wives' breasts torn asunder, and their
troops enslaved. At Corinth, where the worship of Aphrodite
was preëminent, nearly all the temple slaves were women.
Athenian grandes dames for out-of-door excursions preferred
black slaves as attendants, their fashionable veils not blinding
their eyes to the social effects of such possessions. And at home
perhaps some of them studied the *Œconomica,* or guide-book
for girl brides in the management of slaves, prepared by
Xenophon for his own young wife — domestic science thus in
origin a code of servitude. Artists were generally chattels and
always menials, even Pheidias being dependent on the personal
friendship of Pericles for his easy social position. That seventh
wonder of the world, the Mausoleum of Halicarnassus, built
by his widow for the king, was erected by the toil of servile
workers probably in chains.

Such was the dominant attitude toward labor in the entire
ancient world after wars began. Often sold into slavery themselves, the Syrians when they were fortunate enough to own
chattels were fond of using the men as footstools for their
ladies climbing into vehicles. The female slave of a Roman
lady in a later day might be told to confine her attentions to a
lap dog. In Asia Minor she might have to go off to the mountains to chop wood. But Lucian reports a matron who kept a
philosopher among her chattels.

While the distinction between men and beasts was lacking,
mankind of both sexes remained bestial in the sense of continually looking for prey. If in our softened times animals
enter into consciousness as "subsidiary personalities," a curious
paradox long existed in India where certain animals were

deemed sacred while certain human beings were despised and outcast. The fact that men and women could enslave other men and women by means of war, piracy, purchase, sale, and breeding, taking advantage of poverty, injuries, misery and helplessness; that they could torture, mutilate, and murder one another to the limit of their strength; that in the highest stages of culture they could be satisfied on the whole with the manumission of a gifted individual or with a reduction in the rigors of pain and punishment is scarcely a factual or philosophic anachronism even in our time. It was but yesterday that Calhoun on virgin soil was dubbing slavery "a perfect good" while the Sacred Word in all Christendom continues to transmit the ancient command for servants to obey their masters. In backward places over the earth the system endures to this hour unashamed. The British less than a decade ago called a halt on it in Chinese districts under their sway.

From this great division of labor sprang the companion creed that the "rich and well-born" were "by nature" a class apart in privilege — a doctrine which Heraclitus and Aristotle offset with the theory that some were by nature slaves and some by nature free. In any case the division was not one of sex. Even the orderly Plato who wished to perpetuate caste did not propose to reduce the women of the upper set to a position of subordination within that group. Some women were to have leisure, the ancients all decided. Some men were to work. And vice versa.

Though masculine poets of Greece did not have the gods of their own sex performing manual labor by preference any more than female poets voluntarily put upon the opposite sex tasks traditionally theirs, mortal man was somewhat tamed to farming and the crafts by the time critical literature appeared. He had been partially domesticated by youth, old age, weakness in battle, affection for his mate with the desire to help her in emergencies, or by her domination. If such work was transferred as quickly as possible to slaves of both sexes by both, yet all men no more than all women could forever escape the necessity of toiling in the fields and in the little workshops that were opened in the cities. It is necessary therefore to be on guard against the tendency to think of the slave woman and forget the slave man. Or to think of the latter and forget the former; to think of the male slave owner and ignore the female slave owner.

Records imply that Athens in 430 B.C., at the period of her cultural glory, had a population of 120,000 adults classified into 40,000 free citizens, 25,000 unenfranchised free foreigners, and 55,000 slaves. The city kept a supply of chattels on hand to sell to individuals while employing an additional force to act as public policemen, clerical workers, and casual laborers of one sort or another. The whole number of slaves was so small that the richest families could only boast of possessing a few and, while that was enough to create caste sentiments, it was not sufficient to end the necessity of all burden-bearing by Athenian men and women.

For the male citizen, war and statecraft continued to be exacting of energy and thought, since these occupations could not be diverted wholesale to menials, at least of alien races and tribes. For the females, domestic pursuits, especially manufacturing, still required supervision even if servants performed the actual labor; a lively account is given in the Odyssey of the watchfulness the Greek mistress had to preserve in guarding her wine store from her chattels — matched by the study Emily James Putnam made of personnel management in antebellum America. However the owners of slaves considered themselves a leisure class, superior and invulnerable. The free day laborer of Athens, like the poor white of the Old South in the United States, entangled in a gruelling competition with slaves, could scarcely raise his head in their presence. It took a bold philosopher such as Hippias, supported perhaps by his Sophist wife, to declare with pride that he made with his own hands everything he wore. No doubt he was deemed freakish and amiably excused because one freak in the community did not matter.

We have said that war and slavery were joint phenomena. So we must look for reflection on the one to be combined with reflection on the other. Nor shall we be completely disappointed. No Greek seems to have maintained that "slavery was a perfect good." Certainly Socrates and Plato failed to estimate it so highly. The Stoics and the Epicureans had a few brilliant slave leaders who naturally deemed the system less natural than the unphilosophic rated it while among the people at large a strong sentiment against the institution ripened and found expression in the New Comedy. Though slavery was not abolished, the consciousness of its cruelties, injustices, and follies deepened until "fanatics" were ready for emancipation. Aware of the obstacles to freedom, the softerminded sublimated their opposition into the fancy that economic status did not affect the soul — that "with the wise there was no bound or free."

Public opinion was a multiform opinion — a composite of fermenting ideas. "A new sort of people," remarks Ferguson, "these people of leisure and independent means, were asking questions, exchanging knowledge and views, developing ideas. So beneath the march of armies and the policies of monarchs, and above the common lives of illiterate and incurious men, we note the beginnings of what is becoming at last nowadays a dominant power in human affairs, the *free intelligence of mankind.*"

COMMERCE — A REALISTIC RIVAL OF THE PYTHONESS

NOT solely from war experience or the clashes of race, caste and class did the Greeks derive food for thought, substance for speculation. They could have gone on fighting, singing, conquering, and enslaving as long as vitality endured without rising to imaginative heights. Sparta continued on that basis and scarcely a name has come down to our time of a Spartan who did more than fight, try to check extravagances, and institute economic or political reform with a view to the maintenance of vigor. Plutarch charged the Bœotians with being too gluttonous to think.

It was to the businessmen, despised by the Athenian caste, that the Greeks owed the wide-reaching transformation of social life and arrangements which jarred their historic complacency to its foundations and sent creative thinking into almost infinite ramifications. And what was business to have that effect ? It was secular and realistic, instead of mystical. It was the foe of tradition and provincialism. Back of all the far-scattered activities of great businessmen were the merchants of the cities, men and women in stalls or shops, large and small, who ministered in part at least to the living requirements of masters and mistresses, philosophers and kings. Without some possessions, no portion of mankind can be civilised even though too many things may bring decay.

It required mental as well as physical daring to brave the unseen and go off to sea. As late as the century of Columbus, the ocean was still supposed to be inhabited by demons hungry for the flesh of navigators. But as curiosity, overpopulation, and the incitements of trade overcame fear and conventions, interest in adventure increased and the deep came into its own. Naturally the original Greek mariners peopled the

water with gods and goddesses, the tales of Phocæan explorers
nourishing the Odyssey, that immortal epic of the sea. Yet
the first Greek to make astronomical and geographical charts,
Anaximander of Miletus, presumably got his clues from such
early legends, supplementing them by the records of naval
wars and colonies which provided wider and more accurate
knowledge of the universe.

Twelve cities there were on the eastern shores of the Ægean
— Miletus, Myus, Priene, Ephesus, Colophon, Lebedus, Teos,
Erythræ, Clazomenæ, Phocæa, Samos, and Chios — and each
contributed at least one thinker who shot through the old
bucolic myths of nature magic, to which agricultural Sparta
adhered, the penetrating rays of naturalistic inquiry and reason.
Miletus contributed Thales, the father of synthetic thought,
as the West knows its history, and Anaximenes, his loyal disciple. Clazomenæ produced Anaxagoras whom Sihler calls
the "most spiritual of all philosophers," a man of means who
took up astronomical and mathematical research in his birthplace and then moved to Athens in the days of her supremacy
where he became a famous teacher of Pericles, among others.
Ephesus was the home of Heraclitus, "the real Sire of Stoic
cosmology," wealthy and interested in luring science to the
earth. Samos was the birthplace of Pythagoras though his
noted work in numbers and related philosophy was done in the
colony of Sicily where Empedocles, the precursor of Darwin,
was born. The very art of Ionia reflected the naturalistic bent
of her economic interests.

Citizens of the ports began to study the world objectively
without the customary fear that goblins of one sort or another
would "get" them. "Traditions and dogmas rub one another
down to a minimum in such centers of varied intercourse," says
Spengler. "Where there are a thousand faiths we are apt to
become sceptical of them all. Probably the traders were the

first sceptics; they had seen too much to believe too much; and the general disposition of merchants to classify all men either as fools or knaves inclined them to question every creed." But another reason for questioning creeds was the necessity for ignoring tabus that interfered with their business enterprise. Moreover navigation required originality and experiment. The difficulties of a monetary exchange caused brain activity directed to the solution of economic problems. Astronomy and mathematics became instruments of material convenience, found substantial realities with which to work, and lost much of their quality of demonology, or divination.

Thus the economy of commerce, demanding for its advance the physics of navigation, was the first serious rival of the gods; and scientists, of the pythons. To be sure after the physicists had gone far in exploring the universe over which the businessmen roamed, they found themselves face to face with an ultimate mystery. As Aristotle said near the close of the Greek era: "If there is no existence distinct from the concrete realities of nature, physics must be the first science. But if there is an immutable existence, it must take precedence of the former and its science must be the first, and because it is the first it must also be the universal science. And it must pertain to this philosophy to contemplate existence as such, both in its proper definitions and in its essential attributes." But this metaphysics, which meant afterphysics to Aristotle, though it has continued to fascinate the world to the days of Einstein and Jeans, was far removed from the oracular mysticism of the temple mediums. Whatever it was, it was beset by a scepticism ruinous to the divination of the gods.

Rightly did Christian thinkers in the years of the Church's supremacy lay down the maxim: "Where there is difference of opinion, there is doubt; where there is doubt there is no certainty; where there is no certainty there is no revelation," for the Greeks, meeting other gods by trade and exploration, began to doubt their own. Doubt of their deities, their spirit world — the shadow of matter — led to suspicion of customs, including political habits. Doubt respecting native points of view and accepted canons of taste and conduct as eternal verities brought on ethical scepticism.

Thales of Miletus, the trader and politician, divorced the stars and planets from Olympus by insisting that they were not gods and goddesses under whose mandate merchants and statesmen must shape their careers. And before their political demise, the Greeks of the moral Athenian schools had largely outgrown Homer, notwithstanding the fact that Plato cautioned them against raucous laughing and proposed in the Laws to punish it severely. Epicurus insisted that it was positive insanity, an incurable mythological mania, to associate thunder, for instance, with divinity; that while the gods were doubtless a magnificent manifestation of nature, they were not active masters of human destiny to be feared, placated, or supplicated for aid.

Secular concerns were pressing so hard on religious beliefs and their mythological foundations that in the concluding days of Pericles citizens of Athens, frightened at the atheistic tendencies at large, banned by a decree of impeachment any propagator of astronomical theory — an act, exclaims Spengler, "of the deepest symbolical significance, expressive of the determination of the classical soul to banish distance, in every aspect, from its world-consciousness" and thus to live in the "pure present" complacently. Like anti-evolutionists. Aristophanes makes the moon grumble at her treatment when the festivals were changed to the "wrong time of the year" to harmonise with the imported view of proprieties; yet the importation held its sway and instigated fresh and advanced thinking.

Thales got some of his courage to attack conventions in Egypt where he discovered affairs more exciting than the buying and selling of commodities. Even oracular wisdom in Egypt was tinged with scientific curiosity and pythonesses as well as priests studied the heavens assiduously. As early as the forty-third century B.C., in the estimate of Breasted, the priests of the Delta had devised a calendar of 365 days beginning with the time when Sirius shone above the horizon at sunrise. And the need of this device, bearing results in astronomical realism, came from the necessity of a punctual and efficient propitiation of the Fates on the part of rich rulers and traders who endowed clerical establishments; as expertly as possible the priestly beneficiaries tried to systematise the rituals of sacrifice and worship. In India, astronomy developed into a science from an identical demand. With sacrifices related to the movements of the sun, as the naked eye saw the happenings in the sky, the Egyptians combined astrological prophecy — a wisdom presumably derived in part from the conjunctions of planets.

In this particular realm, women were considered seers and there were so many prophesying that when astronomy reached the Greeks, they gave it a feminine name, Urania. The heavens were supposed to control the destiny of man and sorcerers and sorceresses reaped a generous economic harvest from their "readings" of the sky. Plutarch states that Aganice, the daughter of Sesostris, king of Egypt, strengthened her talents for this sort of wisdom by the aid of celestial globes and that Aglaonice, the daughter of Hegetoris of Thessaly, was able to foretell eclipses — verily she insisted that they obeyed her will.

Breasted says that the Egyptians "had much practical acquaintance with astronomy, developed out of that knowledge which had enabled their ancestors to introduce a rational calendar nearly thirteen centuries before the rise of the Old Kingdom. They had already mapped the heavens, identified the more prominent fixed stars, and developed a system of observation with instruments sufficiently accurate to determine the positions of stars for practical purposes; but they had produced no theory of the heavenly bodies as a whole, nor would it ever have occurred to the Egyptian that such an attempt was useful or worth the trouble."

A similar limitation marked their mathematical lore. "All the ordinary arithmetical processes were demanded in the daily transactions of business and government, and had long since come into common use among the scribes. Fractions, however, caused difficulty. The scribes could operate only with those having *one* as the numerator, and all other fractions were of necessity resolved into a series of several, each with *one* as the enumerator. The only exception was two-thirds, which they had learned to use without so resolving it. Elementary algebraic problems were also solved without difficulty. In geometry they were able to master the simpler problems though the area of a trapezoid caused some difficulties and errors, while the area of the circle had been determined with close accuracy. The necessity of determining the content of a pile of grain had led to a roughly approximate result in the computation of the content of the hemisphere, and a circular granary to that of the cylinder. But no theoretical problems were discussed, and the whole science attempted only those problems which were continually met in daily life." For architecture of a high order their knowledge of mathematics and mechanics was competent and dates back, it is said, to the thirtieth century B.C.

But what they had achieved profoundly stirred Thales. For instance the utilisation of geometry in pyramid architecture and the varied shaped tiles covering the walls and floors of majestic buildings charmed him in the way that circles later affected Dante. From the interrelations of lines, Thales developed scientific geometry "the object of which is to establish precise relations between the different parts of a figure, so that some of them can be found by means of others in a manner strictly rigorous." He also measured the pyramids and based calculations on the shadows that they cast. He introduced the theory of proportion — well-spring of harmony — thus making mathematics serve aggressive intelligence. For his successful prediction of an eclipse during a battle between the Medes and the Lydians, thereby ending their belligerency, Thales' mental stock rose high among his own people and his scientific work became popular among the "wise."

Some writers are inclined to believe that the initial curiosity of Thales was awakened by the discovery of the Babylonian calendar causing him to forsake the Greek prophecy based on an examination of the entrails of sacrificial victims for prophecy based on the movements of heavenly bodies. But that also indicates foreign contacts as the stimulus to his thinking. His keen astronomical interest is attributed by one authority to a female wiseacre who conducted him out under the open sky to observe the stars, on which occasion he fell unwarily into a ditch. Then she remarked: "Do you, O Thales, who cannot see what is under your feet, think that you shall understand what is in heaven ?" Naturally he had to make good after that. And before his days were ended, Thales had told the Miletans that the sun and the stars were only balls of fire. He was the first of the wise, it is said, to divorce nature from mythology.

By his pupils science was then expanded and finally Pythagoras, one of the "most assiduous inquirers" of the Ionian community, collected all the learning of the peoples with whom the merchants traded. To his mind travel was likewise such an inspiration that critics declared his vast information to be only the eclecticism derived from his journeys into Egypt and India. He discussed with Egyptian priests their developments; they showed him their records and unfolded their knowledge. So did the Persian Magi instruct him in their astronomical lore and reveal their flight of cosmic fancy; with them he drank mystical draughts. The arithmetic of the Phœnicians, perhaps derived like their alphabet from the Egyptians or the Cretans, if elementary, was like a tonic to Pythagoras. "The laws of moral life and the institutions of civil societies with their excellences and defects he got from the Hellenes. Thus equipped he contended in Olympic contests while refusing the title of 'Wise Man' in favor of the simpler one, 'a lover of nature.'" His choice was revolutionary. Previously the wiseacre, male or female, was merely the transmitter of legend and custom; for example it was in keeping with legend that the Three Wise Men of the Hebrew Scriptures undertook to follow the guidance of the Star of Bethlehem and pay homage to the newborn Savior of their race. But now the wise man or woman was to initiate.

Gradually we are learning the extent and character of the Greek borrowings through the researches of archæologists and philologists, scholars and artists delving into intellectual origins — Persian, Egyptian, Sumerian, Chaldean, Assyrian — and making us acquainted with the early builders of rationalist thought. The story is infinitely complicated and none is bold enough to attempt an explanation in terms of causal inner relations, so tangled are the threads.

But some intensely pertinent facts are plainly revealed. The birthplace of Thales who towers so high among the "wise" as the founder of geometry, astronomy and philosophy, according to the books, was the city of Miletus on the shore of a gulf, at the terminus of a rich valley, with marvelous harbors, from which commerce extended in every direction, to Egypt and the Black Sea. From this busy port merchants journeyed far and wide exchanging and garnering ideas as they exchanged and garnered goods. It was early the seat of letters, philosophy and critical inquiry — inquiry running to the roots of all Greek tradition. In this mercantile atmosphere Thales grew to mental stature. Many notices and some positive statements represent him as a trader himself. At all events he lived in a city of traders and traveled in their ships. The very name "wise man," given him by common consent, rested upon his practical ability demonstrated in several directions. Above all he was realistic in his thinking, as realistic as the merchant who sorted, classified, counted, and evaluated the common things of commerce nearly all related to the care of life. Long before the writings of Aristotle, this master among merchants had cut a deep path on the way to intellectualism.

TRAVEL AS A MEANS OF LEARNING

ALMOST an adjunct of commerce was traveling and like commerce it was a means of changing the direction of inherited interests and reducing localism — in the era of the Greeks as in that of the Crusaders, Marco Polo, Columbus, Balboa or Magellan. Herodotus, driven from home by political winds, used his eyes and ears to advantage and enthralled his audiences, when he was permitted to return, with his accounts of strange places, manners and divergent mentality as they listened to his public readings in Athens from the first books of his history. In our time comparative politics, economic geography, travel books, surveys, anthropology, and world histories do the same thing, namely, disturb local dogmas of might making right, of absolutism and perfection. With this changing vision, collegiate curricula maintain a steady if slow pace, while cosmic speculation and theories of destiny betray the widening outlook.

Most of the Greek philosophers picked up ideas in moving from place to place. It is claimed that Plato was reinforced in his philosophic temperament by a sojourn in Egypt, about 399 B.C., where he observed learned priests ruling a State and was impressed by the relative stability of their theocratic corporation over democratic Athens. It is probable that he lived for a while in Sicily hearing Pythagorean conversations and doctrines and contrasting them with the sybaritic practices of the local merchants. One legend says that he traveled for twelve years or thereabout, encountering strange creeds and conduct, journeying as far possibly as Judæa, home of "almost socialistic prophets," and to the Ganges, seat of spiritual intensity. If the women did not journey as far as some of the men, they listened to tales of adventure and moved around among the Greek settlements with astonishing freedom, considering the facilities for travel.

It was travel that made Aspasia a feminist. The daughter of Axiochus, a learned man of Miletus or Megira, she was educated and eager for more knowledge. All such Greeks who could in time turned to Athens for intellectual expansion. Having the means and the longing, Aspasia followed this rule. But on her arrival she found herself classed with the hetæræ, or courtesans, because she was a foreigner. Her political status was lower than that of an alien merchant who, although he was likewise forbidden to marry a member of the Athenian tribe, was spared the ranking of a prostitute if he aspired to free comradeship with the high-minded and sometimes witty citizens. By a curious irony however no less a person than Pericles, sacrosanct and chief instigator of the law aiming at blood and property, succumbed to her charms, divorced his wife, and took Aspasia into his domicile, legitimised their son, and, until the plague dragged him to the grave, lived with her in a romantic companionate-marriage. Naturally Aspasia had enemies for the very reason that she lived at the center of things Athenian and was known to share in the discussions of politics and policies, of ethics and happiness as if she were a native, granted the privilege. In turn she tried to prove tribal distinctions foolish with respect to mentality. And in Pericles' own time the code was liberalised owing to the falling birth rate among Athenians.

The documentary data for a generous acquaintance with Aspasia are lacking. But so they are for Socrates. It is principally through the latter's disciple, Plato, that anything important is known of the master and, if Socrates had not been forced to drink hemlock as an infidel and corrupter of the young, even his pupils might have neglected to immortalise the aged philosopher. Aspasia therefore cannot be dismissed too lightly in the absence of fuller descriptions of her career. Was she not also charged with impiety and, what is more, with being the power behind Pericles ? There is a reference in the *Medea* of Euripides which is interpreted as pointing to her. She definitely appears in the *Dialogues* of Æschines as a noted Sophist teacher. Socrates names two women — Diotima and Aspasia — as his teachers and Aspasia is conspicuous in the *Dialogues* attributed by Plato to Socrates' leadership. In *Mexamenus,* ascribed to Plato, she is a teacher of rhetoric instructing Socrates and Pericles and attracting many distinguished citizens to her lectures on philosophy. That Xenophon shared Socrates' admiration for Aspasia is clear in his *Memorabilia.* Satirists styled her Dejanira, the wife of Hercules, or Hera, the queen of the gods and mate of Olympian Jove, while other opponents of Pericles attacked his companion with more direct fury in an effort to strike at his power just as they assailed his philosophic friend, Anaxagoras, arguing for the practice of reason. Aristophanes, the comic poet, from whose caustic wit no person escaped, not even Socrates, accused her of instigating the Samian War; naturally she was in sympathy with the Milesians, and Socrates attributed to her authorship the funeral oration which Pericles delivered over Athenian soldiers slain in battle. Some writers say she went to the front with Pericles and that a temple was erected in her honor to celebrate the victory. Though Plutarch declares that the war grew out of naval rivalry and that the power of Athens was imperilled by the trading success of the Samians, he repeats the accusation of Aristophanes without questioning his anti-Periclean bias. In this manner makers of beautiful letters, copying from Plutarch, have placed Aspasia beside Cleopatra and Theodora as a third luminous or hideous example of the baleful influence of women entrusted with liberty. Hermippus, a second comic poet, brought against Aspasia the charge of impiety and of "pandering to the vices of Pericles" while Cratinus styled her a plain prostitute.

Of Aspasia, Leconte de Lisle writes: *"Aspasie est là causant philosophie avec Anaxagoras, morale avec Socrate, politique avec Charinos, hygiène avec Hippocrate, esthétique avec Pheidias . . . Aspasie a sa cour dans ce pays qui est une démocratie; elle a sa liberté dans cette ville dont les lois et les mœurs imposent aux femmes une tutelle permanente; elle préside aux destinées de cette cité où elle est étrangère."* To Aspasia's salon also came several Athenian wives who had risen above their kind in the play of mind. Leisure had been more generously bestowed upon upper class mothers by that time, owing to the rise of surplus wealth and the installation of strong Spartan women in their families as nurses for lusty infants. Manners had been changing in correspondence with leisure and in fact the family was undergoing a veritable revolution. Houses had books. Mothers and wives were de-

veloping social curiosity. The demand was surging for legal
emancipation and equality of opportunity, if not with men,
certainly with the unmarried hetæræ permitted to go everywhere and discuss everything.

With the travel arising from commerce and curiosity must
be associated the involuntary migration known as exile. This
was such a feature of the ancient world that a student of its
culture declared: "Greek history is to a preponderant extent
the work of men who were exiles or virtual exiles: Herodotus,
Thucydides, Xenophon, Timæus, Polybius." First by criticism
of domestic events and then by study of political and social
affairs as they appeared from a distance, exiles made genuine
marks on the evolution of mentality. They found learning
in adversity.

Herodotus broadened the views and interests of the leisure
class by introducing the anthropological approach to learning.
The specific women, such as the Egyptian queen, Nitocris, who
appear in his travel account are there fortuitously. His hosts,
the priests, just chanced to refer to queen Nitocris, perhaps
the builder of the third pyramid and celebrated in Roman
literature as a great heroine of the East, who took a ghastly
revenge on the slayers of her brother, through whose death
she came to the throne, by inviting them to a banquet in a
subterranean chamber and while they feasted admitted the
waters of the Nile, after which she threw her own body into a
bed of hot ashes. Herodotus' information about the queen of
Babylon of the same name appears to have been awry; scholars
say he confused Nebuchadnezzar with some story about a
woman. Anyhow, his tales of the marriage market in Babylon
and of sacred prostitution must have sharpened the wits of
Athenian ladies who listened to the reading of Herodotus or
who turned his pages in their homes. Whatever his opinion

of the marital relations of savage tribes whom he observed, at least he helped to force judgments by others.

His main theme was the contrast between Persian and Greek societies — to the advantage of the latter. But even when he was discoursing on his own Greek culture, comparisons could be drawn between the status of women here and there as he told about the freedom he saw the sex enjoying in other regions than Athens where the original caste equality within the family of chieftains had given way to popular government and masculine democracy. Mahaffy in *Social Life in Greece* deals with the influential position of the wives and daughters of the early chiefs who shared the councils and shaped the decisions as no male member of the tribal rank and file could possibly do; these women despised all lesser mortals whatever their sex and proudly upheld the prerogative of caste. Not until the privileged were forced to yield a voice in government to that rank and file did the mere man with a vote rank and rate himself higher than the finest lady without one. The friendly attitude of Herodotus toward the non-Athenian practices he witnessed, survivals of the ancient régime, compelled a realisation of possible limits to localism at the same time that it awakened a sense of the past.

Thucydides is called the greater artist in handling the raw material of history but his interest was narrower. A rich mine owner of Thrace who entered the military service of Athens, he developed political ambitions which led to his banishment. He has been criticised as "brutally materialistic," resentful of the poverty of Athens in comparison with the luxury of Persia, and impatient for power rather than concerned with justice. Hence he deals with political action, political history, the phenomenon of empire, the personalities of political leaders battling for supremacy. During his twenty-one years of wanderings in exile, Thucydides got a notion of the way outsiders viewed the imperialism of Athens at any rate and from that vantage ground wrote his monumental history of the Peloponnesian War. He grew to realise that the letting of blood alone could not heal political diseases and felt that the exposure of perfidy was a better agency. His study of political capacities and politics at work was a stirring phase of the intellectual development of Greece carried by Aristotle to the point of an attempt at the science of politics.

Thucydides had two children, a son and a daughter. The son Timotheus was a nonentity but the daughter whose name is now unknown was considered by her contemporaries to be so intelligent and clever that responsibility for the eighth book of her father's history was laid at her door. It is true that Marcellinus, the Roman biographer of Thucydides, ridiculed this claim but he based his objection on *a priori* assumptions about the nature of women, rendering him also suspect. If the girl had been incapable, how could the rumor have started ? Some writers declare his wife brought him the mining property. However, the women who figure in Thucydides' work are the prostitutes plying their trade in a time of awful disaster — amid the gloom which darkened the soul of the author. Plutarch, of a more prosperous day, said he agreed with Gorgias about the necessity of considering the reputation more than the bodies of women as Thucydides had done, while we of a still later period believe the rounded story requires a knowledge of both.

Xenophon had a different experience away from home than either Herodotus or Thucydides and possessed a different bent of mind, being primarily interested in agriculture. He spent his exile in Sparta and became enchanted with her form of tillage which at that time held down aristocratic holdings to communist proportions. Sparta remained a kingdom and so it was not difficult for Xenophon to become a monarchist.

In a similar manner through the ages forms assumed by defeat or revenge have often illuminated literature. Thus Dante among the Italians, raging against the birthplace that banished him, shot off sparks of Promethean political fire. Thus Voltaire brought home to France from his English asylum fresh measuring rods. Thus Germaine Necker-de Staël introduced from Germany yard-sticks of a critical nature when Napoleon banished her from Paris.

Isocrates injected a psychoanalytical approach to thinking which awakened more interest in personalities as such, provoking biographies that grew in number with the spread of Hellenism by Alexander. Dicæarchus ambitiously undertook a history of Greek culture; it was colored by the popular belief in a golden age grown mature and paralytic. Lacking the material for pre-Homeric history, the Greeks nevertheless possessed an antiquarian curiosity of considerable range. Finally it led Eratosthenes to claim that Homer belonged to an Age of Ignorance, if not of Innocence.

In the city of Alexandria where the intellectuals continued to pursue learning after the fall of Athens, women also did much looking backward. Thus Hestiæa became a noted archæologist and writer on the Greek classics, a grammarian and a philologist; during a Homeric revival she worked out the topographical aspects of the Trojan War. Agallis commented on the ancient bard. But Nokobule tackled the more modern theme of Alexander's imperialism, writing its history and supplying later authors with material which they used extensively.

THE MEDICAL ROAD TO KNOWLEDGE

MEANWHILE from the realm of healing also came rationalist heresies, or thinking. Was it not from medical observation that Anaximenes derived his theory that air was the one universal and fundamental element of life ? And was not his thesis the most natural one imaginable as he watched the breath vary, saw energy wax strong, and then fade away ? Thus the testimony of the eye reinforced the tradition which held that the surcease of breath meant the vanishing of the spirit to embodiment in some other form. According to Semitic legend, God's breath called clay into life. But among the Greeks concern with this life-giving and life-sustaining element of breath acquired naturalistic implications and, as these were explored, the stream of philosophy was watered from that tributary.

Though mystics with their incantations, making health a question of magic, even demoralised the famous herb women of Thessaly, the Pythagoreans held fast to the habit of reasoning from observation and practice to health, one of their most celebrated medical writers being Theano to whom we shall again refer as a physicist and moral philosopher. Believing that nature could perform feats greater than the Olympians in keeping mortals hale and hearty, she called attention to the value of a planned diet and exercise. Wherever the sect established a branch, vegetarianism was preached, one of Theano's cardinal principles. Socrates also lauds the midwife who was doctor as well as nurse. Abundant evidence exists that Greek women were respected for their major contributions to this field of rationalisation.

More significant is the fact that Hippocrates, the most noted of Greek physicians in later times, makes no mention in his works of the god of healing, Æsculapius, while he does take account of the actual women physicians — general practitioners, specialists, surgeons and pharmacists — who helped to extend the reaches of medical science and reason. Belonging to a family of distinguished medicine-men, or priest-doctors if that term is better, Hippocrates managed to outgrow obscurantism and return to the original feminine approach to medicine through observation and research. Like the Pythagoreans he advocated a selective diet and exercise, belittling drugs and amulets, and thereby pioneering in a realistic direction for a man.

Notwithstanding this development, in the fifth century the Athenians reverted to the worship of Æsculapius, hoping in a period of devastating plague to receive the help from heaven denied them by mortal wisdom. In part borne to their land by African traders, their illness was also caused by malaria home-grown. Instead of draining the marshes properly, the masses resorted to the magic of charms, prophecies and prayers to lift them out of their distress. At this period Athena was given stronger health attributes, possibly in recognition of the devoted women nurses who served during the crisis, and certainly in order that she might add the new protection to her industrial and military care. Polybius describes the swift decimation of the people and the attendant mental ravages among survivors in the melancholia of Letters. But Menander, in the New Comedy he helped to create, maintains a gallant attitude toward the gallant women who attended the sick and the dying.

The ravages of this disease as hostile to armies as to civilians may be one of the reasons why Alexander supplied Aristotle with generous funds for scientific research, Aristotle being a physician and the son of a physician, with a realistic mind. From this vantage ground at any rate the doctor observed Egyptian practices, notably the mode of disembowelling and embalming. It is possible furthermore that the Egyptians vivisected human beings since criminals were turned over to the anatomists. At all events Aristotle realised that medical knowledge was important for the care of life and in that realm employed with great zeal the method of observation and research which ultimately made him the "master of them that know."

SEX IN CIVILISATION

To all this fermenting life what relations did women bear ? Answers are diverse. Those who speak by the records must report wide variations in the status, liberties, and influence of women; but owing to the inveterate tendency of historians to generalise (the simplest way), the ease of extracting neat pictures from legislation, and the inclination of Christians to flee from women as sin or to extol only the "virtuous," tradition has fixed in Western thinking a kind of stereotype of all Greek women as listless in the servitude of the home. The following picture of an Athenian wife, given by Gulick in his *Life of the Ancient Greeks,* has become for the generality of thinking the whole picture, the true picture: "Once settled in the home . . . her interests and pleasures, if she belonged to the upper class, were bound by the walls of her house, which she might not leave without the special permission of her husband. Even then a slave must go with her. Custom excluded her from the banquets and symposia given by her husband in the house. His friends were at most only speaking acquaintances of hers, whom she seldom saw except in his presence. Only at the festivals could she appear in public as a matter of right. No wonder her mental horizon was narrow. . . Further, the wife enjoyed no legal status. Her husband, as her guardian, became her representative before the law." With the formal accuracy of this account as a description of a routine household of Athens at a given age there can be little quarrel, but when considered in relation to intellectual life, it is as pertinent as a similar description of a household on Main Street to the intellectual interests of the United States.

In reality this account contains in itself one fundamental limitation which usually escapes the generalisers, namely, "if she belonged to the upper class." When it is remembered that the majority of women did not belong to that upper or ruling class and that thinking went on throughout society from the slaves at the bottom, who were often from the upper classes of other regions conquered in war, the perils of generalisation are immediately apparent. Still more important are other facts. As specific records indicate, many a housewife was by no means the victim of male dominion and from that center of seclusion exerted an influence reaching beyond the boundaries of cities and states. They also bear witness to the truth that innumerable wives even of the upper class did venture beyond the walls of Athenian homes into public affairs and debates. And in other cities more freedom was generally accorded wives. Was not Hipparchia, a noblewoman-evangelist, the wife of Crates the philosopher ? Was not Themista, friend of Epicurus, herself called "a sort of female Solon," the wife of Leonedor ? It is needless to multiply examples, for the generality, however true within routine limits, fails to reckon with the multitude of women associated with the class known as hetæræ — unmarried companions of men. It is not denied that they were free to attend banquets, theaters, resorts, games, schools, and public discussions. If Christian morality required later intellectuals to look upon them as beyond the pale of "virtue," natural history must admit that they were women — women of deep, far-reaching influence on the life and thought of Athens and of all Greece.

Whether considered as individuals, members of castes and classes, or as a sex, Greek women conformed to no type which particular males deemed efficient for their purposes or statesmen regarded as best fitted to the utilities of the State. As a matter of fact the Ionian cities and then Athens were often rent from center to circumference by efforts to reduce the female of the species to marital complacency. The attempt was imperative if State revenues were to be supplied. The great society, in short, was arising, marked by private property and the need for its definition, regulation, and taxation — a situation demanding that the wife declare her offspring whether the husband did so or not. If he were to meet family requirements, it must be on more romantic grounds than sexual continence. Thus male lawgivers, such as the mercantile Solon, anxious to create a great State adapted to commercial enterprise and provided with a naval exchequer, were far from blind to the relation women bore to the program.

In spite of nature's precision as Thomas Jefferson was continuing to interpret it in the nineteenth century — public freedom must not be granted women so that one may be sure of heirs — marriage and the definition of property rights could not be managed by one sex alone. System had to be introduced into the sexual life of men as well as of women. So the statesmen struggled to prevent spendthrifts from diverting to courtesans the wealth the State needed for its own ends. This political path was a stony one because the courtesans received honors and adulation of unlimited proportions and a traffic in beautiful and clever women reached so high a degree of organisation that the yearly hire of an attractive person rose to fifteen times the auction price of a domestic or common slave, if statistics used by the New Comedy playwrights are accepted. Lascivious men even drew young and handsome boys into their course of dissipation, the very bible of the Greeks approving that excess. Try as they might to cast the onus for the story of Ganymede upon the Cretans who, Plato declared, the Greeks knew had "superimposed this legend, directed at Zeus, in order that following the God they may reap this pleasure also," Ganymede actually dwelt with the immortals. Much of the erotic verse was likewise directed at comely boys. Sophocles entitled one of his plays, "The Lovers of Achilles" and clearly the gilded youths of Athens were reluctant to forsake any companions of joy for the responsibilities of domesticity and obligations to the community as a whole. However in spite of their inclinations, if marriage was to work at all, husbands as well as wives must be held to duties.

Taking note of that fact, our own Margaret Fuller once remarked: "If men look straight at it they will find that, unless their lives are domestic, those of the women will not be. A house is no home unless it contains food and fire for the mind as well as for the body. The female Greek of our day is as much in the street as the male to cry, What news ? We doubt not it was the same in Athens of old. The women, shut out from the marketplace [except working women] made up for it at the religious festivals. For human beings are not so constituted that they can live without expansion. If they do not get it one way, they must another, or perish." In return for the woman's fidelity to marriage, the man had to support her in the circumstances to which she had been accustomed. Naturally this effort to take care of her and their offspring hampered his freedom whatever his wealth might be and compensations had to be offered to persuade him to restrict his liberty. That is where romantic love played its part.

Those who led in the contest for the State against the liberties of sex encountered the obstacle of religion immediately. Some therefore grew very angry over its nature and cast off allegiance to Homer and his Hesiod redaction, declaring them outmoded. Among such dissidents was Xenophanes of Colophon who thus gave vent to his free thought: "But mortals think that gods are born to have their own faculty of perception and voice and shape. . . All these things did Homer and Hesiod assign to the gods, whatever among men is opprobrious and censurable, to steal, to commit adultery, and to deceive one another." Other critics either sublimated the myths into allegorical fancies or purged and refined the tales of the immortals. In such ways fundamentalists and modernists in that "golden day" waged a contest over sex comparable to the present backwoods battle over evolution. Plato retained a yearning sympathy with the god idea and tried to clothe it in beauty and inspiration instead of laughing it out of court. Aristotle, like Xenophanes, felt that the gods were man-made and he remade them into symbols of cosmic principles and continuity. Thus the habit of utilising religion for changing social circumstances was clearly manifest.

Since people at large could not lightly veer in the new family direction, attempts to glorify marriage were countered by allegiance to the Greek goddesses, such as Hera, who suggests the hetæra rather than the wife; to Artemis, a sort of female Apollo who preceded the female Buddha of India; to Athena, motherless and masterful; to Helen, a lovely woman desired of men however much they tried to make her the dawn or the moon "which wanes and disappears." Sculptors immortalised the figures of unmarried boon companions to the neglect of domestic wives just as Japanese artists have made their empire known round the world for its geisha allure. While orators and playwrights inveighed against courtesan gold-diggers, Demosthenes attacking Nicarete, and Hyperides his former mistress Aristagora, "men of the pagan world adorned their chambers with paintings of their pagan gods in attitudes of unnatural lust" and engraved them on seal rings. The theme of physical adventures by courtesans formed the core of legendary education and suggested modes and manners to the "properly" reared.

Without warrant, it seems, the tale was circulated that Thais, whom Alexander carried with him to Asia, persuaded him during a feast to set fire to the palace of the Persian kings — a tale woven into Dryden's *Ode to St. Cecilia's Day*. Lais, the greedy beauty loved by Aristippus among others, war victim, and object of barter, was given a monument at Corinth representing her as a lioness tearing a ram. Gnathæna entered the Athenæum with her witticisms and Callimachus incorporated some of her lines of philosophic verse in a work of his own. Phryne, the mistress of Praxiteles, who had a statue of gold on a marble basis at Delphi, became so rich through lovers' gifts that gossip said she offered to rebuild the walls of Thebes after the havoc wrought by Alexander, provided she might insert the words: "Alexander destroyed them but Phryne, the hetæra, rebuilt them." Lamia, famed for her extravagant feasts, was so popular that Plutarch and Athenæus continued to celebrate her talents and friends of her lover Demetrius proposed to honor him by erecting a temple to her under the name of Aphrodite. She rose from the position of flute player on the stage to the status of joint city-planner with Demetrius of Sicyon — and built a great portico there. Sappho was very bitter against a courtesan by the name of Rhodopis, first a fellow slave with the poet Æsop and then bought and borne to Egypt where Sappho's brother, a merchant, met her on one of his trading trips. Sappho blamed her for getting the brother's property away from him, though of course Rhodopis had been treated in her own person as property for some time. With a portion of the money gleaned by the sex appeal, she presented Delphi with ten iron spits.

Sometimes horrible revenge was wreaked on these fairly hapless victims of war and economic circumstance as when

Periander, tyrant of Corinth, brutally disposed alike of his wife and the courtesans who gossiped about her. At other times, loyalty and majesty of conduct fired the Greeks with ideals of constancy, if not of the legal variety; thus Leæna was honored by the Athenians with a bronze statue on the Acropolis — a lioness without a tongue — for biting off her own tongue and dying in torture to avoid revealing secrets which would harm her lover. If chastity was an incredible concept to the Greek littérateurs, by and large, concubinage had its legends, its heroines, its villains, its poets, its artists, its practices and a tradition which the new monogamy was poorly equipped to rival. Many of the free lovers tried to make poetry of their passions. The lowest grade of courtesan was confined to brothels, made a chattel and source of public revenue as a taxed amusement. Legal marriage was forbidden between an Athenian citizen and an alien; hence some of the most brilliant women of Athens were denied the status of wives. And as some one has declared, there appears to have been "no objective law of conduct anywhere in the Græco-Roman world." One only has to add that it is a very late offering at best.

But this is not to say that the Greek women who did accept marriage were nonentities necessarily. The working class devoid of property had slight reason for making legal choices. But for the propertied class the choice of marriage rested on clear compensations. Her wits alone were the protection of the courtesan, while the wife acquired the protection of the State to a considerable degree. For the sake of security for their children, many free-loving women turned to the legal relation, often finding marriage a romantic satisfaction for themselves in the bargain. We read of men who lavished upon their married mates the extravagances others bestowed upon prostitutes. Marriages for love were known, if not common. Many wives brought rich dowries and were not the sort to lick a hand that smote them, if such were raised against them.

A sample of their pride and its expression occurs in the speech of Panopes to Eutherbulus: "You married me, oh Eutherbulus, a woman of no mean rank or destitute of titles but one ennobled by the blood of both father and mother. Sosthenes of Steira was my father and Damophyla was my mother who united me, an heiress, with you in marriage for the purpose of perpetuating the family by legitimate offspring, but you with an eye easily attracted and loosely directed to every wanton object of pleasure to the neglect of myself and children attach yourself to Galene, daughter of Thalassion, a stranger from Hermione, to whom with a mischief to her band of followers the Piræus has afforded shelter. The young sailors flock to her entertainments and each brings some present which she devours. . . You however going beyond their vulgar presents used your Milesian network, your Sicilian garments and gold besides. Desist from this ill usage and be no longer hunting after every woman you see, or be assured that I shall go to my father who will not overlook me and who will prosecute you for your criminality." It is true that the wife was differentiated from the courtesan by the veil but she accepted that distinction with pride. She too had traditions of freedom if she belonged to the upper class.

The daughters of several Greek monarchs brought whole kingdoms to their husbands as dowries and Simonides of Amorgas speaks for the lesser luminaries when he says: "It is hard to get a wife who will both bring you a good dowry and then do all the work." Straight to a domestic relations court went the wife of the flashy Alcibiades with a bill of grievances when she disliked the way he behaved and, if he is pictured as lifting her up in his arms and bearing her straight home, perhaps victory was not entirely to the strong.

Many a woman by a wedding ceremony healed the breach between rival war lords or competing politicians but Peisistratus, tyrant of Athens, essayed a double experiment for popular favor. He displayed his civic perspicacity by agreeing to marry the daughter of his rival, Megacles. In addition, to satisfy the religious feeling of the public, Peisistratus arranged for no less an exhibition of divine right to rule than the affirmation of the goddess Athena whom some friend kindly consented to impersonate. "O Athenians," the goddess cried, "receive with favor Peisistratus, whom Athena herself, honoring him most of all men, brings back to her Acropolis."

In societies so diversified, in all stages of cultural evolution, swinging from despotism through democracy to tyranny and back again, torn by conflicts domestic and foreign, permeated by bewildering ideas garnered from travel, commerce, and exile, and profoundly disturbed by changing relations of the sexes, there was inevitably a wide variety of opinions. The ground was prepared for the rise of a rich intellectualism. Consequently the history of civilisation, which is the chief source of light for the understanding of men and women, cannot be told in terms of a few towering figures, for they at their greatest but carry forward another step processes already far advanced by hands and minds almost or entirely nameless in the written records.

THE NATURE AND FORMS OF INTELLECTUALISM

It was amid these complex circumstances that intellectualism arose — the habit of inquiring into and thinking about the total situation and all its parts, from the stars overhead to property at one's feet, resulting in a mosaic of inferences, concepts, and beliefs that has ruled in our Western world until the latest hour. And what, when examined, is this mosaic ? In every direction scholars and specialists have analysed, compiled, classified, and schematised. They have followed its growth from Homer, through Pythagoras and Aristotle, down to the scholastics and doubters who held the stage when the flood of Roman armies rolled over the scene. They have built out of it types of philosophical theory and systems of thought ranging from abstract constructions in mathematics, still valid, to speculations concerning the problem of civilisation itself, notably the care of life.

When its inner nature is studied, this mosaic of ideology appears to consist in part of reflections on or descriptions of actuality, considered as a whole, or special fragments, static and in action. In part it also consists of comparisons of similar or different things and situations, the object of which was fundamental conclusions about their essence and possible relations. Finally running through those branches of Greek thought dealing with life and living are efforts to discover either in the substance of things or in the realm of constructive imagination, the ideal, the desirable, and the good. It is true that to the end Aristotle was never certain whether the statesman for instance was a designer and maker of ideal social arrangements or a victim of destiny, nor how far the designs of social life arose unconsciously from the efforts of individuals and classes. But that defeat did not discourage the search for the perfect.

In expressing the various aspects or approaches to conceptual thought, which may be for convenience called philosophy, the Greeks developed forms which likewise rule us today, such as poetry, song, drama, oration, dialogue and solemn treatise. Hence those who explore the rise of Greek intellectualism must range beyond the secure writings of Plato and Aristotle through the whole field of intellectual expression. As in our day a more accurate and vivid picture of American life can sometimes be got from a shrewd and penetrating novel than from a heavy volume on sociology, so the substance of things Greek may be revealed in a song or a play rather than in a tract by a sophist. And when intellectualism, composed of many cross currents, is regarded as an organic growth, then it is seen that all those fragments of thought and forms of expression have intimate links which make sharp pictures of individuals and particular scenes arbitrary and inadequate.

For Greek intellectualism was not the product of a few isolated thinkers working in secluded retreats, as popular treatises on philosophy might lead us to suppose. Those who have gone deepest into the sources of particular systems know best how impossible it is to find beginnings. For example, was Pythagoras a native of Samos or some other island, or a Syrian or Tyrian, as alleged; and did he draw upon the Phœnicians, Chaldæans, Jews, Arabs, Persian magi, Druids of Gaul and Brahmans of India no less than the Egyptians, as traditions insist ? History cannot answer precisely. But it is probable that intellectualism arose in teeming centers of Greek life, especially the trading cities, was associated with groups rather than isolated with specialists, was nourished and matured in salons where men and women gathered for argument and discussion, flourished in schools attended by both sexes and different classes, and was carried forward, modified, and interpreted by followers, dissenters, disciples, and sects.

THE THEME AND THOUGHT OF POETRY

THE oldest form of expression was poetry, and it was meant to be sung. At the fountain, in time, stands Homer but he sang mainly of strife in all its passionate manifestations with an emphasis so destructive and disorderly that Plato and certain other philosophers believed that editions should be expurgated if not disowned. Then came Sappho with a fresh, invigorating tone and theme, singing of redemptive power, of romantic love, and unity. At once she became the inspiration of the Greeks in their deeply sentimental moods — moods provocative of imagination, giving it direction and suffusing it with ideals. The conflict between strife and love led Empedocles to form the theory that these two forces of nature underlie all movement — strife, the separating principle; love the unifier. Always they contest for the right-of-way but are titans unconquerable the one by the other. Love, he said, the ordinary folk called Aphrodite the goddess; the wise knew it was a law of life.

Sappho, the exponent of love, was a product of Æolia, born on the island of Lesbos, where the ferment of monarchical, democratic, naval, and commercial politics had worked on the passions of the people to such an extent that a rich expression of lament, defiance, wit, satire, and reflection burst into poetic flame. To no small degree it was concerned with the interaction of warriors and their captive wives for the latter had refused to be companionable in a marriage by force and the former were resentfully bitter, feeling that after all it would have been better to wed painted odalisques than proud personalities. The misogyny of Ionian poets, who had subdued women through the arbitrament of war but failed to capture their affections afterwards, exerted such influence in Attica that Plato decided poets had no place in a civilised community. Indeed the Ionian school of masculine poetry led by Hesiod had spoiled Homer by transforming the free goddesses of Olympus into common scolds and shrews. Discussing this transformation Jane Harrison suggests that Hera, made increasingly unpleasant with every such redaction, may have been

originally the native queen in whom her captors could see
nothing but spite when she resisted their overlordship, so self-
centered were they. With that psychology as part of their
baggage, rightly or wrongly males accused Sappho and other
female poets, who entered the field of emotional articulation,
of being perverts, without questioning the sadistic impulses
which led to the glorification of war.

Sappho's effort to distinguish between formal and romantic
love was too subtle for the Greek poets in general but it caught
the imagination of the law-givers and philosophers looking
for harmony. To the outpouring of sheer sorrow, conscious
will and sardonic laughter, she added the humanism and joy
of affection, one result of which according to legend was that
Solon, something of a poet himself, after hearing one of her
songs at a banquet, begged the singer to "teach it to him at
once that he might learn it and die." Plato called Sappho the
Tenth Muse, hostile as he was to the general run of poets.
She was commemorated on coins; altars and temples were
erected in her honor. Latin poets of a later time forsook Vergil singing of "arms and the man" to try their skill at equalling
her lyrics and editions of her poetry still come from the press
amid battle pæans and calls for blood. From the exploitation
of local legends the core of which was sexual escapades,
through erotic or misogynic verse, to the sensitiveness of Sappho, the poetic urge led on to mediæval sublimations in the
love of Christ, the Virgin, or Jehovah, and then emerged in
the rapture of Petrarch, Dante, the Brownings, to retreat with
Emily Dickinson behind the garden wall for meditation on
the phenomenon as a whole. Mackail makes a triptych of
Sappho, Catullus, and Shelley.

"Probably no poet ever surpassed Sappho as an interpreter
of passion in exquisitely subtle harmonies of form and sound"
is the tribute of F. A. Wright in his work on *Feminism in*

Greek Literature. The Greek language was in a formative state at the time, indicating thought in a similar stage, and she enriched it with the quality of "proportion, charm and harmony," signifying of course not only linguistic genius but philosophic power. She shared popular lyrical honors with Alcæus of Æolia but hers was the profounder influence. Sappho became the guiding spirit of a poetry society numbering many celebrated interpreters of romantic love.

One of her famous understudies was Erinna who died in her youth chained to her spinning wheel by an industrious mother determined to nip in the bud her daughter's indulgence in the idle art of lyricism. Before breath fled however she was able to write lines which critics classed with Homer. Among them was her autobiographical lyric, *The Distaff*. The mother was soon forgotten but proud Greeks made a statue for Erinna who had composed an epitaph herself for another young girl singer named Baucis.

While the number of known women poets ran into the seventies, they were not all singers of love. Indeed some glorified war and some plain eroticism. Legend for instance said that Homer borrowed from Phantasia, an Egyptian, the daughter of Nicarchus of Memphis, who wrote narrative poems of the Trojan War and the wanderings of Ulysses which she deposited in the local temple of Hephæstus, from one of whose sacred scribes, Phanites, the blind bard got his copy. Though but a legend, Lepsius thinks it indicates the existence of libraries in Egypt at the time and it seems to indicate that women helped to fill them. Ante-Homeric legends also ascribe religious verses to Phemonœ, a priestess of Apollo at Delphi, as well as to the god himself, and both Phemonœ and Phanothea, the wife of Icarius, also a Delphic priestess of Apollo, are credited with the invention of the hexameter verse employed by Homer.

In the temple of Aphrodite at Argos a great poetic festival took place annually in honor of Telesilla, a somewhat legendary lyric Muse. During the celebration the worshipping men and women exchanged clothes as a recognition of her dual rôle in the war of the Argives against the Spartans when she both inspired the soldiers with lyre and song and at the head of a band of women valiantly wielded arms. Her statue in the temple represented her in this double capacity of heroine and singer. Telesilla was the author of an ode to Apollo and other poems to Apollo and Artemis. A scholiast on Homer compares her concept of Virtue with that of Xenophon in the famous fable of Prodicus. Of her work two verses survive composed for a chorus of Argive maidens singing about the love of the river Alpheus for Artemis — a contribution to nature worship. That she "went beyond Alcman in breaking strophes into short verses" is one of the literary claims.

Corinna, born in Tanagra in Bœotia, in the fifth century B.C., was the first and considered the greatest of the Nine Lyric Muses and about her gathered a school of men and women, all writing verse. Pindar was one of her pupils and five times she defeated him at Theban contests, for he was inclined to be excessively florid and to submerge his themes in rhetoric. Her subjects were mainly local heroines and her forms of interpretation, written in the Æolic dialect, were chorals, lyrics, epigrams, erotic and marital verse. Statues to Corinna were set up over all Greece. Corinna said that Myrtis was a competitor of Pindar for a public prize and some claimed that she was his instructor. Aristotle quotes with laudatory comment one of the hexameter verses of Cleobuline of Corinth and Cartinus is thought to refer to her in one of his plays. She seems to have been clever at riddles, more valued then than now, but her genius, we are told, lay in her concept of morality — foundation of all creative thought, as Madame de

Staël sagely declared. Aristomache of Erythræ, who took a poetry prize at the Isthmian games, dedicated a golden book, one supposedly written with golden letters, to the treasury of Sicyon.

Praxilla of the fourth century, B.C., another of the Nine Muses and a very popular one at Athens, living perhaps a century later than Telesilla, was noted for the variety of her meters as well as her skill in their use. Erotic Dorian myths seem to have supplied her with themes though evidences of Æolian emotionalism appear. The statue in her memory is attributed to Lysippus. Iambe, from whom that favored meter takes its name, was a Thracian dancer fortunate enough to make the mourning goddess Demeter smile, with her steps and her jests, her unique achievement provoking a supply of poetic legends, fables and raillery suggestive of the Japanese nature lore connected with the Sun Goddess. First in the Meleager list of lyric poetesses was Amyte of Tegea working in the rhythm of the ancient Doric chorals. She also had a statue and was praised by Antipater as the female Homer.

Poetry preceded politics in Greece but it continued to run as a parallel mental stimulus. In a fragment preserved by Athenæus from the Third Book of the Alexandrian poet Hermesianax, Leontion indicates that the response of such thinkers as Pythagoras and Aristippus to the philosophy of love expressed in the form of song was sensitive, while from other sources we learn of its effect on Socrates. Aristotle found it imperative to deal with the psychology of love in connection with history and politics: was not a tyranny often overthrown by a love affair as well as by the rebellion of the poor ? If order was to follow chaos, the heart and the head must together function socially. It is true that he accepted theoretically and practiced concubinage but he was capable of affection for his second wife, and aware of her devotion to him.

Though Homer and Hesiod were distinctly anthropomorphic, both believing in special creation, though the Ionian poets were largely misogynic, though Pindar was excessively florid, these were the models used for formal education in Europe during recent centuries. The result was a distorted opinion of the range of Greek intellectualism. Knowing that women grammarians and scholiasts wrote considerably on Homer, it would be interesting to discover whether they were critical or pliant themselves. How did Agallis of Corcyra for example or Hestiæa of Alexandria, so learned that male scholars admitted her to their gild, explain the bible of the Greeks? Perhaps the works of the Greek women are lost beyond recovery but, in the discovery of manuscripts year by year, something may yet be found to shed light on such intriguing questions.

THE PYTHAGOREANS

If we turn from poetry as theme and thought to abstract speculation, mathematical and reflective, we meet early in the way — in the sixth century, B.C.— a school rather than a system — the Pythagoreans. At the head is placed Pythagoras as a rule but researches have never disclosed how much he borrowed from neighboring countries. So uncertain about the school was Aristotle long afterward that he always referred, deliberately it seems, to the Pythagoreans, not to Pythagoras alone. But certain it is that the sect made genuine contributions to mathematics and as certain that Pythagoras left no personal writings embodying his own ideas. It may be said that the school "created the science of mathematics." Nor was that all it did. Observing physical phenomena, they drew near to the conception that the world of nature was geared into a common entity ruled not by chance but by laws, foreshadowing by nearly twenty-five hundred years, "the mathematical God," now described by the English astronomer, Sir James Jeans, to an astounded popular audience.

Whatever the larger implications of their speculations, which were often extremely vague, the Pythagoreans made numbers the foundation of all intellectual operations — logic, form, relationships, order, reason — and they developed elaborate symbols to express number thought, or harmony. Health being a phase of harmony, or perfection, they were healers as well as calculators with symbols. They were likewise physicists. By the logic of their reasoning they were also ethical reformers, seeking to subdue disorder and evil to the laws of unity.

Driven out of Samos by tyranny, it is said, Pythagoras settled in Crotona, a Dorian colony in southern Italy, and there became the center of an organisation, sect, or fellowship concerned with the rounding out and application of philosophic doctrines to the ills of mankind.

In terms of religion the movement was one of purification compared by Spengler with the English Cromwellian protest with which it had political as well as religious likenesses. But Pythagoreanism rather suggests the Quaker sect in its gentleness and restraint though its incorporation of music into its system marks it off from that more introspective faith. All life was to be a fine art embracing, as phases of number beauty, the rhythms of music and dancing, eating, gestures, behavior and reflection. A similar idea achieved in Japan in the Tokugawa era a marvelous expression of aristocratic taste and since it has survived sufficiently for an intimate observation, a key to the older Pythagoreanism may lie at hand. It was to quiet the spirit of warriors that the Japanese Noh with its related arts was devised. To unite the world by developing all its parts was the purpose of the ethical and humanistic Pythagoreans.

In the ripening of the Order's philosophy, the whole family of Pythagoras coöperated, proving the application of the theory of universal perfection. The wife, Theano, was a handsome woman of Crotona and their marriage a famous love match. She was learned and had high ethical standards in addition to being lovely and affectionate, her interests ranging from physics, mathematics, and medicine to domesticity and literature. She studied child psychology and corresponded with Callisto on the proper way to bring up a family — quite as vital to a social code as Xenophon's rules for slave management and more original no doubt. She was the author of a treatise on Virtue, Victorian-sounding at this date but a favorite theme of the illustrious Socrates and others who followed the Pythagoreans. This she addressed to Hippodamus of Thurium. It represented early in its career the philosophy of the "golden mean," for which Greece remains the wonder of the world. Certain of Theano's letters are extant, reproduced in his volume on Greek women writers and philosophers by Poestion, but her larger works have been lost. She carried on the central school after the death of Pythagoras. Either Theano or a daughter wrote a sketch of Pythagoras. Myia, a daughter, we discover in the fragment of her work that remains, urged a friend to suckle her child and assume maternal obligations to the full, regardless of the new opportunities to evade them. Another daughter, presumably, mentioned by Suidas, was also a scribe donating to literature epigrams and several manuscripts dealing with the worship and mysteries of Dionysus. A third, Arignote, treasured her father's wisdom and, when gold was offered for his sayings, refused to sell them.

Outside the immediate family of Pythagoras, women were active in the spread, development and interpretation of the faith. While pythonesses continued to deliver divine counsels from their tripods, Pythagorean women taught and wrote for members of their Order and disseminated the theories and practices of the school. By missionaries of both sexes, the creed was carried to Greater Greece and to Egypt where branches were formed. Among its publicists, Perictione took high rank, Aristotle being one of those who considered her work important. In her writings on wisdom and the harmony of women, she developed a theme perfectly attuned to the Greek quest for unity of spirit and body, life and thought, work and mind. Surviving fragments imply that the code called for moral restraint by women in the interest of men and children — a consideration of the larger aspects of love in an age of war and infanticide.

It is possible that Æsara of Lucania was one of the daughters of Pythagoras and Theano; at all events she belonged to the Order and was an illustrious literary exponent. A portion of her work on Human Nature is preserved in Stobæus and she is mentioned in the life of Pythagoras by Bentley; praise for her talent runs through the writings of Roman times, such as the works of Catullus and Horace; Alexander the Sophist lectured on her; grammarians commented extensively on her style; certain authorities ascribe to her the invention of the harp, an instrument exquisitely adapted to the hymns she composed for the gods. Among the effective Pythagoreans, Iamblichus also places Lastheneia though Diogenes Laërtius and others list her with the Platonists.

For more than a hundred years the Pythagorean schools spread and prospered, marked by propaganda, debate, interpretation, and it must be added by conflict, for they were sometimes divided among themselves and were finally the victims of brutal assaults by their neighbors, such as the attack on the House of Milo in Crotona where fifty or sixty members of the society were murdered, early martyrs of a faith. During all the later centuries the ideas of the Pythagoreans, from their most exact mathematical concepts to their ethical teachings, worked like a vigorous ferment in Greece, still leavening philosophy when Socrates, Plato and Aristotle won preëminence. And so intimate were the contributions of women to this movement in its beginning that Pythagoras was known as "the feminist philosopher." Such is the unity that runs through the process of thinking, individuals working in an endless stream of social forces.

THE AMPLIFIERS OF PHILOSOPHY

THE later philosophers of Greece thus worked in an intellectual climate already charged with ideas and speculations set in circulation by the eldest, or the poets, by the dramatists, and by Thales, the Pythagoreans, and Heraclitus, among others. Although in the traditional and popular vision three men, Socrates, Plato and Aristotle, stand out like mountains in a desert, they themselves labored in the midst of that heritage. What was the "state" of philosophy with which they began can never be accurately known, for historians are dependent upon records that are sketchy at best and the ideas, concepts, problems, questions and answers then impinging upon minds in oral discussion have entirely escaped immortality. Nor on account of the fragmentary character of the notions that have come down to us relative to Socrates, Plato and Aristotle is it possible to discover their peculiar contributions to the "state" of philosophy, assuming that it could be recovered.

Yet some filiations may be traced. In his operations as a thinker, Socrates, we have shown in connection with the Pythoness, harked backward as well as forward; he was still conscious of the world where priestesses acted as mediums of the unknown even when he looked about him most realistically. The past hung heavily upon his spirit. On his own confession women's thinking had impinged upon his own. In discussing "the true nature of divine and eternal beauty," he pays generous tribute to Diotima of Mantinea, acknowledging her as his teacher. Tradition makes Aspasia his preceptor in philosophy and politics. It is evident that Xanthippe was not his only companion and his close friend, Xenophon, has him declaring for the equality of men and women, showing that neither study nor experience had given him reason for trusting the masculine mind alone.

From Socrates, Plato derived the art of finding truth by questioning — the art of the temple. Like Socrates he was also influenced by the poetry of Sappho and circumstances indicate that he came within the range of Aspasia's power. At all events he accepted many of her radical ideas and taught that "mentally there was no essential difference between men and women." He drew the logical conclusion that women of talent at least should have the same educational advantages as men of talent. In the *Republic* and in the *Laws,* he makes education compulsory for "all and sundry, as far as possible." He proposes to have girls as well as boys thoroughly disciplined in music and gymnastics and, if this sounds dilettante to us, let us remember that under the head of music he listed reading, writing, literature, mathematics and astronomy. Music was harmony in the broadest sense of the term — a scientific philosophy — not a mere five finger exercise. His view was that of the Pythagoreans.

In the *Republic,* Plato declares: "The gifts of nature are alike diffused in both. . . All the pursuits of men are the pursuits of women." That represented his ideal society. In the *Laws,* his second best ideal, he contends that "women ought to share as far as possible in education and in other

ways with men. For consider — if women do not share in
their whole life with men, then they must have some other
order of life. . . Nothing can be more absurd than the practice which prevails in our own country of men and women
not following the same pursuits with all their strength and
with one mind, for thus the state, instead of being a whole,
is reduced to a half."

Such being his social theory and his feminism, did women
take advantage of the chance to study with Plato? Indeed
they did. Poestion says that Plato was a handsome man and
that species of magnetism would lead nearly every interpreter
of woman no doubt to make that the lure. At any rate
women came from various towns to his academic grove and
when they arrived they had to work. But the first students
seem to have been the wives and daughters of Athenians, and
his own sister, Potone, the mother of his disciple Speusippus
who conducted the Academy after Plato's death, was a distinguished philosopher. Gradually however the courtesans
from all parts of Greece pressed into the school and the outcome was the retreat of the family women to the hearth —
to private tutors, home reading, and discussion in a quieter
atmosphere — a frequent effect of equal opportunity in any
age. Still Plato was not disturbed. The truth is he had a
concubine himself like all the well-to-do men of his time and
was sympathetic with the free love doctrine, making it the
code for his utopia as far as the guardian caste was concerned.
If we are trying to understand women, not wives only, these
facts must be taken into consideration.

Among the women who rushed to hear Plato was Axiothea
of the small Peloponnesian city of Phlius, whose imagination
was caught by reading some of his letters. Her special interest was physics in which field Plato considered her gifted.
Just why she donned the garb of a man for her student career

remains mysterious. She did not have to disguise herself and the explanation must lie in the individual vagary that free women like to display, unless she hoped by her disguise to escape the attentions of citizens. After Plato's death Axiothea worked with his nephew Speusippus and finally she also became a noted teacher of philosophy. From Arcady came Lasthenia who became the concubine of Speusippus and she too achieved reputation as a philosopher in her own right.

Though supposed to be hard and realistic and often quoted in support of tyranny and slavery, Aristotle was a devoted pupil of Plato, revered his master's memory even when he departed from his teachings, declared himself to be a Platonist, and to the end displayed a tenderness that is often called feminine. He married a rich heiress, Pythias, a sister or niece of Hermias, the tyrant of Atarneus, and in his will ordered his executors to provide for his daughter, erect an image to the memory of his mother, and bring the bones of a wife to rest beside him in the grave. Though he ranged over the wide world of knowledge and wrote on ethics, politics, logic, psychology, physics, metaphysics, economics, poetics, zoölogy, meteorology, and constitutional law, Aristotle, like his teacher, was always deeply concerned with the just and the ideal. Being a rationalist in dealing with human relations as facts and hopes, he took full account of women.

Whatever may be the present tradition about the status of Athenian women, Aristotle's views on propriety conform to no neat theory. In his quest for the proper foundations of the State, he inquires into the rôle of the family and says: "The relation of husband and wife, parent and child, their several virtues, what in their intercourse with one another is good, and what is evil, and how we may pursue the good and escape the evil, will have to be discussed when we speak of different forms of government. For, inasmuch as every family is a part of the State, and these relationships are parts of the family, the virtue of the part must have regard to the virtue of the whole. And therefore women and children must be trained by education with an eye to the State, if the virtues of either of them are supposed to make any difference in the virtues of the State. And they must make a difference: for children grow up to be citizens and half the free persons in a State are women," recalling throughout conceptions found in Plato's *Laws*.

While drawing women into the ideal, Aristotle remarks on the unmistakable troubles made by them in the realm of politics. He observes that in Sparta "nearly two-fifths of the whole country are held by women," weakening the military prowess of the State. He notes that women were "friendly to tyrannies and also democracies, since under them they have a good time" but he was constrained to add as a keen student that "the insolence of women has ruined many tyrannies." In a burst of wonderment over the state of affairs in Sparta, he exclaims: "What difference does it make whether the women rule or the rulers are ruled by women, for the result is the same !" Alike in the ideal he hoped to see realised and in the actuality of life which, in some moods, he thought to be a kind of destiny beyond human control, Aristotle pondered gravely on the place of women in society and ethics.

But it is not from the writings of men only that information has come down to us about Greek women. In the ten or more philosophic schools springing from Socratic inspiration, women were usually active. They helped to found and administer, to teach and propagandise, to publish treatises on the particular wing of psychology or opinion at stake, and transmit, as disciples, its tenets. One of the first of the Socratic offshoots was established, about the time the Pythagoreans were being suppressed, by Aristippus of Cyrene, the son of a wealthy merchant who went to Athens to see the Olympic Games and there met Socrates with whom he was so impressed that he was inclined to dawdle in idle conversation without end, until his daughter Arete advised him to return to Cyrene, organise his faith, and diffuse it through pupils. With her help, Aristippus undertook the task. Now Arete was an acknowledged prodigy, interested in natural science and ethics and like her father concerned with a "world in which there would be neither masters nor slaves and all would be as free from worry as Socrates." Their dream allowed room for pleasure and attracted to their school Greek actresses in large numbers from cities where they still had privileges and some cultural training. The outcome was a lively debate on beauty and love, in this particular community. Aristippus bestowed his heart on one of these beautiful women, Lais, the model for some of the finest Greek sculpture, while she improved her mind with Cyrenaic philosophy, having intellectual interests as well as personal charm.

After the death of Aristippus, Arete conducted the school and was said to have taught natural and moral philosophy publicly in Attica for thirty-five years before she died at the age of seventy-seven. More than a hundred recognized philosophers were her students. Then she handed down the educational mantle to her son, Aristippus the Second, with the forty books she had written dealing with such themes as agriculture, childhood, education, old age, war, and the master, Socrates. When Boccaccio turned to classical Letters, he found Arete's mentality and personality exceedingly attractive and extravagant eulogies on her tomb seem to show that her contemporaries regarded her in the same light.

Younger Cyrenaic writers veered from Socratic leadership with its emphasis on extreme self-denial and moved in the direction of Epicurean elasticity. Indeed the Cyrenaics and the Epicureans eventually merged, having a bond in their mutual dislike of metaphysical subtleties. Both believed for example that feelings or instincts were sufficient indices of intelligence. They did not reject concepts of right and wrong, irreducible to sense perceptions, for they knew that sensations themselves are capable either of pleasure or pain. They simply decided that pleasure was preferable to pain and relied on a selective emotional intelligence rather than legislation to provide the basis and law of happiness. In other words they sought æsthetic satisfaction instead of dogma — a quest not necessarily inimical to sacrifice, restraint and dignity.

In addition to the Cyrenaic offshoot of Socratic philosophy there appeared the Peripatetic school — a favorite name for groups who walked while they talked and studied — headed by Antisthenes, but it went in the opposite direction from that taken by the rich Aristippus and his daughter. Antisthenes interpreted the creed of virtue, or excellence, painfully instead of pleasurably and made of the Socratic creed of the simple life a caricature with his austerity. Some critics thought him inspired by vanity. Others described him as foul of speech and raiment saying he lived like a beggar indifferent to family, politics, art and learning — really in a state of nature. In his case traces of feminist leadership or coöperation seem lacking.

The rigorous attitude of Antisthenes, Diogenes his pupil also displayed but his sense of humor preserved his personality. Diogenes was the man who lived in a temple tub and occupied himself, when not in his dwelling, by hunting for an honest man with a tiny lantern. A little masterpiece on the theme of civilising Diogenes was recently published by Edna St. Vincent Millay, her point being that when a woman decided to share the tub shelter with the Socratic philosopher, after she had dressed up the place and landscaped its surroundings, she soon got bored and schemed in every sort of way to dispatch him again on his errand.

Hipparchia who joined Crates the Cynic, another celebrated disciple of Socrates, turned from luxury to stint as an ideal but was not so gross about it. This beautiful sister of Metrocles of Thrace, in the company of her brother, heard Crates denounce materialism and was so moved that she gave up family and suitors, wealthy and noble, to cast in her lot with the holy man, ugly, poor, and even deformed. Clothing herself in the Cynic garb, she accompanied Crates in his wanderings and evangelistic enterprises, sharing not only the actual rigors of self-denial but also preaching the theoretical virtues. Suidas refers to treatises written by Hipparchia, among which was a query addressed to Theodorus the Atheist. She met him at a tavern and, atheist though he was with respect to the gods, he adhered to domestic conventions. So he asked: "Who is the woman who has left the shuttle so near the warp?" And she as quickly replied: "I, Theodorus, am that person; but do I appear to you to have come to a wrong decision if I devote that time to philosophy which I otherwise should have spent at the loom?" His answer is apparently unrecorded.

However the records refer to innumerable replies by Hipparchia when opponents took the side of acquisitive delights. Much of this mental offering reads like Christ's discourses against luxury and concern with things of the flesh. If women had invented the means of being physically comfortable, now when comfort had grown excessive and was obviously demoralising the ruling classes, a few women, sensitive to the dangers, made sacrifices to utter warnings. Like Christ of a later time these Cynics had no place to lay their heads, regularly, at all events. They walked barefoot and ate when they were hungry, foraging for their food. Lukianos, sometimes known as the Greek Voltaire, accused them of living like beasts but the Cynics' point of view was that, like the lilies of the field that toiled not, neither did they spin and weave, yet were clothed in greater glory than the distaff could devise, they had their human justification — an impulsion toward spiritual excellence.

From the political pariahs, after Plato's work was done, sprouted a modified form of Cynicism known as Stoicism for which a Hellenised Phœnician, Zeno of Citium, a merchant's son, was largely responsible. Socrates was still the old master; virtue and restraint were still integral parts of his system; but political circumstances had changed in Athens since the days of the radical tribal teacher, now making inter-racial contacts imperative, however difficult. Hence the individualist species of perfection was outmoded, and Zeno devised a philosophic nexus in a creed of social righteousness and the brotherhood of man — of intellectuals at least, in the Republic of Letters. The Socratic watchword had been knowledge and the Epicurean faith had been pleasant emotion. Taking these as elements for the new philosophy or psychology, Zeno combined them with the Cynic doctrine of suffering together with the Megarian positivism and made of the mélange an ideal of obligation to the whole community in the interests of universal happiness. Trained in dialectics he elaborated his simple fundamentals with a higher phraseology that rendered it attractive to speculators and, in a school which he in turn founded in Athens at the end of the fourth century, B.C., he taught for forty years the Stoic creed. Seneca, Aurelius, and Epictetus found the doctrine best suited to a period of Roman turbulence, racial problems, and tyranny when they went to school to the Greeks. A sensitive rationalisation was to lift mankind over the bumps of passionate prejudices. Stoicism offered a practical, immediate adjustment to a harsh society.

Later we shall see how valiantly Roman women imbued with this philosophy faced realities.

However, Socrates was not the master of every Greek. In fact Epicurus had no master unless, as Bury suggests, it may have been Democritus, the expounder of the atomic theory. Epicurus was the founder of a school of thought in which pure intelligence and suffering were alike derided though there was no resort to mysticism as a consequence. Instead of trying to purify the soul in the fashion of the Pythagoreans, the Epicureans denied that the soul had an existence apart from emotions, feelings and sensations. The Pythagoreans believed in the existence and transmigration of souls while the Orpheus cult also believed in immortality if in another form.

But the Epicureans thought life ended with what is called death. They even sided with the more popular tradition of a dead golden age, though they had distinct notions about the quality of that radiant past and, because they made light of all cultural flourishes, they were accused of being sensualists in the narrow sense. What they were really trying to work out however was a rational sort of happiness unburdened by learning and dialectics. "We cannot live pleasantly without living wisely and nobly and righteously," was their easy way of reasoning, in response to the optimism of a stirring commercial age in which the citizen was losing fear of the gods and acquiring a consciousness of dynamic potentiality within himself. Among those who joined in the discussions in the Epicurean garden-school were hetæræ, whose social crime was often nothing more than the wrong birthplace, and slaves, reduced to a servile status merely by fortunes of war.

Epicurus wrote more than three hundred books on philosophy, and the influence of his ideology was felt far and wide, in Asia, in Egypt and in Rome. Through the Roman Lucretius the creed of the cult was ennobled while some of the tranquillity of Seneca is attributed to his Epicureanism. At the time of Martial, a Greek woman of this faith, named Theophile, who had married the Roman wit, Canius Rufus, enlivened the atmosphere, according to Bilbilis, with her Attican humor, cheerful outlook, taste and literary skill. Epicureanism was one of the four schools of philosophy in the university of Athens which Marcus Aurelius recognised, and much of the mood of the European Renaissance was derived from its lightheartedness — especially the propensity to ridicule theological pretensions and call for a return to nature and nature's god, individualistic, rationalistic, the link with Rousseau. On the other hand a sensualistic discipleship in Rome utilised its doctrine of the inherent right-to-pleasure, for purposes of license and irresponsibility, the truer link.

Nor could every Epicurean disown culture. There were those who insisted that science, letters and the arts no less than fine emotions were essentials of a full life. They denied the necessity of restricting a good and happy existence to the narrow field of the senses and made room for a catholicity of tastes and a generous ration upon which reason could feed.

The development of Epicureanism was conspicuously the effect of a two-sexed debate. We have said that the hetæræ were members of the original garden-school but that did not mean they brought love alone to the enterprise. Judging from their writings they were far more intelligent and witty than the Japanese geisha girls who enjoy a free association with men but usually provide a weak mental challenge. Trained similarly in music, dancing and the art of entertaining, the Greek courtesan was often deeply interested in the art of reasoning as well. In the Epicurean group moreover she associated with legal wives intent on things of the spirit. Within the circle a courtesan might maintain a companionate-marriage with the main educator, the chairman of the discussions, or rise to the status of a wife herself. We cannot be sure in every case what the relationship was between the men and the women of the original school who lived in a common dwelling and studied outside in the garden. Nor were the observers sure at the time. So they charged the Epicureans with advocating and practicing free love though Diogenes insisted that the accusation was the work of maniacs. Still it must be admitted that the easy arrangement for association and the principles which the sect advanced fed the emotions that nourish fanatics.

Take the ideas of Leontium, the girl from a hetæra seminary, painted by Theodorus in a pose of meditation and educated by Hermesianax who dedicated three books of elegies to her. Reading her criticism of the philosophy of Theophrastus, Cicero called it a model of style while Pliny the Elder remarked that the audacity of her analysis gave rise to the proverb, "Suspendio arborem eligere." Seneca translated part of her discussion of the woman question and it was this version which Hieronymus used. On the subject of marriage Leontium observed that, given splendid conditions of health and charming personalities, there were excellent arguments in its favor but for a philosopher, devoted to literature and reflection, the rose had thorns. While he was lost in his studies, his wife would surely try to distract him with her diverse concerns such as the dear children, jewels, household equipment, gossip and society or in any case restrict his freedom of movement, his travel and his friendships. Furthermore he might have to turn from his favorite pursuit to labor for the support of his family if his wife was poor and, if she was rich, perhaps he would have to coddle her in her whims. Besides he must remember her birthdays, be considerate of her relatives, and spend due time in her company. If through force of will she was the actual head of the family, he must be her slave. And such a "to-do" as she could make around the house with her tailors, her tradesmen, her servants and her interests ! If the philosopher needed a servant or even a nurse for periods of sickness, a professional was better; the servant could be dismissed when inefficient while the nurse would be competent without being fussy. Unmarried, he was free from the menace of a sick wife. As for posterity — what does the continuance of one's name mean to a dead person after all ? So many have the same name anyway. Was it not wiser to enjoy such property as one had during one's life than to worry over the use to which it would be put after one's death ? Of course the up-shot was that reason dictated spending it on an "affinity." Such was the doctrine of free love enunciated by a Greek woman in reply to the "godlike or divine Theophrastus," pupil and successor to Aristotle, fretted by the problem of the State. Leontium has also left a letter written to another concubine, Lamia, in which Epicurus and his school were discussed.

If these were all the facts known about the emotions of Leontium, our knowledge of her free-love exposition would be distorted. But there is another side to the shield for which data are also available, proving that she was thinking of the man in the case more than of the woman as she wrote. Actually she bore the brunt of her system. Romantic love upset her calculations. She became jealous — of Glycera — and it was hateful to be cast aside for a rival. Even posterity made its claim upon her whether she willed it or not, and her daughter, Danaë, likewise an Epicurean, became the concubine of Sophorn, prefect of Ephesus. Moreover the very man in the case did not get off as easily as the doctrine presupposed. He too could be jealous and devitalised by extra-legal wives as Epicurus and Aristippus both demonstrated. The truth is that men were so enervated by a scheme enabling them to escape social responsibility and indulge in every mood that their own sex called for checks and balances. Diatribes on the practice of squandering leisure and wealth on courtesans were delivered in public by reformers concerned with citizenship, with the stability of the family and the revenues of the State.

Contemporaries spoke of the Epicurean Themista as a "female Solon" and it is probable therefore that she sided with the family-in-the-making. Themista and her husband, Leonedor of Leonteus, were both teachers in the sect, drawn to the original school by Epicurus himself. Long after they had ceased to transmit directly their notions of morality, the Christian writer, Lactantius Firmianus, who lived in the reign of Constantine the Great, appraised Themista as the grand prototype of female culture and the most distinguished woman philosopher of "heathenism." Unfortunately her manuscripts are not at our service for a modern estimate of her mind.

Standing in the agora waiting for conversation, at prolonged banquets where girl flute players mingled with intellectuals and won commendatory remarks for their wit and judgment, in Aspasia's salon over which she presided and set difficult dialectic standards for conversing guests, or pacing to and fro in academic groves, the participants in the business of being intellectual pursued their careers of learning and illumination, pushing to the periphery of the Prodigious.

From first to last women shared in this enterprise. Menagius states that he found no fewer than seventy-six women philosophers mentioned in the writings of the ancients and extant fragments of their work make the fact irrefutable that Greek conceptual thought matured in the atmosphere of dual sex discussion and criticism. Not to be minimised was the inter-marriage among families of thinkers, more common than the publicity given to courtesans by the fictionists would imply. Thus Isocrates, the magnetic orator-educator, married the widow of Hippias, a famous Sophist. Plato's wife belonged to the family of Solon, it is claimed, and an extended research would undoubtedly extend the list now available of intellectual parents stimulating budding geniuses. But that was only one way to feminine influence.

Her identity hidden by a veil and mantle, Euklides slipped into Athens every evening at dusk from Megara to talk with Socrates and stole home at dawn, in disobedience to the law forbidding Megarians to enter the sacred city. But Euklides must needs defy. She was herself the head of a school of dialecticians upholding a positivist ethics and this question of social morality must be taken up with the great Athenian. One of her own pupils was Diodorus whose five daughters — Argia, Artemesia, Menaxene, Theognis, and Pantakles — perpetuated his interest in the Megarian philosophy. Their writing is no longer available but they evidently made a considerable stir in their lifetime, judging from Hieronymus. Another pupil was Stilpo, a genuine Cynic, disciple of Crates and teacher of Zeno. His daughter and his paramour, growing up in the atmosphere of rationalisation, carried on in their maturity the practice of logical debate.

Possibly it was some of the Megarian women philosophers who joined Plato at Socrates' bedside when he was ordered to drink the hemlock as an undesirable citizen. Waving the ladies away and urging his young student, Plato, to refrain from weeping, the ethical rebel carried out the State's decree, after which Plato and other Socratics retreated from intolerant Athens for a time, partly in grief and bitterness, partly for security. Plato went to Megara and there his idealism deepened.

On account of their own philosophic proclivities and from theories of statecraft, women were included in most of the schemes for education. As early as 600 B.C. Kleobolus proposed such equality of opportunity and his own daughter, Kleobuline (or Eumetis as she was sometimes called) became a distinguished thinker. Therefore when Plato opened the portal of his Academy to women, he was but following a seasoned practice.

THE DELINEATION OF LIFE AND THOUGHT ON THE STAGE

It would be a mistake to assume that the whole circle of Greek thought, or perhaps it would be better to say thoughts, is to be found in the speculations of the formal thinkers, for the world is more than physics and mathematics, logic and laws. Aristotle was so severe in his logic that commentators can determine interpolations in his writings by the break which they make in his closely-knit structures. But the biological, economic, social and political manifestations of life cannot be enclosed in any such iron-bound scheme. So the dramatist, hampered by no such intellectual rules, may in fact be truer to life as reality than the most expert logician. Within the technical forms of his art, he can catch and reflect every mood, opinion, and suspicion — illuminating by hints and foreshadowings the course of life which defies and disrupts systems of thought.

Since the theater in Athens was a state institution, actors ranked higher than teachers, philosophers, poets and physicians, giving specific encouragement to playwriting. Lyricists and dramatists had private patrons who helped them prepare for the grand contests and in order that popular participation in the award might be as wide and as enthusiastic as possible, partly for reasons of State, poor freemen were given seats in the vast arena where the prizes were handed out. From season to season every form of literary expression was tested in that arena and, in the fortunes which bore awards this way or that, even empiricism was somewhat directed. Madame de Staël names glory as the secret of Greek poignancy and the failure to win the coveted laurel in a competition, some think, drove Socrates further afield in his search for Truth while the victor contentedly delivered his "Oration on the Crown."

Perhaps the Frenchman who raised the question in the early days of the American Republic with respect to the compensations for genius possible in a democracy had the Greek experience particularly in mind. "What could Americans do to draw talent to the service of the State ?" he asked. "Dramatise politics in a national theater," replied the theatrical-minded Dunlap.

The Greek theater was the State forum, church, school, art center and amusement place all in one. For the great religious festivals, the State ordered and directed the plays which were performed. Naturally men got the commissions and they also got all the parts to play. God was sometimes one of the actors — a type of drama still to be seen in Japan, retaining its early realism, and in the Wagnerian operas reminiscently. Even when the problem plays superseded representations of Fate, such authors as Sophocles and Euripides, Aristophanes or Menander had to continue to work within the prescriptions of State politics and culture.

It was Æschylus (525-456 B.C.), a veteran of the wars, who seems first to have lifted the drama above the loyalties of the temple and the camp. He was born in a noble family of Eleusis where the sex rites in honor of the Earth Goddess Demeter, symbolising the mystery of life as life itself, were vivid to the extreme. In his youth he fought in the Persian Wars and was one of the heroes at Marathon — a circumstance which saved him from death later in the theater when he was accused in one of his plays of disclosing the Eleusinian secrets, the most sacred of all. But Æschylus had entered the army with a zeal for national independence rather than affection for arms as such and he was peculiarly sensitive to the horrors that warfare inflicted on women non-combatants and children. His experience in childhood surroundings, his personal observation of cruelty, his rugged and virile service at the front were supplemented by visits to Sicily where poets, playwrights and men of letters in general were the invited guests of the court, especially of the magnificent Hiero the First, tyrant of Syracuse. On one such visit Æschylus was asked to produce a play in honor of a new city, Ætna, and, having begun to build his plots on the actions and reactions of women to religion and to war, he called his work *The Women of Ætna*. His was the nascent art of experimental drama and many devices are employed to express his sense of human tragedy; but his concept of tragedy was romantically simple. He disapproved of violence toward women, he was sorry for captives and refugees, he was moved by the supplications of the opposite sex, especially when they were humbly made, he was aware of women's dramatic rôle as weepers relatively helpless in a community of fighters, he felt that they had capacities of brain and soul, he had no imprisoned war mate in his own abode resentful and defiant, he was no Ionian degenerate. Æschylus hated the idea of non-combatants calling for protection upon men or the gods in vain and unresponsive warriors were handled without sympathy. In short, Æschylus wanted his people to be free but enlightened, and gave his service to both designs.

As it happened, his genius was operating in the theater at the time of a sex crisis, economic and social, following, as is its way, the crises of war. The proposal to fix in the marriage code a regulation that the bride's property should pass to her husband or nearest male relative was in review, as the defense of national independence brought in its train the issue of the

State and its corollary, the control of private property Æschylus liked the civil form of violence no better than its military type and the removal to male guardians of the girl's own will seemed to him an invasion of her rights. Besides, Homeric goddesses taught another lesson. So one of his earliest plays is named *Supplices;* it represents fifty daughters of Danæus complaining against the rigors of a code which would automatically place within the power of their father's brother their betrothal to his fifty sons. By the treatment of their protest in choral form, Æschylus raises it to the level of a general sex plaint and, as the plot unfolds, their protection and satisfaction come through their submission of their cause to the people at large who defend them when the king proves hesitant. Here the hero of the wars is a gallant democrat in a time of peace.

Notwithstanding his advocacy of a liberal adjustment to meet the necessities of the State, the marriage code with its strict masculinity became a law. Still interested in the status of women, however, Æschylus goes on to write problem plays of a more complicated nature which the situation demands. Thus he poses questions such as this: What if force meet force in private life ? Nearer to our own time was the same issue and the same answer when Peter the Great attempted by fiat to subdue free-ranging Russian females to property subjection at the hearth; they replied with suicide, arson, murder and poison, setting the themes and the plots for Russian writers for generations. When the Greeks tackled the problem, they were fortunate in having a dramatist who could write what Wright considers the "greatest play in world-literature," namely, *Agamemnon,* built on the query as to whether a woman is ever justified in killing her husband. Then there came succeeding plays — to constitute a trilogy — *Oresteia* dealing with such rights as that of a son to slay the mother who had previously

disposed of an errant father — a model for the immortal
Hamlet; and Eumenides, speculating on inheritance. Shakespeare's concentration on nobility was of a piece with the patrician perspective of Æschylus.

We witness in the feminine review by Æschylus a queen,
Clytemnestra, unyielding to the "intolerable callousness and
brutal pride of Agamemnon who has sacrificed his daughter's
life to help on his political schemes and now brings home with
him from Troy the concubine whom he has compelled to share
his bed;" Cassandra, the prey, first of a betrayer, Apollo, and
then of a mortal master; Electra, a woman of direct action who
knows no remorse; an aged nurse, gentle and intelligent. So
are the choruses significant: the male group of feeble old ad-
visors; the maidens who are both friends and furies. One of
the neatest issues is that treated in the *Eumenides* with regard
to the definition of the nearest relative: is it the mother or the
father of a child ? If Æschylus believed that the Fates controlled destiny, at least he had a tragic sense of female reckon-
ing in that circumstance, and gave a graphic portrayal of the
process through which the Fates operated. He must have
had models for his direct actionists and history reveals their
probable personalities.

Of softer clay was the next great dramatist, Sophocles the
Serene. It is true that he too served in the wars but he served
differently; late in life at the age of forty-five he was a commander under Pericles in the Samian War, an affair of short
duration. Nor was he away from Athens so much of the time
as Æschylus. Sophocles was an urbanite primarily — one of
the gilded men of a wealthy and leisured Athenian period,
when surplus property had enriched the State and marriage
was fairly well established. In his idler hours, music and
poetry were cultivated, while an alignment with the oligarchic
faction made his economic and political life assured. He too

had traveled but differently from Æschylus — rather to Ionian cities and as a diplomat running errands for the State. Naturally when Sophocles turned to coöperate with the State in play production his attitude toward life and its sex connotations was a variant from that of Æschylus.

Æschylus was able to visualise women as individuals. Sophocles saw instead law and order which, at that stage of politics, meant men. There was no longer a question of restless wives breaking out and slaying husbands. Sufferings and martyrdom therefore become transformed into fidelities to domesticity. Homer accordingly is revamped to serve the concept of marital tranquillity. When Antigone appeals for protection, she now symbolises the unwritten law of the gods, foundation of the recently established legal code designing her for wedded bliss. Feminists, direct actionists, and critics become adventuresses, represented by Eriphyle and Procris; Helen of Troy in the new incarnation is no longer the victim of a despoiler of the domestic sanctuary but a wilful deserter of the hearth — a harlot, in short; Pandora is a symbol of sin; there are wantons, such as Tyro the unsubduable; Penelope has turned into a shrew fuming like any virago instead of sitting contentedly at her loom while the years roll by and the suitors come and plead; and Sappho enters the drama as a vicious rather than a romantic lyricist. As if his public now preferred their notes, slave women repeatedly constitute the Sophoclean chorus. And the upshot is that watch and ward had better be maintained on the female sex even if the system of marriage and male guardianship of property do seem to be working pretty well. To Sophocles, divine honors were awarded after his death.

His views admirably fitted the Periclean dictum relative to law and order: "A woman's highest glory is not to fall below the standard of such natural powers as she possesses: that woman is best of whom there is the least talk among men, whether in the way of praise or blame." That was for public consumption. Pericles addressed the galleries like any demagogue while privately he divorced his mouse-like wife to live with the most talked-of woman in the whole city of Athens. So he prated of Athenian liberty and splendor, while he was utterly blind to the fact that the State of which he was head was a "task-mistress and a tyrant" whose brutality brought her to a collapse like a thing of shreds and patches. "Every year her allies sent her 600 talents of tribute and their soldiers and sailors at half the Athenian rate of pay came to serve in her armaments. Every year hundreds of her allies were forced to make the wearisome journey to Athens, to spend their savings in hotels, in shops, in custom-houses, in law-court fees to swell the national resources of Athens." And yet, said Pericles, like any modern juggler with words, "We have made our friends, not by receiving but by conferring benefits."

Sophocles tried to write a play or two eliminating female characters entirely but these have not been popular with posterity and how much favor they won at the time is uncertain. His greatest play, generally conceded, is the one with a vital woman character, and if he had known more anthropology, his eulogy of man might have comprised woman. He himself is the personification of the Man of Letters grown oversoft. Nevertheless the liking for a stable State was not to be condemned. The theme of *Antigone* lives on — only now with a less sexual emphasis. Rather would we ask in our time whether an individual of either sex can set up his or her own conscience as a superior law to that of the prevailing jurisprudence ? Sophocles answered in favor of the law. In his *Antigone* occurs the passage which, as Bury says, marks a stage in the growth of man's consciousness: "Of all strong things none is more wonderfully strong than Man. He can cross the

wintry sea, and year by year compels with his plow the un-
wearied strength of the Earth, the oldest of the immortal gods.
He seizes for his prey the aery birds and teeming fishes, and
with his wit has tamed the mountain-ranging beasts, the long-
maned horses and the tireless bull.   Language is his, and swift-
winged thought and city-founding mind; and he has learnt
to shelter himself from cold and piercing rain; and has devices
to meet every ill but Death alone.   Even for desperate sickness
he has a cure, and with his boundless skill he moves on, sometimes to evil, but again to good."   Here in these lines we see
that man "has suddenly, as it were, waked up to realise that he
himself was the wonder of the world."   He had become aware
of what he had done.   In the eighteenth century, A.D., he was
to take the second great step by discovering the idea of progress,
of what he could yet do should he turn his powers to the service
of his imagination.

That his mother, Clito the green-grocer, marketed herbs in
the agora was offered by the comic poet, Aristophanes, who
considered everyone a buffoon, as one of the explanations for
the "vulgar" tastes of the third great Greek playwright, Euripides.   Little is actually known however of the parentage of this
fierce rebel against tradition.   Deeply interested in the common
people Euripides undoubtedly was — especially in women.   He
was opposed to slavery, hostile to war, inclined to regard the
farmer as superior to the urbanite, and critical of the pretensions
of the giddy youth of Athens to intellectual and social primacy.
He was bitter, but in behalf of human rights.   Like Æschylus,
Euripides was away from Athens enough to view it with a
different perspective from Sophocles; indeed he died in exile.
Moreover he saw politics, economics and sex more closely in-
tertwined.   Yet if there had not been in fact another Athens
than that to which Sophocles appealed, Euripides could not
have played to the large audiences of men or gained from them

a prize at the age of thirty-nine. A contemporary of Sophocles, but sixteen years younger, he had to compete with the friend of the oligarchs and he did so by direct opposition to every creed loved of his rival. He regarded the old deities as positively foul. He wrote in the speech of the populace. Not that he was a democrat exactly; he damned rather than constructed. At the same time he was a humanist and by exposing the follies of pride, he restored a certain balance to the sexes.

Euripides brings the woman back into the center of the drama but not romantically in the style of Æschylus. He is above all a realist. Where Æschylus "moralised," Euripides satirised. He displays female vagaries and passions starkly beside their strength and capacities for charm. His *Electra* contains one of the most horrible female characters in all literature; his *Andromache* one of the most sensitive. One by one he offers the living types that were matters of every-day observation, instead of derivatives from Homeric myths used as symbols of Fate or legends to be redacted in the interest of purity. He deals with war captives, concubines, slaves, the betrayed and the deserted, mothers, grandmothers, the maternal and the promiscuous, the cruel, selfish, jealous, crafty, sweet, simple, faithful, faithless, witty, clever, intelligent, rebellious, sacrificial-tempered, and idealistic. Instead of grounding them in religious mysticism, he plants them firmly in the economic and legal soil of the State and handles their reactions to factual environment. Down his social gamut race the heroic, the villainous, the frightened, the tame. He insists on the variety of personalities which women manifest and refuses to permit the whole of womankind to be charged with the mind and conduct of any single type. He has his syntheses, however, such as the defense of girl babies at a stage of evolution when it was the privilege of the father to decide whether one should be reared, pointing out that, if such decision must be made, the mother is the one to make it — an utterly revolutionary doctrine.

If woman is shown in her weaknesses, so is man whom Euripides also passes in review, with the shallowness of his pretensions to a monopoly of intelligence and soul skilfully analysed. The synthesis is that the age of the gods must yield to the age of reason; that nobility of spirit must supersede convention and fear; that neither enmity nor neglect is an avenue of escape; that the ruling class must be charged with cruelty and tyranny. Murder, suicide, revolt, and wantonness prove nothing; mutual esteem and dignity may prove everything. His is the philosophy of the naturalist, carried into the theater, denying ruthless destiny manipulated by Olympus, critical of human machinery, economic and political, interested in education, hopeful of liberty and humanism.

Through Euripides' use of subtle irony, bitter and comic, through his laughter and his tears, one must get impressions of this playwright of the people talking to a gilded age of Athens. In his chorus — that forceful instrument of all Greek drama — is revealed his animus. Æschylus had treated choruses of suppliant women as the symbol of social events; Sophocles had employed choruses of old men typical of the elder statesmen who controlled the politics of Athens; Euripides again turns to a chorus of women but it now chants of the manifold experiences of their lives — from the hardships of war to the simple gossiping at the washing meet. Realist though he is to the core, he has gone a long way beyond the misogynic Ionian poets of whom he disapproves. There were many *Dolls' Houses* in his landscape, it has been cleverly said. In the *Medea,* Euripides writes: "It is men now that are crafty in counsel, and keep not their pledges by the gods; the scandal will turn and honor come to a woman's life. 'Tis coming — respect for womankind. No longer will pestilent scandal at-

tack women, *and women alone* [italics mine]. The music of
ancient bards will die away, harping ever on woman's perfidy.
Phœbus is the guide of melody and in my heart he never set
the wondrous music of his lyre. Else I would soon have raised
a song that would have stayed the brood of male singers. The
long years have many a tale to tell, of men as well as of
women." It was not the identity of interests and personalities that intrigued Euripides. He recognised and admitted sex
differentiations. What he advocated was an end to superiority-
inferiority chatter and its ridiculous consequences.

While the tragedians had been developing the depiction of
suffering and pathos, the comedians had been busy with the
portrayal of sheer folly. Of these Aristophanes was a leader.
A merry companion of Socrates and Euripides, he turned into
melodious wit the "grouches" of the radical group. His
father was a country landlord — an added reason for his ability
to observe certain Athenians with detachment but also a reason
why he could laugh more than his poorer friend, Euripides,
perhaps. Aristophanes regularly burst into robust guffaws,
often ribald, if penetrating, at the modes of the ruling class
while simultaneously he could poke fun at the Sophists or the
"thinking-shop" of his moral friend, Socrates, or the tragic
productions of the emotional Euripides. Some of his parodies
of the playwright are among his best plays. However beneath
his general rollicking, designed for public entertainment,
State-subsidised, was an anti-war, anti-anthropomorphic, anti-
exploitation fervor comparable to that of Euripides himself.
Not so understanding and steadfast a feminist as the tragedian,
he nevertheless wrote *Lysistrata* which is as up-to-the-minute in
its attraction as it was when he composed it for his fellow-
citizens.

On the thesis that household management is a fine apprenticeship for State administration and that the latter may as

well be placed in the hands of women who care less for war and would abolish it, he built a gay and effective satire about the mentality of the masterful male. *Women at the Festival,* a parody of Euripides, assume charge of themselves and reverse the tables on the men; while *Women of the Assembly,* a burlesque on Platonic feminism, is a study of the socialistic State. An opponent of Pericles and the war party, Aristophanes attacked Aspasia, as a means of reaching the chieftain, but that did not signify a preference for the "vegetable" women who lived out of the sunlight and aloof from the public eye, for he complained that "They dip their wool in hot water according to the ancient plan, all of them without exception, and never make the slightest innovation. They sit and cook as of old. They wear out their husbands, as of old. They buy sweets, as of old." When he has them take over the government, he reports their first act as the abolition of prostitution, prophetic of the prime concern of early suffragists.

There are many immortal lines in Aristophanes and among them are these: "Let man stand by woman and woman by man. Good luck to all, and pray God that we may make no more of these mistakes." Peace was to have its victories, not one whit less than war. He counted on the representation of the follies of belligerency and the horrors of blood-letting as a method of settling disputes, to stir up resentments against the whole business, preferring, like many of the Greeks, including veterans of the wars, a civilised arbitrament.

With forthright scorn he lashes out against the war hawks who were trying by force to transform Athens into a military monarchy, grabbing empire by the agency of the sea power, who were applauding the death grapple between Sparta and Athens, who thought that by carrying off the Megarian girls on the frontier to be their slaves they could terrorise that neighbor into an alliance. Cleon, the die-hard, was the chief of the trading militarists, and so powerful an advocate of expansion that it was daring to oppose him. True it is that Nicias was also for arbitration and that a peace party was fairly vocal. But Aristophanes was savagely pacifist. As the war proceeded, in spite of his alarm and disgust, refugees swarmed into Athens, prostitution expanded enormously, famine came and the plague followed. The whole place was hungry and debts alone were abundant. In despair utopias were written by those who still had the strength to hope. Accordingly Athens being filled with women, native and refugee, while the men were at the front, Aristophanes made them the crux of the political crisis. Thus *Lysistrata* means Dismisser of Armies, *Ecclesiazusæ* is a socialistic utopia introduced by women, and *The Thesmophoriazusæ,* the third woman play, is a satire on Euripides showing the problems he raised for women and proposing to solve them by disposing of the playwright who called attention to them.

INTELLECTUALISM AS A CULT

PENETRATING and realistic as were the writers of plays, mirroring all moods, incidents, clashes, and tempers, conceptual thought remained among the Greeks the operation of a class far removed from labor with common things. All the immediate productive processes were consigned to the poor and slaves of both sexes. Intellectual speculation therefore, with or without the aid of oracles, was carried on in an artificial realm created by conquest and economic subjugation, making it essentially intuitive and deductive.

Vocal, voluble, forensic, combative, didactic and individualistic, the Greeks gave to the Semitic religion a turn which shaped the course of Christianity to a large degree, injecting an argumentative quality as well as an abstraction into European theology that kept its mysticism full of battle while contributing to the sterility of scholasticism.

Not until physical science was united with engineering could thought keep forging ahead and that possibility was blocked with the Greeks by their system of servile economy.   As Millikan points out: "The method of empiricism can go a certain distance and no further. . . No caveman, no Tutankamen, no Pericles, no Cicero, no Galileo could think about the kinetic energy of a molecule because the concept of kinetic energy was unborn, and it could not be born in the era of pure empiricism, for it is an analytical concept involving the integral or work function."   No inspiration was present for an effort to make heat accomplish labor when slaves could be captured or bought to undertake it or poor freemen could be compelled to do so or starve.   Human life was exploited.   There was little effort to exploit nature's powers.

Nevertheless meditation made great strides beyond occultism. The Greeks were not ascetic by nature.   The gods had their proper sphere and mortals had theirs — State-making, social defining and researching.   But even this dichotomy limited the range of thinking.   Nor did leisure automatically turn its beneficiaries to brain exercising of any sort.   Many members of the rich ruling class of Athens devoted themselves wholly to pleasure without conscious rationalisation; some idle folk were satisfied with comforts, amusements and sex.   It was therefore the "civilised minority" only who were reflective and made of their freedom a noble opportunity to consider life in the large.   There were a few who lived modestly from choice that they might save their souls for moral philosophising: Heraclitus and Hipparchia were two of this species.   Others managed to use their minds amid somewhat luxurious surroundings: Plato and Aspasia were shining examples of that possibility.   Surplus wealth enabled certain individuals to become articulate respecting the divergent tastes and manners on exhibition all about them. It enabled some to become articulate by proxy as they bought thinking talent for their diversion, their defense, or to further what they regarded as the interests of the State.

While leniency toward slaves developed in Athens, humanistic interests did not extend to merchants and the business class in general. The intellectuals remained precious in their scorn of buying and selling, the mercantile procedure, and its ethics, in spite of the fact that some of them belonged to the middle class as sons and daughters of merchants, artisans and tinkers. The father of Socrates, if called a sculptor, was socially classed as a laborer. Demosthenes was the son of a cutler or cabinet-maker. Plato was a member of the landed aristocracy but Aristotle's father was a physician and he himself may have practiced medicine. The women of the intellectual circles came from every station in life and slaves were admitted to some of the cults. Yet among all the philosophers dislike for manual labor, including commercial transactions which involved both physical work and mental bartering, was vigorous. It was in keeping with that scorn that so many preached the simple life.

Their hostility to commerce was in harmony with self-sufficing household industries but it lasted into the time when the population could no longer feed itself and, seeking for grain in the spacious fertile regions along the Black Sea, found itself compelled to devise exports in payment for imports. Indeed after the Athens-Sparta combination which held back the hordes of Asia Minor from the Greek peninsula in the fifth century B.C., until further invasion seemed improbable, Sparta settled back in agricultural complacency and had no middle class, whereas Athens retained her navy and went forward into sea adventuring. She was led in this course by merchants who

pressed up to the great metropolis from the Ionian coast after
political misfortunes had driven them from home and helped
to tap the grain regions capable of supplying Athenian needs.
They organised the potters and textile workers, the leather and
jewelry artisans, the shipbuilders and bankers essential to the
business of exchange.

For this service the philosophically inclined were far from
grateful. As many writers today deride the machines and their
manipulators who provide labor-saving devices and luxuries
which the penmen and penwomen, the verbal artists, enjoy,
so the Greek intelligentsia stood almost as a unit in their disdain
for the busy traders buying and selling, dickering and becoming
absorbed in the profits of the market. The merchants tended
to think in terms of commodities while the philosophers wished
to think in terms of general ideas. But the intellectuals in
their turn were heartily disliked by the aggressive business men,
anxious to prod them into strange folk ways and elaborate their
wants. Thus raged a fierce contest that was economic at bottom. "I take my stand," on the older mores, avowed the
landed gentry and their literary friends hostile to a business
civilisation. "Come, let's be up and doing," urged the aggressive traders. A veritable class war promoted thought but defeated social unification.

In the period of Pericles, a powerful representative of the
commercial interests, a native Athenian, struck back at the
intellectuals' chatter about knowledge, virtue, truth and beauty.
Cleon this was, the owner of a profitable tannery business left
him by his father. Cleon had scant patience with the landed
gentry and the sages seeking moral values through the process
of thought. He was an imperialist economist — a war hawk
of his time, popular among the masses in whose interest he
framed a political program as against the classes. Some assign
to him at any rate the authorship of a plan to levy a definite

property tax on landowners then permitted to make voluntary gifts to the State and in those conditions remiss in their donations.

Nowhere was that scorn for labor and merchandising in common things given more articulate and determined form than in the writings of Aristotle, which must be taken more seriously than any idealistic speculations of Plato. While he feared the machinations of a plutocracy, he despised the turbulence of an urban democracy. "The best material of democracy," he said, "is an agricultural population; there is no difficulty in forming a democracy where the mass of the people live by agriculture or tending of cattle. Being poor they have no leisure, and therefore do not attend the assembly, and not having the necessaries of life they are always at work, and do not covet the property of others. . . The people of whom other democracies consist are far inferior to them, for their life is inferior; there is no room for moral excellence in any of their employments, whether they be mechanics or traders, or laborers." In these few words are summed up the underlying substratum of Greek intellectualism. The landlord of moderate estate, freed from toil, is the best fitted to rule, while laborers, artisans, small farmers who meddle in politics, and the merchants are troublesome, mobile, and inferior persons to be elbowed aside in government and deemed unworthy of moral excellence. It is small wonder, therefore, that when he wrote on the physical world and its objects, where the laborer works and the merchant deals, he scarcely rose above the childhood of the race. When he treats of the subject-matter of mechanics he runs off into metaphysics and makes no substantial contribution to the advance of thought and understanding, however ingenious he may be in handling the arts of the governing class to which he belonged.

The tendency of intellectualism to become a cult was ac-

celerated by the rise of the teaching class. Admitting that
Plato and Aristotle were teachers, it must also be recognised
that they were thinkers in spite of their occupation rather than
on account of it. They were thinkers first and teachers second.
Great hordes of commonplace scholars gathered round every
center of learning, imbibed a smattering of wisdom, and then
went forth either in the streets or to distant regions to dissemi-
nate thought as a profession, receiving compensation from fees,
patrons or the State. One group, known as the Sophists, in
operation when Socrates began his popular questioning of
opinion, undertook to prepare young men for civic responsibilities, especially in the law courts, by training them in rhetoric,
politics and disputation. At last they degenerated into
reasoners of the main chance for contending partisans. Other
schools or sects, proud of their wisdom, assembled cliques of
"earnest thinkers" given to praising this or that form of intellectualism and dedicated to this or that interpretation of some
famous philosopher's ideology, without the goal of application.
Since learning was a monopoly of small groups within major
classes, seldom disturbed by upthrusts from below, it was gar-
nished with affectation, idle speculations, and vanities, rendering it powerless against the dissolution of the very economic
and social world in which it thrived.

THAT FREEDOM OF SPEECH

JUDGING by the wide variety of opinion among the Greeks,
casual readers often assume that, with the exception of Socrates,
they had at least reached freedom in the intellectual realm. It
would truly be enchanting to be able to believe that in one
golden age things of the spirit actually had complete sway in
a portion of the earth. But was free speech always welcomed
and protected in illustrious Athens in very fact ? Could the

spirit be sure of a haven ?   Could critics question custom and legend without fear or favor ?   Were ideas supreme over the sheer will-to-power ?   Let us see.

Zimmern makes it indisputable that nice distinctions in matters intellectual were not as common as one might be led to suppose from the halo that has encircled the classical tradition. He says that "Gorgias the rhetorician was a greater attraction than Socrates, the critic of his phrases; that Isocrates, the founder of journalism, was a more fashionable name than Plato." But leaving such considerations aside, what was the power of prejudice ?

Anaxagoras, who taught the Athenians how the moon became eclipsed and who sublimated God into Intelligence, was banished for his pains.   In sorrow at the verdict, Pericles accompanied his beloved teacher a part of the distance into the hinterland when he set off to live the life of an outlaw, as Roger Williams and Anne Hutchinson were compelled in a later day to forsake New England Puritans for the forests.   In accordance with the decree that one who disputed the existence of the gods or introduced novel opinions about celestial appearances should be tried before an assembly of the people, Socrates, Aspasia and many other citizens and foreigners in Athens were brought up for impiety.   The judgment against Socrates will probably be remembered forever as well as his sublime indifference to his judges and his philosophic acceptance when his jailers placed the cup of poison in his hands.   He might well have said: "Lord, forgive them.   They know not what they do."   Coupled with the charge of impiety against Aspasia was one brought against her by Hermippus, a comic poet no more friendly than Aristophanes toward Pericles, who said she received prostitutes of the free class into her home to entertain Pericles — a doubly heinous offense.   Only the personal appeal of Pericles, in tears for his companion, saved Aspasia from banishment or death. Even the male beauty and wit, Alcibiades, was summoned to trial and disciplined as well as the female beauty, Phryne, whom Praxiteles chose as the model for his Cupid and his Venus. Nor was the artist secure against envy and intrigue by jealous rivals bent on elimination. Thus the great Pheidias was accused of graft in connection with the modelling of the statue of Minerva and actually died in jail, while the accuser received honors and material reward.

On the scene Grote comments as follows: "It was not only against the lives, properties and liberties of Athenian citizens that the Thirty [Tyrants] made war. They were not less solicitous to extinguish the intellectual force and education of the city, a project so perfectly in harmony both with the sentiment and practice of Sparta, that they counted on the support of their foreign allies. Among the ordinances which they promulgated was one, expressly forbidding any one 'to teach the art of words.' The edict of the Thirty was, in fact, a general suppression of the higher class of teachers or professors, above the rank of the elementary (teacher of letters or) grammatist. If such an edict could have been maintained in force for a generation, combined with the other mandates of the Thirty — the city out of which Sophocles and Euripides had just died, and in which Plato and Isocrates were in vigorous age, would have been degraded to the intellectual level of the meanest community in Greece. It was not uncommon for a Grecian despot to suppress all those assemblies wherein youths came together for the purpose of common training, either intellectual or gymnastic, as well as the public banquets and clubs or associations, as being dangerous to his authority, tending to elevation of courage and to a consciousness of political rights among the citizens." It is plain that social fear, as old as the tribe, and suppression of thought, no less than the pursuit of Truth, have their roots in ancient Greece.*

Immense then were the complications of the Hellenic world in which rose the intellectual heritage of the Western civilisation — with its hoary mythologies of gods and goddesses, its wars, its clashes of caste and class, its adventures into politics, its explorations by merchants and travelers, its conflicts of sexes, and contests in prowess and wits. Rich and varied were its constructions of conceptual thought about life and the universe. Societies and minds, economies and systems, men and women were evolving together through time toward our own age. And as a modern scholar has remarked, if it is highly important to consider how much the Greeks did not know, the later mental unfolding which emerges into our living present can only be understood, in case it can be understood at all, in the light of Greek experience and rationalisation.

* For a concrete case in the history of free thought, which is worth a book of generalities, see "The Trial of Socrates," in *Selected Essays of J. B. Bury,* pp. 75ff.

PART IV

OUR GREAT PRECEDENT OF ACQUISITIVE POWER AND POMP

HATE and love, war and peace, men and women, sentiment and passion, aspiration and bigotry. Unless one's philosophy is all inclusive, nothing can be understood.

Believing that history is primarily a record of the passions and follies of mankind, on the contrary, Edward Gibbon chose the Roman Empire for his great theme. Certainly it is our shining Western example, or precedent, of acquisitive power and pomp — a clue to our behavior as human beings which must in any case be set beside our liking for physical comfort and our effort to reason. In the mammoth territory dominated by Rome for many centuries, extraordinary play was given to the physical might and accumulative mania of the male and the female. No other vast empire demonstrated more convincingly the human forces, fairly blind, positively selfish, against which industry and agriculture, science and morality must battle, perhaps forever, for survival and advancement.

Among the expressions of this demiurgic sweep of energy may be listed the reigns of terror, the extortions and cruel punishments, the confiscations, uprisings, crimes, treachery, conspiracies, blackmail, insanity, judicial injustices, and talents for wasting presented so graphically by historians. Acquisition was the social diapason deepened in quality by contacts with Oriental despotism, especially its penchant for magnificent display. The Roman philosophical plumage was largely borrowed from the Hellenes, little of value was added by the

Latins, and the effect was an exaggeration of its forms, if not exactly a caricature. Hellenism decorated Roman force and greed with cultural flourishes and the sensitive indulged more and more in the habit of brooding in the place of social planning.

Considering the procession of murders and plots, sexual excesses and judicial depredations, greed and brutality, even the Roman imperial "triumph" was one in name more than in reality. What could one believe? "Nothing," said the Cynics. "One must," answered some philosophers. "Enjoy," remarked the Epicureans. "Adjust and salvage what you can of spiritual concepts," thought the Stoic. "Read, for heaven's sake," urged Pliny. "Have faith in the mysteries," pleaded this religious and that, and many of the finest Roman minds in the end sought so earnestly for eternal verities that they minimised the passing show, allowing it to pursue its way with scant intervention on their part. Passion thus moved to its nemesis rather proudly on the whole.

The curtain on this Roman drama was raised eight or nine centuries, B.C., by happy warriors from the forests of Italy scarcely inured to the plow and knowing little of the sea, restricted in their diet through their ignorance of the vegetables and fruits used in Greece and Egypt, crude of clothing and shelter, through force of arms making themselves masters of the world and thinking they had boxed the compass. Speaking of the Romans in their great day of power, Gibbon says they finally felt that "the true principles of social life, laws, agriculture, and science, which had been first invented by the wisdom of Athens, were now firmly established by the power of Rome, under whose auspicious influence the fiercest barbarians were united by an equal government and common language. They affirm that, with the improvement of the arts, the human species were visibly multiplied. They celebrated the increasing splendor of the cities, the beautiful face of the country, cultivated and adorned like an immense garden; and the long festival of peace which was enjoyed by so many nations forgetful of the ancient animosities and delivered from the apprehension of future dangers."

The curtain falls on a play of one thousand years or more with armies of rats scurrying through the silent halls of the Cæsars; on dust piled high over Nero's house of gold; on crumbling circuses and monuments erected to heroes.

What then happened to warriors whose State, founded by the sword, rested to the end upon that instrument of power ? The question has always presented a problem in human understanding but concerning its substance there can be no doubt. It was in fact the sword on land and sea — if we may use that generic name for the assorted spears, javelins, axes and battering-rams — which established Roman "unity" and maintained it for so long. Cato the republican and Augustus the emperor alike believed that a military force was the basic strength of government though the latter was aware of its odious aspects and tried to promote justice and peace by the personal assumption of the duties of consul and tribune. In truth this simply made him dictator and threw him back upon the army for his guarantee. Try as they might to veil the source of their imperial power through the administration of civil offices, the emperors who were not direct creatures of the army either reigned through the agency of terrorism of their own fashioning or relied on the army for its automatic execution of their decrees.

From the simple days of the early kingdom to its end in 509 B.C., through the years of the expanding republic until it was slowly merged into the empire at the turn of the Christian era, through the four centuries of empire until night fell upon the theater, the sword, used first for defense and then for conquest and subjugation, ruled Roman society. If at times it was kept in the background, in periods ostensibly dominated by civilian forms, those at the center of things, high and low, knew upon what implement reliance was to be placed. In the epoch of Augustan peace, when nobles and grandes dames basked in the sunshine of order, the senate was there, of course, the forms of popular government, to be sure, but the emperor depended for his own strength and, in arranging for succession, upon the strength and loyalty of the army. Theoretically elective he knew that his fate hung upon the whims of military leaders and common soldiers and, when the acquisitive passions that governed civil society crept into the army, they undermined the rigors of its discipline. Once that virus had begun to work in the center of power, rewards, bonuses, divisions, and other favors flung out to keep it intact only accelerated the disintegration until those who ruled by the sword perished by their own device.

One dictatorship after another was the fruit of government by force. Mommsen describes its unfolding: "The dictatorship is doubtless to be conceived as an institution which arose at the same time with the consulship, and which was designed, especially in the event of war, to obviate for a time the disadvantages of divided power and to revive temporarily the regal authority; for in war more particularly the equality of rights in the consuls could not but appear fraught with danger; and not only positive testimonies, but above all the oldest names given to the magistrate himself and his assistant, as well as the limitation of the office to the duration of a summer campaign, and the exclusion of the *provocatio,* attest the pre-eminently military design of the original dictatorship." And the extension of one-man rule beyond a summer campaign was steady if gradual. Campaigns became all-year-round affairs. They occurred at home as well as abroad. More and more they were resorted to as a cover for civil encroachments and exploitation until they broke down of their own weight, bearing racketeers to the earth with them. One learned that there could be an over-production of wars. But the truth was not discovered until the mischief was complete.

"Æ," the Irish sage, insists that twenty percent of a State's population must remain in the fields if stability is to be maintained. Other political thinkers have declared that, if more than a hundredth part of its people live in idleness or arms, a State's doom is sealed. It is also important to consider the kinds of persons who bear arms and how far, in the case of Rome for instance, the effort to control subject races by force made demands on the soldiers themselves which eventually destroyed their morals, their organisation, and their ability even to protect Rome. As Gibbon shows, to have military discipline on any scale, science is imperative but that very scientific training and discipline are machine guns that can be turned on instructors with deadly effect. Before Voltaire, Jesuit-tutored, used the implement of logic to defeat his teachers in that arena, the soldiers of Rome, organised to work coöperatively in the interests of the republic or the empire, discovered that they could also work in their own interests. If an army is disaffected or infected with unofficial ambitions, its reliability is at an end and the State is at its mercy. That became the situation in Rome as the centuries rolled on. For example, the Prætorian Guard, formed by Augustus, "to protect his person, to awe the Senate, and either to prevent or to crush the first motion of rebellion" finally conceived the idea that it possessed the inherent power to make its own dictator.

Military men grew ambitious for self-aggrandisement. Civil wars and conspiracies, devastating in their effects, were dependent on military support for success or for failure. By the sword of great Romans, races and classes were held in check. But by the sword dissidents broke that famous peace, the Pax Romana. And by the sword of alien armies the way was prepared for the sack of Rome and the ensuing feudalism of Europe.

At times an emperor would deliver an oration on peace while making war his practice. Thus Severus fomented civil strife. Then to hold his troops in line, he permitted them to wear gold rings on their fingers and have their wives in camp — a relaxation of discipline which put civil notions into their heads and reduced their fighting temper. When their families were compelled to live elsewhere and other women were allowed in camp, the soldiers were weakened by disease. War was tough business and refined gentlemen could not carry it forward. Softening occurred among the officers and privileged underlings in the environs of Rome, permitted to hang around the court and palaces. Severus recruited from the frontiers but it was impossible to keep the happiest warriors always in that condition by the best of military science. A sanitary cordon could not be stretched around the acquisitive practices and ideas and invasions from that source into the army sooner or later led to the exercise of force in the interest of greed. Factionalism spread through the ranks of soldiers as it did through politics. The army became a house divided against itself and could not stand the strain.

But after all the sword was only a symbol of something else. Behind it were the complex motives and passions of families and classes in the great Roman State, the ambitions of individuals and the hopes of multitudes. Hence an understanding of its manifestations runs deep into the texture of Roman society — its forms, processes, and forces of government, its economic structure and practices, its struggle for riches and luxury, and its integument of ideas and beliefs, swiftly changing after contacts were formed with the speculations of the

Greeks and the superstitions and ideals of the Near Orient. Between the older world and the Western world, Rome formed a kind of plot of destiny — a bridge over which mankind passed into the new age of religion, in theory the antithesis of the sword, and onward into the era of positive knowledge, in theory the age of reason.

THE SWORD AND SEX

EVEN when the sheer military aspects of the vast operation are narrowly considered, it is found to be no simple masculine game in course or in results, whether attention is given to conquests abroad, to social wars and proscriptions at home, or to the clash of families for possession of the government. All along the line there was an abundant, if not an entirely equal, opportunity for women to fight and perish in fights — an opportunity that might well represent a goal of perfection to the intransigent feminist of our own time.

Whether it was at the siege of Carthage, where women shared the perils of defense, or in the conquest of the Iberic peninsula where women committed suicide in shoals to escape enslavement, the Romans struggled with the female of the species. Again and again they came face to face with military women no less ambitious and determined than themselves. In 22 B.C., Candace, queen over a part of Æthiopia, invaded Egypt and defeated the Romans; then they regained their hold, drove her home, and wrested some of her land away in retribution, though she managed to have a portion of the tribute laid upon her remitted through the skill of the diplomats she dispatched to Augustus.

The classic military feminist of the Roman age, however, is Zenobia, queen of Palmyra, that great neutral trading ground between East and West, off in a wilderness — an important meeting place of two great empires. Under cover of serving the Romans, Zenobia was permitted by Claudius to be joint ruler of Egypt which she occupied. She was also allowed to plant garrisons in Asia Minor as far west as Ancyra in Galatia and Chalcedon opposite Byzantium. Finally throwing off this loyalty disguise, she took the war path to expand her empire and make herself Queen of the East. Aspiring to incorporate all Syria, Asia and Egypt in her realm with the grand manner of an Alexander the Great, Zenobia was ready to pay the price by personal command of her troops. In uniform, on horse or on foot, she lived with her soldiers and fought with them. Yet it was her fate to "grace" a Roman triumph in the year of Our Lord 272. Aurelian, her conqueror, had Zenobia, famed for her beauty, loaded with jewels and shackled with gold to prove how magnificent was his victory over the Arabian queen. Aggressive to the limit of imperialist possibilities, Zenobia was withal a capable ruler, "at once liberal and prudent in the administration of revenues, strict in dispensing justice, and merciful in the exercise of power," Gibbon declares. Traditions refer to her religious discussions with the Archbishop Paul of Samosata and she is mentioned in the Talmud as showing favor to the rabbis, the inference being that the Jews in general had tolerant treatment in Palmyra. The imperialist queen appears to have been a distinguished linguist, knowing the Greek and Latin, Syrian and Egyptian tongues and studying Homer and Plato with Longinus. A scholar was ordered to prepare an abridged Oriental history for her use. A life so broad in its interests and so vigorous in its activities was rounded out in a villa near Tivoli presented by the Roman emperor who, after showing off his war prize, spared Zenobia's life. There she spent her last years in the style of a Roman matron, and her daughter married a Roman noble.

Women who were exhibited in the train of conquering

heroes to the Roman crowds were usually unseated rulers or proud rebels attempting in vain to hold out against tribute collection or the acknowledgment of Roman supremacy. The revolt of Civilis in central Germany during the reign of Vespasian nevertheless was inspired by Veleda, a prophetess, revered as a divinity by most of the nations in central Germany, confident of a successful outcome; victories did follow for a while but luck changed and in the final defeat Veleda herself was borne to Rome as proof positive. One queen, Arsinoë of Alexandria, a sister of the renowned Cleopatra, was released after she marched in the train of Cæsar but on her return to Alexandria, Antony put her out of the way at the instigation of Cleopatra, notwithstanding the fact that she had fled to a temple for safety.

No humiliation before the Roman mobs was to disgrace the queen of Britain, Boadicea, a valiant fighter for freedom against the invaders, commanding her soldiers in person from her chariot and rallying them to what proved to be their last stand after the aliens had ravished her two daughters, beaten her own body, enslaved her relatives, and seized the family property. Rather than fall an utter victim to the Romans, she poisoned herself just as they prepared to mete out "justice" to the "rebel."

Occasionally a great queen played for high stakes in Roman favor at the cost of her own autonomy; thus Cartimandua, of Britain, turned over an important local chieftain, Caractacus by name, a proud and fierce opponent of the Romans, and received praise and wealth in compensation; when she divorced her husband, matriarch-like, a little later and "took up with" his arms-bearer, a civil war dethroned her and all she had left was Roman sympathy. If the Stratonices and Laodices, the Bernices and Arsinoës of the age of Alexander "cannot be reproached either for cowardice or for scrupulousness," neither can the "heroines" of the Roman conquest.

By her beauty and wit Cleopatra managed to escape marching behind a warlord's chariot to be jeered at and insulted. For some twenty-two years she held her own, first captivating Julius Cæsar, who made her younger brother, her Egyptian-style husband, share the throne of Egypt with her, and then, enchanting Marc Antony, a joint ruler with her for the last fourteen years of her life. Emil Reich declares: "She spoke most languages and there were few of the foreign ambassadors whom she answered by an interpreter. She gave personal audience to the Ethiopians, the Troglodites, the Hebrews, Arabs, Syrians, Medes and Parthians. Nor were these all the languages she understood, though the kings of Egypt, her predecessors, could hardly ever attain to the Egyptian and some forgot even their original Macedonian." Amours were thus aided by intelligence in staving off defeat. Even Cleopatra's religion — the divine right of kings — was an asset applied to encouraging Cæsar to believe himself a god. When disaster loomed before her, in spite of all her arts, in the shape of shackled decoration for a triumph of Augustus, like Boadicea she poisoned herself. Augustus thought he was sure of his prey when he threatened to mistreat Cleopatra's children, but his exhibition was evaded and she brought about a more dramatic climax to the plan of her Roman conqueror. Plutarch is more liberal toward the character of Cleopatra than modern sensationalists are prone to be. He says: "Cleopatra certainly possessed the virtues of fidelity and natural affection to a very eminent degree. She had several opportunities of betraying Antony could she have been induced to do it either by fear or ambition. Her tenderness for her children is always superior to her self-love; and she had a greatness of soul which Cæsar never knew."

Into the political contests at home, interwoven with imperial conflict at the ends of the empire, were drawn the ambitions of women at the capital. While Cæsar and Antony were at swords' points, Fulvia, the wife of the latter, moved heaven and earth to ˙ fend her husband's interests during the time he was ostensibly engaged in the Parthian campaign. Promiscuous before her marriage, Fulvia had been ardent and loyal afterwards; in fact, determined that he should be the head of the state at any cost; when Antony was declared a public enemy, she made a speech in person to the Senate in an effort to force an annulment of the declaration. But she was a creature of steel as well as sentiments and gazed with rapture on the heads of the murdered Cicero and Rufus, victims of her husband's brutality during the proscriptions in 43 B.C. When noble ladies called upon her for assistance in a protest to the triumvirs against an order commanding them to deliver up their treasures for the support of the army, she treated them with contempt. She also opposed the program of Octavianus for distributing lands to soldiers. On the other hand, harsh words of Antony, when they met again at Athens, blaming her for the need of fighting, are thought to have broken her heart. Her death, soon afterwards, removed from·the scene one of the many women over whose personality much controversy has occurred, though there can be no dispute about her political energy.

With Fulvia out of the way, a marriage was effected between Antony and Octavia, widow of Gaius Marcellus, one of Cæsar's sternest foes, sister of Octavianus, and regarded as even more beautiful than Cleopatra. Those behind this marriage hoped it would reconcile Antony and Octavianus and it was especially gratifying to the army. Her efforts to keep the peace between these stormy petrels were for a time successful. But when Antony went back to the wars, he renewed his liaison with Cleopatra. Since Octavianus suspected Antony of scheming to remove the capital to Alexandria, Octavia tried to hold her philandering mate to his military task and wean him from his royal companion in the interests of Rome no less than of herself. She took reinforcements and money to Antony in 35 B.C., reaching Athens with her aid; however he refused to see her, while accepting her material aid, and indeed divorced her three years later.

Meanwhile, Octavianus challenged Antony to a naval battle off the coast of Greece, Cleopatra fled, Antony pursued, was trapped, and took his own life. Octavia then protected Antony's children, legal and illegal, whether born of the union with Fulvia or Cleopatra, her numerous virtues winning the sympathy of the Roman people so completely that on her death public honors were paid her. She had refused to be a cat's paw for fomenters of civil war. Her beauty and integrity were lauded by many writers and love for Octavia was largely responsible for the acceptance of her brother, Octavianus, as the first Cæsar Augustus. Whether Octavia directly or indirectly through Augustus erected the Porticus Octaviæ, housing a library and art gallery, where the Senate often met, is not positively known today but the woman was certainly capable of doing it.

In the later days of the empire, as well as in its stormy emergence, women still operated at the center of military politics. Near the middle of the fifth century A.D., when the "barbarians" again converged on Rome, a chain of events made Galla Placidia, daughter of Theodosius the Great, widow of a Gothic chieftain, and mother of Valentinian III, the real ruler of Rome. Valentinian was only six years old when he was proclaimed emperor; so his mother acted as counselor-in-chief — that is, dictator — without the formal trappings of empress. No tables of law could control her self-indulgence and the boy was clay in her hands, in other words, profligate and incompetent.

His mature years of rule were filled with troubles brought on by a conflict with his sister, Honoria. Fearing that she had designs on his prerogative, he raised her to the rank of Augusta, which prevented her marrying and ruling through a Roman husband. Whereupon, tongues reported, Honoria, resentful at this interference with her liberty, sent a eunuch to Attila, king of the Huns, conveying an offer of marriage. To counter this move Valentinian announced that Honoria, being a woman, was not entitled to the family inheritance and, to make her disqualified as a bride, declared that she had philandered with a steward; in fact was his wife. At all events using the "wrongs" of his affianced wife as a pretext, Attila made demands on the court, and finally marched in and took possession of Rome, bride or no bride. In days of strength and of palsied weakness, from first to last, women were conspicuous in the military pageant and energetic behind the scenes.

THE INDOMITABLE MATRIARCHS

So much has been written on the patriarchal law of Rome that it has long been the habit to think of Roman men as heads of their families, acting alone on their own wisdom in affairs of State, and enjoying at home the power of life and death over their wives and daughters, until late in history the law was liberalized, bestowing property rights and other civil liberties on "the weaker sex." Nothing could be more unreal. Besides the formal law of the State, there were the fortunes of circumstance and the custom of the family, making women of the propertied or ruling classes the chieftains of the great households, when the adult male guardians were away or dead and the boys were too young for responsibility. And the innumerable wars, assassinations, and proscriptions frequently threw the headship of the family, even in imperial circles, upon the shoulders of matriarchs, who usually proved equal to the situation as the ancients saw it, rivalling in power, cruelty, cupidity, or moral idealism the male members of the species.

Not merely in terms of individual personalities, therefore, can the true history of Roman power be written. Yet Gibbon misses the connotations of the family system in history, betraying a woeful confusion through his failure to understand the rôle of the family in war, government, and economy from primitive times to the modern era. At one moment, thinking of formalities and theories, he writes: "In every age and country, the wiser, or at least the stronger, of the two sexes has usurped the powers of the State, and confined the other to the cares and pleasures of domestic life. In hereditary monarchies, however, and especially in those of modern Europe, the gallant spirit of chivalry, and the law of succession, have accustomed us to allow a singular exception; and a woman is often acknowledged the absolute sovereign of a great kingdom, in which she would be deemed incapable of exercising the smallest employment, civil or military. But as the Roman emperors were still considered as the generals and magistrates of the republic, their wives and mothers, although distinguished by the name of Augusta, were never associated to their personal honors; and a female reign would have appeared an inexpiable prodigy in the eyes of those primitive Romans, who married without love, or loved without delicacy and respect. The haughty Agrippina aspired, indeed, to share the honors of the empire which she had conferred upon her son; but her mad ambition, detested by every citizen who felt for the dignity of Rome, was disappointed by the artful firmness of Seneca and Burrhus. The good sense, or the indifference, of succeeding princes restrained them from offending the prejudices of their subjects; and it was reserved for the profligate Elagabalus to discharge the acts of the senate with the name of his mother Soæmias, who was placed by the side of the consuls, and subscribed, as a regular member, the decrees of the legislative assembly. Her more prudent sister, Mamæa, declined the useless and odious prerogative, and a solemn law was enacted, excluding women forever from the senate, and devoting to the infernal gods the head of the wretch by whom this sanction should be violated."

But this same Gibbon, in the very next breath, exclaims realistically: "The substance, not the pageantry of power, was the object of Mamæa's manly ambition." Then he goes on to show how she gained her object. "She maintained an absolute and lasting empire over the mind of her son, (Alexander Severus) and in his affection the mother could not brook a rival. Alexander, with her consent, married the daughter of a patrician; but his respect for his father-in-law, and love for the empress, were inconsistent with the tenderness or interest of Mamæa. The patrician was executed on the ready accusation of treason, and the wife of Alexander driven with ignominy from the palace, and banished into Africa. Notwithstanding this act of jealous cruelty, as well as some instances of avarice, with which Mamæa is charged, the general tenor of her administration was equally for the benefit of her son and of the empire. With the approbation of the senate, she chose sixteen of the wisest and most virtuous senators as a perpetual council of state, before whom every public business of moment was debated and determined. The celebrated Ulpian, equally distinguished by his knowledge of, and his respect for, the laws of Rome, was at their head; and the prudent firmness of this aristocracy restored order and authority to the government. As soon as they had purged the city from foreign superstition and luxury, the remains of the capricious tyranny of Elagabalus, they applied themselves to remove his worthless creatures from every department of the public administration, and to supply their places with men of virtue and ability. Learning, and the love of justice, became the only recommendations for civil offices; valor, and the love of discipline, the only qualifications for military employments. But the most important care of Mamæa and her wise counsellors was to form the character of the young emperor on whose personal qualities the happiness or misery of the Roman world must ultimately depend. The fortunate soil assisted, and even prevented, the hand of cultivation. An excellent understanding soon convinced Alexander of the advantages of virtue, the pleasure of knowledge, and the necessity of labor. A natural mildness and moderation of temper preserved him from the assaults of passion, and the allurements of vice. His unalterable regard for his mother, and his esteem for the wise Ulpian, guarded his unexperienced youth from the poison of flattery."

As a matter of fact the power of women as leaders of families in the imperial age, which Gibbon thus described without recognition of the implications, had precedents in the republican period and was manifest in every direction as the republic changed into an empire at the turning of antiquity into the Christian era. Indeed the story of that political transformation is the story of a family — the Augustan family — and within it is contained the epic of matriarchal rule. It might almost be said that the Augustan plot centers in two women, one the republican, the other an imperialist — Livia, called by Caligula after her death "Ulysses in women's apparel," and Messalina, the siren, luring the Ship of State upon the rocks.

The tempestuous events which attended this political transformation are apt to be ignored as phases of the family law. But verdicts on Livia, such as those rendered by Tacitus and Livy in Roman times or by Ferrero in these times must meet the test of the larger implication. Ferrero comes close to that realisation, in his explanation of such a tribute as Livy's who said she "held her head above all vices" and of another statement that she was "a woman in all things more comparable to the gods than to men, who knew how to use her power so as to turn away peril and advance the most deserving." Ferrero after years of study now believes that the charge she murdered right and left for the gratification of a personal ambition is unwarranted but, if she did dispose of individuals inimical to the program she was executing, still she must be judged with reference to the demands her family responsibility imposed upon her. Livia was in the extraordinary position of being a representative of two semi-divine clans, and Cæsar Augustus, a social upstart in comparison, surrounded by enemies, knew he could best establish himself in popular esteem by making her his empress. Livia already had a husband but when the marriage proposal was submitted to her, there could be but one decision. The call to a supreme aristocrat to maintain the weight of her ancestors in the councils of State, as she alone could do, overcame all other considerations and she accepted the seat beside the Cæsar Augustus as a duty. Henceforward until she died in 29 A.D., at the age of eighty-six, Livia watched over the fortunes of Rome in the light of her family morality and the republican code of honor and Ferrero thinks she played her act with great valor and consistency. Sensitive, like every proud Roman, to the authority of the great Clan, Augustus relied on Livia for his precise program as well as guidance in its execution, while she brought her "prodigious stock of learning" and a courage instilled by the warlike spirit of her people to bear upon situations as they arose.

Lest Livia's aristocratic program be interpreted as one of reckless extravagance, it is important to realise at once that the exact converse was the case. Republican aristocracy, which she symbolised, if proud beyond all cavil, required ladies of the first families to assume in full the elaborate domestic obligations, including household industries, and to be modest and frugal as well as industrious. Roman stability for some three hundred years was in truth guaranteed by their labor, restraint, sagacity and marital fidelity. These codes of honor Livia set herself to defend at all costs and guardianship was now no light matter for the *nouveaux riches* were pulling hard in the direction of idleness, frivolity and self-indulgence and the court was beginning to feel the effects. Hoping by legislation to check the trend toward indolence with respect to private and public obligations, Augustus presented to the Senate in 9 A.D. laws aimed at celibacy, adultery and luxury, offering them for consideration as models of virtue exemplified in the Empress Livia, scion of republican honor. During their reign Ovid was banished from the court under somewhat mysterious circumstances, the presumption being that his panegyrics on the non-mother and his devotion to the cult of beauty alone, luring the *jeunes filles* of the upper classes to exalt pleasure above labor, were deemed hostile by Livia to the best interests of the governing caste. In short, the guardian of an old régime sagaciously tried to fend off excesses derogatory to its vigor and offensive to popular sentiment.

But within the matriarchal household, the young generation was fighting its battle for liberty or license. Julia, the only daughter of Augustus, Livia's step-daughter, was its ringleader, encouraged by the "smart set" who found her escapades and defiance of her elders diverting. Macrobius was among the admirers of the self-willed girl, witty, educated, charming, proposing to enjoy life rather than to consider family or futurity. Macrobius preferred her to intellectual women. But Augustus had no choice in his attitude toward Julia. Though he had tried to educate his daughter and hold her to industrious habits, the haughty young descendant of a haughty caste threw virtue to the winds and paid an awful penalty. Her father was compelled to enforce against his own offspring the rigors of the law he had written on the books for other Romans. So Julia was banished to one of the islands off the coast of Campania where she died of neglect and tuberculosis. Sinning, she was also sinned against, for she had been a victim of family politics. Her mother had died soon after Julia's birth. Married first at the age of fourteen, she was given as a third husband none other than Livia's son by her former marriage, Tiberius, in order that the family line might be cemented and the succession secured. Both Tiberius and Julia had to pay the price of matriarchal law — the code of the clan.

The times were harsh and the rulers like their times. Women found even less protection from the fairly blind fury, to no small degree of their own stimulation, which largely determined the careers of the great families of Rome. A contemporary of Julia, Prisca Publia, whose husband, C. Geminus Rufus, was assassinated, when she was accused of being a party to the same conspiracy through which he suffered, rather than face the charge, stabbed herself in the Senate House. And what with self-annihilation or murder, the list of men and women of the major clans who died unnatural deaths was appalling.

Yet Livia was a cautious politician when circumstances demanded leniency. For example when the question arose regarding the proper punishment to be inflicted upon Cinna, a conspirator, she gave this opinion: "An enemy who has been generously pardoned, when one has an opportunity of punishing him, has no longer the power to hurt his benefactor." For the clemency showed to Cinna, Livia received abundant credit.

While Augustus lived, everything went Livia's way and the emperor basked in the sunshine of popular favor. His reign was called the golden age of Rome for, if the court was stern of honor, it gave play to the intellectual flights of Vergil, Horace, and so many other poets, major and minor, that the age became an outstanding period in Latin Letters. But neither Livia nor Augustus was immortal like poetry and other standards of virtue made headway, until Messalina entered the political arena with demands so averse to republicanism that the lays of ancient Rome must be shunted aside at this point for the story of a new-style matriarchate.

For a time Livia lingers — in fact into old age, the years of her widowhood being stormy ones for the head of the clan. For instance there was the question of the succession and she left no stone unturned to settle it in favor of her son, Tiberius. So anxious was the army on the Rhine to seat Germanicus on the throne that his wife, Agrippina I, the granddaughter of Augustus, during her husband's absence on duty, had to prevent the march of his admiring cohorts on Rome with his coronation as their goal. Had her elder sister not been the wife of Tiberius, Agrippina might have behaved differently but she was not inclined to destroy her sister's career to further her own.

Livia took little cognizance of such restraint, it appears; she saved the life of Placina, a close friend, when on the accusation of Agrippina she was brought to trial with Piso, her husband, for poisoning Germanicus at Antioch. Rumor whispered that Livia was behind the conspiracy to dispose of Germanicus as a peril to Tiberius but Piso sealed his lips by self-destruction. And the circumstances surrounding the death of Germanicus, already a military hero, raised him in popular favor and made his widow more revered.

So many members of the Augustan family died strange deaths during the régime of Livia whom Augustus had made its arbiter that suspicion often fell upon her. Ferrero however thinks that physical degeneration may be a sufficient explanation of the decimation which carried another of the great old Roman families down the long hill into the darkness. Against that deterioration Livia's frugality was no protection. Nor was she a seer capable of appreciating the weaknesses of blue blood. As long as she was the twin sovereign with her son — actually his dictator — she seemed satisfied and that position she long enjoyed. Letters on public affairs were addressed to them jointly and together they signed public documents. Livia did not appear at any time in the senate or before the army and the people but her matriarchal sway was so complete that there was no necessity for claiming its existence. She even forced Tiberius to divorce the wife he deeply loved and take Julia for dynastic ends, embittering his life and increasing the family distress. When he could bear conditions no more, he fled from the court and left the government entirely to his mother. Nor would he return for her funeral or permit her apotheosis. Her very will was long suppressed — until Caligula was crowned. He carried it out and paid its legacies.

Tiberius succeeded in restraining another woman who might have been a matriarchal ruler, namely Agrippina I, whose "masculine preoccupation," Tacitus said, "left no place for such feminine frailties in this domineering and ambitious soul." But the judgment of Tacitus deserves closer examination under the microscope of his republican biases. Other Roman writers describe her as a woman of integrity and strong ideals and even Tacitus valued her *Memoirs* for their data on the Germans, utilising them in the preparation of his history. Whatever the character of Agrippina I might be, she had a son, like Livia, and fear that she might try to seat him on the throne, with a like determination, led Tiberius and his favorite, Sejanus, to deport her to Pandataria, a barren island off the coast of Campania, where she expired, some declare in a hunger strike while others say as the result of slow starvation regulated by imperial arrangement. Her portrait hangs in the Capitoline Museum at Rome and a bronze medal in the British Museum pictures the return of her ashes to the capital through the decree of her son, Caligula, who succeeded Tiberius in spite of everything. Caligula became Egyptianised and one of the first results was his deification of his mother and sisters — the Egyptian claim to the throne acquiring its justification only on the basis of descent through divine women, the unqualified matriarchal law.

Meanwhile the aristocratic republican tradition upheld by Livia, the matriarch, was perpetuated in a more diluted form by Antonia, Marc Antony's daughter, whose quiet watchfulness prevented Tiberius from becoming the victim of a plot framed by Sejanus to steal the scepter from the son of Livia as soon as she was dead. Equally noble and somewhat gentler than Livia, Antonia yet permitted her daughter Livilla to starve herself to death when jealous ladies-in-waiting plotted against her life and her fate seemed dark in any case.

It is still the story of family law in its matriarchal form which envelops Agrippina III and her son Nero after Livia and Augustus, Germanicus and Agrippina I, Tiberius and Antonia are all in their graves. But the political and social ideals have now been modified, upsetting the republican code of honor, entailing industry and thrift, by an individualistic flair for wealth and indolence. As we have seen, the "modern" urge began in the court of Augustus, sacrificing the Emperor's giddy daughter in its heedless drive. However the third generation, "snappy and up-to-date," has at last put the old folks " in their place" and we are at the stage of dynasties guided by individualists. First however there was a tooth and claw struggle, with women in the spotlight close beside wilful men.

Tacitus limns the group which turned the world topsy-turvy and though it is a related blood clan, the star actors are now

Agrippina III, Nero, Tiberius, Claudius and Messalina, with Messalina pointing the arrow in the new direction and the others studying the target. Messalina was a child-bride of fifteen when she became the wife of the Emperor Claudius, a man of forty-nine, but she was by no means cowed in her position as the third wife of a dotard. Did she not have freedmen at her beck and call ? Who was to define her purposes or set bounds to her desires ? No one until the mother of Nero undertook the task.

According to Ferrero: "Messalina thought only of acquiring wealth, that she might dissipate it in luxury and pleasure. The wife of the emperor had been selling her influence to the sovereign allies and vassals, to all the rich personages of the empire, who desired to obtain any sort of favor from the imperial authority; she had been seen bartering with the contractors for public works, mingling in the financial affairs of the state every time that there was any occasion to make money. And with the money thus amassed she indulged in ostentatious displays which violated all the prohibitions of the Lex Sumptuaria, leading a life of unseemly pleasures, in which it is easy to imagine what sort of example of all the finer feminine virtues she set. . . Messalina then, with her peculiar levity of character and violence of temperament, continued to emphasize the modernising Asiatic tendency introduced by Caligula into the state, and was influential in destroying the puritanic traditions of Rome and replacing them by the corruption and pomp of Asia."

The prisons were filled with the victims of Messalina's wrath, male and female, Claudius not being so much as consulted as a rule. She put Julia, the youngest child of Germanicus and Agrippina I and the sister of Gaius, to death on a charge of adulterous relations with Seneca though she spared his life in a decree of banishment to Corsica. During her rampage Pætus and Arria, the parents-in-law of the Stoic, Thrasea, committed suicide together to evade assassination.

Wilful while Claudius was in Rome, Messalina at that time maintained considerable secrecy in the matter of her sexual divertissements in palace and in brothel. When he was out of the city she made no attempt to hide her conduct. Messalina was truly a racketeer. "The only escape for a victim was the surrender to her and her satellites of an estate, province, office or person; the rights of citizens were sold for a price; she disposed of legions and provinces without consulting Claudius or the Senate; she corrupted or intimidated judicial tribunals; she filled the offices with her hirelings. . . During the absence of Claudius she forced a handsome youth named Gaius Silius to divorce his wife and go through a regular marriage with her. The freedman, Narcissus, warned by the fate of another freedman, Polybius, who had been put to death by Messalina, informed Claudius of what had taken place and persuaded him to consent to the removal of his wife. She was executed in the gardens of Lucullus, which she had obtained on the death of Valerius Asiaticus, who through her machinations had been condemned on a charge of treason." Thus a girl of twenty-six, led solely by her passions, especially of avarice, battled fiercely with gods and men until her power was cut short by her own excesses.

That Agrippina III should have been the true cause of the overthrow of Messalina is often interpreted as another demonstration of cave politics. The fact seems to be that it was a second Livian effort to restore traditions to their old authority. There was a difference nevertheless in that Agrippina III did not wait for her uncle Claudius to initiate the marriage which would dispose of Messalina and unite the scion of the beloved family of Germanicus with the Claudian line. She herself made the proposal that she should now become his wife. Yet

Ferrero thinks that in doing so she prepared to sacrifice self to political stability and family integrity. It is undeniable that, like Queen Elizabeth of a later age, Agrippina was inured to crime and that she exhaled some of the poisonous breath inhaled in her youth. But at least she restored Claudius as Livia elevated Octavianus to the status of a popular Augustus. The laws against adultery required imperial enforcement even though they hurt the royal household. Hence Claudius, the "semi-sacred magistrate," by judicially murdering his wayward wife, upheld his own integrity in the eyes of the people. His marriage then with Agrippina was approved by the prætorian cohorts and the legions, ever mindful of her illustrious ancestor, Germanicus. So something of the glamor of Augustan days returned as the aristocratic standards of a prouder morality revived. The clamor had grown strong for the recovery of reputable principles of modesty and frugality and Agrippina III was aware that, unless the survivors of the old ruling family hung together, they might all hang separately.

With this in her mind, she took every precaution against errors on the part of Claudius. She was always at his side, not at his solicitation as Livia had been consulted voluntarily by Augustus, but ever on guard anyway, reviewing the army, watchful of its designs, zealous in financial matters in order that funds should be conserved for political necessities, and dominant over freedmen who under Claudius had been looting the treasury. For these reasons she pleased the aristocracy trained in republican manners and abhorrent of the tastes and performances of the parvenus led by Messalina.

In dealing with the ways of politics, Ferrero also deals with the ways of history in this connection: "The government of Agrippina was from the first a great success. From the moment when she became empress there is discernible in the entire administration a greater firmness and consistency of policy. . . A certain concord and tranquillity returned to the imperial house, to the aristocracy, to the senate, and to the state. Although Tacitus accuses Agrippina of having made Claudius commit all sorts of cruelties, it is certain that trials, scandals, and suicide became much less frequent under her rule. During the six years that Claudius lived after his marriage with Agrippina, scandalous tragedies became so rare that Tacitus, being deprived of his favorite materials, set down the story of these six years in a single book."

And now we come to Nero, her son by a previous marriage, whom Agrippina enthroned just as Livia had made her son a Cæsar. And again there was an ominous conflict between noblewomen shaping political events. Agrippina III saved herself from the clutches of Claudius by disposing of him before he attacked her. Her next task then was to see that Nero behaved properly. "Nero's restoration of the republic was Agrippina's masterpiece," says Ferrero, "and marks the zenith of her power. It followed, as a result of her decision, that Nero, who was to go down to history as the most terrible of tyrants, was that one of all the Roman emperors who had the most limited power. . . Most historians, hallucinated by Tacitus, have not noticed this, and they have consequently not recognised that in carrying out this plan Agrippina is neither more nor less than the last continuator of the great political tradition founded by Augustus. In the minds both of Augustus and Tiberius the empire was to be governed by the aristocracy. The emperor was merely the despositary of certain powers of the nobility conceded to him for reasons of state. If these reasons of state should disappear, the powers would naturally revert to the nobles. It was therefore expedient at this time to make the senate forget, in the presence of a seventeen-year-old emperor, the pressure which had been brought to bear upon it by the cohorts, and to wipe out the rancor against the imperial power which was still dormant in the aristocracy. This restoration was not, therefore, a sheer renunciation of privileges and powers inherent in the sovereign authority, but an act of political sagacity planned by a woman whose knowledge of the art of government had been received in the school of Augustus." And of Livia.

To preserve the appearance of legitimacy Agrippina III married Nero to Octavia, the daughter of Claudius, killing, some insist, the husband Octavia already had in order to make the new arrangement legal. These obstacles to Nero's rule all settled and the deck swept clean, Agrippina took up the task of making his reign notable. And the years which Trajan commended for competence and achievement were the early years when his mother was erect at the wheel. The sway of freedmen which had made of Claudius' reign a horror was ended. She recalled Seneca from exile and made him her principal adviser and tutor to her son. Drawing into the court other presumably wise men such as Afranius Burrhus, she and they together prepared a splendid program for the empire which Nero presented in a vigorous speech before the Senate. This included imperial free trade, a better administration of the corn supply, recognition of Senatorial responsibility, and other measures looking to public welfare — all before he was twenty-one.

What started so well administratively however ended savagely notwithstanding all the alleviating circumstances that may be cited. Agrippina III plotted, a court party led by Seneca and Burrhus was formed against her, Nero came under the influence of other women and courtesans, and the question of the succession once more arose. At this point Nero turned against his mother who then threw her influence to the original legitimate heir, Britannicus, whereupon the son she had made sovereign had his mother murdered in cold blood.

Thus before we take up the story of women and monks, it seems imperative to know more about women and monarchs. In this Roman chapter it is the custom to say that vice got the upper hand. However it had the lower hand as well. Seneca the "noblest of the Romans," to use the language of innumerable appraisers, was active in leading the emperor he was assigned to tutor into sexual digressions, insinuating the freedwoman, Acte, into the young man's affections and preparing him for an alignment with the party working against his mother by the time Poppæa, the notorious prostitute, became his favorite. The true villain in the drama of the "monster" plot to slay one's own mother may conceivably therefore be the "noblest of the Romans" notwithstanding the fact that Seneca's influence with Agrippina was strong to the very end. He contrived to save some of her intended victims from schemes for their annihilation and Nero more than once suspected the philosopher of intriguing against his government on that account. Nero feared to permit Seneca out of his sight and finally ordered him to commit suicide to relieve the strain.

Advancing into the later imperial period from which Gibbon drew the illustration previously cited, we still encounter the family system with the matriarch at the center of all the operations of State. Owing to the exigencies of space, a single case must be taken as typifying the movement of feminine force and solicitude. Shortly after Caracalla ravaged Mesopotamia because its king refused to give him a daughter in marriage, he was murdered at the instigation of a prefect of the prætorian guard. In the absence of an adult male to perpetuate the family in authority, his aunt Mæsa Julia, who succeeded him for a brief moment, assumed charge of its fortunes with only imperial eunuchs to assist her at the outset. And the first thing this female chieftain did was to beat a strategic retreat to her native Syria carrying with her an immense fund, "the fruit of twenty years' favor," together with her two widowed daughters each of whom had with her a young heir or pretender to the throne. Soon the group came back to Italy at the head of Syrian troops and the little lads, in turn, in accordance with their grandmother's program, received the scepter of the Cæsars. The young men got the glory. The women got the State.

Of course Mæsa was powerless to keep the family in power without an army behind her. Neither could a man. But she knew how to get her fighting men. As the Syrian soldiers wavered, she had the mother of one of the youngsters lift her exceptionally beautiful child high in her arms for them to accept as a stimulus to fiercer effort, thus turning what would have been defeat into victory. Then the mother of the youthful Roman had a second flash of genius. She told the soldiers that Caracalla was the child's father, rendering doubly sacred the heir of a dead and deified emperor. Objectors were silenced by lavish bribes until they actually saw the features of the holy ruler reproduced in the lad, Varius Avitus, selected as their emperor. Still they had to fight in defense of their idol when Macrinus, a reformer, challenged his claim to the throne, and the outcome of a battle over the point was dubious. At the crucial moment however the claimant, mounted on a steed, charged boldly on the enemy, the eunuch Gannys displayed the talents of a general, while the interested women climbed down from their chariots and kept the soldiers infuriated until they had crushed the opposition. The path to the throne was now clear for the family and Varius Avitus' mother, being a widow, was charged with the responsibility of guiding its career from that stage.

The fact that Varius Avitus took the name of the Syrian Sun

God, Elagabalus, helped him to find favor for a time with the
Eastern Army who bore him back to Rome. In the form of
a black conical stone, presumably heaven-sent, the Sun God
was worshipped by the Syrians and its transplanting to the
city by the Tiber was attended with lavish rites. There was
plenty of wine, sacrifice, perfume, sinuous dancing and chorus-
ing of maidens, barbaric music, and loving. The new emperor
tried to remove the Roman religious symbols but the Vestal
Virgins, by a ruse, saved a part of them and hid them away.
Political and military leaders were ordered to clothe themselves in long Phœnician robes and perform duties of homage
to the ruler and his horde of strange gods. "Pallas had been
first chosen for his consort; but as it was dreaded lest her warlike terrors might affright the soft delicacy of a Syrian deity,
the Moon, adored by the Africans under the name of Astarte,
was deemed a more suitable companion for the Sun. Her
image, with the rich offerings of her temple as a marriage portion, was transported with solemn pomp from Carthage to
Rome, and the day of these mystic nuptials was a general festival in the capital and throughout the empire."

Dion says the subjects had to make liberal presents to the
newly-weds and Mæsa saw that the subjects carried out their
pledges. That too was her privilege and obligation as chieftain of the clan.

The mother of Varius Avitus, Sœmis Julia, also enjoyed herself for a while, as Augusta. She took a seat in the Senate,
the first to be held by a woman, and was the president of a
woman's parliament which held sessions in the Quirinal and
drafted codes of conduct for the public. But when rumor
whispered, and people believed, that mother and son performed
human sacrifices in secret, the play ended. Even the soldiers
revolted and the pair were slain by a centurion who threw the
body of the mother into the sewer.

Meanwhile the old matriarch Mæsa foresaw this "eventuality" and prepared for it previous to her natural death by guaranteeing the succession to the second young claimant, Alexander Severus. When he took up the reins of government according to the grandmotherly schedule, it was his mother's turn to rule Rome as regent. Now Mamæa Julia, on the advice of her mother, was careful to see that no repetition of the vices which had undermined the power of Elagabalus and threatened the family took place. Besides, she had begun to be interested in the Christian cult and had her son taught its tenets together with poetry, history and philosophy. So catholic in his tastes did Alexander become that according to Gibbon he received into his chapel all the religions of the Empire, Jesus Christ thus mingling liberally with Orpheus in the palace while the Jews were granted extraordinary liberties in civil life.

Unfortunately Mamæa Julia was greedy — the miserly sort of person who possessed in order to hoard. In the end, her stowing away of money was to be as disastrous as the religious orgies of her predecessor had been. Extreme parsimony on the government's part alienated the soldiers, who rebelled in 235 A.D. Alexander and his mother were their victims, the emperor with his last breath gasping out denunciations of the matriarch as the cause of all his woe.

Nor was the matriarchate simply the aftermath of Caracalla's death. It was known before. In a fit of rage at family dictation of that variety, Caracalla almost murdered his widowed mother, Julia Domna, with his own hands. He did go so far as to slay his brother lying in her arms and, though the parent's life was spared for the time being, a battle continued to rage between the two for supreme power as long as Julia Domna lived — she laboring to preserve her clan prerogatives, he to free himself from that law and to rule in his own right.

Domna Julia was the widow of Septimus Severus and a person of uncompromising will as a family chieftain was supposed to be. The truth is she had been largely instrumental in lifting this particular family to its regal estate in the beginning and she saw no reason why she should abdicate in the end. A humble Syrian by birth, on marrying Severus, by means of readings with her horoscope she persuaded him to make war on Pescennius Niger and Clodius Albinus, as obstacles to his inauguration, the outcome of which was success at arms and politics. Yet while Severus reigned, the empress had little control over his conduct. He was jealous of her many lovers and, being of a gloomy disposition in general, turned to astrologers for companionship and counsel. But Julia Domna outlived Severus and as matriarch she then undertook to manage her two sons, Caracalla and Geta, who divided the empire between them and started out to be independent of each other. However, the dynastic power which she had won for her family almost wrecked it finally. Caracalla could not remain content with half the empire as his domain and murdered Geta together with twenty thousand persons of both sexes, it is said, slaughtered for their friendship with his brother. Against his wife, Plautilla, wilfully forced upon him by both parents before his father's death, Caracalla swore eternal vengeance, early executing one measure in that program by having her father slain in the presence of his own. Eventually by physical intimidation he even conquered his widowed mother — the matriarch. Compelled to retreat to her boudoir in the plight of a subject, for a while she tried philosophers as consolation but found her position intolerable and committed suicide.

Caracalla was the "common enemy of mankind. . . In the midst of peace and for a time upon the slightest provocation, he issued his commands, at Alexandria, in Egypt, for a general massacre. From a secure post in the temple of Serapis, he viewed and directed the slaughter of many thousand citizens, as well as strangers, without distinguishing either the number or the crime of the sufferers. An oracle called him a savage beast but he apparently liked the appellation. According to Dion, his gifts to his army mounted annually to seventy millions of drachmas (a sum which would amount in English money to about 2,350,000 pounds). Not only were increases in pay made from time to time but the size of the army enlarged correspondingly and was one of the reasons assigned for the final ruin of the State." The ball set rolling by the emperor the women of his family who survived him had to follow. But that law of family politics — matriarchal-patriarchal — matriarchal — Gibbon misses, resorting to the codes of a more individualistic age for his judgments of Mamæa.

THE POLITICAL ECONOMY OF ROME

UNDERNEATH the public stage on which a few families — with women always active, sometimes as directors and again as negotiators, counselors, and manipulators — played for great stakes of supreme power lay a vast social order or array of classes, whose interests, ambitions, aspirations, and discontents furnished the motives and energies for immense movements in time. The imperial ambitions which carried Roman eagles to the ends of the Mediterranean world sprang from the interests of class, even though they were mingled with the necessities and ideas of defense. The conflicts of politics, aristocracy and democracy, bringing changes in forms of government and social wars in their train, likewise had their roots in the antagonisms of the economic system. And it seems probable that the final collapse of the magnificent show was due mainly to the failure of jurists, governors, women, and philosophers alike to comprehend the operations of the deep-lying forces that were bearing ruling orders and the State as well to dissolution and doom.

At the top of the economic structure was the aristocracy of the land composed of noble families. Their number varied with the ebb and flow of fortune but judging by the fragmentary documents a few thousand always made up the dominant element, and within the few thousand was a nucleus of hundreds or scores that actually determined the fate of the whole. By heroic efforts, scorn, exclusiveness, and legislation, this aristocracy managed to restrain the infiltration of plebeians to a small stream and until the end was able to avoid being swamped, like the British aristocracy, by newcomers of wealth from below. At later times there was intermarriage between the members of the aristocracy and the orders just beneath, but the rule that senators should never engage directly in trade kept them from sinking into the rising flood of bourgeois. They borrowed from the plutocrats and occasionally gave daughters in marriage, but they were on guard to keep the lines of class distinct. Even Cicero, a new man, was careful in his correspondence with members of blue blood to observe the proprieties of subserviency.

Broadly speaking, members of the nobility supplied the leading officers of State from the beginning of the republic until the close of the empire. There were times, to be sure, when plebeians broke through the upper crust or had to be conciliated with favors. Yet as a rule, when there were ferments below, some member of the aristocracy turned popular, either to stem the current, direct it, or ride into power upon it. From the nobility came all the members of the senate, a few hundred in number, which formed the dominant governing body, actually in the days of the republic and formally under the empire, with varying fortunes, as plebeians, armies, and masterful emperors contested its authority. As long as the noble families devoted themselves to the management of their estates and to the discharge of public obligations, avoiding luxurious and easy living, the senate was powerful; but when riches had corroded their spirit of enterprise, reduced their energy, and clouded their minds with doubts as to the utility of their labors, the senate neglected its business, dawdled, and finally became a mere rubber stamp for militarists.

Below the ruling aristocracy were the business adventurers engaged in trading, banking, money-lending, the execution of State contracts, and the collection of taxes — a class that increased in size as Rome passed from the primitive agrarian life to imperial activities on a huge stage. Its members owned land and speculated in land. They had town houses in the cities and luxurious villas in the country. They handled the business of the provinces, enriching themselves as tribute poured into the imperial city. They entered into understandings with senators and augmented their fortunes through lucrative contracts that might make any modern "grafter" turn pale with envy. Unchecked by the sense of clan honor and public service which made some senators conservative in manner and living, individualistic traders plunged into the acquisition of riches by every method that their ingenuity could discover, from trafficking in slaves to buying Greek books for the libraries of plutocrats in the Eternal City. If excluded by blood from the select landed circle, the business men and their wives were not indifferent to the manipulations of politics carried on within that charmed group and in fact it is impossible to separate sharply the two bodies in action. Again and again the money that high officers of the State used to maintain their clients, feed the proletariat, and amuse the multitude came from loans obtained from the money manipulators, under conditions that had both economic and political significance. And in the later days when the army put up the office of emperor for sale, a swollen plutocrat, spurred on by the social ambitions of wife and daughters, would buy the bauble for a brief moment of glory, ending as a rule in tragedy for the entire family.

Below the business class in power, if often proud of their blood, were the poorer landed families and the free farmers. In early days the basic population of Rome was peasant. In republican times efforts, usually ineffectual, were made to provide each free family with a farm. When soldiers demanded their rewards after great wars, some large estates were confiscated for the purpose of satisfying their demands. But in time the great landlords gained over the small, compelled them to work on their vast holdings, purchased slaves for houses and fields, built defenses, and were so masterful, near Carthage for instance, that in 238 A.D., in a quarrel with the local procurator, they armed their tenants and drove him out. Pliny the Elder said that six men owned half that province, reminding one of recent Mexican conditions. When the government adopted the policy of turning devastated and confiscated land over to private persons in great holdings, particularly favoring Generals, the soldiers on the whole were found to be poor agriculturists and many soon forsook the soil. Only where it was especially fertile could the regular peasants manage to survive. It was fertile in Africa yet Pliny describes the minimum of existence which the local farmers had on their tiny parcels, their ploughs dragged by an ass and a woman. The poorest peasants and the slaves were alike driven to their tasks by overseers seeking rapid profits. In times of depression parents were apt to sell their children into slavery or leave them by the wayside to be picked up for servitude, a practice encountered in China to this day.

Some of the great estates were as unproductive as similar property in England in the twentieth century — pleasure holdings with vast game preserves. Others were self-sufficing as long as the supply of slaves lasted. The slave-artisans carried on such industries as weaving, cheese-making, the production of wine, oil and honey, the quarrying of stone, the growing of lumber, the handling of sand for cement, construction, grain milling, and baking. Incorrigibles might be chained to the manor house, mutilated or crucified. Eventually the supply of slaves gave out.

Originally they were war captives shackled for sale in the markets of Italy and other cities of the Empire. Every triumph of arms meant a new sort of chattel. Thus South Italy, Sicily, Greece, Greek Asia, Africa, and Gaul, Spain, Thrace, Numidia, Germany and Britain enriched the stream in turn. Then slave-catching expeditions, kidnapping, and the search for abandoned children augmented the supply and kept the price low. Marriage experiments were tried with a view to heavy breeding. Inevitably when the supply was abundant and the price cheap, the worst treatment was meted out to chattels.

They resisted on occasions and the menace of revolt was an ever-abiding terror though it did not destroy the market. Cicero charged Catiline with trying to achieve his ambitions with the allegiance of the slaves. And undoubtedly in the strife of great families for possession of the State, resort was had by some of them to the middle and lower classes for support against the others. Sicily was particularly a hotbed of rebellion and it may be that the temper of modern Sicilians still exhibits a residuum of that fierce struggle of their kind in imperial Rome.

In general, the rich Romans owned more slaves than the rich Greeks had done. Ten were considered a minimum of Roman respectability and Cæsar and Pompey were said to have sent a million men to the capital alone in bondage. This was an easy disposal of prisoners and no distinction was made by the government among the "blacks from Egypt, swift runners from Numidia, grammarians from Alexandria, house servants from Cyrene, beauties from Greece, scribes, accountants, teachers and artists, experienced shepherds and hard and sturdy laborers," except in the matter of price.

As long as Rome which seemed eternal could get sufficient labor and keep it in bondage, could import its fruits, grain and glass from Egypt, its wool and silver ore from Spain, its wine and oysters from Greece and the Ægean Islands, its spices, ivory and jewels from India and Arabia, its prosperity and its suzerainty were assured. But both had a termination. In the contests between provincial and royal governors, American fashion, in efforts to lighten colonial rule, British style, in the struggle to maintain Roman parasitism on outlying regions, the usual imperial style, in the increasing reluctance of the native stock to fight the battles of Empire, Indian style, and its evasions of service even by mutilation or suicide, the "death-knell" of Empire was rung. The provinces finally rebelled and announced their independence.

The balance sheet was wrong. Probably few of the Roman colonies paid — any better than colonies pay in these times. Trade could not all flow one way. Italy could not import everything and export nothing. Agriculture decayed and domestic manufacturing was hampered by the constitution of the Italian system. Just what effect slavery had on industry it is difficult to say since authorities disagree so emphatically on the point.

However, certain facts stand out in the debate. One is that during the time when the slave supply was lavish, industry was principally operated by chattel labor. Duruy and Guizot, in their studies of Roman society, refer to the great households of the republic containing anywhere from 400 to 20,000 slaves; in the latter case numbers of them were often hired out to manufacturers, and in the former necessities were all produced at home. Unskilled slaves acted as porters, stevedores and navvies. The skilled were artisans, mechanics, smiths, carpenters, bricklayers, masons, seamen, shop assistants, waiters, cooks, artists, architects, scribes, musicians, actors, teachers, and physicians. To an astounding extent carvers of wood and stone, designers of furniture and furnishings, the fashioners of mosaics and indeed mural painters and decorators were slaves, bought and sold in the market. Moreover the incorporation of slaves in the great households where fine goods were produced, high finance planned and executed, and political schemes formulated gave many of them apprenticeship to power which poor freemen could in no wise obtain.

Within the high-caste villas, where all work was done by chattels, business and financial enterprise was often entrusted to them and slaves who acquired freedom were thus prepared to earn handsome livings. Often a favored slave was both emancipated and made heir to the estate of a rich man or woman, using the inherited capital for large scale adventuring in commerce or industry. Fortunate marriages of freedmen with patricians lifted many into positions of political power, though actual membership in the senate was denied to them and Nero even refused to enroll the names of their sons in the Roman album. Claudius had taken a similar stand against the social pretensions of freedmen and delivered harsh speeches against two "ungrateful" emancipated slaves, Pallas and Narcissus. Nevertheless under Hadrian freedmen won secretaryships in the palace and became virtual ministers of State. Tiberius made a Spanish freedman prefect of Egypt and "thus clothed a man who had stood with chalked feet in the slave market with vice-regal powers as the deputy of the Cæsar and the successor to the Pharaohs." Ex-slave women were often well dowered, though they never attained quite such political heights.

Outside of politics freedmen likewise played an important rôle. That they achieved economic distinction is proved by inscriptions on their tombs boasting of their progress and position. They made their mark as bridge-builders, coopers, stone-cutters, oculists, plumbers, and merchants. In many cases they evolved into *nouveaux riches,* founded great houses, and learned to despise more than anyone else manual labor and all that it implied. They discovered illustrious ancestors for themselves, and, not stopping with Æmilus Paullus or Scipio, they harked back to Æneas or Agamemnon. Power and pomp stamped the most menial servant of the large household with the seal of pride and prejudice.

The pride of slaves in great families and the haughtiness of freedmen, set on the way to fame and fortune, operated in such a way as to depress free labor of every class. Their prejudices were reinforced by the inveterate contempt of the aristocrat for workers and merchants. "All gains made by hired laborers," declared Cicero, "are dishonorable and base, for what we buy of them is their labor, not their artistic skill: with them the very gain itself does but increase the slavishness of the work. All retail dealing too may be put in the same category, for the dealer will gain nothing except by profuse lying, and nothing is more disgraceful than untruthful huckstering. Again, the work of all artisans is sordid; there can be nothing honorable in a workshop."

In such an environment there was little opportunity or incentive for freemen to rise out of their class or to attain for their class in which they remained a position of consequence in the State. From early times, it is true, artisans and merchants were organised in gilds or "colleges," as they were called, which had their ups and downs through the long evolution of Roman society. Some of them established fraternities of a high order, with rites, codes of ethics, and chests for the aid of the poor and unfortunate; but the long course of gild development is shrouded in obscurity, so meager are the records of the humble. Occasionally workers emerge in an unfavorable light when they attempt political action and sell their votes for magistrates in return for favors of one kind or another. Again they are used by the State in the execution of a particular economic policy. Often it was necessary to propitiate them by providing doles from the treasury. But at no time did they rise to such a power that they could materially sway the fortunes of rulers or incorporate themselves in the sovereignty of the empire. While the unions chose gods to worship, assembled in colorful conclaves, marched, banqueted, and displayed their emblems as proudly as the emperor his crown, they were pawns of the State or perils to policy, and never masters of the political scene. In the later days of the empire many of the gilds were virtually absorbed into the State, ordered by legislation to discharge stipulated functions, and formed into rigid corporations from which members could only escape by death. As Dill has tersely put it, "the property, like their persons, was at the mercy of the State."

By this time the ordinary system of "free economy" had practically ceased to function efficiently. The capital of the empire had become the seat of aggressive and insolent masters, aristocrats and capitalists, without grand policy, and of depressed artisans whose ranks were augmented by unsuccessful farmers. Unemployed a great deal of the time, housed like rabbits in warrens, surly or spiritless and in either case a peril to order, they could evoke little consideration from the upper classes save in the form of bread and circuses. The arteries of industry, like the arteries of agriculture, had hardened, and no remedy was at hand.

This development inescapably affected women. Many of their historic domestic arts had been taken from their hands — but not for better organization with the object of distributing more widely comfort and leisure for reflection. On the contrary the removal of food and clothing industries from the homes of the poor, too cramped for kettles and looms, for gardens and a sheep and a cow, actually meant less food and clothing instead of more. Public bakeries and workshops sprang up to supply tenement needs and by the end of the republic ready-made garments were on sale in various towns. During the empire the clothing trade assumed large proportions and a finer quality of garment was produced. Aware of opportunities to clean as well as make garments, public fullers put in their appearance. Equally alert shoemakers, vegetable and fruit dealers opened public stalls in the market places and women found chances in various of these business fields to make a meager living. With shopkeeping, some of the cunning combined hospitality — of a variety adapted to the tastes of masculine customers — thereby adding to their stock of coin, if not to their own welfare. Many of the new business women, however, such as fishmongers, modistes, laundresses, bar maids, accoucheuses, masseuses, actresses, dancers, and plain prostitutes were foreigners, principally Greeks.

Meanwhile in the great houses, cloth and bread and other commodities long associated with women's labor continued to be manufactured domestically, though the women who now superintended the processes as bosses of slave labor were frequently harsh enough to destroy whatever virtue and poetry were once attached to the system of domestic industry. The records flame with stories of their cruelty and greed. Younger women in the household, who were not needed for the task of supervision, were hard to confine to their looms and their needles and went the way of Julia, Augustus' daughter, in seeking sheer amusement beyond the guardianship of the hearth. Some matrons went into business, indeed into big business, the indication of feminine monopolies being found in the names of great ladies inscribed on bricks, for one thing. A pearl dealer who operated on the Via Sacra, her epitaph reports, provided for the burial of her freedmen and freedwomen by her side — evidently a spiritual ancestor of the Grimké sisters. Initiative and energy were not wanting among the ladies. It was the political economy that was at fault.

A change from domestic to workshop production did not guarantee buying power to the populace, often hungry and ragged in the shabby quarters surrounding the bakeries, tailoring establishments, shoe shops, and counters for the display of pearls. The poor did not necessarily fare well even when the corn distribution was placed in the hands of the working class. Sometimes it was given to the bakers who diverted so large a proportion of the public food to their "over-head" accounting or personal use that cries of corruption and extortion, familiar in connection with provincial governors, ascended in Rome itself against those charged with popular responsibility.

The attitude of the upper social crust affected the mental processes of the lowest. That psychology was one of utter contempt for the underdog, slave or free. Conscious of the significance of this robber psychology, this social blindness, a few writers, notably Juvenal and Petronius, standing at opposite ends of the caste ladder, produced copy in dispraise of folly. Thus Juvenal declared: "No virtue, no gifts, no eminence of service will be noticed in the poor. A great fortune will conceal the want of talent, sense or common decency. Everything is forgiven to the master of moneybags." The poet

Horace exclaimed with complete honesty: "I hate the common crowd !" It was evident that such hatred was general,
for no more attention was paid to an unfortunate pedestrian
hurt by a chariot than is paid by the captain of a Yangste
steamer to a native who happens to fall overboard. When the
worm turned, as Spartacus led a revolt of the poor and enslaved in the very year that Cicero was inveighing against
extortion, a hundred thousand soldiers were called into action
and stamped out the uprising in blood.

But until the last hour of the empire the upper classes, those
who speculated on politics, ethics and economics, no more
than the thoughtless engaged in the pursuit of happiness, gave
any fundamental consideration to the system by which they
lived, its inhumanity, or the conditions of its continuance.
In the day of splendor no Roman writer, even on agriculture,
conceived the possibility of slaves entirely emancipated and
labor placed on a basis of dignity and humanity. Nor, as
Fowler puts the case, "did any Roman writer recognize the
fact that slaves were potentially human beings, until Christianity gave its sanction to dutiful submission as an act of
morality that might be consecrated by Divine authority." So
it may be said that Roman State policy, though founded on
economy, kept it out of purview, save in allaying discontents
with bread and circuses and suppressing revolts. It remained
to the end a policy of exploitation for the benefit of the ruling
classes, tempered only occasionally by heroic efforts such as
were made by the Gracchi; and those who profited by it went
on their way enjoying the fruits of acquisition, though often
quarreling over the distribution, until they were no longer
able or inclined to bear the burdens of sustaining the economic
structure by manifestations of physical courage.

Nor did agrarian uprisings, slave revolts, or poor-white af-
frays accomplish anything of enduring significance. Beggars

could not by wishing climb into the saddle. The rich could not be unhorsed by upthrusts from below. Money was power, while it lasted. If the Stoics taught brotherly love and mutual aid, their preachment was not bodied forth in political parties. And after all, theirs was merely a plea for charity, though refined beyond bread and circuses. The very Gracchi, plebeian and agrarian reformers, who in the republican era sought to rehabilitate the freeborn on the land, launched the practice of doles. In time of crisis, the rich rushed to divert the attention of the hungry and the restless with food and "amusements" in the theater. But even this palliative, as we have said, was often manipulated by corruptionists diverting the doles for the poor to their own pockets in the face of famine and revolution. In reality the corn distribution swelled the long list of political scandals which the money that was power evoked.

So doles solved nothing. Poverty increased. Unemployment received no remedy. Then philosophers prodded while benevolence aspired to inject something more fundamental through the agency of education. In this direction Vespasian led off and his successors provided liberally for higher studies, hoping, it seems, to reduce avarice and instill some sense of honor among the rulers of the Empire. Nothing worked. Education was not applied and idle intelligence could only be poignant about the course of events. Rome was without a social plan.

WOMEN IN SOCIAL POLITICS

THE structure of society, thus roughly described, and the concentration of political authority (once actively and later formally) in the senate, composed of a few hundred members representing as many families, all contributed to the power of women among the classes at the top, whether as domestic educators of young men destined to rule, as ambitious manipulators, or as counselors. The case is well stated by Ferrero: "When Rome became the master of the Mediterranean world, and especially during the last century of the republic, woman, aside from a few slight limitations of form rather than of substance, had already acquired legal and economic independence, the condition necessary for social and moral equality. . . During the same period, indirectly, and by means of juridical evasions, this independence was also won by unmarried women, who, according to ancient law, ought to have remained all their lives under a guardian, either selected by the father in his will or appointed by the law in default of such selection. To get around this difficulty, the fertile and subtle imagination of the jurists invented first the *tutor optivus,* permitting the father, instead of naming his daughter's guardian in his will, to leave her free to choose some general guardian or several, according to the business in hand, or even to change that official as many times as she wished.

"To give the woman means to change her legitimate guardian at pleasure, if her father had provided none by will, there was invented the *tutor cessicius,* thereby allowing the transmission of a legal guardianship. However, though all restrictions imposed upon the liberty of the unmarried woman by the institution of tutelage disappeared, one limitation continued in force — she could not make a will."

In keeping with their economic position, as members of ruling noble families and as independent personalities possessing rights, women acted as informal advisers and counselors, mingling ambitions with care for the State. Tacitus is authority for the statement that their "counsels and assistance were considered of peculiar value by the commonwealth. For when some of the sterner old moralists wished to exclude women from all participation in affairs of State, the Senate, after a heated debate, decided by a large majority that the coöperation of women in questions of administration, far from being a menace, as some contended, was so beneficial to the State that it should be continued." Under Tiberius an effort was made to prevent wives from accompanying husbands to the provinces and for two reasons: one was that the custom of carrying women wherever the army went undermined discipline; the other was that wives of governors were sometimes dangerously extortionate toward the natives or were centers of political intrigue. Unquestionably there were avaricious wives bent on grinding the very face of the poor, to use the vulgar parlance. Yet Messia Castula, one of two magistrates in Africa, in her own right *duumvira,* was praised for her "intellectual capacity and administrative ability."

Early conflicts tore Rome from center to circumference and women were always involved either as moving spirits or as victims. Out of the first great struggle of the plebeians to curb the plutocracy and force a redistribution of wealth, especially in the form of land, in the second century, B.C., emerges the woman perhaps best known to modern times, Cornelia, mother of the Gracchi, though her true consequence in history is buried beneath a cloying sentimentality which makes her famous but for one remark, removed from its context, namely "These are my jewels," made as she pointed to her sons. In the popular mind, Cornelia is pictured as a sheltered creature reveling in maternity to the exclusion of political and social interests. That is far from an exact picture as it happens. It is true that when Ptolemy suggested to her a second marriage to be marked by diadems and pomp, she said she found her young "jewels" preferable. But that was because she was a partisan of the plebeians in their long and fierce domestic strife with the ruling class of Rome. Cornelia and her jewel sons stood with their backs to the wall fighting for the plebs against their oppressors and, when these men fell, the public had no more such defenders.

Cornelia's first espousal of the plebs was made when she chose for her husband an anti-capitalist reformer, Tiberius Sempronius Gracchus, in opposition to the traditions of her caste. While he lived her father, the mighty Scipio Africanus, conqueror of Hannibal and Carthage, refused his consent to their marriage. When he was dead, Cornelia quietly wed the man of her choice and remained loyal to plebeian-agrarian interests through her remaining years, transmitting to her sons, whom she personally educated, her own enthusiasms and her culture. Her sway over them was wholesome; their respect for her was deep. The Gracchi men were both idealists and gifted orators.

When Cornelia's son, Tiberius Gracchus, was made tribune, he revived the Licinian Law restricting land ownership to three hundred acres, encouraged by the mother in the face of terrific hostility on the part of the great landlords. But this reform brought on a civil war in the course of which Tiberius Gracchus was slain, in 133 B.C. In time the second son, Gaius Gracchus, became tribune and again attempted to reduce the autocracy of wealthy senators by forcing land reform. He too lost his life in the process, in 121 B.C. Cornelia had presented her jewels to the Roman people.

But Gaius Gracchus had failed to select a wife of equal calibre, though she had her own side of the story, poor woman ! Unwilling to hide as a refugee, Gaius strode to his martyrdom with his eyes wide open to eventualities, unarmed in a moment of danger. His wife tried to save him from the inevitable fate with these words: "You do not now leave me, my dear Gaius, as formerly, to go to the rostra in capacity of tribune or lawgiver, nor do I send you out to a glorious war, where, if the common lot fell to your share, my distress might at least have the consolation of honour. You expose yourself to the murderers of Tiberius, unarmed, indeed, as a man should go who had rather suffer than commit any violence; but it is throwing away your life without any advantage to the community. Faction reigns; outrage and the sword are the only measure of justice . . . for what confidence can we have either in the laws or the gods after the assassination of Tiberius ?" What was expected happened. In fear the people deserted their leader without remorse and, when his end came, he could but pray that Romans might forever be slaves, not wanting liberty.

The social movement led by the Gracchi family culminated in the establishment of Cæsar's empire. The very warp and woof of that social transformation, analysed in detail, reveals the ambitions of other families, the loves and passions of women touching Cæsar, Pompey, Sulla, Marius and Cicero, the celebrated actors in the drama. The setting must be summarised in a word however. Pompey and Cæsar, like the Gracchi, were "friends of the people" or made pretensions in that direction for a while. When Pompey went over to the patrician faction, he gave shows to the public as a solace. Cæsar did more for the people: master of Rome with popular backing in 48-44 B.C., he admitted the plebs to the Senate, revived the Licinian Law for which the Gracchi had labored, built homes for 80,000 landless folk, permitted local autonomy in the method of collecting taxes, reformed the calendar, rebuilt Corinth and planned to reconstruct Carthage. But Cæsar had developed vast imperialist designs, which in a large measure he executed. He conquered Gaul in eight years, from the Rhine to the Pyrenees, destroying eight hundred cities, hundred of thousands of soldiers in the process, and heaven only knows how many women. Suddenly his enterprise was cut short in the traditional manner of the ancients by assassination and that at the hand of his friend, Marcus Junius Brutus, principally.

The Pompey-Cæsar rivalry, the Sulla and Marius attempts to crash into power, and the civil war led by Catiline, frightful happenings as they were, involved the interests of many women who therefore took a hand. For one thing, through the politics of marriage, aspirants to power sought to rise on dead men's bones or to pacify living competitors. Consequently it became the practice, systematically inaugurated by Pompey, to change wives according to the political weather. Pompey violated traditions by divorcing a wife without her consent, marriage being considered a contract; in fact he had five in turn selected with a view to advantageous connections, each being dismissed peremptorily as his political requirements veered. This established a new fashion. However, it was one which Cæsar was loath to adopt. He did not object to several marriages but he preferred to marry for his own satisfaction. Therefore when Sulla, omnipotent in 82 B.C., ordered him to divorce Cornelia, the daughter of Cinna, whom he had chosen as his second wife in preference to a union with a plutocratic commercial family, and marry into the bourgeois group, he refused, thereby losing his property which Sulla confiscated, his priestly office and almost his life. Nothing but the intercession of his patrician relatives and the Vestal Virgins saved him from death. Cæsar had a genuine affection for Cornelia and it was not until she had died that he married again — the third time, Pompeia, a niece of Sulla. Then Pompeia was unfaithful and he set her aside after a sensational trial marked by the inquisitorial ardor of Cicero. His fourth wife was Calpurnia, the daughter of none other than Piso whom Cæsar planned to have succeed himself in the consulship.

Finicky for himself, Cæsar played open politics in selecting

a husband for his daughter Julia. He gave her in marriage
to Pompey to bind that antagonist in closer communion and
while she lived Julia kept the peace between these two politicians and fighters. On her death Cæsar then tried to marry
Octavia, his grand-niece, to Pompey, the widower, on the
understanding that if Pompey was favorable to the proposal,
Cæsar would see that her existing husband, the consul C.
Marsellus, was divorced to make the wedding legal. This tie
could not be effected and the two rivals drifted apart — a
rupture dreaded by aristocrats as the probable harbinger of
anarchy. Six years after Julia's death, in 50 B.C., Cæsar definitely started war on Pompey and their breach was never
healed.

Such political alliances M. Porcius Cato roundly denounced.
He said it was scandalous that army posts, governorships, and
the chief offices of the State should depend on marriage agreements. He especially referred to Cæsar's marriage to Calpurnia. But she mourned him in all conscience and after his
murder she went to the home of Marc Antony with whom
she divided her property in order to help him finance a
revenge.

Since the history of Rome was a history of family rivalry —
the thing Plato sought to abolish in Utopia — marriage alliances regularly decided the control of the State. Take the
case of Marius, hailed by the people as their savior from the
barbarians in Spain and the Cimbri and Teutons of the North.
When the selection of a supreme military commander followed, the office was given to Sulla instead because Marius was
of plebeian origin. He had likewise been denied the ædileship
on that account. But his revenge was bitter: aristocrats were
slaughtered wholesale and their property seized, the estate of
Sulla falling a prey to the angry partisans of Marius. Sulla
in turn sought revenge and Cæsar had to say where he stood

as between them. As chance set the stage, Marius was Cæsar's uncle, and Marius' wife, Julia, had reared Cæsar. Moreover Cæsar's father-in-law, Cinna, supported Marius in his wrath.

So the civil war, as far as Cæsar was concerned, involved not only popular emotions and programs but regard for the women of his family distributed among warring factions. He had to be wary of Marius but he had other problems besides. His defiance of Sulla in the matter of women when the latter made overtures for peace had helped to drive him into a tangle of debts and worries over their payment. In the circumstances amid the massacres and confiscations of Marius and the proscriptions and reign of terror under Sulla, Cæsar firmly planted himself in the ground where his affections lay, watching for a chance to be freer economically, and scheming whenever he saw light.

Fortunately for Cæsar, Sulla wearied of the dictatorship after he had had his surfeit of strangling men in cold blood, of orgies with actresses one of whom lavished treasure upon him, of planting soldiers on lands taken from freeholders and bona fide farmers following the permission he had given his men to plunder at will in Greece and Asia. The "favorite of Venus," as he styled himself, a great orator and adroit diplomat, had been educated in literature and art and as his life of blood and iron was ebbing away, he resigned political power, withdrew from Rome to an estate, composed poems and wrote his memoirs. Then Cæsar wormed his way to the dictatorship in Sulla's place.

If consideration for women affected events, it was not a sentiment born entirely of chivalry. Nor did the women simply take passively what chanced to come their way. They made things happen themselves. If men could divorce women at their will, women determined to do the same with men. Thus Polla assigned no more reason for divorcing one husband to marry Decimus Junius Brutus, a foe of Cæsar, than Pompey expressed when he acted for his own designs. Nor is the story of Roman power and pomp in this age a story of wives alone. One commentator on the times declares that its history "cannot be written unless Servilia appears on every page." Now Servilia was the favorite mistress of Cæsar, after her husband, the first Marcus Junius Brutus, was slain at the order of Pompey. When Cæsar became consul, he gave her a pearl worth $250,000 and later he presented her with several confiscated estates which the tribunes let her retain. It is thought by some students that M. J. Brutus the second, who finally slew Cæsar, was his illegitimate son by Servilia and that the son turned against the father because Octavianus, a member of an equestrian family of a small village, was made his heir. At any rate Servilia tried to prevent the enmity between her son and Cæsar ripening into rebellion. Courage in another case took the form of eliminating a clause in a senate decree she found objectionable. Beautiful Servilia seems to have been, but this "most influential woman of the republic," a half-sister of Cato of Utica, relied on the arts of the mind as well as of the body to win her command over men.

That Servilia failed to prevent the murder of Cæsar by her son was partly due to the counter-influence of Cassius, whose wife was her own daughter, a half-sister of M. J. Brutus, by the name of Junia Tertia, or Tertulla, a very rich woman who gave property to many of the great men of Rome. Tertulla was able to help finance revolt but whether she aided Brutus directly or not historians fail to state. Porcia, the wife of M. J. Brutus and a staunch republican, killed herself, it was believed, by swallowing hot coals at the news that the assassin of Cæsar had fallen on his own sword when death at the hands of the enemy was the only alternative. She foresaw the end of the republican movement to which they were both dedicated.

Sallust, "the Roman Thucydides," preceptor of Tacitus and Seneca, argues that the conspiracy of Catiline was largely the work of women, beyond the age when love affairs could bring bounty without stint but still possessed of extravagant tastes and habits demanding unlimited expenditure. They would stop at nothing to pay their debts. Knowing this, runs the Sallust theory, Catiline counted on their assistance in drawing their husbands to his side or putting obstreperous ones out of the way for the purpose of a revolution, ostensibly in favor of the oppressed masses of Rome. Sallust makes Sempronia, a wife of D. Junius Brutus, a relative of the murderer of Cæsar, one of the arch conspirators in this civil conspiracy. Undoubtedly she was a type of the ancient politician of either sex capable of any private or public crime. She wrote verses à la mode, talked gracefully and even wittily, was a patron of literature and art, found marriage incompatible with a career, played fast and loose with money, and apparently overlooked nothing likely to advance her personal interests.

Nevertheless it is extremely difficult to comprehend the true nature of the Catiline affair. That he fought oligarchy with a view to cancelling the heavy debts of himself and his friends was the belief of the opposition aristocrats. Cicero and Sallust and Dio Cassius who wrote about Catiline were all aristocrats and Sallust was especially ardent in his hatred of the democracy which Catiline openly championed whether sincerely or not. At one time Cicero admitted that he had almost been persuaded of Catiline's honesty and merit and had gone so far as to seek a political alliance, even considering his defense; but his proposal for the union was rejected, an election was at hand, and Cicero actually delivered orations against the conspirator as a profligate and murderer.

Certainly the record of Catiline lent countenance to the view that his mercurial temperament could not be interpreted as sincerity. A supporter of Sulla, he was a cruel ally during the proscriptions. In official capacities, such as governor of Africa in 67-66 B.C., he was as willing to make debtors of the helpless, to slay and to torture, as to expatiate on the charms of the people. He was thought to have killed his wife and son, the latter at the behest of the dissolute Aurelia Orestilla whom he married. He was suspected of undue intimacy with the Vestal Virgin, Fabia, a half-sister of Cicero's wife, Terentia, and this according to Plutarch was really responsible for Cicero's prosecution of Catiline.

And what a powerful antagonist Cicero was, once the resolute Terentia stimulated his vacillating resolve to the supreme effort ! Among the charges he brings to bear against Catiline is also that of Sallust, namely, that bankrupt women were leaders in the conspiracy. But when Cicero himself was head over heels in debt, what did he do ? He simply divorced Terentia, then over fifty years of age, Terentia who had tided him through many a hard crisis in his career, Terentia who had tried to hold his interests together, with Cæsar's forgiveness problematical, when her husband fled to Greece leaving everything at sixes and sevens after the defeat of Pompey. Terentia swept aside, Cicero married his wealthy ward, Publilia, a youngster whose family evaded the law with respect to a married woman's property right by placing her inheritance in Cicero's hands as a trust. Tiring of his girl-bride he was legally bound in divorcing her to return her dowry. That he failed to do voluntarily but her family was careful to attend to the detail and Cicero had to scurry around to find the necessary cash. During the civil wars Cicero complained that Terentia did not give him and his daughter enough money, such a complaint implying that the eloquent public advocate was less successful as a private pleader.

Sempronia, attacked for complicity with Catiline, brought the counter-charge against Cicero of moral turpitude. She averred that he had no financial honor at all, that he refused to acknowledge his debts to her and misused her funds. Beyond question he was embroiled in continued financial and sex intrigues. On one occasion when he slipped into the home of Sulla, disguised as a slave, for a rendezvous with Fausta Cornelia, Sulla's daughter by a fourth wife, a rival lover caught and flogged him. Perhaps it was a case of the pot calling the kettle black.

While Cicero was consul the Catiline conspiracy was betrayed by a woman — Fulvia, an avaricious and disgruntled mistress of Q. Curius, one of the plotters. Unable to amass more riches through the agency of the sex game, she decided to take what she could from the senate in the shape of its proffered reward for light on the trouble-makers.

Another of Cicero's great cases was the Claudian affair, a maze of love entanglements. Dressed as a woman in order to be with Cæsar's wife, Pompeia, Claudius entered her home during the rites and festivities connected with a celebration of the Bona Dea mysteries "by women only." This disguise did not deceive Cæsar's mother, ever watchful of his interests, and Claudius was brought to trial, charged with impiety. Cæsar's sister gave evidence and Cicero prosecuted. Having bribed the jury, Claudius was acquitted in spite of opposition eloquence, but his resentment was so great against the prosecuting attorney that he resigned his patrician rank and became a tribune of the people as a means of revenge. Accordingly Cicero's property was confiscated, his house burned, and the site bought up by Claudius at auction. Nor was Claudius satisfied with that punishment. The distinguished advocate was sent into exile. Later the tribunes recalled him and rebuilt his villa at public expense while Claudius insulted the workmen and assaulted Cicero in the street.

More women complicated Cicero's career. His troubles were not confined to law courts and verdicts. Clodia, the sister of Clodius, though married at the time, was madly in love with Cicero and determined to win his heart. He repulsed her and her pique led to the persecution of Cicero's family during his exile; she turned her brother Publius against the recalcitrant one and Publius had a wicked way. But when Cicero finally came home, he had his own innings. He defended and secured the acquittal of a paramour-deserter of Clodia, M. Cælius, whom she tried to blackmail on the charge of attempting to poison her. And it must not be thought that this was a minor incident in the lawyer's life, because Clodia was very rich and prominent socially, the patron of young poets and intelligentsia, the Lesbia in fact who had driven Catullus into his passionate verse for and against the courtesan. Cicero himself was tormented into more of his wonderful prose by this adventuress. Yes, of course, Terentia was jealous. Yet when he prosecuted Verres, charging that his extortions were influenced by the demands of his greedy mistress, Chelidon, no such explanation for his eloquence can be raised; one wonders however whether Chelidon who left all her property to Verres when she died was really a mistress or a powerful plebeian client able to take care of herself. In Cicero's defense of Cluentius, we are introduced to Sassia, "a monster of guilt," as he described her. It is astonishing how many *causes célèbres* argued by the sonorous orator really concerned the fortunes and the litigation of women.

Some women were able to defend themselves oratorically at law. Hortensius, the florid advocate always ready to approve corrupt provincial practices, a sybarite who introduced peacocks as a table delicacy, owned handsome estates, spent lavishly for entertainments, wrote erotic verse, patronised art and composed minor works on oratory and historical events, had a daughter who followed in his footsteps as far as protecting her own interests was concerned.

When she undertook to defeat legislation hostile to her income, she made some clear-cut distinctions between sex forms of politics and was complimented by the great rhetorician Quintilian for her forensic gifts. A special levy having been laid on women for the equipment of an army to proceed against Brutus and Cassius, Hortensia and her feminine cohorts reduced the number of matrons on the list of the assessed from 1400 to 400. Lictors could not restrain them as they marched through the forum to the tribunal of the triumvirs where Hortensia expounded the doctrine of no taxation without representaion — long before the good American Fathers saw the dawn. In the presence of the authorities, Hortensia gave voice to these extraordinary principles: "(1) Let war with the Gauls or the Parthians come, and we shall not be inferior to our mothers in zeal for the common safety; but for civil wars may we never contribute, nor even assist you against one another; and (2) why should we pay taxes when we have no part in the honors, the commands, the statecraft, for which you contend against one another with such harmful results ?" All women have not agreed with her about supporting civil wars but the tendency is to universal acceptance of her second maxim at any rate.

Hortensia was not an isolated illustration of a litigious woman. Afrania, sometimes called Gaia or Caia, the wife of the senator Licinius Buccio, always stood for her rights before the prætor and set such an example of feminine individualism that an edict was issued forbidding any woman to "postulate." But those who were trained in the rhetorical methods and en-

joyed public speaking often broke through the tabus and
braved the whips of lictors to display their art like their
favored brothers. They had vested interests themselves over
which to exercise verbal gifts.

Long before the age of the Cæsars, during the Punic Wars
when their husbands were absent from home, wives were
granted or assumed the control of property — a privilege they
were unwilling to relinquish when the heroes returned from
the front. But throughout Roman history fortunes came to
women in many ways. In the reign of Trajan, Quadratilla
Ummidia, a wealthy old fellow of eighty, left one-third of his
estate to his granddaughter, if he gave two-thirds to his grandson. The property of Æmilia, wife of Scipio Africanus I and
mother of Cornelia of Gracchi fame, was very large and it
passed on her death to her grandson, Scipio Africanus II, who
gave it to his mother Papiria divorced by his father. Cæcilia,
Sulla's wife, according to Pliny, bought in a huge share of the
property confiscated in the proscriptions. Olympiade, an
enormously wealthy widow, was temporarily deprived of her
property by an emperor for his own family exchequer; later
he restored it in order that she might continue to distribute it
in charitable enterprises.

That ladies had the run of the forum where business transactions took place, at least by proxy, is attested by an illustration
from Fowler: "In the passage from the *pro Cæcina* . . . a
lady, Cæsennia, wished to buy an estate; she employs an agent,
Æbutius, no doubt recommended by her banker, and to him
the estate is knocked down. He undertakes that the argen-
tarius of the vendor, who is present at the auction, shall be
paid the value, and this is ultimately done by Cæsennia, and
the sum entered in the banker's books." Whether women were
bankers, members of corporations, contractors and share-

holders, some monographist must say but it is already known that they were manufacturers, shopkeepers and landlords.

It appears that Roman women from the earliest times were on the *qui vive* for moves designed to interfere with their prerogatives. When in the third century B.C. the Lex Oppia, limiting their property and habits of luxury, was on the carpet, for instance, they canvassed the voters, threatened its supporters with vengeance, and in fact almost made a feminine riot; several years later they saw it repealed. In reply to critics dubbing such feminists vicious, Lucius Valerius, a tribune, reminded the public that female liberties were an ancient Roman tradition and that the State would remain secure if it stopped short of sharing its offices and careers with women. Of course this qualification was formal, if not absurd, considering the number of women who selected and managed office-holders; but Romans had not the modern suffragist view that direct and open responsibility on the part of women is the best way of suppressing any of their activities which run against the public interest.

LUXURY AND POMP

As territorial expansion continued, bringing slaves, booty, and revenues to the capital city, the passion for acquisition and enjoyment flamed high. Then classes joined families in struggling desperately over the spoils. When ease, luxury, idleness and pomp could be attained by the exercise of wits, the use of political influence, and the manipulation of markets, avarice knew no bounds. Although the critics, such as Cato the Elder and Juvenal, must not be taken too literally, there is enough fact and truth in their laments to prove that the old republican virtues of thrift, prudence, and plain living were submerged in an orgy of spending, ostentatious display, and gormandizing. Certainly vast resources that should have been devoted to capital account, the maintenance and improvement of property and estates, went into baubles for the decoration or delight of males and females alike.

Cleopatra not only made Julius Cæsar believe himself a god; she made Roman matrons sigh for the ornaments that hung around her neck, shone from her breast, and drew magnetized glances to her arms and ankles. Soon ladies by the Tiber were fired to outshine her, covered with gems, especially pearls. One which Cæcillia Metella wore in her ear was valued at £8000 current money. For the thrill of tasting so magnificent a sum, the son of Æsopus swallowed it at a gulp. In spite of edicts and efforts to check extravagances the flow of specie eastward to pay for luxuries never lagged. Pliny declared that "at the lowest computation, India, Seres . . . and Arabia drained from the empire a hundred million sesterces [about five million dollars] every year, so dearly do we pay for our luxury and our women."

Warmington describes the situation by further quotations from Pliny: "Beginning with the Jewish philosopher, Philon of Alexandria, and St. Paul we find moralists lamenting the wearing of pearls by women and girls, while Pliny becomes almost incoherent with wrath in his contemplation of this form of luxury, which he said reached the extreme of expenditure and necessitated travel in Indian seas over large distances and in torrid climes, and perils undergone amidst wild beasts — presumably sharks. . . He speaks, with a gust of anger against feminine luxury, of the wealth drained by India and the Chinese from the Roman Empire. He grieves that people should love the sound of clashing pearls . . . should wear them on their shoes. . . Even the poorer classes desired them, since the pearl was as good as a gentleman-usher (lictor) to a woman in public. . . Again and again do Mar-

tial and Statius mention the Oriental 'lapilli,' their high value,
their dearness to the hearts of women; the frivolous Gellia
lavishes all her affection upon them; the adulteress glitters with
them; the coquette in silk and rings wears pearls in her
ears . . . Pliny saw Lollia Paulina, wife of Gaius, covered head,
neck, ears, and fingers, with strings of pearls and emeralds,
the produce of spoliation but not of trade, placed alternately
to the value of 40,000,000 sesterces."

To jewels and silks which disturbed the Puritans were
added the most costly perfumes that merchants could find
anywhere. Everything that the æsthetes wanted some one
prepared to import however difficult or hazardous the undertaking. If a Roman dame owned a recipe calling for nard-
leaf in her oyster sauce, somebody had to travel from Randa-
marta into the far-off regions of the earth to bring it home.

It was not the ladies alone who rejoiced in the new standard
of Roman living. They received the major part of the blame
for extravagant tastes — were made the scapegoat according to
Hoyle — but a few writers were just enough to point out the
equal flair for lavish expenditure on luxuries which possessed
the males. Quintilian tells how Nero "consecrated in the
Capitol his first beard, decorated with the most valuable
pearls." Tiberius calls attention to the use of silks for both
sexes and its economic peril. All of which was a phase of the
Orientalising of the West. The very Christians who reverted
to puritanism exalted the New Testament as their most
Sacred Word and allowed it to inculcate as the dream of
paradise — the Heavenly Jerusalem — a city of flashing jewels,
with streets of jasper and gold.

In China of old, emperors and upper caste men wore
precious chains. Indian princes to this day are a blaze of
jewels. Amid the peasants and pigs, Balkan rulers, like kings
and queens in the fairy stories, emblazoned in gems and

crowns shine above the masses. Czarist Russia — the land of shabby mujiks — was noted for its regal magnificence. So men and women alike of ancient tyrannies found in personal bedizenment the satisfaction of their pride.

Wealth in time sat brazenly in the seats of the mighty. Wealth was power and wealth was law. The pride of birth, of prowess or of industry, gave way to the pride of possessions. City villas and country estates multiplied in number and magnificence. Size soon became the desideratum and the fact that his palace "covered more room than many cities embrace within their walls" distinguished one friend of Augustus beyond his status of eques. Rare marbles went into construction while landscape gardening beautified the environs. Statuary was brought from afar to adorn interiors and Greek artists were employed to paint the walls and do the finest designing. Long before Americans became "bath-tub minded," the Romans made luxury in baths a veritable religion; "marble and crystal ceilings, statuary and silver faucets were vital accessories of the baths," the water for ablution being carried over giant aqueducts, one of which in Africa was forty-three miles long. In the colder climates central furnaces made bathing comfortable. Cicero had eight villas in Italy and several more scattered along his favorite traveling routes. Nero built a house of gold and made Rome more splendid generally. Seneca declared: "We have reached such a stage of delicacy that our feet no longer tread on anything but precious stones," and Horace complained that the great estates were obliterating the plow.

Nor was that the crux of the situation. Service to domiciles began to supplant service to the State and thus to defeat the very object which underlay the effort to confine the economic enterprise of patricians to the land. Previously a noble had the State constantly before his eyes. He was eminently successful in proportion as he filled political positions. It was his ideal "to be a quæstor at the age of thirty-one, curule ædile at thirty-seven, prætor at forty, consul at forty-three; that is, to get the great State magistracies at the earliest age permitted by law." He was not above defending the State with his own muscle and sacrifice.

Devotion to the State opened opportunities for self-aggrandisement however which were well-nigh impossible to resist. And the most loyal of public servants found themselves little by little exacting tribute from vassals and spending it on themselves as a matter of course. Held to the landed interest by traditional philosophy and political ethic, their incomes were stretched by the reception of gifts, voluntarily or by request, which in the case of a governor with rich subject princes sometimes amounted to regal proportions. Lawyers' fees came in the form of presents on the spot and remembrances in wills. With a horde of slaves to take care of all manual work, life grew soft and the acquisitive instincts had freer sway. The outcome was that interest in the State developed a more personal bias, pleasure outweighed obligation, money became god, and traditions and legalities were offset by direct or secret commercial transactions until every patrician became his own law. "The soil of Italy ceased to produce even flowers. There were not even children to inherit the vast riches so eagerly sought and amassed. Much of it went to the emperor or lay idle in marble baths or theaters. The Roman nobility gradually died out through its own lack of descendants." Money was flung to soldiers, increasingly alien, to keep them from destroying the show.

Those who like the younger Pliny revolted at certain of the vulgarities of the Roman gilded age tried to inculcate a love of books and strengthen family life. Occasionally the sensitive built and endowed a local library and set up a local academy so that students might remain with their parents through the years of adolescence. Other funds supported hospitals, orphan asylums and homes for the destitute and aged. But the most popular philanthropy was a grand municipal banquet marked by circus entertainments when men fought with men or with beasts and, on extremely grand occasions, noble ladies with their kind in the ring. Of course such events did not always run more smoothly than true love and heavy disappointments might come to the benefactor and his beneficiaries, as it did on that unlucky day when Anglo-Saxon prisoners strangled one another in their pens in preference to fighting one another for the delectation of the Roman mob. As a regular thing the happy banquet and fight were heightened by a generous donation from the emperor, such as ten thousand gladiators to contest in their strength with hungry imported beasts or delicate Christians of both sexes condemned to martyrdom without a chance. When the crowds were hungry and restive in spite of such a program, corn was doled out to them, and sometimes a little cash was distributed, down to the tiny slave girls in the audience.

By the time of Severus women were "discriminated against" in the ring; a prohibition was placed on their fighting in the arena but there was no law against their financing of fights. So they indulged in that form of "public work" to some extent. On fête days they were frequently the patrons and hostesses. At the banquet, occasionally the male patron entertained the males ensemble and the patroness the females. Political wiles sharpened such occasions. Long before politics, American-style, was devised, Cæsia Sabina of Veii invited the female attendants of the decurions to a feast "with the additional luxury of a gratuitous bath." Whether they were told to "bring your bathing-suits, girls, and have a good time" we cannot say but no doubt that detail was also remembered if bathing-suits were needed. However, women's benefactions were not solely imitative. There has just been discovered by French excavators in Numidia a small shrine to Fortuna Augusta erected by two women in the reign of Hadrian. A priestess of that locality, at Calama, gave generous funds for a theater. In addition to private sums for the poor and the sick, the gifts of women went to the industrial societies charged with the care of dependents. Thus Marcellina in the age of Antoninus Pius presented to the college of Æsculapius and Hygeia — a combined religious and benevolent society — a banquet hall, money for burials as well as feasts and a general aid with "overhead."

In such an atmosphere flourished the tyrants, their way paved by Julius Cæsar's acceptance of an inscription to himself, on a statue erected in a temple, as a dedication "To the Unconquerable God." Some students blame Cæsar for undermining the dignity of the senate, for treating republican institutions with contempt and for bending what might have become a grand council of the various races and nations which composed the empire into a creature of his own will. But his megalomania was fanned by warm currents from outlying sections of that empire, such as Egypt, where the god-king was the only kind known. The very constitution of the universe seemed to shape the product of imperial progression.

To quote from Dill: "The lust of despotic power which Tacitus regards as the fiercest and most insatiable of human passions, has been intensified by the spectacle of a monarchy commanding, with practically unlimited sway, the resources and fortunes of a world. It was a dazzling price, offering frightful temptations both to the holder and to possible rivals and pretenders. The day on which a Nero or a Caligula awoke to all the possibilities of power was a fatal one. And Tacitus, with the instinct of the tragic artist, has painted the steady, fatal corruption of a prince's character [Nero's] by the corroding influence of absolute and solitary sway. Of all the Cæsars down to his time, the only one who changed for the better was the homely Vespasian. . . In Tiberius, Caligula, and Nero, some of this deterioration of character must be set down to the morbid strain in the Julio-Claudian line, with its hard and cruel pride, and its heritage of a tainted blood, of which Nero's father knew the secret so well. Much was also due to the financial exhaustion which, in successive reigns, followed the most reckless waste. It would be difficult to say whether the emperors or their nobles were the most to blame for the example of spendthrift extravagance and insane luxury. Two generations before the foundation of the Empire, the passion for profusion had set in, which, according to Tacitus, raged unchecked till the accession of Vespasian. Certainly the man who would spend £3000 on a myrrhine vase, £4000 on a table of citrus-wood or £40,000 on a richly wrought carpet from Babylon had little to learn even from Nero. Yet the example of an emperor must always be potent for good or evil. We have the testimony of Pliny and Claudian, separated by an interval of three hundred years, that the world readily conforms its life to that of one man, if that man is head of the State. Nero's youthful enthusiasm for declamation gave an immense impulse to the passion for rhetoric. His enthusiasm for acting and music spread through all ranks, and the emperor's catches were sung at wayside inns. M. Aurelius made philosophy the mode, and the Stoic emperor is responsible for some of the philosophic imposture which moved the withering scorn of Lucian. The Emperor's favorite drug grew so popular that the price of it became almost prohibitory. If the model of Vespasian's homely habits has such an effect in reforming society, we may be sure that the evil example of his spendthrift predecessors did at least as much to deprave it.

"And what an example it was ! The extravagance of the Claudian Cæsars and the last Flavian has become a piece of historic commonplace. Every one has heard of the unguent baths of Caligula, his draughts of melted pearls, his galleys with jewel-studded sterns and gardens and orchards on their decks, his viaduct connecting the Palatine with the Capitoline, his bridge from Bauli to Puteoli, and many another scheme of that wild brain, which had in the end to be paid for in blood. In a single year Caligula scattered in reckless waste more than £20,000,000. Nero proclaimed that the only use of money was to squander it, and treated any prudent calculation as meanness. In a brief space he flung away nearly £18,000,000. The Egyptian roses for a single banquet cost £35,000. He is said never to have made a progress with less than a thousand carriages; his mules were shod with silver. He would stake £400,000 on a single throw of the dice. The description of his Golden House is like a vision of lawless romance. The successors of Galba were equally lavish during their brief term. Otho, another Nero, probably regarded death in battle as a relief from bankruptcy. Within a very few months, Vitellius had flung away more than £7,000,000 in vulgar luxury. Vespasian found the exhaustion of the public treasury so portentous that he had to resort to unpopular economies and taxation on a great scale. Under Domitian, the spectacles and largesses lavished on the mob undid all the scrupulous finance of his father, and Nerva had to liquidate the ruinous heritage by wholesale retrenchment, and the sale even of the imperial furniture and plate, as M. Aurelius brought to the hammer his household treasures, and even the wardrobe and jewels of the empress, in the stress of the Marcommanic war."

From early days until it was too late, critics assailed the pomp and luxury that accompanied accumulating riches. In the second century B.C., Cato the Elder raged against them and in the manner of the Spartan, Agis, pleaded for a return to harsh, military virtues. He advocated and supported legislation against expensive dressing, against adornments, grand dinners, and habits of ease. As censor he ousted Manlius from the senate because he kissed his wife in daylight in the presence of their daughter. He worked hard himself and believed that slaves should be kept as busy as endurance would permit. Elaborate mansions and gardens he regarded as sources of sloth, idleness and selfishness. In later years Cato had his successors, protesting, protesting, and protesting, but little effect did they have on the course of riches through Roman society. The empire that had been built up by physical valor and sacrifice was the reservoir from which wealth flowed and provided employments to enrich governors, who expected to return to Rome with enough loot to pay the debts incurred in buying office, bribe their judges if accused of robbery, and live on the fat of the land until death closed their joyous career. That which virtue and valor had erected, amid blood and tears, brought the very canker that ate away the public spirit with the courage that alone could sustain it. And none of the protestants could provide any real remedy. Prohibitions by the hundreds were established in law. But the causes of decay lay deeper than the reach of legislation.

THE MORALS OF THE MAIN CHANCE

In such conditions the sex passions ran full riot, at least among the irresponsible slaves at the bottom of the social scale and the scarcely more responsible rich at and near the top. A single standard of morals largely prevailed in practice whatever the law and that single standard was a freedom for all who dared and did. Though Livia and Augustus battled against an evident loosening of marital standards, the very mother of the emperor had set a new pace by claiming Apollo as his father, and Ovid, if banished for his comments on the social scene, contended during the reign of Augustus that "the temples of Isis often became places of assignation and guilty intrigue." A Roman lady in the reign of Tiberius was seduced by her lover in the guise of the god Anubis. Dionysiac and Bacchanalian orgies raged like plagues and sometimes the mischief to society they caused had to be "stamped out in blood." In the train of war lords returning for Roman triumphs marched not only slaves and beautiful queens but cults deadly to health and social responsibility. These fortified many of the natural lusts of the weak and made it possible for Hadrian to adopt as his successor a voluptuous nobleman renowned for his deification of a male concubine, named Antinous. Commentators on Greek sex perversions have occasionally been inclined to attribute them to devices for escaping overpopulation but it is difficult to see that connection when religions from early times made sex their core.

In the hands of the irresponsible, wealth naturally represented the power of vice. It lead to such extremes that innumerable writers found little else to engage their minds. To read Catullus, Horace, Propertius and Tibullus, among others, is to feel that the Roman matron who kept the home fires burning was a fiction. The very fact that moralists counseled downcast eyes for women indicated that the degenerate Romans were objects it was best not to behold. But such degeneracy worked both ways. Tacitus blames Crispinilla Calvia for the vicious traits Nero developed; rich and childless, she lived with the emperor and his eunuch, Porus, until the ruler came to his end; then, enraged at his murder by the Romans, she went to Africa to try to effect a grain boycott against them and barely managed to escape losing her life in their return resentment; her great wealth enabled her to survive by bribery. But

Poppæa is the more famous mistress of Nero; she was of noble birth, beautiful and rich, witty, energetic and ambitious to the limit of greed. It was she whom Agrippina, Nero's mother, saw undermining her own influence with her son; it was she who finally persuaded Nero to dispose of his own mother; it was she who made him divorce, then slay, his wife, Octavia, the girl-bride; it was she who seated herself by his side as empress, decidedly the ruler. It was said her mules were shod with gold and that five hundred asses daily furnished the milk for her bath. For her efforts to protect the Jews, Josephus calls her pious. Yet after achieving her goal as Augusta, she died from a kick of Nero's foot. Lonesome without her, Nero pronounced her funeral oration in person, placed her name among the gods of Rome, built her a temple, and married a boy who resembled her. Not that the people enjoyed this "romance" exactly. Her very slaves under torture refused to admit that Octavia was an adulteress when a ground was sought for her divorce and, when she was dispatched to Campania under guard, they insisted on her recall and received her with demonstrations of joy. But the outcome was in keeping with what usually occurs when one side is persistent and the other is not. Poppæa adhered to her course while the popular interference was temporary.

Of course enemies may have exaggerated or maligned the wives of Roman rulers in certain instances. Ferrero seems sure that they did in particular cases. The families represented in the senate were always jealous of the family in power and ready to foment or to heed rumors of incapacity. Every capital of the world is more or less a vicious whispering gallery. Marcus Aurelius consulted a soothsayer in search of a remedy when gossip convinced him that Faustina was enchanted by a gladiator. But he was loyal to the mother of his eleven children and so grieved when she died in Cappadocia by his side that he had her statue placed in the temple of Venus, making her one of the titular gods of Rome, and founded orphanages in her honor. Bewildered by life and its whirl of emotional impacts, he accepted initiation into the Eleusinian mysteries when he passed through Athens after the campaign in Syria and at another time was attracted by proposals for birth control. Brooding on the obstacles to happiness, he could with difficulty find it for himself.

Undoubtedly writers still somewhat misrepresent Theodora, wife of Justinian, ruler of the Roman Empire in the east. Traditions concerning Theodora can be traced back to Procopius whose *Anecdota* Gibbon utilized, his disciples copying him ever since. Now Procopius may have been a disappointed courtier, for he wrote two very different kinds of histories — one flattering the twin rulers, Justinian and Theodora, and dwelling on their noble public work such as the building of churches, palaces, hospitals, roads and bridges; the other a secret document written ten years after the death of the empress and filled with invectives against her and against everybody else around the court. Naturally the popes disapproved of Theodora because she took a different stand from that of Justinian on religious matters and was the power behind Belisarius whose dealing with the popes she directed. This empress was especially stern in her determination to root out prostitution in Constantinople, enforcing the laws and immuring five hundred courtesans of the city to repent in a house on the Asiatic side of the Bosphorus. Had she not earned her own living in her youth as an actress-courtesan — a geisha girl, in others words — reformed herself, gone in for spinning, married the emperor and remained faithful to him ever after? She had courage of various sorts, exhibiting another during the menacing Nika insurrection of the year 532 A.D. when she refused to flee from the rebels and saved the imperial crown by her daring. Her political zeal took the form of joint planning with Justinian of wars and legislation, the famous *Institutes* of Justinian being marked by decided favors to women in such directions as the emancipation of comédiennes, hitherto slaves, the right to divorce, legitimation of offspring and dowries.

To read large segments of Roman literature is to believe that only the courtesan or beautiful slave girl made the slightest appeal to Roman men. The same emphasis and interest ran through Greek writing and still dominates the literature of certain Oriental peoples but the Roman man was a more lascivious creature apparently, emperors being known to command their very wives to display their charms to banqueting guests — perhaps a precedent for the European custom of having palace walls covered with nudes. Greek critics who had assailed their fellow citizens for bestowing property upon parasitic hetæræ occasionally cautioned them against spoiling their wives; they would have been paralysed by the degree of conspicuous waste attained by both castes of women in the days of Roman riches and pleasure.

Vespasian, coming to the throne after a prolonged season of debauchery, found the treasury empty and instituted reforms but these only filled the coffers for another bout of extravagance and dissipation. His own granddaughter died of abortion after seduction by her uncle Domitian. Cities were named for concubines, coins were struck in their honor, statues were erected to their memory, and divine honors were paid them on their death. However, these were fairly innocent expressions of amours and in some cases might actually symbolise a genuine affection. Apparently some of the mistresses deserved funeral orations about as well as some of the wives who received them.

Throughout wide circles sensuous prodigality enslaved multitudes of youth of both sexes in the service of passion. "A long train of concubines, and a rapid succession of wives, among whom was a vestal virgin, ravished by force from her sacred asylum, were insufficient to satisfy the impotence of the passions" of Elagabalus. "This master of the Roman world affected to copy the dress and manners of the female sex, preferred the distaff to the sceptre, and dishonored the principal dignities of the empire by distributing them among his numerous lovers; one of whom was publicly invested with the title and authority of the emperor's, or, as he more properly styled himself, of the empress's husband."

The presence of great aggregations of soldiers and the return of their heroes boasting of arms, the enthronement of the mysteries and temple approval of conquest, wealth won by exploitation and confiscation instead of by labor, reliance on forms of commercial gambling for accretions, display and waste to the extreme of human ingenuity could in no time or clime serve as the foundation of aught but illusory power and pomp — gaudy and transient exhibitions of rule through the agency of the senses.

HELLENIC AND ORIENTAL PLUMAGE

INTELLECTUALLY considered, in the maze of economic and political developments, Roman history proceeds from the simple psychology and reactions of a primitive forest people to curiosity about the world at large and to a toying with philosophies. They began spiritually with a multitude of gods, tribal, household and clan, the forms of propitiation and exorcism common to primitive life, and the protective thought of classes struggling to keep what they had, gain more, or accomplish favorable arrangements in times of conflict. But soon they came into contact with other peoples more highly civilised — the Greek colonists in Italy, who transplanted there some of the finest arts of the mother country, and eventually in the later days of the republic the Greeks of the homeland whom they conquered and absorbed.

In due time rich Romans were educating their daughters at home in Greek literature and sending their sons to the Greek universities that survived the conquest. In those seats of learning the student could select his courses and his teachers or he might enter the classes of all the teachers indiscriminately. There he heard all the conflicting philosophies of the Eastern Mediterranean discussed, not by great masters like the departed Plato and Aristotle, but usually by pedagogues engaged in working over old ideas and adding glosses more labored than edifying. By the time he got through with Platonism, Pythagoreanism, Sophism, Stoicism, and Epicureanism, his mind was a perfect whirl. Frequently he was bewildered if not paralysed by the clashing doctrines that were discussed, debated, and expounded for his edification; and when he returned home his parents and friends often wondered whether Hellenic rhetorical training did more than fit students to laugh at Roman ideals and religion and resort to chicane for advancement.

Through other channels Greek culture seeped into all parts of the Roman Empire. Slaves, courtesans and merchants acted as purveyors. Greek women carried on as teachers and doctors, entertainers and intellectuals the occupations they had widened during the Alexandrian period. They also appear in lists of painters and designers. Intermarriage was another source of culture transmission. Roman rulers from Cæsar to M. Aurelius read Greek works and found ways to display their learning. Augustus was enthusiastic about Hellenism; Tiberius and Caligula were lukewarm; Claudius took pride in quoting Homer in the senate and wrote history in the Greek tongue. Nero revelled in Greek festivals and tried to compete with Greek actors in the theatre; Vespasian financed the teaching of Greek rhetoric; Domitian organised athletic meets on the Greek model and replaced a Roman library, destroyed by fire, with manuscripts brought from Alexandria. M. Aurʌlius had among his tutors a Peripatetic and a Platonist and reached such a point of reflection that he preferred meditation to gladiatorial combats.

A few details may be given to show just how contacts between Rome and Greece were formed and what results they brought. We may begin with Æmilius Paullus, the conqueror of Macedonia, who was the first important patron of Hellenism. Owing to him, the learned Polybius slightly more than a hundred years before the Christian era settled down in Rome as an instructor of the young people in a leading household. Being a commander of cavalry, he taught them in addition to grammar, rhetoric, philosophy and the fine arts, love of the out-of-doors, the care of horses and dogs, hunting and physical exercises.

A son of this household then bore into the family where he was adopted, the Scipio family of which Cornelia, the mother of the Gracchi, was a member, the Hellenism he had imbibed at home. Next, the Scipio family "opened out new ways in manners, in literature, in philosophic receptivity and lastly in the study of the law which was destined to be Rome's great contribution." And as oaks from little acorns grew, so the history of civilisation in terms of Roman expansion arose from this transplanting of the Greek scholar to the seat of Italian empire. Polybius became the close and lifelong friend of Scipio Africanus who protected him, introduced him to the leading figures in Roman military and civil affairs, enabled him to see with his own eyes the siege and destruction of Carthage, gave him the leisure and the funds for prolonged travel and study of the archives and monuments, topography and geography essential for a bigger and better history than the world had yet known — in the Greek tongue.

Polybius made the most of these advantages and accomplished the feat. His history dealt with Rome and comprised forty volumes. It aspired to impartiality and perhaps achieved all that could possibly be expected of one who had been drawn so intimately into the Roman ruling caste. He did not gloss over all the Roman follies and faults; he suffered with his own people in their defeat and used his position to mitigate the rigors of the post-war settlement; he recognised forms of incipient anæmia among the masters of the world. But he was a pragmatist in his belief that Roman supremacy was inevitable and must be accepted as a *fait accompli*. His benefactor therefore shines in high lights and the history flashes with an optimism created by the conviction that there is a destiny which guides human ends, Rome being the instrument of Providence. After an examination of her previous record, her republican strength, her constitution-making, and her military prowess, the author amplifies this belief in the Manifest Destiny of Rome, his didactic style fitting his theme. The thesis supplied Rome with a romantic view of her power. But this complacent attitude did not sway the young Cornelia to the exclusion of interest in economic affairs. Her share in the agrarian revolt has already been described. When it failed, she retired to her country estate where she was often visited by Greek savants and writers, as her parents had been, for, notwithstanding her excursion into radical politics, she remained one of the most distinguished of Romans.

Polybius introduced a second Greek to Rome, the Stoic, Panætius of Rhodes, who enlivened this factual study of power with philosophic notions of universal law. Manifest Destiny then straightened its shoulders still more proudly. His disciple, Posidonius, on the eve of Christ's birth, called "the most learned man of his time" on account of his electicism — natural science enthusiasms leading him to try to discover the distance and size of the sun, the diameter of the earth, and the effect of the moon on the tide — by personal contact and by writing spread the Stoic philosophy far and wide through the Roman territory. In fifty-two books Posidonius set down the history of the period between 146 and 88 B.C. Cicero was one of his pupils.

At length in the schools and universities of Italy itself Greek ideas and cults were expounded and acclimatised either by Greeks imported for the purpose or by Romans trained in Greek learning. Philosophers from the East found welcome in patrician homes and circles, where they lectured to and instructed the simple. Rich families bought Greek tutors in the slave market to train their children and decorate their banquets. Wealthy Romans collected libraries of Greek books which they may or may not have read, such evidences of culture at least looking well when *novi homines* were entertained. Some of the fierce energy they had displayed in political conspiracies, women now turned to intellectual pursuits. They flocked to the readings of poets or the discourses of agitators and philosophers with a fervor akin to their zeal for the defense of property rights. Possessing the means, they were generous in their financial patronage of foreigners. Gemina and her daughter, prominent members of the intelligentsia, opened their fine home to Plotinus, a learned Greek Neoplatonist, who lived and taught there while he was providing Rome with a sort of political theory. The emperor Gallienus and the empress Salonina were so attracted by his teaching that they considered turning over several towns to be governed according to Platonist ideals. Some of the ladies were however satisfied with the mere interlarding of their remarks with Greek quotations, much to the disgust of certain men who thought that form of diversion ought to be restricted to their sex.

The upper class generally "went Greek," even Livia of the Augustan age saving time from her knitting to study philosophy with foreigners at her court. Ladies-in-waiting took to it with spirit and in the reign of Aurelius the habit of such instruction was well formed. Laugh and scoff as they might at rulers and profiteers enlightening themselves in ideologies, Juvenal and Lucretius were in the minority and the classical grammarians in the great majority.

While the sponsors were legion and important, it would be a mistake to assume that either Hellenism or Orientalism was received with cordiality by all classes of Rome. On the contrary many a proud Roman of the old school fought against them both as forces working for decay and ruin in the good republican order received from the fathers. Among these stout opponents Cato the Elder was the most invincible. After discharging his heavy military obligations, he devoted his energy largely to assailing Hellenic culture, regarding it as his supreme mission in life to check its invasion. As Censor, he struck from the lists of senators and knights men trained in the new "immorality." His effort to restrain the property rights of women was in part the result of his fear that they would be the major factor in the foreign triumph. Naturally the Bacchanalian mysteries were inimical to the old Roman gods and Athenian philosophers were critical of republican puritanism. So he had three such ambassadors deported. Even physicians who were chiefly Greeks in his day he regarded as public enemies. It is true that Cato was not personally familiar with Greek literature and did not venture to begin its study until he reached the safe age of eighty but that was no handicap to his confidence that Hellenism was a menace to Rome. And from his era in the third century, B.C., until the degenerate days of the empire, there were spiritual heirs of Cato who kept up the fight against imported culture.

The women of Cicero's family were among the "Philistines." They were aristocrats of the old school but urbane and noted for the elegance and dignity of their diction and manners. It was their Latin tongue which Cicero first embodied in his majestic speeches. This debt he admitted in a measure, saying: "When I listen to my mother-in-law Lælia — for women preserve a traditional purity of accent the best because, being limited in their intercourse with the multitude, they retain their early impressions — I could imagine that I hear Plautus or Nævius speaking, their pronunciation is so plain and simple, so perfectly free from all affectation and display; from which I infer that such was the accent of her father and his ancestors — not harsh like the pronunciation to which I have just referred, nor broad nor rugged but terse, smooth and flowing." Cicero's wife, Mucia, and the granddaughters of Lælia continued to transmit the graceful old Roman speech, all being lauded for their Latin accomplishment. In his later work Cicero departed from this simple, flowing style and adopted a form more Hellenic in type, more florid and involved, that found in Seneca its sentimental adept. The strife between the tongues was a phase of egoism but it was also a contest in sound and fury. Romans loyal to Latin felt that it had a vigor and cadence absent in the more graceful and delicate Greek. In the face of stubborn opposition, Latin itself was steadily Hellenised until the Roman world fell under the sway of Christianity. Then there came a rebound.

The last flicker of Hellenic naturalist philosophy was snuffed out at Alexandria in the fifth century after Christ by Christian antagonists of the Greek teacher, Hypatia, head of the

Neoplatonist Academy founded by Plotinus. And to appreciate the significance of this dénouement we must sketch the course of Neoplatonism, if briefly.

After the death of Plotinus, whom we have met teaching in the home of Roman ladies, his sect divided. The eastern wing was led in Syria by Iamblichus and grew mystical and esoteric, possibly in response to the craving for relief from the savage economic and political strife of the period. One of his pupils was Sosipatra, wife of the prefect of Cappadocia; and women adherents of Neoplatonism in that sector were especially adroit at mystical explanations of life like the older oracles. Under the reign of Julian, Christian apostate, this eastern version of Neoplatonism was given hospitality at Athens with Plutarch, the son of Nestorius, as sponsor. On his decease it was perpetuated by his son Hiero and his daughter Asclepigenia who lectured and conducted classes. The girl finally married the wealthy Archiades and after her death her faith was transmitted by Asclepigenia the Younger.

There was also a western wing of Neoplatonism under the charge of Hypatia at Alexandria who made of the creed a scientific rationalism. Pascal calls mathematics "the highest exercise of the intelligence" and by all philosophers agreeing with him Hypatia must be revered. Several hundred years elapsed before she had a peer in the field of physics, that is until St. Hildegard made up the cultural lag. And about twelve centuries more intervened before natural philosophy, based on mathematics, caught up with the past and began to shape destiny toward the age of positive knowledge and invention. No further progress was made in the mathematical sciences, as taught by Hypatia, until Descartes, Newton and Leibnitz, among others, took up the challenge. Hypatia was not only "one of the most eminent teachers of antiquity but one of the ablest of the later Greeks of either sex."

It is thought that Hypatia got her initial training from her celebrated father, Theon of Alexandria, and from student-apprenticeship in the school of philosophy conducted by Plutarch the Younger and his daughter Asclepigenia. Nevertheless Hypatia went so far beyond her father or her teachers in the sweep of her imagination that she was invited by the magistrates of Alexandria to lecture on mathematics and philosophy at the capital of Hellenism. The historian Socrates reports that she taught magnetically, that students from the civilised world crowded to her lecture hall, and that "her knowledge was so great that she far surpassed all the philosophers of her time." In a period when the science of algebra was in its infancy, Hypatia wrote commentaries on the Conics of Appolonius and the Arithmetic of Diophantus to serve as text books for her students — no light mental operation or mean educational task. The importance of the foundation of naturalistic thought laid by Appolonius of Perga, "the Great Geometer," was well understood by illustrious European mathematicians of the later day, such as Borelli, Viviani, Fermat, and Barrow while the English astronomer, Halley, studied Arabic simply to examine a text of Appolonius translated into that tongue. Diophantus was of similar value for the induction of students into mathematics.

But with algebra and mathematics and geometry, Hypatia joined the teaching of astronomy out of which these other sciences had largely evolved. She published an Astronomical Canon containing tables for the movements of the heavenly bodies that may or may not have been a commentary on the work of Ptolemy. And what is the more noteworthy, she was not afraid to use her hands.

One of her pupils, the wealthy bishop Synesius of Ptolemais, who had keen scientific interests himself, highly valued his intellectual association with Hypatia and credits her with the invention of an astrolabe and a planisphere, while Mozans claims that she invented an apparatus for distilling water, another for measuring the level of water, and one for determining the specific gravity of liquids — an areometer as it would now be described. The earliest known reference to areometry is in a letter of Synesius addressed to Hypatia.

Though a great teacher and inventor, Hypatia was a philosopher of power, well aware of the implications of science for the social order. Her interests were naturalistic and realistic, affecting the attitude of Synesius, who accepted a bishopric on the condition that he should be free to dissent at least in his own mind from the accepted view of "the soul's creation, a literal resurrection, and the final destruction of the world" — beliefs dear to the heads of the Christian Church whom he served. For her persistent paganism, in the full light of her fame and eloquence, Hypatia fell a victim to the resentment of Christians — who were satisfied with nothing short of her life.

Cyril, the patriarch of Alexandria, an inquisitor, violent against all heretics alike — Jews, pagans, and critics generally — made it one of his first official acts to close the churches and confiscate the ecclesiastical possessions of the Novatians — a sect of puritans — anti-idolaters and zealots proud that their founder, Novatius, was a Roman martyr. Cyril also directed armed troops to attack the Jewish synagogue, drive the race from the city, and pillage their houses and property. And in the vortex of this religious frenzy stood the arch pagan Hypatia, her position complicated by the fact that she was the friend of the pagan prefect, Orestes, making a brave effort to stem the tide of hysteria. Fanatical sectarians finally dragged the learned philosopher from her chariot, cut her veins with oyster shells, and let her blood flow out upon the highway. Since the murderers were officials of the Christian

Church, Cyril was considered to have inspired the attack. At all events, passionate irrationality destroyed the rationalist at the height of her power and even her writings were consumed in the flames when the library at Alexandria burned down.

The next great effort to blot out paganism was Justinian's order for the closure of the schools at Athens and Greek women shared the fate of their male colleagues on the faculties. To cite a particular case, his decree silenced Theodora, a Neoplatonist. By this time Christianity, Semitic in origin but tinctured with Greek and Roman philosophy and faiths, was becoming firmly entrenched in the western provinces of the empire. The elder Cato must have turned over in his grave.

With the philosophic and moral speculations of the Greeks came their gods until the Romans were so confused that they could scarcely tell their own fetishes from the new deities. Superstition and credulity were piled on superstition and credulity. To the Greek religions were added the mysteries of innumerable cults garnered from other shores. From the East came the worship of Magna Mater with its sanguinary ritual and cruel sacrifices, its frightful power over the imagination of the masses, and its "processions of effeminate figures with dripping locks, painted faces, and soft womanish bearing;" in 191 B.C. a decree of the senate gave the Great Mother a shrine on the Palatine Hill not far from that of Apollo.

Competing with the Roman cults and that of Magna Mater was the worship of Isis and Serapis which for half a millennium filled the empire with an awe and confusion born of bewildered Egypt and transfused with creeds from other sources. Finally in the last three centuries of the empire the religion of Mithra, originating in a cult of nature worship and associated with the Sun, seemed to overshadow all the older rituals — a strange combination of mysticism and humanism possibly facilitating the progress of the last great invasion, Christianity. Such were the emotions that made turgid the stream of Greek rationalism, small and thin as compared with the total volume of foreign influence in Rome, and confounded rather than clarified efforts to think realistically about the world the Romans were trying to organise.

ROMAN INTELLECTUALISM

In the Latin language, modified by Hellenic and Oriental influences, a great body of literature flowered, in all the forms known to the Greeks. Yet for philosophic grasp and penetration into the nature of things it contained few models to tower forever with the peaks of Greek learning. Of all the Roman writers, Lucretius perhaps deserves to be placed at the head, for physicists still marvel at his insight into the constitution of the atom and social speculators wonder at the reaches of his thought running into the past of the race, into primitive life, and considering the long struggle of mankind up from savagery. In passages of rare eloquence he struck at the prime source of superstition and distress, fear of death, declaring that nothing happens after mortal clay is dissolved — no torments, no troubles, no unsatisfied longings. He was Epicurean in that but he had independent vigor.

Roman literature in general was full of pæans and rejoicings respecting the State and its destiny, leaving little room for factual thinking upon what was actually transpiring. Thrilled by the Homeric treatment of another great race, Vergil dramatised the Latins in a similar vein and thus helped to increase their self-pride. Horace, his contemporary, shared this patriotic fervor, addressing even the plutocrat Mæcenas as a symbol of Roman glory. Vergil and Horace were both country-bred men of the Augustan era who exulted in urban magnificence and political prowess during a time when a city of brick was being transformed into a city of marble. Since agriculture remained at this period in a fairly healthy condition, their sins of omission are not heinous. And with Horace the delights of Roman peace were in themselves an excuse for being.

Like these poets the historians contributed to the celebration of Rome's splendor rather than to an understanding of the factors that were shaping an inglorious fate. Most of them produced nothing more than simple annals and those who did were careless in the use of sources and given to a kind of futile moralising. If they were critical of their own times, as some of them were, they usually believed that all would go well when the old Roman virtues were restored — virtues of military prowess, industry and thrift. To this school belonged Livy. Referring to his own age he declared: "Into no State were greed and luxury so long in entering; in these late days avarice has grown with wealth; and the frantic pursuit of pleasure leads fast towards a collapse of the whole social fabric; in our ever-accelerating downward course we have already reached a point where our vices and their remedies are likewise intolerable." But this was all due, he thought, to a departure from ancient morality: simplicity, equity, piety, order and obedience to law. While Tacitus could be severe in denouncing evils and tyrannies and was haunted by a mordant fear of avenging gods, he could speak of the prince under whom he lived in terms of praise and faith as if he really believed in his greatness and had hopes for the future of government could it be entrusted to such enlightened rulers.

Among the patriots of various degrees must be reckoned the orators, with Cicero as the master, who never wearied in singing the praises of the senate and people of Rome and assailing with heavy vituperation those deemed enemies of the State.

Usually the "undesirables" were of the noble order or new men who had attached themselves to the ruling power. Cicero himself was of the latter origin and had intimate connections on both sides of the line. A senator, affiliated with the nobility, he knew their moods and interests. Forbidden to engage in business because he was a senator, he formed trading alliances with the *negotiatores,* awarded public contracts, and made money in indirect ways. Thus he was a type like the English Burke, coming to the capital from the provinces, young but clever, to accumulate a fortune while serving the State. In his numerous villas, he lived in the fashion of the best landed aristocrats; yet as a shrewd investor in the slum property of Rome he was familiar with other kinds of income. Obsequious to those above him in blood, he was utterly indifferent to "the homeless crowds in the rabbit-warrens of Rome." Fowler, a specialist in the Ciceronian age, says the sonorous orator thought only of citizens within his own circle and never troubled his mind about the vast majority. So when his resounding periods in praise of the senate and the people of Rome are read, there can be no doubt of whom, for whom, and of what he speaks. Cicero's Rome was the Rome of the "best people" and it was good to behold, in his opinion. That he thought and taught.

The chant of patriotism written by poets and confirmed by orators was sung to the drop of the curtain by one who is known as "the last genuine representative of the old pagan tone in letters," namely Rutilius Namantiamus. He came from the imperial office-holding class and was associated with the nobility whose virtues he lauded. The span of his life crossed the fateful years when the barbarian invaders were laying waste Roman estates; he had even seen his ancestral home in ruins; and he may have been in the city when the Goths ravaged Rome. But nothing prevented his writing in the tone of Vergil as if Roman glory endured and he clung to the Roman religion as if the myths were a revelation of the gods. He hated Jews and intellectuals criticising the noble structure of the fathers. But he was sure of Rome's future and her immortality, just as sure as Cicero, rejoicing that the temples were still standing and gladdened by the cheers of the multitudes in the circus at traditional amusements. Though critical events were occurring around him, he refused to regard them seriously. The enemies of Rome had been conquered in the past. Rome stood for "triumphs of law and equal justice" and, despite vicissitudes, the might of Rome, good old Rome, would continue, bringing peace and security again to the earth. Such was the mental calibre of the "last genuine representative of the old pagan tone in letters," after the borders of Rome had been invaded by enemies, the capital had been looted, and the social order set afloat.

At the other extreme were the Cynics laughing long and hard at the effusions of the patriots. Some of the Cynics were blatant and vulgar. Some were relatively refined and diverting. Others were sensual, using criticism merely as a cover for indulgence. Because so much of their ridicule was directed at superstition, which increased steadily in the last days of the Empire, they were a source of particular irritation to the piously disposed. Those Cynics who made money by laughter were apt to forsake the cool philosophy of their master Diogenes and for this reason they were highly obnoxious to Dion Chrysostom, the friend of Trajan. He honored Diogenes as an idealist rather more than the Greeks had done but despised the disciples who harangued "with coarse buffoonery a gaping crowd in the squares and alleys or in the porches of the temples. He thinks that these men are doing no good, but rather bring the name of philosophy into contempt. . . The vulgar Cynic, with his unkempt beard, his mantle, wallet and staff, his filth and rudeness and obscenity, insulting every passer-by with insolent questions, exchanging coarse jests and jeers with the vagabond crowd which gathers at his approach, is the commonest figure in Greek and Roman literature of the time." During the Syrian dynasty of the third century, however, Cynics of a subtler school won their way to favor at court.

Dislike for the Cynics inspired much of the work of Lucian, a contemporary of Tacitus. While he does not try himself "to solve the riddle of the universe by a single formula or by the fine-drawn subtleties of dialectic," he cannot take their course toward a renunciation of all social obligations and he charges them with gross inconsistency between theory and practice in verbally denying the rôle of pleasures and refinements while greedy to accept them when they come within their grasp. Yet he does not hark back to the Greeks for examples of sincerity; his research reveals too many similar contrasts between precept and practice, such as Plato flattering the autocrats in Sicily and Aristotle sycophantic before Alexander. Lucian has been ranked with Thackeray as a satirist of manners. A Syrian by birth, a Greek by education — trained as a rhetor and lecturer — he became a Roman through politics. Life had few delusions for him. Charletanry he saw wherever he turned. The transcendental value of Greek philosophy he felt to be worthless owing to the prevalent idolatry and crudeness of superstition among the throngs imbued with the Greek religion. While Antoninus and Aurelius, it was true, made philosophy fashionable in a sense, the gods which the Greek thinkers had tried to sublimate and refine were now mere themes for the comic stage: thus an enormously popular pantomime dancer built success on a decidedly mortal representation of the amours of Ares and Aphrodite. Oracles took advantage of plagues and other disasters to reap personal gain and, in general, ideals in the hands of human manipulators turned into futile or vicious imaginings.

Another critic was Arulenus Rusticus, author of a eulogy on Thrasea Pætus, the Stoic "saint" of Nero's reign executed by Domitian for his teachings. Thrasea refused to kow-tow to Nero, to pay divine honors to the emperor and his paramour, to be present day by day in the senate and watch it perform its venal acts. Thrasea was praised by his admirer as "the noblest and wisest member of the Stoic opposition." That means he behaved "nobly and wisely" with reference to senatorial ideals. And all the members of his family apparently behaved the same way as their ideals were tested. When Nero, at the instigation of Messalina, passed sentence on Thrasea, his wife, Arria, proposed to make the suicide a double one in honorable protest at abuse and only refrained at her husband's urgent pleading that she live for the sake of their children and accept exile instead. Arria's own mother had set her an example of such fortitude and honor — she of "the smoking dagger" fame who stabbed herself first and then handed the weapon to her husband, Cæcina Pætus, sentenced to death for his part in the plot against Claudius, saying as she passed it over: "Pætus, it does not hurt." To the Japanese such pride is still one of the sublimest concepts of nobility.

To the tradition of her parents Fannia, the daughter of Thrasea and Arria, succeeded. When her husband, Helvedius, a staunch republican, died, she asked Senecio to write a panegyric, thinking that the man who had brought peace and order to Armenia on the basis of provincial self-respect, who had served as a quæstor in Achæa and as tribune under Nero well deserved it, even though his opposition to Nero's notions of propriety had led to the joint exile of man and wife, and his continued criticism of the government under Vespasian to his execution and the confiscation of his property. The outcome of her effort to secure this panegyric was the execution of its author and a decree for the perpetual banishment of herself.

The more thoughtful of the Stoics held that man is a rational animal and that in the judgments which he makes, facing the world, lies his force. The women of the sect shared the ideology, the onus of a puritan "repression," and the hardships that came with persecution. They stood shoulder to shoulder with their men through all the trials that beset their idealistic circle, making it possible for this branch of Greek philosophy to root itself so deeply into Roman soil. Their literary ornament was Seneca, wealthy minister of Nero, unable to remain aloof from political life and yet inclined to meditate upon social evils and prescribe remedies. His works are Stoic homilies. When he seemed by retreating to his villa to be losing interest in the court, Nero commanded his presence lest he concoct revolt; but very often, from the very nature of his musings he fled voluntarily back to Rome. Steeped in the philosophy of the Pythagoreans and of Chrysippus relative to the virtues of simplicity and the refinements of restraint, Seneca was withal a member of one of the most extravagant and vicious courts the world has known. Hence he constantly ran from the logic of his position either at the capital or in the country. Philosophy for him could never be a complete escape and indeed he was such a creature of the courts that when flattery of Claudius was of no avail, he went so far as to compose a panegyric on Messalina, the very cause of his early expulsion from the court. He knew that Roman intellectualism was thin, that citizens of the motor type such as Cæsar, racing up and down the world and merely jotting down impressions casually, were not contributing anything to a knowledge of life and destiny, but what he desired was a righteous tone and emphasis on virtues rather than trenchant criticism and analysis. He could not be an ascetic. In his delicate youth he had inclined that way until his father checked the tendency. Consequently he could never resolve the dualism of flesh and spirit. Sombart calls attention to one of his maxims: "Cease to forbid gold to the philosopher; no one has condemned wisdom to poverty." And his own practical application is seen in his forcing on the Britons a loan of forty million sesterces at an usurious rate of interest which caused a revolt of alarming proportions. He turned from the super-rationalist wing of the Stoic school to an evangelistic modification somewhat resembling Platonism in its moral over-tone. He was never as dogmatic as a Christian. Nor as sacrificial. "The men whom he wishes to save are masters of great households, living in stately palaces, and striving to escape from the weariness of satiety by visits to Baiae or Præneste (the slum and sailor quarters). They are men who have awful secrets, and whose apparent tranquillity is constantly disturbed by vague terrors, whose intellects are wasted on the vanities of a conventional culture or the logomachies of a barren dialectic. They are people whose lives are a record of weak purposes and conflicting aims, and who are surprised by old age while they are still barely on the threshold of real moral life."

Though Seneca did not advocate martyrdom he was finally ordered by Nero to commit suicide and then his second wife, Pompeia Paulina, a general's daughter whom he had married late in life, proved her Stoic principles by suggesting that they open their veins together. Only the imperial command that hers be tied again saved her from Seneca's doom.

Akin to the Stoics in spirit and emphasizing as they did ethics as a guide to life, Quintilian, expert in oratory, a writer and teacher, believed that by an independent "modern" education the Romans might regain their virtue and political competence. He was restive under the tyranny of Domitian and under the tyranny of Hellenism as well. Rationalist in his conviction that the Romans could not be helped by "culture" alone and abhorring cheap rhetoric in particular, Quintilian insisted that his people must take stock of themselves and begin a rejuvenation with mothers and infants, providing equal education for women and girls in order to restore a sense of realities and provide for its application. He proposed a patriotic education but not the blind worship of the blind. His thesis that lost verve and personality might be recovered by educational innovations was a potent influence in the later middle ages. Vittorino in Italy tried to apply Quintilian's dicta to the training of young men and women in the very shadow of theology and Erasmus apologised for his own proposals in view of the fact that Quintilian's *Institutio Oratoria* had already been written.

In the circle in which Quintilian moved and discussed Roman life were several women of such superior integrity and mentality that he could not possibly have made their sex the major scapegoat for the weaknesses of society. What he did believe was that women's psychology was a fundamental asset or loss to the State and he sought to diffuse more widely through the State the quality of his associates. Instead of ranting about the effeminacy of his generation, he really tried to provide more play for the sterling vitality of the male sex. That is, he was not misogynic. Amid the adulterers, poisoners, murderers and acquisitors was a class, doubtless large in numbers, of Roman matrons of exceptional industry, administrative talent, education and idealism who were overlooked by poets celebrating concubinage and by essayists concentrating on "bad women" but who inspired writers such as Seneca, Plutarch, Musonius and Quintilian to believe that the same training and the same high standard of morality was possible and desirable for the two sexes.

While the patriots boasted, the Cynics ridiculed, and those who searched for a median way discoursed, each after his kind, critics of a passionate bent raged against the plutocracy without stint. At the head of this literary school in the first century A.D. was Petronius. Whoever he was and whatever his motive he knew the aristocracy for which he spoke and the plebeian world for which he had contempt. He was an expert in the vice he ascribed to others. He was an observer on the side lines. If he did not spare his own kind and was merciless in dealing with literary dabblers, he was cruel to refinement in portraying the rich and luxurious merchant, swollen with pride, gorged on fine wines and dishes. In his account of Trimalchio's banquet, he gave vent to his scorn of a class supplying Rome, it is true, with its commodities but aping meanwhile the splendor of persons to the manor born. What the upshot was in terms of social policy it is difficult to say but there stands the picture he painted of the new plutocracy.

Juvenal, of this literary school, who scoffed and blasted, had the background of primitive simplicity as his approach to Roman scenes. "Satisfied by the kid and eggs and asparagus of his little farm at Tibur," Juvenal damned without qualification, much as Zola, the country boy, "blew up" Paris in a later time — from the underworld perspective of poverty and crime. In his position, Juvenal could scarcely plead with rulers for righteousness and he felt that there would soon be no place for Romans of any sort because the Greeks were taking possession of the citadel. The imported culture seemed to him as ridiculous or harmful as French imitation appeared to the independent farmer in early nineteenth century America. So he wrote: "Material civilisation, without any accom-

panying moral discipline, has produced the familiar and inevitable result, in an ever-increasing appetite for wealth and
enjoyment and money distinction, which ends in perpetual
disillusionment. . . When the secret (of life) is learnt, their
buildings may be less stately, gold and silver will perhaps not
be so abundant, there will be less soft and delicate living, there
may be even fewer costly sacrifices as piety increases; but
there will be a clearer perception of the true values of things,
and a chastened temperance of spirit, which are the only security for the permanence of society. And the moralist points
his audience to the splendid civilisations of the past that have
perished because they were without a soul. Assyria and Lydia,
the great cities of Magna Græcia which lived in a dream of
luxury, what are they now ? And, latest example of all,
Macedon, who pushed her conquests to the gates of India,
and came into possession of the hoarded treasures of the great
Eastern Empires, is gone, and royal Pella, the home of the
race, is now a heap of bricks."

Dill helps to point the moral: "It is also to be observed that
Juvenal seems to be quite as much under the influence of old
Roman conventionality as of permanent moral ideals. He
condemns eccentricities, or mere harmless aberrations from
old-fashioned rules of propriety, as ruthlessly as he punishes
lust and crime. The blue-stocking who is a purist in style,
and who balances, with deafening volubility, the merits of
Homer and Vergil, the eager gossip who has the very freshest
news from Thrace or Parthia, or the latest secret of a tainted
family, the virago, who with an intolerable pride of virtue,
plays the household tyrant and delivers curtain lectures to her
lord, seem to be almost as detestable in Juvenal's eyes as the
doubtful person who has had eight husbands in five years,
or one who elopes with an ugly gladiator, or tosses off two
pints before dinner. We may share his disgust for the great

ladies who fought in the arena and wrestled in the ring, or who order their poor tire-women to be flogged for deranging a curl in the towering architecture of their hair. But we cannot feel all his contempt for the poor penitent devotees of Isis who broke the ice to plunge thrice in the Tiber on a winter morning, and crawled on bleeding knees over the Campus Martius, or brought a phial of water from the Nile to sprinkle in the face of the goddess. Even lust, grossness, and cruelty, even poisoning and abortion, seem to lose some of their blackness when they are compared with an innocent literary vanity, or a pathetic eagerness to read the future or to soothe the pangs of a guilty conscience."

A clear sex bias runs through the writings of many Roman men. When they are not making women the source of their own woes, they are sneering at them in the temper of the Ionian Greeks, or lapsing into the laudation of obscenity. Thus Juvenal, as staunch as the elder Cato in his dislike for Hellenism and resembling the more ancient Aristophanes in his contempt for aliens in general, attacked women, amenable to foreign influences, with the virulence of a Schopenhauer. His *Legend of Bad Women* is a great document as the confession of a country boy appalled by urban horrors ranging from vice to philosophy.

In most marked contrast perhaps is the later poetry, the light and transient compositions made by the pupils of the rhetors. Among these verse-makers a few rose to professional status and enduring fame but the crowd of amateurs was legion. Martial like Juvenal and Seneca bemoaned the thin literary talent which concealed its feebleness behind the pomp and faded splendor of epic or tragic traditions. He roughly tells the whole crowd that genius alone will live forever. He seems to think that Sulpicia among the few was worthy of consideration; her poetry was read in Gaul in the days of Sidonius.

Of, by, and largely for women were produced *vers de société,* novels and lyrics — a way of working off the energies of two sexes which could not find other outlet.

To Longus, a Greek Sophist, of the late fourth or early fifth century is attributed the "first gentleman in ancient literature." This was the hero in *Daphnis and Chloe,* a story of romantic love. Plutarch also argued for tenderness in the marital relation and maintained that it was not incompatible with an interest in philosophy as Greek courtesans had declared; his wife was a woman of good sense, independence and ability to reason. Plutarch was a popular lecturer to Roman women before he published his biographical studies and his research into Pythagorean humanism and feminism may have deepened his sympathies with the sex. His friend Favorinus echoed some of the Greek women's doctrines with reference to the importance of maternal solicitude. And Dion Chrysostom came out unequivocally against the organised traffic in beauty, debauching buyers and bought; during years of exile and the observation of non-Roman societies he learned to hate hypocrisy and fear Roman degeneracy.

Of the patterns of thought woven by Roman talent, jurisprudence, by the agreement of those most competent to speak, is the most marvelous. Scholars who know it best are lost in admiration at the logic of its arrangement, the practicality of its principles, and the perfection of its reason. Yet when viewed as an instrument of statecraft designed to perpetuate and uphold society, Roman jurisprudence must be placed among the failures of Roman intellectualism. The purpose of justice, its great aim, we are told, was to give every man his due; but when Roman society is analysed into its parts, from nobles at the top to slaves at the bottom, it is impossible to find just who this "everyman" is, and when the distribution of wealth in Rome is examined from period to period it is equally impossible to discern just what is his "due." Moreover when in the later days of the empire jurists were trying to repair the disorganised public service, to restore the army to defensive power, to uproot corruption in office, to make the rich assume their share of the financial burden, and to relieve the producers of wealth from crushing taxation, their instrument of thought and government broke in their hands. Their smoothly drawn lines, in the best style, increasing the penalties on the wrongs they sought to suppress, only betrayed their powerlessness to stem or divert the tide. Jurisprudence was mighty but it could not prevail. The reasoning of the lawyers could not rearrange the dissolving social pattern and give to it the health of endurance.

Indeed in all the vast literature which flowed from the intellectualism of Rome there is visible little or no comprehension of the movement of social forces which determines the fate of societies and almost no mention of the precise modes of living and working pursued by the free poor and the slaves. Granted that there are innumerable references to rustics, warriors, slaves, and the rabble, in poems, letters, and treatises of one kind or another, still it is true that there is no reasoned consideration given to the proletariat of Rome. "The upper classes," says Fowler, "including all writers of memoirs and history were not interested in them. There was no philanthropist, no devoted inquirer like Mr. Charles Booth, to investigate their condition or try to ameliorate it. The statesman, if he troubled himself about them at all, looked on them as a dangerous element in society, only to be considered as human beings at election time; at all other times, merely as animals that had to be fed, in order to keep them from becoming an active peril. The philosopher, even the Stoic, whose creed was by far the most ennobling of the (Ciceronian) age, seems to have left the dregs of the people quite out of account;

though his philosophy nominally took the whole mass of mankind into its cognizance, it believed the masses to be degraded and vicious and made no effort to redeem them. The Stoic might profess the tenderest feeling toward all mankind, as Cicero did, when moved by some recent reading of Stoic doctrine; he might say that 'men were born for the sake of men, that each should help the other,' or that 'Nature has inclined us to love all men, for this is the foundation of all law;' but when in actual social or political contact with the same masses Cicero could only speak of them with contempt or disgust."

That deficiency was never rectified. In all the literature of Rome it seems impossible to find any grand conception of statecraft notwithstanding the political and military prowess. There was no attempt to reconcile the idealism of Plato with the realism of Aristotle binding them into an efficient plan of action and social redemption. And no individual Latin philosopher came forward with innovations of planning. The sword could conquer, money could buy, but intelligence could not yet avert the flood that buried the great Roman State of acquisitive power and pomp.

PART V

DERIVATIVES FROM THE AGE OF THE GODS

A CONSIDERATION of physical comforts, the habit or art of reasoning, and the love of power and pomp must be supplemented by a study of the gods if we are to get our bearings for an understanding of women or of men. Back of all thinking are the mysteries and in the highest stages of monotheism, many gods have been sublimated into the more abstract unity. This is an inescapable fact and must be taken into account in every effort to comprehend human life, belief, and conduct.

There is for instance a popular view of Christianity to the effect that it conquered all the old deities and by power of truth and the law of Rome was substituted for previous religions and schemes of thought. But the fathers of the Church knew full well the continuous battle that had to be fought with ancient creeds and rituals while modern scholars, both Catholic and Protestant, have long been aware of the distant anthropological origins of much that still passes current in religious thinking. Yet even they, in emphasizing their faith, have tended to minimise the tenacity of the historic heritage and what is more unfortunate have generally confined their observations to the relatively small part of the world of fact and opinion which for convenience is called Western.

In sketching the background for an understanding of modern people and the world in which men and women must now work, it is necessary therefore to widen the canvas and rub in the deep colors of the ancestral background on which our positive knowledge and rationality are laid. While huge fragments of the primitive have been discarded in the course of the movement of humanity, there has never been a break or total substitution. Nor is it possible. Perhaps not even desirable. An age of reason may well be an age of many new superstitions. Small minds engaged in sharpening minor antagonisms may easily add to confusion rather than illumination. The total process of thinking cannot be grasped but, unless an effort is made in that direction, no single pattern of specialised thinking can escape being warped.

Every bold warrior in history sought for his deeds the sanction of a god. Psychic civilians, "in tune with the infinite," pronounced oracular judgments on opinions and events. Great dreamers, sensitive to the mysteries, erected great systems of thought in correspondence. And the humblest of mortals, faced with the exigencies of existence and looking for protection against the buffets of fortune, turned to the guardianship of the deities. Thus the highest and the lowest common denominators of human imagination have been swayed by concepts of superhuman wisdom, mercy, authority, or power to whose mandates mankind was subject during the long age of the gods. Exceptional thinkers among the Greeks made an effort to reflect without reference to such imponderables but the genuine sceptics were few in number and, when the French took up their methods, most of them made a Goddess of Reason.

It seems to be in the very construction of the mind that a power not ourselves should make for righteousness —"certainly not *ourselves*" comments Bernard Shaw — for intelligence, beauty, morality, security, and hope. And limitless are the psychological explanations of the phenomenon which can be traced to the pre-historic records of man. Petronius said that "fear first made the gods" but some religions even in Rome were essentially gay. Lucretius thought that "dreams peopled the heavens with gods" and that view predominates in modern studies of primitive society. Ancestor worship has been offered as the source of religious rites; in the age of Alexander the Great a Sicilian by the name of Euhemerus insisted that "religion arose from the respect and reverence paid to kings and heroes during their lives and continued after death" with or without the ministration of priests. Empedocles, a fifth-century-before-Christ Greek, classed religion as a nervous malady and Feuerbach, a late European, specified the malady as pernicious anæmia induced by hallucinations.

Others have been concerned with the evolution of the idea of God or the gods — with the continuously creative flow of the concept. Thus Brinton says: "The psychic origin is the recognition or assumption that conscious volition is the ultimate source of all Force." In other words, the rise of religion marks the dawn of a faith in mind. In whatever way the first human mind surveyed the universe, it fancied that it could know something about the cosmos and set forth its interpretation. Intrinsically religion in this perspective was a form of mental awakening however involved it became with emotional excitations. The primitive child of nature was puzzled by its surroundings but began to acknowledge them and arrange ways of thinking about events, such as dreams and coincidences, life and death, light and darkness, the sunshine and storms, rains and winds, fertility and famine, space, old age and infancy, happiness and sorrow, friends and enemies.

Older than the social sciences and helping to shape them in spite of the independence which they like to claim, religion often upset the best laid schemes of the rationalists and in all times and places it has presented notions of life and destiny that have had to be reckoned with by every thinker of the word or doer of the deed. Studying many religions, Hegel found elements of truth in them all and on that discovery erected his argument of a divine unfolding. Kant in effect made God perfect Intelligence, a return to the Socratic view. And now with the popular reversion to natural philosophy, wizards of mathematics such as Einstein, Eddington, De Broglie, Schrödinger, Jeans, and Heisenberg, asked to name the law of the universe, call God a mathematician revealing himself through their species of symbols. The deity has become in their hands more abstract than ever — nothing less than a pure scientist.

The consciousness of Mind, though not at first as Mind but just as a yearning to know and express ideas, was usually accompanied among the primitives by a belief in eternal life. Nothing really died, as they viewed the matter. It was reincarnated or survived as a ghost for better or for ill. This gave rise to the doctrine of souls and to the countless creeds and guides respecting the life hereafter.

Then as the speculative sense enlarged, everything beheld by the eyes or heard about through the ears was invested with the mystery surrounding life itself. Polytheistic was early religion, showing itself in the worship or propitiation of sticks and stones, trees and sounds, colors and forms, beasts and birds. Professor Pinsero of Palermo declares that the anthropoidal apes have a religion in which they display rites related to their great enemy, the snake; they bury it in the ground and put insects into its tomb to keep it satisfied. But whatever the reaction of the ape may be, certainly the human in history has been obsessed by the serpent. It appears as a fundamental feature of early religions, rides high in the arms of Dionysian priestesses prancing to the temples, and stamps itself on some of the sublimest art of the earth. So do doves, eagles, ravens, frogs, fish, tortoises, cows and cats and dogs, horses and swans, sun and moon and stars, bulls and deer and foxes loom as the prime subject matter in the ancient quest for an understanding of the universe, that is, of the mind adjusting itself to environment. Sacred trees and totem poles, mountains and the echoes, birth stones and crystals for gazing, bird songs and their wings, eggs for Bacchus or for Easter, a hundred-breasted Diana, a multiple-armed Brahma, a two-faced Janus, and on through the reaches of wonder and its embodiment in phraseology or plastic form run the symbols of religion — the objective aspects of the inner self-revelation.

THE EARLY POLITICS OF RELIGION

The crystallisation of all such amazement in the presence of a Nature dimly comprehended begins with the temple organisation synchronous with the settled agricultural society. Agriculture being the mystery of mysteries to primitives, the women who planted and reaped, the sun which shone upon the soil, and the rain which watered the crops were all regarded as gods or demons, and medicine-men, or priests, soon undertook rites designed to woo their favor and make the food industry work smoothly. Then gradually the whole tribal life fell under priestly control — not only the gods of fertility and the elements — but also labor and law. It was this temple organisation — the first civic culture — based on agriculture and a settled society which once flourished by the Nile and the Euphrates, in the Ionian Isles and along the Mediterranean. Incidentally it thrived as a vested interest, priests being able to exact a goodly fee for their service of intermediation with the deities. The entire land of the tribe might be owned in theory by the temple as the property of the Mother Goddess administered by her priests. It was they who governed by divine right — stewards of the god. Thus when a warrior contested the right to dominate the economic life of such a community, his success was naturally proportioned to the credence he could arouse for his own pretension to divine favor. Sometimes the chief priest became a genuine king himself and sometimes he accepted a partnership with a mighty man of arms. At any rate, whenever the warrior triumphed, priests stood ready to resume their mastery in case the monarchy developed anæmia.

The Greeks possessed unusual ability for controlling miracles and mediums but perhaps there is an explanation. They were invaders and conquerors of a local temple organisation and it did not regain its pristine vigor and form. Hence the old gods of fertility and the elements, losing much of their fanciful symbolism, took on the concreteness of human beings.

In Egypt a conscious attempt was made by one pharaoh, Ikhnaton, to modify the god of his fathers, the Sun God, Ammon Ra, a tribal deity, and institute a worship more representative of the broad trading empire which Egypt had become. But Ikhnaton was not a militarist. His empire shrank and Egypt dropped back into religious tribal complacency. In the popular imagination the ruler was primarily a priest granted his right to preside over destiny by virtue of the god's approval. Lacking that divine sanction, his strong right arm alone could maintain his power and in any case the favor of the god was an asset. More than once the temple organisation was weakened by a man of Mars but it returned with his degeneration. A mere philosopher like Ikhnaton was unequal to the task of reform.

Well aware of this rhythm, Alexander the Great sought adoption into the family of native gods when he conquered Egyptian soil. At Babylon he was not so ambitious because the god, Bel-Marduk, who had blessed Cyrus when he set up the Persian empire, had lost too much ground to be feared; but in Egypt Ammon Ra could still awe the doughtiest wielder of the battle-axe. Though he had his men-at-arms at his heels, Alexander therefore felt he must also have this god on the side of his battalions. Yet he was not merely a religious "snob" as a leading historian has dubbed him. Alexander had been nurtured in the creed of the gods. Life does not represent or display such breaks as his sudden assumption of divinity considered by itself would imply. Philip, his father, had been devoted to the mysteries in his youth while Olympias, his mother, rounded out her years as high priestess of a cult. Alexander and God accordingly "carried on." He ordered the cities of Greece, unaccustomed to a living god, to set up his statue for worship.

His Roman imperial successors, who felt the practical need of drawing upon the mystic reservoirs of their subjects or allies for the veneration withheld from a sheer man of might or who romantically dramatised themselves as gods, rationalising their real or fancied authority, succeeded better in their claims to divine right with the Oriental element of the empire than with the European. Indeed the Egyptian queen Cleopatra helped to make the first of the Cæsars view himself as a holy man, thus far outshining the simple mother of George III summoning him to be "every inch a king"; Cleopatra demanded that Julius be every inch a god. And just prior to his launching of the Mesopotamian campaign, he tried to be, with senatorial confirmation. He was already Pontifex Maximus, or high priest, director of the religious affairs of the Romans, and by virtue of that position he had installed the priesthood within the regal walls. But Julius Cæsar's assumption of the ultimate prerogative was his downfall. Roman citizens promptly slew him. Then his heir, Cæsar Augustus, played more cautiously upon the susceptibilities of a public, amenable to deification of a ruler after his death but unwilling to accept living gods, by calling himself the son of the divine Julius and leaving the implication to sink into opinion with its own avoirdupois. His mother, Atia, thinking this far too uncertain of effect and wishing to see her offspring a living god, declared that he was the child of Apollo with whom she had mated in the temple, the god assuming the form of a dragon for the occasion — the old serpent continuing to be a tempter. However even her "bit" failed to produce the desired triumph. Nor did Caligula or Domitian attain his purpose of being worshipped as *deus* while he was alive; the Jews, who had to be considered, opposed that status for the former and the natives for the latter. We have already seen the awful end that came to the Syrian emperor posing as the Sun God, Elagabalus, and to his maternal ally, when their rites proved excessively obnoxious.

Nevertheless the anxiety to be directly divine continued to bother Roman rulers, just as it lingered in Egypt, notwithstanding all the obstacles. Aurelian made gains, with the aid of his Eastern troops, by erecting his own variety of Mithra worship; he aspired to be the son of Mithra and almost got admission to the divine family before he died. Nor was this the worst selection of an ancestor which Aurelian could have made. Originally Mithra was a Persian Sun God but, through accretions and modifications, the cult had lost the more orgiastic impulses among the Syrians, and, in the opinion of Biggs, had become "the purest and most elevated of all non-Biblical religions." To Mithra monuments were built throughout the Roman Empire as far from its center as Britain. The rites took place underground. An annual celebration occurred on the twenty-fifth of December. There were baptismal ceremonies, a consecration of bread and water of symbolic significance, concepts of atonement, resurrection, redemption and immortality. The cult was one of the ecstatic religions and its fervor attained such force that when Diocletian became emperor, though he was of humble birth and the mere choice of his army, the miracle happened — he actually ruled as a living god, priest-emperor of the Unconquerable Sun !

Centuries afterward a little Puritan theocracy appeared in the American wilderness. It had nothing so sinful as a Sun God. But it had priest-magistrates acting as self-appointed deputies of Jehovah and it banished to the frontier a dissenter in the community, Anne Hutchinson, for laughing outright. Finally she was slain by the Indians. More recently a Chinese militarist, Yuan-shi-kai, thrown up as temporal master in the local political arena, sought acknowledgment as the Son of Heaven in order that his scepter, wrenched from the former priest-emperor, might extract power from the adoration of the populace. Although the times were out of joint for that victory in China, across the Yellow Sea the monarch of Japan to this day holds his crown by mandate of the Sun Goddess, Amaterasu, who bestowed it upon his ancestor some two thousand years ago. She adopted the Japanese founder of the monarchy into her divine family and none of the heirs has disowned the exalted ancestor. The truth is, it is a crime in Japan to deny the tribal goddess.

OFFICIAL CHRISTIANITY

When either a priest or a king was sacred, diversity of religious opinion was of course out of the picture. And yet one divine ruler, Diocletian, the Roman, became bored with that dictatorship and abdicated to enjoy his own changed mood. There was much to alter his whim, for the empire was breaking apart and the divine honor was becoming an empty bauble.

This dissolving State, Constantine the Great, in the fourth century, A.D., undertook to govern nineteen years after Diocletian laid down the scepter. The new problems he had to face he saw clearly and handled judiciously. Chief among these was the problem of unity within a State seething with factions. It was idle for him to wear the aureole of a Sun God when his temporal authority over the people was obviously so weak. But there was a way out of the dilemma. The masses had a proposition to offer: namely that they be allowed to worship a new God that had taken possession of their hearts. He might do what he could to save politics if they might have the new deity. The solution seemed a happy one, as it was presented by intermediaries, and the compromise was accepted.

Thus instead of arrogating to himself the quality of *deus,* Constantine elevated Jesus Christ as the Light of the Roman world. Now in the eyes of certain of his disciples Jesus had been a simple carpenter of Nazareth, a lowly Roman subject, when he lived three centuries before; while in the opinion of others he was always the Son of God loaned to the earth temporarily that he might lead humanity to Heaven. When Constantine adopted the new faith, barbarian arms were rattling menacingly on the Roman borders and, unless factionalism in religion could be reduced, the Empire might collapse within before it had a chance to fight for its life with enemies at its gates. The old Roman religions were tenacious, making the religious warfare triangular, and Constantine had to sink or swim. So he swam.

In other words, he made a religious revolution in an effort to prevent a political revolution. This was in the year 310 when he set up the Cross. Henry Adams declares that in its symbolism of mysterious energy the Cross was the grand precursor of the technological revolution of 1900 when Langley fathered new rays of light, "occult, supersensual, irrational," destined to correspond more exactly with modern cravings for a revelation of the "divine substance." Anyway

Constantine first saw the Cross in the sky flaming with the words, By This Conquer, and he at once determined to follow their advice, having been prepared for a heavenly vision by his Christian mother. At the same time he was tactful enough in the circumstances not to attempt the overthrow of paganism by force. He chose instead the method of personally endorsing a sect and its god hitherto despised and persecuted by the crown. With his brother-in-law Licinius, Roman ruler of the East, Constantine arranged for their mutual toleration of the Christians, the Milan Edict to that effect in 313 A.D. embodying the contract.

So sensational was this step that the fathers of the Church always held it to be a distinct innovation in the history of religion, ignoring earlier and stronger acts of toleration, such as that of King Asoka in India. Professor Luigi Luzzatti, in a volume entitled *God in Freedom,* directs attention to the fact that some five hundred and forty years before Constantine, the Buddhist monarch not only established general toleration but restrained his own religious expressions in order to promote an atmosphere of utter liberty to believe. In his case toleration was ethical, as Buddha had conceived it. As for Constantine's political precedent, one hundred years before, the Persian emperor, Ardashir I, had undertaken to consolidate the State through a religious revolution; on special terms of intimacy with his Jehovah, Ormuzd, he adopted the old Persian Zoroastrianism as the unifying faith. Constantine had the same choices for procedure — either a complete and uncontrolled religious liberty or the erection into a monopoly of a single religion which had proved its vigor by surviving incredible persecutions and had converted the ruling class in impressive numbers. He took a third course. He gave the new religion the right-of-way through his personal approval while permitting paganism to live if it could. Paganism was then stronger in Rome than it was in the East and a false step might have defeated the very political unity which he sought to promote. His proclamation of a religious truce between paganism in decay and Christianity in the flood tide of youth was therefore the work of a statesman and not of a scholar like Asoka.

However, Licinius gave him trouble in the matter, violating the toleration agreement where he was governing and launching a new persecution of the Christian movement. In this emergency Constantine transferred the capital of the Roman Empire to the Bosphorus, taking the political rein from the hands of Licinius, enlarging and beautifying old Byzantium into his rechristened stronghold, Constantinople, and inducing Christians to regard it as their holy city, the center of the new drive for a defense of the frontiers. The city was dedicated to the mother of Jesus; Christian priests performed the inaugural rites for Constantine; he received Christian baptism on his death bed, and was buried in the local Church of the Apostles.

Before his baptism Constantine had taken measures to reconcile the warring Christian factions and his leadership in that respect was a phase of strategy. If the sect was to be tolerated, one must know what the State was defending. Several times Constantine summoned its leaders to assemble and iron out their disputes. Of humble birth himself, possibly the illegitimate son of a general and a Slav innkeeper's daughter of Nish, positively ignorant about the antecedents of the Christians, he had to look on at the proceedings without much intimate comprehension of the arguments that were advanced. But at a conference in Arles in 313, the year of the Milan Edict, he sat on a golden throne while the Christians tried to compose differences often so violent that fists flew and riots, near or actual, interrupted the proceedings. Later at a grand council in the East, at Nicæa in 325, to which the West sent several representatives, an adjustment was accomplished, culminating in the settlement of the moot point as to the divinity of Christ — in its favor. On this occasion Constantine delivered an oration and affected the result appreciably.

Victory thus went to the wing headed by Athanasius, the prince-bishop of Alexandria, a Trinitarian, who insisted that God had himself entered into humanity through his Son Christ Jesus in order to avert the doom of death pronounced on Adam for his disobedience; in other words, the Son of Man was Jehovah reincarnated. The Father, Son, and Holy Ghost were a Three-in-One God. This disposed of the opposition centering around Arius who disagreed with St. Paul's conception of the divinity of Christ and argued that Jesus was not actually the son of God but the embodiment of a divine principle of righteousness enunciated by Jehovah. Arius made Christ a little less than God and the angels. He was inclined to the view that the Messiah's call to reason and loving kindness was sufficient for his worship. But it was decreed by the Assembly of one hundred and fifty laymen and thirty-six Macedonian bishops in solemn conclave that Jesus Christ, the equal of God, was a living God; that the newest religion like the oldest was to rest on the supernatural. Arius was then banished and his adherents scattered. In this manner a union of souls was achieved by disciples of Christ "recently persecuted, vilified, torn to pieces by wild animals, burned alive, crucified . . . maddened by irrepressible sorrow but illuminated by the thought of imminent redemption. That meant it was to be an emotional, ecstatic cult."

From the fortress on the Bosphorus decrees followed which step by step intrenched the Trinity of Christendom and reduced paganism to the status of a superstition just occupied by Christianity. Again the Heavens were to be called upon to bolster politics as long as arms could give any substance to the State. Some feeling for what life means must keep society unified and the gods, being the oldest, were long the major expedient.

This concern with an earthly State could not be attributed to Jesus who displayed as little interest in its design as the Buddha had manifested. But before the hour of his crucifixion and even before the agony of Gethsemane, the disciples of Jesus gave to his words a political complexion. And steadily the manipulators of the sect took full possession of this verbal texture.

Many women agreed with Arius about the divinity of Christ and stated their opinions openly while others were suspected of boring through subterranean channels to secure the eventual triumph of the Unitarian philosophy. In Constantine's own family indeed they helped to disrupt the political unity based on religious accord which the emperor thought he had made rigid. Both his half-sister, Constantia, and her husband, Licinius, wandered from the path of political rectitude after the Milan Decree of Toleration had been signed. The husband remained a pagan in spite of his signature and renewed attacks on the Christians of every brand; while his wife, though baptised by Sylvester at Rome, went over to Arianism and used her influence to procure the recall of the exiled leader of the Unitarian wing of Christianity. So Arianism was in reality no more dead than paganism.

The successor to Constantine, Theodosius I, discovered that. No sanctions had been laid down for the safeguarding of the Nicæan creed, its chief authority resting on the admonition delivered by Constantine at the imperial banquet which he gave to the bishops and priests in conference. That was a kind of Washington Farewell Address to factions — and it had a similar effect. The old discussion over the divinity of

Christ broke out afresh after Constantine's death, with women aiding and abetting.

Galla, the second wife of Theodosius, was not considered orthodox, though his first wife, Placilla, was canonised for her conformity and piety; it has been hinted that Ambrose probably failed to mention Galla among his faithful adherents because the orthodoxy of the great lady was suspect. Arius had a strong following not only in the East but in Rome and later among the Goths, Suebi, Vandals, Burgundians and Langobardi. It was said that hundreds of nuns forsook orthodoxy for his faith. From the very throne room operated an advocate in Justina, the Sicilian wife of Valentinian I, who was so tenacious that she tried to persuade her young son, Valentinian II, when he was made emperor, to do what his father had refused to do, namely, promote Arianism, that is Unitarianism, in Europe; at the very least to appoint a bishop from that group. This brought her into collision with Ambrose the irreconcilable and, while he served her on several delicate missions, he would not yield an inch to her religious preferences.

Loyal to the great ecclesiastical organisation now taking elaborate form, he replied with heat, when the young emperor Valentinian and his mother Justina in 384 asked for a few churches for the Arians: "If you demand my person, I am ready to submit; carry me to prison or to death, I will not resist; but I will never betray the church of Christ. I will not call upon the people to succor me; I will die at the foot of the altar rather than desert it. The tumult of the people I will not encourage; but God alone can appease it."

The influence of Ambrose was a factor in the harsh decision which Theodosius reached with regard to religious conformity. Like Constantine, Theodosius had a war vision revealing the strength of Christian concepts. In fear of losing that divine aid, he took the creed as defined at Nicæa and gave it the missing sanction. That is, he ordered every Church to surrender to the Trinitarians — and no other branch of the Christian faith or any form of pagan religion was to be tolerated. Though the Emperor tried to make the transition peaceful, zealots overcame his objections to persecution. When the Jewish synagogue in Constantinople was destroyed and reparation was demanded by the victims, Father Ambrose would not listen to his suggestion of clemency and so God alone suppressed the tumult in the grand old Semitic style. In 390 Theodosius ordered the huge statue of Serapis at Alexandria destroyed. And steadily the new religious passions drove all before them like a hurricane. The world had been revelling in the blood that flowed from the veins of Christian martyrs. Now it was to be treated to the sight of Jewish and other human sacrifices offered to the Christian Trinity. No arms have ever been so delightful to human beings as those which cause the life-stream to run in libations to the gods and Christendom was to experience as deep a joy in that respect as ever pagan had felt. Probably more — because in the age of the latest religion righteousness was organised on an immense scale while the soldiers of Christ looked forward to eternal compensations. Europe now displayed for religion's sake its tragically barbaric soul without the soothing balm it might have derived from an older East that had passed from activism into Nirvana. And so partly by arms the latest temple corporation, founded on a Christianity of zealotry, grew into a worldly estate of proportions unknown to any previous "golden age" when priests and war lords were at swords' points.

Behind the weak Theodosius II and his decisions, his sister Pulcheria, highly educated in linguistics, art, literature and such science as the time afforded, was the power. She was exceedingly orthodox and, becoming Augusta, in 414 she practically ruled the Eastern empire for many years during her brother's incompetency, his mother having neglected to prepare him for responsibility. In her Christian ardor, Pulcheria built and adorned churches and convents.

During the controversy with Nestorius, who insisted that Mary was not to be called the Mother of God because God could have no mother, St. Cyril called on her for help and she corresponded with him on the subject, taking the opposite view from that held by a noted female contemporary, Hypatia, whose letter in 431 complaining of the condemnation and banishment of Nestorius appears in the synodical book of the great ecumenical council of Ephesus summoned by the emperor. In 450 Pulcheria carried on a long correspondence with Pope Leo and his archdeacon Hilarius relative to another heresy — Entyches and the Monophysite, which the empress Theodora, the wife of Justinian, a century later was to espouse. In defense of the council of Chalcedon, Pulcheria wrote to the monks of Palestine and to Bessa, the abbess of a convent at Jerusalem. An official had previously taken up with her the matter of taxing his episcopal city of Cyrrhus and the clergy of Ephesus, the concerns of the episcopate of Bassianus. Much of her time and attention was given to religious affairs and she helped to elaborate the ritual by such acts as the transfer of relics, notably those of St. Chrysostom, to Constantinople, with great pomp. For political purposes she had married a General. And for similar reasons soon after her enthronement she took the veil, not however to retire from the world of activity for she kept in intimate touch with public affairs. Her largesse to the poor and the suffering was but one phase of her manifold energy and interests. And after her demise a granddaughter, Pulcheria, bred in that tradition, "for forty years reigned like a saint and a great empress and this period was for the Church a golden age."

When Pulcheria converted Eudocia, a beautiful, rich and learned heathen, the wife of Theodosius II, a disciple of Christ, likewise equipped for great service in many directions during the struggle of the church for political power, was drawn into the cult. Eudocia was educated by her father, Leontius, a sophist and noted grammarian of Athens, who relied so much on her scholarship and personality to carry her through life that he gave his property to his sons, apparently considering them insufficiently dowered with charm and brains to make their way in the world unaided. But the father was mistaken in thinking life would be easy for any girl in such times. It is true that her emperor-husband enlarged the town of Antioch with its surrounding walls and rendered many other favors to his empress, made Augusta in 423. Nevertheless since Pulcheria was far from a meek follower of Jesus, she and Eudocia became seriously involved over appointees to religious offices. Jealousy and crime made life at the court tempestuous and perilous for both these learned ladies but solace came to Eudocia when she was able to visit the Holy Land in her declining years and turn to good works and pious verse. She repaired the walls of Jerusalem, built monasteries and hospitals and churches, financed priests and cared for the poor, communed with Simeon Stylites and other holy men, wrote paraphrases of the prophecies, poems on the martyrs, and, it is thought, a history of the fall and redemption of man under Christ.

Valentinian III came to power with an uncompromising mother-regent, Galla Placidia, a daughter of Theodosius I, who made orthodoxy so violent that heretics, such as the Manichæans, were banished from Rome, astrologers were outlawed, Jews and other pagans were forbidden to hold public office and a general intolerance set in. Yet, as might be expected, in the light of the psychological history of persecutors, she was instable in her personal conduct. Profligacy and conspiracy, if not direct crime, involved her in the civil wars which occurred at the time of the Alaric invasion. She was accused of the murder of her cousin Serena, widow of the Teuton chief Stilicho, lord at Ravenna, and suspected of actual dealings with Alaric demanding Roman entry. When she fled to Theodosius at Constantinople, he sent her back to Italy with reinforcements of troops and afterwards she married Romans and barbarians at will and had a very strenuous life religiously and secularly, tasting some of the vengeance she sought to wreak on others.

Under the ægis of the empire, Christianity of the more violent type spread like fire. But Persia checked it for a time at her frontier. Suspicious of the political motive behind the religious prowess of her rival at Byzantium, Persia secured a treaty in 422 which recognised her right to her own sphere of influence and to the enjoyment of her god-king, protector of Zoroaster. Peace however did not flow from that mere document for Christians tried to sweep away every competitor. Thus for three centuries the East was a battleground of religious intransigence.

THE SOCIAL AND RELIGIOUS REVOLUTION

ALTHOUGH Christendom was for a time legally a unit in its creed, in the fifth century it lost its uniformity. Persia gave shelter to the Nestorian Christians who refused to accede to the request of the Latin-speaking wing of the Church that the Holy Ghost be allowed to proceed from the Son as well as the Father God and on this disturbing point they broke off relations, each wing to go its way in extending the gospel of

Christianity. This division relieved the tension in the East considerably, not only because the physical power of the Christian sect was thereby weakened but also because Nestorian monotheism, being in fair harmony with Persian thought, strengthened the Eastern faith. The Nestorians carried their creed into Russia and on into China. Moreover with the dissolution of the Roman Empire, religious factionalism reasserted itself in the Roman provinces until the Egyptian and Assyrian churches achieved independence and worshipped as they pleased. Later we shall deal with attempts to heal such breaches by the agency of Catholic Crusades, remembering as we do so that all the leading faiths of the world have had a similar inner conflict, great conferences seeking adjustments, compromises resulting, and failures to agree disrupting the sway of particular mysteries.

Though Christianity spread rapidly after the authorisation given it by Theodosius, no fiat could accomplish the miracle of smoothing out all the involutions of the pagan brains which held to their habits of thinking. Dreams of mutual toleration lingered among the liberals of the two faiths for a time. Furthermore there were competent advisers among the pagans whom Theodosius and Honorius needed in their administrations and these were allowed to retain their personal beliefs until 416 A.D. when all offices were closed to pagans. Indeed for a century after the conversion of Constantine who gave official encouragement and Theodosius who made Christianity the State Church, Romans of the patrician class remained sceptical to a high degree. At the opening of the fifth century, the majority of the Senate members were still unaffected by the new faith and pagans held office in the prefectures. Pagans "might still meet . . . to hear one of their number expound the sacerdotal lore of Rome and another set forth the Stoic or Alexandrian interpretation of the myths, or the command of

augural science possessed by Vergil. Their great poet, as if
he were writing in the age of Augustus, could invite the
Christian Emperor Honorius to survey the shrines of the gods,
which still in all their old splendour surrounded the imperial
palace with a divine guardianship. Another pagan poet, who
had been prefect of the city, a quarter of a century after the
death of Theodosius, could pour contempt on the Christian
profession, and rejoice at the sight of the villagers of Etruria
gaily celebrating the rites of Osiris in the springtime. Magic
and divination of every form had long been under the ban of
the State. Yet a prefect of Honorius proposed to employ the
Tuscan sorcerers who offered the aid of their arts against
Alaric, and Litorius, fighting against a successor of Alaric in
Gaul, consulted the pagan seers before his last battle, under
the walls of Toulouse. In the last years of the Western Empire, the diviners of Africa were practicing their arts among
the nominal Christians of Aquitaine."

Educated Roman Christians had in many cases but added
a new color to their Joseph's coats, and that of a pastel tone.
In academic groves, professors seemed blind to social and religious revolutions. In the *Letters* of Symmachus — imperial
orator and office holder, consul, senator, governor — in the
poems of his friend Ausonius — professor at the university of
Bordeaux — and in the *Saturnalia* of Macrobius — a third
member of a congenial circle of intelligentsia — no hint of
their being disturbed by the evangelistic ardor of the Apostles
gleams through the lines. Symmachus associated both with
Father Ambrose the intransigent Catholic and Prætextus the
pagan but he was devoid of "vulgar" enthusiasms and equally
complacent about the barbarian menace; in a letter to his son
written in 402 while the terrible battles of Pollentia and
Verona were raging, he merely refers to them as obstacles
necessitating his detour en route to Milan. Notwithstanding

the doughty Alaric, the noble Roman seemed to feel no alarm — perhaps because another change of rulers meant nothing to a people even of the upper caste accustomed to continual battling for the throne. No doubt it was impossible at the time to know whether or when Rome had fallen or to imagine that it had. Neither did Ausonius in Aquitaine betray a consciousness of fear, contenting himself with framing sketches of his university colleagues and the bright and shining lights within his family. He drew a gentle picture of country life among the landed gentry loyal to traditions of literary interests and Roman family concepts and still confident of their future. One member of his family had remained unmarried to carry on her medical work and a sister had become a Christian devotee but these heretical flashes were simply incidents in a patrician life continuing along well-trodden paths.

The *Saturnalia* also represents this coterie of literary men chatting together amiably, placid in the presence of war clouds and the growing religious absolutism, still undisturbed by perils to their way of life. Inured to the superiority which had long been theirs by right of birth and wealth, they seemed to think nothing could destroy their security. They were accustomed to having Roman matrons perform deeds of charity. For one of them now to do so in the name of Christ, if a bit exotic, seemed little more than that. The wife of Prætextus was his intellectual companion and for Ambrose and the other Christian fathers to cultivate sacred learning with women friends appeared a very natural thing. As for the rise of Christianity among slaves, well, the Stoic school had infected all the upper caste with a more lenient attitude toward servants, anyway. Paganism therefore sank down slowly.

Apollinaris Sidonius himself, Bishop of Auvergne in the latter part of the fifth century, saw in the landscape chiefly his own imperial caste of pagans as his writings reveal. He was a grand seigneur, celebrated for a poetic panegyric on the last emperor of the West, Avitus, his father-in-law, an adept in the classics of Greece and Rome, and far removed by economic circumstance from the lower classes of the State. Sidonius seems quite unconscious of the passing of his order, indifferent to the miseries of the masses, sweetly satisfied with the elegance and refinements of the pagan society of which he was still a "brilliant" member, notwithstanding the fact that he had become a Christian.

Two or three times paganism legally returned to Rome after its suppression seemed assured. Nevertheless there were Catholics of unyielding metal whose tenacity withstood every assault and finally they got the upper hand. Not without hate and ferocity characterising the contest, however, for their climb to political power and with it their prohibition on dissent produced a pagan defiance of the law which reacted on the Christians with such intensity that the ancient habit of religious warfare regained its original strength. For a long period in Rome religion had been polytheistic, the exigencies of empire demanding a toleration of conquered and allied gods — a catholicity of tastes in the true sense of the word. So it was extremely difficult for minds cooled by that stream of thought to become hotly sure that there was but one true God whose high priest was the Pope. Themistius, a gifted orator, in the reign of Valentinian managed to save some blood and preserve some room for tolerance by his calls for loyalty to the ideals of the past. On the other hand strenuous evangelism flourished in part as the result of fear that economic right and emoluments would melt away unless a fierce effort were made to regain by religious unanimity the ground that was being lost through political factionalism. The thesis was advanced by Christian leaders that Roman political power diminished through the lukewarmness of the

Christians, because they relied too little on the new faith and in their heart of hearts sought protection from the pagan deities — a species of assertion still used by the Christians in Japan after earthquakes.

Coupled with such a motive in the case of Justinian, who closed the University of Athens in 529 A.D. on account of its heathen atmosphere, was his undoubted personal ambition. He was a born organiser and fancied he could control minds as well as physical energies.

In any case it was a great victory for the Roman Christians when the barbarian invaders succumbed to their cult — a bloodless triumph moreover, since the newcomers were profoundly impressed by the rites and ceremonies of the Church and only too glad to derive what security and power might lie in homage to the dominant local god — reflecting Alexander the Great's reaction to Egypt. Before the doughty Clovis yielded to the Christian religion, he became convinced that the deity who could enable St. Genevieve to maintain such a marvelous resistance to his siege in Paris was well worth adoption. He was only too happy therefore when his Christian wife, Clotilda, a Burgundian princess, seemed able to lure her powerful divinity to his side and give him the victory. With this triumph Clovis became the great champion of Christianity in western Europe. Because he took the Church under his own wing instead of acknowledging the Pope as its protector, the Papacy however had some hard sledding with Clovis and often had to do his bidding. Even so, he ordered all his subjects baptised and on the whole the cult made great gains.

To "please his Gothic masters" converted to Christianity, Priscus Attalus, a Hellenist naturalist serving as chief of state when Alaric became ruler of Rome, gave up his paganism — as lightly and adroitly as the South Slavs in Bosnia and Herzegovina resigned Christianity at a later day for Mohammedanism when their estates were endangered by the Turks. Alaric's demand for ransom was paid in part from the temple ornaments and golden plate of the ancient régime and the native pagans were no doubt pleased to get off so well.

As the barbarians mounted the throne of the Cæsars, they were told by the Popes that they would also lose their grip unless they were more steadfast in the Christian faith and more enthusiastic in their worship. Serena, the niece and adopted daughter of the Roman emperor, Valens, married to the barbarian chieftain Stilicho who rose to power within the State before the hordes of Teutons invaded the scene, evidently was deeply impressed with this opinion. A learned woman and scarcely less of a political chief than her aggressive mate, in the presence of a notable assembly and before the very eyes of the Vestals, she snatched the necklace from the throat of the pagan goddess and put it around her own.

Without, no less than within the old confines of a political empire, the new religion expanded until it was supreme over the destinies of assorted races and classes — the most amazing temple corporation in history. It is impossible therefore to think of what we call the Middle Ages apart from terms of religion. Mediæval kings of Europe often felt a duty to Rome which transcended their local obligations. Sylvia Benians points out that "some rulers cared for their own country to the neglect of Christendom but these did not earn the living fame given to the memory of Richard I of England and Louis IX of France who were thought to have placed the service of the Christian commonwealth above that of their kingdoms." She thinks this Christian unity "was founded on fact — on the broad geographical and climatic sameness of the Mediterranean area, on the spiritual unity of mankind proclaimed by the Christian faith, on the memories and remains of the world-wide culture of Rome." Undoubtedly these were elements but there were other and perhaps more fundamental ones.

THE PAPACY AND WOMEN

At bottom the unity of this religious empire depended mainly upon skillful management by the chief pontifex, the Pope of Rome. Now on first thought nothing would seem more remote from the celibate head of a celibate priesthood than women and their ways; but on second thought coupled with some examination of the facts in the case a contrary conclusion must be reached. As heir to the pomp and dignities of the Roman Empire in the West, including no small part of its temporal authority, taxing power, and legal jurisdiction, the Pope was the master of a great estate. The honors, emoluments and prerogatives of the office made it the object of ambition for families whose interest in the teachings of Jesus was, to say the least, not their sole motive. Since under the rule of celibacy, the Popes were precluded from erecting a hereditary dynasty, a new incumbent had to be elected on the death of each pontifex. If in the days of the Roman Empire where attempts were made, sometimes successfully, to assure succession according to the hereditary principle, the office of emperor was a prize over which families and politicians contended, it is only natural to suppose that similar considerations would enter into the selection of Popes. And this is exactly what happened. As a corollary, places in the electoral body became much sought-after prizes. Hence we meet as late as the sixteenth century Italian noblewomen still demanding positions of ecclesiastical power for their husbands or sons. As we shall also see, women had a hand in the selection of the Pope himself on occasion.

They were concerned not only with ecclesiastical dignities

and financial perquisites. For the Pope was the head of an organisation possessing enormous control over marital relations acquired through contests over divorce, in the main, and that bore watching too. Indeed the repudiation of Teutberga by Lothair II of Lorraine in the ninth century and the Papal defence of the lady marked a critical stage in the political history of Christendom by demonstrating that a powerful court of appeal against temporal rulers existed at Rome. A few cases like that enabled the Popes to emerge from quiet diplomatic channels to open assertions of their supremacy over all questions of morality. It was not easy for the Papacy to master feudal lords and one of the most ingenious weapons they had to use was participation in the strife within a family. It is necessary therefore to dwell somewhat upon the evolution of the Papacy and indicate some of the leading points of contact between women and that institution.

When the Council of Nicæa settled the issue of the divinity of Christ it also recognised Pope Damasus of Rome as the grand representative of the God on earth. Later when Christendom divided like the Roman Empire into a polemic West and a mystical East, each retained the priestly character of its creed. The God of each was to have an intermediary with mortals. Neither could be communed with directly — a situation against which many good Christians were to rebel in the centuries to follow.

The center of Catholicism was the altar where consecrated priests, directed by the papal head, performed rites for the living and interceded for the dead — a device in vogue among the Hebrews and other ancient peoples. It was familiar to St. Augustine during his boyhood in North Africa where priests were an accepted institution. His later reading of Plato but strengthened that inherited perspective giving to his *City of God,* written in the fourth century A.D., the combined viewpoint of a temple corporation and idealism. This Augustinian concept of a holy Christian city directed by priestly guardians, the various Popes then expanded into the vision of a whole world administered from Rome by vicegerents of the Trinity — providing live unities for the decadent. The peace of Christ was to succeeded gloriously to the Pax Romana.

That was the dream but it was not realised all in a day and not to its final degree without shrewd diplomacy, considerable terrorism, some open fighting, and not a little chicanery. The Papacy had riches to begin with, partly obtained from the gifts of wealthy Roman ladies, a large share of which it spent in the founding of churches far and wide, even in Cappadocia and Arabia. Its property Diocletian confiscated but Constantine restored it and things were running smoothly until the barbarians seized Rome. The bargaining then was a difficult affair but the High Priest was adroit. Through the mysteries he accomplished much for the conquered Romans in the way of protection and he awed the barbarians to some extent by his intimacy with the gods. Yet in spite of his management of a difficult situation, a great deal of the papal wealth was dissipated by seizures on the part of the invaders.

On the other hand the clerical force of the Papacy was of great service to the invaders who required experts in the native Latin tongue and skilled legal advisers to make their rule a success. Holding the balance of power, the Pope thus became in some respects supreme over subjects and masters alike. The High Priest of Christ Jesus was in a very real sense the dictator of affairs.

Kneeling at the feet of the Pope Leo III, no less a man of Mars than Charlemagne, in 800, received his crown from the High Priest in recognition of the prime power of the mysteries. What Charlemagne had evidently intended to do was to pay homage to the God of the Christians instead of to the Pope but the high priest neatly arranged the matter in such a way that, in receiving his crown and rank of emperor from the Pope, the temporal ruler should be admittedly inferior to the priest. This gave the Pope a more strategic political position than he had hitherto possessed. Strong monarchs such as Justinian had been wont to dictate to the steward of God, ordering him to appear at Constantinople on occasion, or bullying him in this fashion or that. Now with the Frankish monarch under his orders, the Pope could potentially defy the masters of the East and Charlemagne in fact proved to be a great asset of the Roman Church. Victory over Charlemagne, who would much have preferred making himself emperor, was the beginning of the "Holy Roman Empire" of strange memory. And when the Pope acquired such honors and such allies, he learned to be still more zealous in economic and political relations as well as in spiritual affairs. The truth is he began to claim an overlordship over all European rulers. And bitter as the strife often became between the temporal and the spiritual arms, the Holy City with its temple corporation asserted an authority over mind and matter in Europe for a thousand years of so masterful a nature that the barbarian invasion of Rome is really of secondary importance to the Roman invasion of Europe through the religion of the Christian potentates.

In the eleventh century Pope Gregory VII, in consolidating Christendom, declared that Constantine had left Rome body and soul to the Pope when he removed the capital of the empire to the Bosphorus and this donation combined with the gift of the keys to Heaven made by St. Peter endowed the Pope with legal and spiritual supremacy over all mortal concerns in Western Europe. Accordingly Gregory took from other bodies the privilege they had been exercising of selecting the Pope and passed it over to the College of Cardinals, a transfer which eliminated nobles, reduced the control of powerful families, and elevated the humble to positions of influence.

Gregory was of lowly birth himself, having acquired his office by irregular means. And for the new program he framed, he needed financial backing. This came in a generous measure from the Empress Agnes and from Matilda, the Duchess of Tuscany. It came openly for they traveled to Rome to show that leading representatives of the feudal class were behind the Pope's power. With Matilda as his ally, the Pope was then able to force the homage of Henry IV and Frederick Barbarossa, whose surrender to the Pope no one enjoyed more than the devout daughter of the pious Boniface II and Beatrice of Bar. In fact it was on her splendid estate at Canossa, the richest in Italy, that Henry IV made his obeisance. Hence enemies of the papal pretension who hoped to outwit the Pope had to consider outwitting Matilda.

They tried to make depredations on her wealth but she formed a league of Lombard cities and fought back. For more than thirty years she upheld a series of Popes — Gregory VII, Victor III, Urban II, and Paschal II. In 1074 she supplied funds for the papal attack on the Normans, the great robber barons of Europe at the time, so menacing alike to the Pope and the ruler of Byzantium that they doubted whether even their alliance would be a sufficient barrier against these buccaneers. The following year Matilda was present in person when the Church condemned Guibert, the Norman chief, and deprived him of the archbishopric of Ravenna; two years later she bestowed her property on the Holy See, renewing the grant in 1102, a source of wealth for the Papacy which constituted its major strength although family opposition checked the complete surrender of her inheritance. Matilda was not only able to help with her riches. She had personality and learning — invaluable reinforcements. A linguist, her equipment included Italian, French and German; she owned a goodly library and wrote letters in Latin; she supervised an edition of the Pandects of Justinian. St. Anselm was among her correspondents and from Canterbury he sent her his *Meditations*. On her death she was interred appropriately in St. Peter's. And she has come down in history as St. Matilda.

Now this Pope Gregory, whom Matilda so ardently patronised, was especially rigorous on the point of celibacy for the priests and tied them to the Papacy with economic ropes by depriving them of family and state alliances and making them dependent on the ecclesiastical treasury for their maintenance. His idea was to divert the priests from worldly enterprise and confine their interests to the Church. And his plan worked so well that a large element of the male population of Europe was found in undivided loyalty to the Pope when he struggled for empire with refractory kings. It is true that his scheme of sovereignty seemed overthrown when William of Normandy and other feudal lords forced Gregory into exile and he died at Salerno. But he had chosen his successor and the struggle went on to uphold papal prerogatives based upon the Donation of Constantine which some of the temporal rulers of the Middle Ages declared to be a betrayal of imperial trust. In 1440 Laurentius Valla, an Italian nationalist, stated that the whole thing was a forgery. However the Papacy was on its guard and, by explaining that the forgery at any rate was not committed in Rome, helped to prolong its theocratic power. In such ways the priest-emperor — with occultism, with arms, and with personal management — held the temple corporation in a straight and masterful course and the ship of theocracy sailed the seas of economic and politics in confidence, not without tempests and many torn sails, it is true, but with astounding success.

In fact far beyond the periphery of the old Roman Empire

was stretched the sphere of the Pope's influence, the divine monarch of Christendom uniting Celts in Ireland, Scandinavians in Norway and Sweden, and Teutons all over Germany, in theory and to an amazing degree in practice, as loyal subjects. Such a vast religious "Amphictyony" would have paralysed Greek minds.

Like the pythoness of old, the Pope made and unmade heroes, determined economic and social policies as religious adviser to war lords, or went over their heads to give orders to the people in a time of crisis. Yet a masterful temporal ruler now and then dared to dictate even to the High Priest. And occasionally a powerful female made of the Pope a puppet. Thus the "fair but wicked" Theodora and her daughter Marozia installed the favorite of the former and the son of the latter as Popes John X and John XI respectively. John X, the infallible Christian director from 914-928, while deacon at Bologna, had caught the fancy of Theodora, the wife of Theophylact, a great Roman noble, who persuaded her husband to promote the deacon first to the see of Bologna and then to the archbishopric of Ravenna. "In direct opposition to a decree of council, he was also at the instigation of Theodora promoted to the papal chair as the successor of Lando." Then Theodora's daughter, Marozia, caused his downfall though he had been hardy enough to fight against the Saracens and to labor for the unity of Italy. Her son, John XI, Pope from 931 to 935, according to rumor the child also of Pope Sergius III, was raised to the high priesthood through the intrigues of his mother whose behests he obeyed until another of her sons rid the stage of maternal and fraternal rivals. For a considerable period a "pornocracy" presided over Christendom, inaugurated by Sergius who had strangled his enemies.

In marked contrast to such masters of the Papacy was St. Catherine of Siena who lived long after these hot-blooded females of the species and their male companions had done their worst for the religious estate. St. Catherine was an extraordinary personality. The daughter of a dyer, she was by birth as humble as Jeanne d'Arc; in a similar fashion she saw visions and dreamed dreams. According to a custom of the times she felt on her own body the wounds of Christ, thus proving that she could suffer with the Savior. Some nuns felt more kinship with the Virgin, distraught by the sacrifice of her son, but Catherine was attuned to the woes of the Crucified One himself. Nevertheless she would not enter a convent, being in every fibre a woman of action like the sturdy Sienese in general, capable of defending their town against the Florentines, against the armies of the Pope, against French, Spanish, and German attacks. It is true she made a compromise in the strife between the Franciscans and the Dominicans over the right to a monopoly of wound impressions; when the Dominicans were forbidden to compete in this line, she, who was of that order, yielded the point to Pope Sixtus IV and his Franciscan Brothers.

But Catherine had large objectives and was determined to realise them — nothing short of church pacification — a political task which challenged her talents and was executed brilliantly. She achieved what neither Petrarch nor Dante could accomplish, namely, the healing of the schism between the Guelphs and the Ghibellines in Italy that had led the Pope to leave Rome and make of Avignon the Holy City. Catherine tried to reconcile the Pope and the Florentines first by letters and, when these failed, she went herself to talk things over with Gregory XI until he agreed to restore the papal seat to Rome if she would prepare the way by arranging a preliminary peace settlement. He came as far as Genoa to discuss her arrangements, holding conferences with her in the home of a noblewoman, Madonna Orietta Scotti, where she was visiting, and as a result of that interview he returned to Rome. Nor was Catherine's work finished when Gregory sat again in St. Peter's chair. He alienated friends and failed to win enemies to his side. With no money for an army and fretful by disposition, he had to rely on Catherine for next steps. So in 1378 she went to the Florentines, strife with whom had caused the breach in the beginning, and sued for their pardon and sympathy. While she was in Florence on this mission, Gregory died. Then tumult once more rent the Church and Catherine barely escaped with her life. Perhaps she did not care to escape for the "red rose of martyrdom" was still an allure to the pious.

Anyhow the new Pope, Urban VI, was accepted by the Guelphs, peace was signed, and the holy woman returned to her birthplace of Siena. However it seemed that even Urban could not prosper without her ambassadorial assistance and she was summoned to Rome where she "wore out her slender powers in restraining his impatient temper, quieting the revolt of the people at Rome, and trying to win for Urban the support of Europe." Catherine herself died in 1380 —the link between St. Francis and Savonarola; having the humanistic magnetism of the one with the great political genius of the other. Quarreling Italian aristocratic families composed their disputes under her guidance but, when some one in gratitude presented her with a castle, she turned it into a monastery. At their own solicitation usually, she gave counsel to kings, popes, cardinals, bishops, societies, political corporations and private individuals. She was the master spirit of a group of religious people who labored to reform individuals, the State and the Church. Among the elect her Prayers were classics. And between worldly missions in the interests of Christian progress, she wrote on religious doctrine using the vernacular which Dante employed. "In a language which is singularly poor in mystical works," her *Book of Divine Doctrine* stands with the *Divina Commedia* as one of the two supreme attempts to express the eternal in the symbolism of a day, to paint the union of the soul with the supra-sensible while still imprisoned in the flesh." Other critics rank her close to Petrarch as a fourteenth-century letter writer, "handling the purest Tuscan of the golden age of the Italian vernacular with spontaneous eloquence."

RELIGIOUS HISTORY-MAKING A JOINT ENTERPRISE

WOMEN's participation in the direction of a religious cult was nothing unusual in the case of Matilda or Catherine. From its early formative processes women had shared directly in the development of Christianity. Was not the Messiah accredited with Virgin Birth? Women friends took care of the Christ's needs as he went from place to place proselytising. They accompanied him to the very cross at Jerusalem where he died to save sinners. They waited by his side sorrowing and ready to administer the last rites. According to St. John he reappeared first to Mary of Magdala, a point which may have made some appeal to the forceful ladies of the upper classes who were among the earliest converts Paul secured in Macedonia. Everywhere women joined the first congregations. At Corinth where Paul made enemies of the divine-image-makers by his attack on their lucrative craft, the talented Priscilla, wife of the tent-maker from Pontus, Aquila, a Jew, joined her husband on a tour with Paul to Ephesus and other cities, propagandising. When the life of Paul was menaced from time to time, they acted as a bodyguard. And then when the cult spread to Rome, women fairly leaped to its support and defense, counting no sacrifice too great to demonstrate their loyalty.

In the East the movement acquired rich noblewomen as patrons in its primal stages. In Rome it grew from underground channels into the light of day, but women helped to lift it from the underworld. "Pedlars, weavers, shoemakers, merchants, sailors, slaves as they met in the marketplace or on lonely highway, exchanged for a moment their blissful tokens all for love of the Good Shepherd — that radiant figure depicted so often on the walls of the Catacombs — aureoled with eternal youth; smiling, serene, sublime; with a lamb on His shoulder." After their eunuchs or their maids converted them, grand ladies slipped from their households to commune with the followers of Christ, bringing husbands and sons eventually into line.

At this distance the communion of noblewomen with humble Christians in the Roman catacombs seems rather weird and unreal. But in fact there was a fine tradition about secret burials underground and oracles had long spoken from caves. The worshippers of Mithra held their rites in subterranean quarters and such performances had a sacred quality through inheritance; so much so that the Church fathers explained the similarity as the work of the devil trying to make Mithraism attractive. Of course the darkness had no terrors to the poor of Rome accustomed to living in the tenements and there were even precedents for the mingling of high and low at religious assemblies while the practice was prepared for philosophically by attacks on slavery in Hellenic and Roman literature. But the satisfaction which chattel servants hoped to glean from the new cult in the way of redemption and joy in the next world, their owners now hoped to derive from pitying the poor and having their sins forgiven for so doing. If few of the Christian leaders took without strong reservations the side of the slaves in their preachments, St. Jerome despising them fully as much as any pagan before him and the very Christ himself stopping as short as Abraham Lincoln of a positive condemnation of the system, the ideal of ultimate brotherhood in another world did something for immediate gentleness and mercy. The effects are discernible not only in multiplying private deeds of kindness but also in Roman law.

And as Christianity began to reach the upper air, an emperor's mother became curious. Thus Julia Mamæa invited Origen to tell her about the new faith. It is her influence behind the reluctance of Alexander Severus to persecute the Christians; he kept a statue of Christ in his palace among his Roman gods and he was deeply impressed by the Messiah's Golden Rule. Of ethereal cast was Cecelia, the Christian saint of music, who spread the new religion in its ascetic form among the nobility during the same reign and was so effective in her campaign that Severus felt compelled to remove her and her converts, including her husband, from the scene, whatever the Golden Rule might offer in objection, because he had ordered no proselytising. His wife and daughter were the very first persons whom Diocletian commanded to offer sacrifices to the Roman gods, when he launched his persecution of the Christians, owing to reports in the regal whispering gallery that they had inclinations in that direction, or sympathies at all events. Instead of choosing martyrdom, if they were really inclined to be Christians, these women complied with the imperial order and therewith, in the opinion of Tillemont, struck a great blow at the sect.

Seven women, seventy years of age and unmarried, noted for their public benefactions, however, paid the full price of their conviction and are remembered as the Seven Martyrs of Ancyra. Macrina, the grandmother of Basil and Gregory, great Church Fathers, had to flee for safety leaving her property to be confiscated. And as the persecution swept on, the way women stood torture of every sort for their faith astounded the beholders. Their very persecutors were unable to understand the sublime fidelity of the sex to the new belief. Sometimes girls rebuked male companions for a comparative weakness. When torture proved futile among her young friends, Dionysia was put to the sword without further delay by bored enforcers of paganism. Petronilla, who, legend said, was the daughter of St. Peter and was healed by him of the palsy after he had brought it on her to display his magic, died a virgin rather than marry Flaccus against her will. In fact it seemed that marriage was to innumerable women in itself a supreme anguish beside which all else was as naught. They were eager for a union with Christ and bliss in the hereafter but they would not consider marriage with anyone short of a god if they had to die for their obstinacy.

The tutelary saint of nuns and virgins is St. Catherine of Alexandria represented in plastic art with the wheel on which she was broken during the persecutions in the reign of Maximus after she had tried to convert him. Young, beautiful, and intellectual, the daughter of a king named Konetus, Catherine tried to mend the minds and manners of pagan scholars, rulers, and men-at-arms. Scourged and flung into prison, she made Christians of her guards. Even the empress, sent to restore Catherine to reason, was profoundly moved by her appeals. But her blood was the wages of her eloquence. When the wheel had done its worst, she was beheaded. Preachers, poets, mechanics, and scholars as well as nuns worshipped at the shrine of St. Catherine, monasteries were erected to her memory, and the university of Paris honored her by taking her name.

Perpetua, seer of visions, and Saturus were the professed authors of martyr biographies completed for publication by an unknown third person, after the woman collaborator had paid the penalty of disobedience to the State. From the incitements of martyrdom, prayers arose over the dead, adding a fresh compensatory rite to a rapidly evolving clericalism and symbolism. The truth is that interest in the martyrs and in the ideology of martyrdom superseded concern for civic problems and worldly needs. A sense of the prodigious got in the way of everything else. Or was this concern with martyrdom only the opposite side of the shield from the sadism which produced it ? Its antithesis ?

Nine official persecutions there were by the rulers of Rome, marked by every conceivable form of torture and horror including the throwing of men, women and children to wild beasts to be torn limb from limb in the arena, while glad Romans watched them devoured. Virgins, staring lions in the face, were careful only to arrange their robes over their limbs that they might not be exposed to the gaze of the jungle men who watched their torture from the galleries. Accused of burning Rome himself and needing an alibi, Nero first thought of selecting the Jews for a pogrom but his mistress, Poppæa, on that occasion shifted his animus to the Christians and on a great holiday multitudes of the worshippers at the new shrine were destroyed in a gorgeous spectacle. Nevertheless persecution could not eradicate the sect. It merely made its worship more ecstatic. The faith of the Christians crept in, swept over the people, bore them along on its current by its promise of life more abundant, and undermined the harsh police system of the imperial city itself.

The story of woman's participation in the spread of the Christian faith has many parallels with the history of Buddhism in India — precursor of Christianity. For the same reason that the lower castes of men rallied to Buddha, women rushed to his side. His leadership was anti-Brahmanistic. Primitive India had been subjected to the rule of the conquering aliens whose militaristic régime demanded an idealisation, a deification, of the masters and a corresponding disciplining of the subjects, particularly of women. Mothers had ceased to sing pæans to maternity and virgins no longer offered counsel to kings. The Brahmans, as the new rulers, concentrated on their own souls' beauty and excellence and created their own heaven for themselves. They were especially afraid of granting philosophic equality to the sexes lest women question arms and the man. Consequently the attacks made by Gautama Buddha on all Brahmanic presumptions to soulfulness and worldly superiority were a welcome release to Indian women at large as well as to men of the oppressed orders.

Regarding him as their equal liberator, women joined the masses in the Buddha's intellectual war on the classes of India. The aunt who had reared him and the wife whom he married, then deserted for the "Way," became ardent apostles. During the period of his wandering, young girls brought him food. "During his preaching, so stormy at times, when the gates of Bhadramkara were closed against him and when its inhabitants had promised the Brahmans not to yield to the call of him who desired to wrest them from their tyranny, it was a Brahmani who, braving all dangers and obstacles, was the first to disobey the open prohibition and to throw herself at the feet of Buddha and prevail on her countrywomen to follow her example. When he explained the system of ideas contained in the lotus of the good law, the six thousand women whom he had permitted to embrace the same ascetic life as himself were present." Thus nearly five centuries before the Sermon on the Mount, with its denial of castes and ambitions, a similar doctrine — defeatist in political essence — was set forth by the Buddha: "Those who abandon riches, relatives and the pleasures of the world, and submit themselves to harsh discipline in order to gain for themselves the joys of heaven, become in reality riveted to a stronger chain. Some strive for this world, others for the world beyond. Meanwhile all men, disappointed in their hopes, their designs ending in failure, fall into evil because they seek the good." In other words those that sought life, Brahman style, were to lose it. But not by an armed rebellion. Only by the indifference of their subjects to the world of physical affairs — among which Buddha named, specifically, concern with such a miserable thing as a soul.

That women could "come back" as they did within the new religion shows how persistent had been their religious consciousness throughout the Brahmanic era. Having in the *Upanishads* discussed the knowledge of the absolute with the greatest of Indian minds, women could carry intellectual habits into the militarist régime. And even in that cult of force which required caste aloofness, among the very Brahmans themselves forbidden to marry non-believers, grew up the denial of its own caste presumptions.

Though Buddhism vanished from India it drew large areas of China into its fold and thence was borne to Japan — by women. In the latter country imperial princesses remained its chief priestesses until the early years of the reign of the Emperor Meiji in the nineteenth century when Princes or Peers were assigned that office and given a host of clerical assistants. Japanese history often refers to the Empress Suiko who ordered five thousand *bonzes* (priests) to foregather at the Nara Todaiji and hearken as she read to them from the sacred Buddhist books. She was instrumental in carrying forward the plans for the giant Buddha sculpture at Nara. Her Buddhistic religious impulse led her to insist upon a law forbidding the killing of any living thing, under severe penalties for infraction.

Though far removed from Buddhism in spirit and in forms, Judaism was in many respects a religion of the household with the mother serving as a sort of high priestess. The older Prophets of that faith were sympathetic with outcast women as Jesus was with Mary Magdalene. For instance Ezra related in a sensitive way the story of Ruth, the Moabite wife of Boas, who suffered hardships by reason of proscriptions against intermarriage. Malachi appreciated such difficulties also and throughout the traditions and sacred lore of the Jews ran the consciousness of women, of their matriarchal power, of discriminations against them imposed by law, of marital problems, and the issue of sex. Stimulated or perpetuated by the transfusion of ideas from neighboring sources, the Jewish tradition molded the attitude of the Savior, if his apostle Paul tried to uphold a puritan view of sex.

From the Jews and the Christians, Mohammed borrowed many elements for the making of the last world religion. Since the Jews could have a Messiah to lead them out of the wilderness, why could not the poor people of his race find a leader in their misery, Mohammed asked himself? And he found his answer not in Arab prophecy but in his personal imagination, aspiration, and holy wars.

Perhaps such a warlike religion as Mohammedanism, Christianity's chief foe in the Middle Ages, would seem unsuitable for feminine coöperation, at least in the eyes of a follower of the Buddha or of Jesus. Nevertheless Islamism was unmistakably assisted by the daring, faith, and financial backing of a woman, Khadija, during the life of the Prophet, and after his death widows and heirs kept the movement going. Khadija was a rich Koreishite merchant, member of the upper class of Mecca, who took to her heart Mohammed when he was a poor ex-shepherd youth in her service, engaged in driving bargains for her in Syria whither he journeyed with her caravan. He drove good bargains and his colorful report of returns made him doubly attractive in her eyes no doubt. Having enlarged her patrimony in such ways, Khadija needed no dower for a wedding. She therefore drugged her father for the duration of the ceremony which united her to Mohammed and when that was over, she was her own mistress in every way.

Her class had been for some time buying poets and philosophers to make life more entertaining and so it was a fairly natural thing for Khadija to provide herself with an interesting egotist. For them both it proved a diverting existence. As they shaped the Moslem gospel, it spread in the households of their friends until it was mature enough for world diffusion. Since Mohammed was illiterate and despised as low caste by her "set," Khadija placed her own education and experience at his service, bestowed wealth upon him, drew other members of her important family into his sphere of influence, retreated with him to the caves on some of his meditative excursions, and, after helping to convince him of his divinity, enabled him to employ it for empire. During their long married companionship, Mohammed was devoted to Khadija as she to him. In those years when he pondered on the Day of Judgment and Hell Fire, of which he heard in Syria, he genially admitted women to his Paradise.

Then after the death of Khadija, when Mohammed was fifty-four, he became polygamous and his "carelessly-compiled harem" not only affected his late religious effusions but embroiled the Moslem disciples in family rivalries and bloodshed. Unbelievers were threatened with hell fire after death or menaced with earthly murder prematurely. Widows and heirs took possession of the Church and Islamism continued to advance by the route of passion and piracy. The Prophet's final years and concepts are a strange medley of sex and worldly adventuring, leading Wells, in commenting on Mohammed, to remark that there is no fool like an old fool. Yet he remained the skillful organiser and diplomat which he had been in his commercial days and achieved the position of an Arab king consolidating loose tribes into a religious monarchy bent on imperialism by means of a holy war. Accordingly his widows and heirs had patterns already set for them in ruthless, emo-

tional aggression when they took up the mantle after he laid
it down. As in the Rome of family feuds, Islamic men and
women fought like tigers for the possession of the Caliphate.
Islamism was not a priestly faith; hence there was no third
party to hold them in abeyance. An ex-wife of the Prophet,
Ayesha, even in her old age led a battle-charge mounted on a
camel. And to this very hour the Moslem world is separated
into factions, each claiming to be the one true adherent of the
divine teacher. Hence the shepherd boy started more than
religious dissent when he left the desert with its traditional
liberties and laws for the field of cosmic speculation.

Nor must the Prophet's adaptation of Christianity to his own
moods be ignored. Some scholars think that his sensitiveness
to the superstitious nature of the worship of the Kaaba, a
magic black stone that provided the only unity for three hundred or so Arabian tribes, came from observing the scorn of
the Jews whom he encountered on his trading journeys to
Syria. He may also have seen and been impressed by the
Christian churches in Syria. That he knew much of the belief in the One novel God is indisputable for he speaks of
Jesus in the Koran. That he confines his attention to the rôle
of Jesus as the Son of Mary, the Mother, indicates that his
knowledge came from the Christian faction which adored the
woman more than Jehovah himself. She was venerated with
sex rites in Syria.

So it may be said that every holy man and prophet of old
had a retinue of devoted women supplying funds for the spread
of his gospel and encouraging particular interpretations of life
and destiny. The Christians then were no exception. Nestorians and Catholics were alike in that respect. From whatever angle these rich and capable followers surveyed the mysteries, they defended their positions with their resources and
attacked opponents with spirit. Fathers Ambrose, Jerome,

Chrysostom, and Augustine were never aloof from the necessity of courting women's approval for their doctrines. Thus while many ladies among the Roman nobility agreed with Chrysostom's criticisms of their luxurious habits and his analysis of the effect of their social manners, one Eudoxia turned her guns on the saint, while another spelling her name Eudocia gave all she possessed to the Church of the Resurrection he wanted to found.

Chrysostom, 347-407, has been repeatedly described as the "greatest pedagogue of his day and probably the greatest preacher of all time." On his scholarly career he was set by Anthusa, his young mother widowed at twenty, who belonged to a distinguished family and felt the responsibility for upholding its traditions. So she provided the best possible tutors for her son and watched his intellectual progress intently until the time came when he was to go out in the world where other women were to help shape his mind and his fortune.

The most famous of the women in his entourage was Olympias, born in 368, a young heiress orphan converted directly from paganism. Owing to her change of faith she had a long struggle to get possession of her inheritance but it came to her when she was thirty and, living frugally herself, she devoted it to the Church of Christ. Every visit of a bishop or other holy man was an occasion for her largesse and she was exceedingly popular. Indeed Gregory Nyssen dedicated to her a commentary on a portion of the Song of Solomon composed at her request. Sometimes her benefactions took the form of land and sometimes of coin. Her home was a famous shelter for monks and nuns who swarmed from all parts of Christendom to feed at her hand. Whereupon Chrysostom advised and warned her, managing to direct her gifts both locally and in the distant sectors of Christendom. While she was still no more than a prospective heiress, Nectarius had made her deaconess of the Church of Constantinople, consulting her in ecclesiastical problems and heeding her suggestions — a position she retained under Chrysostom, his successor. But the influence of the holy father over her funds aroused enmity for them both, leading to his expulsion from the bishopric, her own persecution, and the disbanding of the convent she had founded, when the resident nuns refused to commune with the new bishop Arsæius. During his exile Chrysostom wrote the long religious tracts and letter of praise and courage to Olympias, more famous with posterity than the lady who inspired them.

Another of Chrysostom's well-known deaconesses was Salvina, the daughter of a Moorish chief, brought to the court as a hostage by Theodosius. She was a Christian and when she married the emperor's nephew, she was placed in a post of strategic value giving access to funds. Consequently she was a great benefactor of churches and their clergy. Jerome heard about her when he was in Palestine and wrote in the hope that Salvina might be weaned from fellowship with Chrysostom to his own coterie; but she remained faithful to the end to her first love.

With other women Jerome was more successful. When persecution of the Christians started in Egypt, for example, Melania, a Spanish-Roman lady and granddaughter of an earlier Melania who had been persecuted for the faith, supported Jerome, Rufinus, and several other religious men in a retreat near Palestine. And later when Alaric's victory seemed assured, she left for her African estates with several prominent Christian workers in her train. The property in Gaul and Italy which Melania had inherited she gave away though she retained her lands in Sicily, Africa and Spain — a happy haven as the sack of Rome commenced. By the grandmother whose heiress she was, Melania had been reared in ascetic ideals and when she married, for her father's sake, she chose a man with similar inclinations whom his friends had hoped to make into a priest.   In time the two swore continence and, leaving their son in the care of a local prætor, they went for a sojourn among the monasteries of Thebaid before they finally separated — he to head a monastery and she a convent in 414 managed by Paula the Younger in Bethlehem, with her mother as her companion.   Photius says that in Constantinople Melania made a monk of Evagrius.   Family as well as friends she besought to take vows of chastity and divert their interests from secular affairs to the Church.   The holy fathers had won a hardy advocate indeed.   At Alexandria Melania had visited Cyril and discussed religious matters with him.   She knew Augustine. She accompanied Rufinus to Jerusalem and founded a convent in that city — afterwards returning with him to Rome in a crisis.   Her settlement at Bethlehem with the friends of Jerome healed the strife between the two religious camps and amicable greetings were exchanged. His correspondence shows Jerome exceedingly sensitive to power.

In the Pelagian controversy this group of learned women submitted a questionnaire to Augustine to ascertain his attitude toward points they felt were confused.   Naturally no holy man was going to admit that his light was dim on the issues, and Augustine explained everything including priestly vestments.

In the writing of complacent old Romans, such as the professors in the province of Aquitaine, no inkling was given, as we have said, either of the deathknell of empire or of paganism, at the very time when alien arms were battering down the Roman gates and men and women were overthrowing the Roman gods.   Thus it is not to the academicians that one turns to learn of the pilgrimages to the holy places, the debates and correspondence on practical and theological affairs, the family divisions that weaned young maidens from the university groves to radical religious affiliations. It is Apodemius, a young priest of the fifth century, who gives the clue to such developments. He was a friend of a rich widow belonging to one of the first families in the academic world celebrated for contributing a teacher of rhetoric to Rome and two or three to Bordeaux. The family, it was claimed, had descended from an ancient Druid line, which the Romans had fused with their State by identifying its Celtic god with Apollo. But two ladies within this proud group, Euchrotia and Procula, fell under the spell of Priscillian and became Christians. And when Hedibia, a rich widow, began writing to Jerome, a third apostasy from the Romanised Druid ancestors caused a sensation. Euchrotia and Procula found ecstatic satisfactions in the change of faith but Hedibia wanted rational novelty. So she inquired about the practical way to serve the Christian God and requested replies in elucidation of contradictions in the Gospels, such as the conflicting accounts of the Resurrection, together with explanations of some of St. Paul's less lucid passages.

The epistles which Apodemius carried to Jerome included the queries of other women besides Hedibia. Algasia, for example, presumably of the diocese of Cahors, wanted to know why John the Baptist sent his disciples to ask of the Christ: "Art thou He which should come?" when he had already called attention to Jesus as the "Lamb of God." And she submitted two other puzzles: "What is the meaning of the text, 'If any will come after me, let him deny himself?'" and "Who is the steward of unrighteousness commended by the Lord?" She is evidently troubled by the threat of barbarian triumph, if Ausonius is not, for she asks Jerome to interpret for her the lines in Saint Matthew: "Woe to them that are with child and to them that give suck in these days. . . Pray that your flight be not in the winter, nor on the Sabbath." Jerome soothes her with the answer that the coming of Antichrist is meant.

Into the dispute over theology which arose among Jerome, Anastasius, Rufinus, Origen and other religious leaders, another noblewoman, Marcella, plunged with zeal. Discussing with the Pope passages in the writings of Origen to which she objected, Marcella urged him to ban Anastasius and Origen both. Jerome gives her the palm for their excommunication: "Of the glorious victory Marcella was the origin." Two friends, who had gone on to Palestine, urged Marcella to come there with Jerome but she preferred to stay in Rome, notwithstanding the approach of Alaric. On her mother's death she took a tiny house with a friend, Principia, outside the city and gave the rest of her life to philanthropy, loving her neighbors as herself beyond the customary charitable practices of her race. Marcella witnessed the sack of Rome but Alaric spared her life and she was able in her will to gratify her sense of Christian proprieties by leaving all her property to the poor. Unhappily her correspondence has been lost; it might have contained valuable pictures of early Christian ideals and customs.

Marcella's friend, Paula, a second young widow, helped to give asceticism a bookish bent. She had plenty of wealth at her disposal when her husband, the senator Toxotius, died, leaving, among other properties, the town of Nicopolis, or Actium. He remained an irreconcilable pagan but Paula, a Christian, deciding against remarriage, radically altered her mode of living, freed her slaves, dedicated her riches to the Church, and devoted herself to its intellectual foundations. Paula was a descendant on her mother's side of the Scipios, the Gracchi, and the Pauli and on her father's it was said, of the half-legendary kings of Sparta and Mycenæ. And yet like the earlier pagan, Hipparchia, she turned from the traditions of caste and the manners of her set to don the coarse garb of puritan reformers and help them propagate their gospel. She opened her home to clerical visitors and ecclesiastical conferences; during the synod of 382 at Rome which followed the council at Constantinople, she entertained the bishops, Epiphanus of Salamis and Paulinus of Antioch.

But her fame now rests on the amount of literary work she managed to wrest from the Dalmatian monk, Jerome. Highly educated herself, she installed him in her home as instructor for a distinguished group of converts, tried to check his tendency to quarrel with everybody about everything, and succeeded at last in holding him to scholarly pursuits. The students were curious and insisted on knowing so many details about the new faith that he had to work to keep ahead of them. But that was not enough to satisfy Paula or her learned daughter Eustochium. So they sat down at the tables beside Jerome for a long and difficult labor in the production of the Latin version of the Bible, known as the Vulgate edition. Since this task called for familiarity with Hebrew, Paula acquired that tongue for the purpose. The two women also bought at great expense the manuscripts essential to the enterprise and, if Jerome manifested a disposition to falter at the labor involved, they were always at hand to spur him on. He submitted his translations for their criticisms and made the revisions they proposed with "touching humility."

Moreover Jerome was firm and honest in his acknowledgment of their invaluable coöperation, notwithstanding the objections of anti-feminists. In the preface to his Commentary on Sophonius, he wrote: "There are people, O Paula and Eustochium, who take offence at seeing your names at the beginning of my works. These people do not know that Olda prophesied when the men were mute; that while Barach was atremble, Deborah saved Israel; that Judith and Esther delivered from supreme peril the children of God. I pass over in silence Anna and Elizabeth and the other holy women of the Gospel, but humble stars when compared with the great luminary, Mary. Shall I speak now of the illustrious women among the heathen ? Does not Plato have Aspasia speak in his dialogues ? Does not Sappho hold the lyre at the same time as Alcæus and Pindar ? Did not Themista philosophise with the sages of Greece ? And the mother of the Gracchi, your Cornelia, and the daughter of Cato, wife of Brutus, before whom pale the austere virtue of the father and the courage of the husband — are they not the pride of the whole of Rome ? I shall add but one word more. Was it not women to whom our Lord first appeared after His resurrection ? Yes, men could then blush for not having sought what the women had found." Evidently the ancient Hebraic record had equipped the scholar for a worldly wisdom which many of his Roman flock lacked. On Paula's tomb near her convent in Bethlehem Jerome had an epitaph inscribed.

It was not solely for her literary labors that Paula was famous. Such an activist for the faith was she that she turned her young son, in tears, over to the local prætor as Melania had done in Gaul, and left a marriageable daughter in despair, in order to sail to the East with her intellectual child, Eustochium, who cared naught for nuptials, and sit at the feet of the hermits. There she wandered about for a while, visiting the holy places and the holy men. Finally she settled in Bethlehem where she founded a monastery for men and a convent for women, both to wear the same coarse dress and meet for the purposes of worship. Her own penance Paula carried to the extreme. Debts piled up as she gave her wealth to the cult and her children were left with the burdens her charity imposed. However this did not dampen the ardor of a granddaughter, also named Paula, who followed in her steps. Even her son married a Christian girl, Læta, whose mother was a friend of Jerome, though he did not give up his pagan faith. By such mixed marriages the newer religion was to be perpetuated even if motherhood, non-immaculate, seemed to the Christian saints an evil.

While he reports rather faithfully perhaps on his women colleagues, Jerome remembers to mention some of the male kin of the innumerable ladies who forsook the world and its goods for prayer, Bible study, meditation, and holy work. Occasionally husbands and sons joined the cult as eagerly as their women but that was by no means the rule. Whether the women's intuition was stronger or their courage weaker, the fact is that as the sack of Rome impended and while the Pope Damasus was officiating as Roman dictator, some of the noblest, richest and best educated Roman matrons, as if aware of political dissolution, organised a retreat on the Aventine, called the *Ecclesia Domestica,* or Church of the Household — a residential club in which some women lived all the time while others used it only for spiritual conferences. They were abetting the aristocratic withdrawal from worldly interests, regarded by Aurelius as a sign of the political and moral wreck of Rome, to find solace in self-perfective, that is emotional, creeds. Thus did Buddha before them, though without faith in charity like that of the Christ these women followed.

On the financial support of women the Church depended heavily for its expansion. Of course the natural outcome was the shaping of the rites, ceremonies, and the very organisation to some extent in accordance with feminine tastes. If woman therefore was pronounced the sinful symbol of sex, she had a direct hand in framing the ukase. Some women preferred to give their property outright to the clergy; others let it filter piecemeal in the purchase of regalia and decorations for the rites. The office of bishop of Rome and then of Pope was prized as a worldly possession no less than a spiritual opportunity and Roman women helped to emphasize the earthly character of the Holy See as well as its heavenly connotations. One little thing led to another in the quest for material support until monks went to the utmost lengths to gain the favor of the women of wealth — the pinnacle of their ambition being the chance of "riding in elegant apparel through the streets, and giving banquets of more than regal splendor." The pagan Prætextus, himself no mean popular idol, remarked to Pope Damasus that his office was a tempting one.

If wiles failed to win the hearts of the ladies, something more drastic might be tried, not excluding theft and murder. The emperor Valentinian I in fact had to issue an ultimatum. Transcribing from Jerome, Dill says that he "sternly prohibited monks and ecclesiastics from entering the houses of widows or orphan wards and made illegal both *donatio inter vivos* and testamentary bequests in favor of the Church. It may be doubted whether the law was strictly obeyed. The higher clergy generally seem to have lived in a very unevangelical worldly state and luxury. They often entertained at sumptuous feasts great magistrates and prefects. The clerical epicure, brought up in a hovel and fed on milk and black bread in his boyhood, develops an extraordinary delicacy of taste in his later years. He has the nicest judgment in fish and game, and the provinces are distinguished by their ability to satisfy his palate. [Remember our Methodist forebears and their chicken dinners with parishioners.] Holy Orders become the passport to social distinction and dangerous influence. The doors of great houses opened readily to the elegant priest whose toilet was managed by a skillful valet. The clerical profession, so far from imposing restraint, furnished facilities for intrigue. The priest was admitted to the intimacy of superstitious women of the world, which was pleasant and lucrative, but perilous to virtue [like that of Eastern Holy Men in Western situations !] . . . The passion for wealth invaded all ranks of the clergy. Many were engaged in amassing fortunes in trade. They will perform the most disgusting and menial offices for some heirless lady on her deathbed. . . If we believe St. Jerome, numbers of these clerical and monkish impostors became far richer than they could have been, if they had remained in the world. They go about asking for alms to be distributed to the poor, but secretly enrich themselves; making a parade of their bare feet, black cloaks, and long unkempt hair, they creep into houses and 'deceive silly women laden with sins' [shades of Mormonism !] Pretending to live in the greatest austerity, they spend their nights in secret feasting and sensuality."

So much for the men portrayed by Jerome. Now for the painting of numerous women. "On a not much higher level are those virgins of the Church, whose peculiar dress is their only title to the name which they disgrace, and who strut about the streets, nodding and leering. In many so-called Christian circles the gay, supple 'virgin' who would laugh at jests of doubtful freedom, and who had a relish for spiteful gossip, was much more popular than the 'rough and rustic' person whose religion was not a fraud. Many other sketches of female character have been left us by the pencil of St. Jerome — the sot who justifies her love of wine with a profane jest, the great lady puffed up by the honours of her house, and surrounded by a herd of sycophants, the great lady who passes through St. Peter's, attended by a crowd of eunuchs, doling out alms with equal parsimony and ostentation, and repulsing the unfortunate widow with blows."

Naturally the further women could be weaned from their family ambitions, the deeper into the religious movement they could be drawn. And when they arrived at asceticism, they often led the men of their families with them. While anchorites of both sexes were no novel phenomenon — in fact one of the oldest — the ambitions of senatorial houses and the aspirations of the nobles had run their course in Rome and, with the collapse of the acquisitive society, there seemed no alternative for large numbers of the upper classes other than a retreat to the religious asylums. After Alaric had sacked Rome and ruined many leading families, Demetrias, a young girl of the great Julian clan, yielded to the persuasion of Jerome and a devout mother and agreed to remain forever a virgin. Jerome was obsessed by the idea of perpetual virginity, partly from his acquaintance with the holy anchorites in cloisters along the Nile and possibly, in part, from his anxiety to preserve the purity of Roman blood. How else could one interpret his comment on the decision of Demetrias to the effect that her vow of chastity was a consolation for a Rome in ashes and his declaration that Italy threw off her mourning at the news while the most remote Roman villages were radiant at the tidings ?

When Buddha began to organise the Indian anchorites of both sexes for the spread of his faith, a protest was raised that he had come to destroy the family. A similar opposition to the Christian ascetic trend was voiced and a veritable hue and cry followed the fasting and premature death of the noblewoman Brasilla. However antagonism merely fanned fanaticism. On special solicitation, Ambrose wrote three books about virginity for his sister, the nun Marcellina, and some of his most important letters were addressed to her.

A throng of disciples believing that family and political obligations stood in the way of inner light or personal perfection followed Jerome at the end of the fourth century to erect convents at Bethlehem, in the Syrian and Egyptian deserts, to the islands of the Tuscan Sea and into the forests of Gaul. Women were especially besought to lead the perfectionist movement and they responded to the appeal, from various motives no doubt. The prevalent system of concubinage may have influenced the more sensitive but in certain cases both husband and wife took vows of chastity. Either despair at life as it was lived, or the sway of mysticism attracted some in that direction. Luxury and vice bringing their antidote in boredom or desire for a novelty, however extreme, carried others down the stream of tendency.

Another of the noblewomen thus recruited for the faith was Fabiola, an extremely rich divorcée who had left her husband on the ground that his vices were unendurable. She was less ascetic by nature however than Christian propriety required and so she married a second time to the horror of the sect. But she redeemed herself in its estimation by a public repentance, after the death of her second husband, coupled with the gift of her property to the Church. She was again received into holy communion and her benefactions extended to monasteries in various parts of Italy and the adjacent islands. In person she nursed in a hospital which became famous from Parthia to Britain. Though she visited Bethlehem, she refrained from participation in the heated theological dispute which her women friends were helping to keep alive. However there were many things in the Christian ritual that she wanted explained, perhaps with financial support in mind. On such details as the mystical meaning of the high priest's garb Jerome enlightened her. At the time of her death she was casting about for ways to spend her money and outlets for her energy. The Christians gave her a splendid burial.

It was apparently his unmarried sister, Macina, who made a monk of Basil, spoken of as the founder of Christian monasticism. Rich but studiously inclined through association with her grandmother and taught by her to look among the Christian writers for excellences no less than among the heathen poets, Macina became a devout disciple of Jesus. And when

Basil's university training and honors were complete, he was persuaded to take the vow of chastity as she had done, yielding during a particularly sensitive mood caused by the death of a beloved brother. Then Macina and Basil settled on opposite banks of the Iris River running through their family estate, each with a group of anchorites drawn from illustrious Roman families and aspiring to live the life of holiness. To another brother, Gregory of Nyssa, likewise a great theologian, Macina uttered on her deathbed such an impressive exordium on resurrection and immortality that he wrote it down and circulated it. This was an approval of the concept of purgatory in the interests of purification — still high Catholic doctrine.

Yet in part asceticism was compulsory. The foundation of retreats afforded places for the incarceration of enemies, real or imaginary, and women as well as men were often victimised by the powerful. In this manner Theodora, the daughter of the emperor Constantine VIII, in the eleventh century was confined by her jealous sister on a charge of conspiracy, until a political upheaval released her. Others became prisoners for life. An incorrigible child was regularly threatened with such isolation. Hence involuntary and listless servitude sometimes supplemented the voluntary and fervent devotion to the Christian Trinity.

Naturally many desperate people rushed to the church asylums for safety and succor in times of distress. Gregory of Tours, the historian of the Franks and called the Herodotus of the Barbarians, paints a lurid picture of such an invasion in the sixth century with its direful consequences. He said that the "combination of abject superstition with shameless license, of a desire to share in the privileges of religion with a readiness to defy all laws, human and divine," exceeded the ability to describe. Vice in one form was finding a substitute in another.

Nor could the Church control the situation entirely. If it

sheltered a refugee from the wrath of an overlord, it might have to face itself the vengeance designed for the refugee — in other words, cause "a Merovingian army to ravage the lands of the see and block the doors of the basilica." Not even a poor slave could be received in every case with assurance of clerical immunity from the anger of a master. Moreover, if a vassal proved to be of the same metal as the master or the lord from whom he had fled, he might "pollute the sacred precincts with bloodshed or scandalous excesses . . even offer insult to the bishop himself in the very sanctuary." Consequently holy men and women suffered a new sort of martyrdom from time to time in which arson and rape, murder and torture, confiscation and outlawry followed, as ineradicable companions, organisation and propaganda.

After the firm establishment of the Roman episcopacy, one might suppose women were working under Papal direction placidly. But that is hardly the case. There was a great trouble-maker for the Pope in the eighth century, the Empress Irene, widow of the feeble Leo IV, nominal Emperor of the East, who ruled in the name of her young son, Constantine VI, and wished to see the Eastern and Western churches united after their quarrels and their schism. In 787 she initiated a new church council which she summoned to historic Nicæa not only to declare the two branches again one but, what is more, to revive image worship, that great love of the mortal soul which the holy fathers had been trying to suppress. But the Pope was alarmed. He suspected that the real objective was Eastern domination of the West. Accordingly he declared that "Irene, being a woman, could not possibly be a Cæsar" and "flung off all dependence on the East." With Charlemagne as his ally he was now in a position to do so for the first time. Knowing the value of that great alliance, Irene herself, gossip said, had previously tried to marry Charlemagne. She had been unsuccessful, however. Her disappointed rage was so great that she was suspected of blinding her son to prevent his marriage with Charlemagne's daughter. Later the son was murdered when he attempted to get the reins into his own possession. Hence, if Irene was not Cæsar, for ten years she had her own way in a large measure, holding her throne through intrigues with bishops and courtiers, overriding military opposition, and appointing a favorite, Tarasius, as patriarch before the nemesis came. Then she was exiled to Lesbos where she was forced to spin for a livelihood, dying within one year of that harsh experiment. At that point it seemed that the Pope's easy contempt was justified. But was it in fact ? While Irene did not by her own will immediately revive image worship in the West, in the East she became a saint of the Church for the success of that movement. Moreover the people of the West took the matter into their own hands in time and insisted on worshipping images whether the Pope, who was a Cæsar, willed it or no. So Irene ultimately defeated Charlemagne in that respect for he and the Gallican church had been much opposed to image worship.

In 842 another woman, Theodora, widow of the emperor Theophilus and guardian of her infant son, Michael III, again called a church council which was presided over by the patriarch Methodius I. This council officially restored image worship for the East, removing the antagonistic clergy in order to execute the decree. Theodora was a better financier than her idolatrous predecessor. She defended her realm against the Bulgarians and steered the ship of State in her own course until the boy's uncle got possession of the helm and cloistered her in a monastery. However, a second saint was enrolled by the Church among the zealots who worked to exalt devotion to images.

Against the natural tendency in this direction, Paul had

struggled with all his power in the beginning of the Christian movement. Convinced of the divine character of Christ, he nevertheless felt that image worship would lead to degeneration. On the occasion of his first visit to Athens, he had stood aghast at the extent and character of idolatry and so he pleaded for the transfer of affections from graven images to the living God. In spite of his views, he could only stem the natural tide for a time, his strength being no greater than Canute's. Steadily the belief in outward signs and symbols settled down on the newest religion and not until another sort of Paul, named Martin Luther, visited in the fifteenth century the great center of material pomp, called Rome, was the sway of images again broken to some extent, and "opposition to idols" once more raised to an equal obsession.

For its "magical equipment" the Mohammedans despised the whole of Christendom. Able to suppress that anthropomorphic habit more successfully than the Christian leaders, Islam made the "barbarism" of the Christians one of its main excuses for its efforts to crush the West. In the same way Buddhism was at first free from material symbols, though it finally yielded to the natural man and woman and even became famous for those very images and accessories. Indeed Buddhism and Catholicism grew to be so much alike in this respect that in places they became scarcely distinguishable.

Unquestionably "social service" was a close second to martyrdom in popularising the Christian faith. Japanese Buddhists of today, analysing the respective appeals and values of the two religions, uniformly agree that the spirit of benevolence is the greatest asset of Christianity. Consequently the origin of that spirit is pertinent and revealing. In a work entitled *Military and Religious Life in the Middle Ages,* Paul Lacroix ascribes to women the initiation of charity as a fundamental practice of the Church. Not that charity itself was novel exactly but its Christian administration was peculiar. Sporadic philanthropy marked the earliest stages of the sect's advance and within little more than two centuries it reached such a stage that Helena, the wife of Constantius Chlorus and the mother of Constantine the Great, dedicated her entire fortune to poor relief. "Simple and modest, kind to the suffering and the needy, she tended and consoled the poor with maternal solicitude. . . She recalled the exiles, ransomed the captives, released from the mines the unfortunate men who had been condemned to labour underground, and obtained for them the means of living in open daylight, thus causing them to bless her name and that of her God. Her daughter Constance also devoted herself to works of charity; she was accompanied by a band of maidens whom she animated with her example. And this was in fact the first School of Sisters of Charity." In time the Pope was persuaded that deeds of mercy were as vital as rites and ceremonies — even more stabilising than political intrigue. They were an aspect of economics highly useful to the Vatican and a secret of religious authority which the Soviet Republic has well understood in its effort to separate deeds from faith.

The philanthropic zeal of one Christian woman, Adelaide of Italy, actually menaced public finances in the closing years of the tenth century. When she married the German ruler, Otto I, the Pope crowned her Empress immediately after her husband was crowned Emperor and she refused to play the second fiddle. Her superior education, particularly in Latin, tided Otto over many a crisis and her influence over her son, Otto II, was very great until she began to pour her resources into the coffers of the Church for buildings and charity to such an extent that he feared the State would be bankrupt. At that point a breach came in their affections.

EVANGELISATION AND STRANGE FRUITS

By organisation and theological exposition Christianity penetrated to the confines of the earth.   The Christian missionaries
who converted the "great, proud, voluptuous City of the Seven
Hills to the religion of Jesus" and laid the foundation for a
Church, able to dominate the incoming pagans from the North,
were emulated by a long succession of evangelists who moved
like Buddhist emissaries to the corners of the earth with the
gospel of a new religion.   And the species continues to move,
into the heart of China, the depths of Africa, or the jungles
of the American tropics with the tidings of Christian salvation.
When asked a few years ago just why he risked the perils and
faced the hardships of an Oriental campaign, a Christian missionary en route over the wide Pacific replied that he dared to
brave everything in the confidence that he possessed "the keys
to Life and Death" and so could open magic gates to those who
groaned in benighted sorrow.   Such were the skeleton successors to the tools which Peter, according to the Scriptures,
received from Christ and transmitted to the Pope.   They have
been borrowed by Christian sects of assorted molds, on fire
with zeal to tell those that still sit in darkness about the pearly
gates before which they will appear one day to find they need
these keys.

Nevertheless there were many sorts of missionaries in every
age.   There were the dogmatists, the superior-minded, con-
temptuous of native customs and mentality, the mercenary, the
artful and the artless, the learned and the ignorant.   That was
inevitable since the new religion was of democratic origin and
highly emotional in its temper.   Evangelisers outnumbered the
medical and social service workers and often quarreled so hard
among themselves over ways and means, if not theology, that

occasionally a strong people among whom they settled had to suppress the entire profession.   For a time Japan did that when the internecine bickering of Christian missionaries in her midst menaced the political stability of her State.   After they quieted down, Japan became one of the most liberal hosts to the Christians.

It was not only with the rulers of countries they invaded that Christian missionaries waged their contest for mastery over the mass mind.   With the scholars and schoolmen of the State their contention was perhaps more bitter on the whole.   Repeating the Master's dictum that "not many wise are called," Paul made light of the pedagogues' opposition in Rome but that did not end the calling of names and the contest for survival.   Not relishing a reinterpretation of Homer by a Christian Jerome, any more than a Confucianist enjoys the Christian redaction of the Chinese Master, the Roman emperor Julian tried to put more life into Hellenistic teaching.   At the same time he ousted the members of the faculty of the Roman schools who had turned Christian.   It had been an academic scandal when one of the richest and noblest students of the pagan professor Ausonius, of Bordeaux, became a Christian — an awful shock to the professor and a public sensation.   Besides it was rumored that his rich and noble wife, Therasia, was largely responsible for his transgression after her conversion by the monk of Nola, who had previously forsaken his high class and renounced his wealth for the revolutionary movement.   In time, however, the Christians got possession of the Roman schools and wherever the missionaries went beyond the Holy City they established new schools for Christian teaching.   The adoption of the religion by a king or feudal lord also meant the employment of missionaries as tutors in the palace or castle.

If women were not in the beginning the traveling envoys of the Christian Church to the Barbarians, they often formed the reception committee which invited, received and introduced the visiting mystics. Thus Bertha, the wife of Ethelbert, king of Kent, induced the monarch to give ear to the Roman emissaries and that audience brought about Ethelbert's baptism into the Christian faith. Bertha, already a Christian, was the daughter of Caribert, a French king. At their marriage, Ethelbert, though a "heathen," permitted Bertha to retain her religion and have a bishop of her own. As the opening of England to Rome resulted, Gregory wrote her a fine appreciation, comparing her with that "patron of the faithful," the empress Helena, canonised mother of Constantine the Great, who gave costly presents to churches, founded new ones, and made pilgrimages at the age of eighty during which she was supposed to have discovered the site of the Holy Sepulchre. Bertha was urged to be a true servant of the Church in England and this she was qualified to be, by reason of her education.

The time was to come when women would join the traveling missionaries and falter before no peril in their labors over the earth. "I have given you sisters," said the Pope Paul III to Ignatius Loyola, founder of the Jesuits, as he sanctioned the Ursuline nuns organised by Angela Merici. During the first hundred years of its existence the Ursuline order established more than three hundred schools in France and its pupils spread out over the globe, teaching. In the New World they suffered molestations not only from the savage natives but later from other Christian sects and in no less a cultured center than New England where their convent at Charlestown, Massachusetts, was burned in 1836. Philadelphia wrecked their institution in 1850 during the Know-Nothing riots but the original American foundation at New Orleans lived on from 1726 through the ravages of civil war and the hostility of Protestants.

Often in lands to which the Christian ideals were borne, strange by-products appeared. For instance when monks took to Ireland the idea of asceticism, natives decorated it with their own romantic imagination. They accepted monasticism as offering a realistic solution to the problem of starvation in times of agricultural distress and the problem of protection during wars so frequent in the island.

SEX IN THE MYSTERIES

PARTLY because it was at first so simple a religion — so plain that "the wayfaring man though a fool could not err therein" — did Christianity rise and thrive. Cultured enemies said it had no philosophy behind it at all; that it was an intellectual let-down. Certainly it represented a lesion in the great dialectic systems of reasoning developed for other ends. It had none of the rationalisation of Ionian speculation or Athenian morality and with its priestcraft and symbolic rites it seemed to be more of an anachronism than a sign of development, critics insisted. And however earnestly the evangelists tried to adorn it with Hellenic flourishes in their chagrin at the contempt of scholars, it remained a simple faith for the mass of its adherents. The theologians mingled the Proverbs of the Semites with the poems of Pindar, the natural speculation of Heraclitus, Thales and Anaxagoras, the legends of the Odyssey, and carried Plato back to Moses. But this was a diversion of their own rather than the system of beliefs closely related to the functioning of everyday life which the people took to themselves.

Nor with all its militancy could the Church control the reaction of its baptised multitudes to the mysteries. There were things to which human nature was vulnerable; things which troubled it, perplexed it, charmed it, comforted and enraptured it; things which no amount of pressure from above could eliminate or modify to an appreciable degree through decretals and administration. To cite a particular, the Church-State was almost helpless in the presence of Sex.

Sex had been the foundation, or a prime element, of nearly every preceding type of religion. And sex was prone to reconquer territory alienated by scientific curiosity. Astronomy and physics, as distinct from astrology and metaphysics, had no interest for the Church Fathers who classed them as heresies — an attitude continuing for centuries to narrow the field of religion to the age-old sex obsession. Deeds of mercy no doubt multiplied. Certainly a "cause" was provided for which the Stoics had searched in vain, namely a treasure in Heaven awaiting the religious which "neither rust can corrupt nor thieves break through and steal." For the Roman weary of thinking to no purpose or inaccessible to the complacent rationalisation of caste, Christianity offered a reason for existence and an exciting goal for effort. But most of all the Christian converts seemed to want ecstasy.

Several times before, ecstatic religions had appeared to rejuvenate the spirit of man. In his study of religion *From Orpheus to Paul,* Dr. Macchioro argues that Paul may have been a Dionysian initiate precedent to becoming a Christian; that in any case he drew his spiritual nutriment from that mystical faith. To Paul, he thinks, Christ was a new sacrifice of the Dionysian order — the spotless lamb — and the discovery of Orphic symbols in the Christian catacombs lends countenance to this thesis. Unmistakably the miracles and magic of archaic cults were clung to with fidelity, the Scriptures fortifying custom. The altar and incense, the ancient symbols of blood and sacrifice, remained such essential parts of the Christian rites that when the clash came with Islamism, it was over these major aspects that the battle raged. For their symbol the Knights Templars took the Old Testament "Lamb" and "washed in the blood of the lamb" became the testimony of

Christian purification throughout the reaches of the faith. In its closing years Rome had forbidden the actual sacrifice of animals in religious ceremonies but that did not prevent a sublimation into symbols or the relapse of the worshipping masses into the conventional view of their living reality.

Thus while the richer converts may have derived satisfaction from the idea that, when the sheep and the goats were separated in heaven at the Day of Judgment, through their acts of loving-kindness to the poor they would continue to be patricians rewarded for their bounty, at the same time they were delighted to see the new priests wear the vestments of the old Roman magistrates — the dalmatic, chasuble, stole and maniple — as if they were ruling an empire of benevolent aristocrats headed toward Paradise.

As years abundantly proved, the pulsing heart of the new religion was still the heart of the old; in other words, of the oldest. Of religious origins, T. W. Rhys Davids says: "A much more solid basis [than ancestor worship] seems to support the argument that as the oldest recorded gods are goddesses, and as man makes God in his own image, the original deities must have arisen at a time when women were the leaders, as in other things, so also in theology. They were born of women, for it was woman who conceived them. And we must make room in our theory at least as much for the awe inspired by Mother Earth, and by the mysteries of the stars, as for the worship of ancestors. We have to explain how it was that the oldest divinities were almost, if not quite, exclusively feminine. We have to explain why the moon was worshipped before the sun and certain stars before either, and the Mother Earth before them all."

Certainly Hera was older than Zeus. Cecrops was apparently the first to call Zeus the All Highest.

In the quest for origins we are taken far afield. Buddha

even loses his maleness as he moves from land to land and yet sometimes the sex of the god was vague. The Incas of Peru, high in the cultural scale, revered and sang hymns to a deity they called Uiracocha, "Creator and Vivifier." One of these Radin reproduces:

> O Uiracocha, lord of the universe,
> Whether thou art male,
> Whether thou art female,
> Lord of reproduction
> Whatsoever thou may be. . .

Believing that the matriarchal or patriarchal forms of early societies were "matters of local accident or incident," Brinton thinks that the sex of the reigning deity was largely a question of the interplay of language and religion. "Those languages," he writes, "which have grammatic gender almost necessarily divide their deities according to sex; those in which the passive voice is absent or feebly developed will be led to associate with their deities higher conceptions of activity than where the passive is a favorite form; those which have no substantive verb cannot express God as pure being, but must associate with Him either position, action, or suffering." Among the Algonquins, as an illustration of the working of this principle, there was no grammatical sex distinction but there was a distinction between animate and inanimate objects so that fetishes, as we should call them, were worshipped as warm realities. Carried down through the ages the same habit enables the cross and the beads and other objects to assume the warmth of living things. In his Hibbert Lectures, Professor Sayce states that the Sumerian tongue of ancient Babylonia was without gender and that the local gods were first endowed with sex when they were adopted by the Semites. A similar confusion seems to mark the rhapsodies of Rama Krishna and other Indian mystics.

In the face of every proscription and every insistence that

woman was a synonym for Sin, Virgin Worship triumphed in the minds of Christian men and furnished them with emotional loyalty, while the Crucifix worked a similar magic for the women.

More frankly the Hindus gave expression to the sources of their spiritual inspiration. Dealing with the holy man, Rama Krishna, one of India's great saints, Mukerji shows how he pushed day and night toward the ultimate mystery, his mother trying to rescue him from this "god madness" by marrying him to a nice young girl, just as the parents of Buddha did — only to find that Rama Krishna linked her with him in a more intense search for the solution of the riddle of the universe. Placing his bride in a tower which was made as pleasant for her as any ivory tower could be made, the holy husband said: "You will find everything there that you will need. Go, and meditate and pray to God to give me an illumination. Why should you do it ? — because it takes two women to make a man holy — his mother and his wife. My mother has brought me thus far; now it is your task to be my other mother, not my wife, and to take me across the river of delusion to the House of Heaven." And the young wife accepted the mission.

Describing his spiritual experience to an interlocutor, Rama Krishna said: "I never studied profound books, but I have heard scholars discuss them. Having heard — and gathering what rang true for my own needs — I made a garland of them and put them around my neck. Then I flung every inch of it at the feet of God saying, *'Mother,* take all your erudite tomes and laws. All I want is love of Thee !'" But his inquisitors pressed for an answer to what seemed to them contradictions in his craving for Heaven, or *Samadhi,* Oneness with the beloved, saying to him: "Will you please resolve what seems to us a contradiction ? People say that you have attained Identity: you are He. Yet you go about giving all the credit to the

Divine Mother. You never say 'I'; you speak of God, Mother, She, Thou. If you are 'I am He,' why do you call God 'Thou' ?" Then the Master answered: "That is the ultimate matter of conduct. I have seen Him and embraced Him. I was infinite existence, Absolute Intelligence, and Bliss. But I could not stay in that unconditional state and yet be here in the conditioned. There, there is no limit; each and all are one infinite existence, Unconditioned, Indescribable. You cannot use words about It. No matter what you say becomes finite. Naturally you say 'Thou, She, Mother.' " . . .

Now the god that Rama Krishna worshipped was Kali, "the symbol of Time and Eternity, of Death and Immortality. . . She is the Mother of the Universe as well as its destroyer. Out of Her all things come, and into Her all return. Her image, which is that of a dancer, is hewn out of black marble, for Time is invisible; it has no color. And yet because we experience ceaselessly the succession of Time's moments the symbol of Time lies in the art of dancing which is a succession of movements. Moments of time are but movements of men. When man sees with his eyes he beholds only space, but when he dances he experiences Time. Hence Kali, the symbol of our experience of Time, must needs be an image of the dance. And she must also wear a garland of human heads around her neck, for those are the epochs of man's life-history that time wipes out of existence. Besides these weird ornaments she has four hands which are emblems of the three features of time: the past, the present, and the future. The first two hands, holding a sword and a human head each, mean: that man, the latest embodiment of human destiny, is being wiped out by death. Her other two hands are raised to indicate hope (the future) and memory (the past). Such is Kali."

" 'I reign, I command,' exclaimed Indrāni, wife of Indra, in a hymn of striking lyrical beauty, attributed to the goddess herself. 'My voice inspires terror. I am the victorious one: may my husband recognise my strength. O Devas ! it is I who made the sacrifice from which the great and glorious Indra received all his strength.' "

Master of Man that she is, of Time and Eternity, Kali the Mother had one rival whom she could not conquer — namely, the god of renunciation. Ascetics alone could hold their own against the woman's culture. However, associated with that mother mastery, was compassion as an equally essential quality of motherhood. Hence another Holy Man, Turyananda, explains the twofold magnetism of woman worship: "Men and women nowadays are in a great hurry. Hence they will take short-cuts to the Infinite. In Kali Yuga, this age, the only thing they have to do is to go on wanting the Lord secretly. . . He is like the mother-cat who cannot resist the crying call of her kitten very long. Look at Rama Krishna. He found the Mother by simply crying and pleading with her. Do so yourself and she will at once take down the mask of the sun from Her Face, and reveal to you Her Face of Compassion that is within you. Oh! it is so easy to find God in our own time! Look, my child, the Sun is setting. It is time to commune with Her. Come into my dwelling and meditate with me. Hari Om, Hari Om."

What Rama Krishna through prayer learned directly about life and death from the lips of the mother goddess, Rama Mohn Roy acquired through strenuous study and reasoning. The one holy man simply lived in accordance with the idea of unity and brotherhood; the other gave scholarly expression to its principles. And the same thing happened in the divisions of Christian experience. Mlle. Clarisse Bader writing on this theme maintains that, with all the warlike symbolism, the Indians were unable to discard the sense of the creative power which woman typified.

Apparently, at one time, Buddha would have liked to disown the women if his aunt, Gautami, and his female cohorts had permitted. Professor Luzzatti reproduces a charming Dialogue in which the quandary was presented, Professor Pavolini, Sanscrit savant, being his authority. Buddha's most beloved disciple inquires:

"How, O Blessed One, must we behave toward women ?
You must avoid looking at them, O Ananda.
And if, notwithstanding our endeavor, we look at them, what must we do ?
You must not speak to them, O Ananda.
And if we spoke to each other, O Master ?
Then, O Ananda, you must watch yourselves."

To this revelation of the male sex, the Master adds his lore of all sex: "If, O Ananda, entrance into the order and the law had not been granted to women, the life of sanctity, O Ananda, would have lasted for a long time; for a thousand years the doctrine would have preserved its purity. Now that access has been permitted to women, not for long will the life of sanctity last, and only for five centuries will the doctrine remain pure."

In Christendom as elsewhere, the eternal issue worked vexation of spirit. Before the priests and people at large took the settlement into their own hands, there were fierce debates among the Church Fathers over the part woman was to play in the new religion. The Ebionites, Encratites, Montanists, and Epiphanes were all aroused over the question and each spiritual director wrote voluminously on the subject. Had they been as familiar as we are with anthropology and human history, their distress might have been relieved. But in the circumstances the Old Testament — "that arid nightmare of desert sorrows" — freighted with terror of an over-supply of girls, as we see in the Mosaic law and in other parts of the

Scriptures, got in the way of understanding. Said Tertullian, Carthage bred, scornful of Greek learning but steadfast in his devotion to the Hebrew text which unhappily he read selectively: "The sentence of God on this sex of yours [referring to women] lives in this age. You are the devil's gateway. You destroy God's image, Man." The great matriarchs of the Old Testament were thus overlooked in order to give the feebler Adam his day in court. But it was out of his own experience that St. Augustine drew the fire which condemned sexual desire as a hellish possession and the lure of women as man's major enemy.

Christ had not viewed life in that fashion nor with all the seclusion of Athenian wives had sex antagonism gone that far in Greece. The Greeks had made provision for women's participation in the holy days and festivals; State archives were kept in the agora within the metroön, a temple dedicated to the Mother of the Gods; the hearth of Hestia, "symbol of State dependence on the family," close by, was sacred to male philosophers; the wife of the second archon who had charge over religious affairs was given in a symbolic marriage to Dionysus and she participated in the ceremony for the honoring of the dead, known as the Anthesteria, precursor of the Roman Saturnalia and the early Christian Christmas; the third archon had to perform the sacrifices to Artemis Agrotera to whom every girl of ten was dedicated; stewards were required to raise the funds for the endowment of Athena directly; and indirectly the Greek men were exceedingly busy providing space in their religious life for women who in their minds were not the gateway to the devil — but to the gods. Herodes Atticus of the second century was wont to offer one hundred oxen on a single day as a sacrifice to the Virgin Goddess, mother of all the pagan gods.

Of the Egyptian cults which not only ruled the land watered

by the Nile but penetrated the heart of Athens and later affected the city by the Tiber and the Christian religion, the Mother of God was the heart. Isis was the Madonna with Child. In her arms she held the infant Horus, fathered by Osiris, and the babe grew up to be ruler of Egypt. Osiris, Isis, and Horus were thus a clear Trinity, and the idea of Immortality was its adjunct. While the Egyptian priests threw their support to male successions, they could not overcome the general belief that imperial divinity came through the queen by whose authority the male ruled. When the Semites came into contact with Egypt, they refused to succumb to this form of theism or take a deep interest in a life after death. Nor were the Persians overcome by the creeds of the Nile valley. The Jews clung to Jehovah whom their Prophets had set above them and the Persians to the Sun God. But the Egyptians were always intrigued by the desire for immortality and they saw no solution short of the miracle of sex.

The cult of Isis was a priestcraft with celibates, tonsure and a uniform, holy water and prayers. It had a sway of untold centuries though in modified forms; Hellenic ecstasy utilised it for the Eleusinian mysteries, Delphi for its oracles, and the sophisticated philosophers for their cosmologies. Ptolemy adopted it for political ends; it arrived in the homes of Roman grandees through returning diplomats, merchants, and slaves until the very emperors were given the tonsure, proud to build and adorn temples to Isis and walk in her parades. One could recognise in Apollo, Dionysus and Demeter — Osiris, Isis, and Horus; and in Græco-Roman society the Trinity survived with the worship of Serapis, a substitute for Osiris, and her attendant gods. Even an intermediary, precursor of the Pope, was present to conduct souls to heaven, Hermes and Anubis acting as magic go-betweens. Rituals and disciplines were the media set up for the successful accomplishment of this mission.

Egypt thus stimulated Greece and Greece shot back to the land of its origin rays from her own Orphic and Pythagorean cults. To the Romans coming into close relations with Egypt, this final cult was magnetic. Also into the remoter East percolated the infusions of the religious movement, dividing the Semitic race into partisans, influencing Christianity.

From time to time in history a new religious expression was demanded at Rome by jaded appetites, by the exigencies of social control, or by the criticism of reformers. For long stretches, emotion claimed the right of way and fanaticism burned itself out with orgies, sexual and evangelistic; only religious frenzy could satisfy the hunger for an answer to the riddle of the universe or provide food for exhausted nerves. Even though the theory of Good and Evil grew in influence, it embodied itself in divine personifications. Thus Lucius dreams of Isis as the cleanser of the human heart, its comforter, its guarantee of life everlasting. She was addressed by penitents at her altar as "Thou who art all." Freedwomen and mistresses of the penmen in the golden age of Augustus were priestesses and the worshippers at her shrine, while the multitude clamored so hard for her recognition as early as 42 B.C. that the triumvirs had to give heed and erect a temple in her honor. Her guardianship of childbirth made particular appeal to women while men revelled in the adoration of maternity and enjoyed the great ceremonies of the death and resurrection of her infant. Grumble as they might at the excesses of the men and the adherence of the women to Eastern cults, the old Romans never succeeded in reducing to any appreciable extent their popularity. Vergil came under the Orphic spell. Juvenal raved. Orgiastic cults grew in favor as materialism manifested its inability to do more than exploit humanity.

Yet Isis had her ups and downs. There were scandals in the temples with murders and plots against the State. Punishment was administered. Regulation was attempted. Emperors introduced rival gods; thus Nero would honor none but a Syrian goddess. No less a conscious patron of letters and prudent administrator of finances than Vespasian maintained a solitary vigil in the temple of Serapis and felt himself rewarded with the gift of divine healing. Domitian in the midst of civil war donned the sacred robes of the priests surrounding the altar of Isis and thus made good his escape from the Vitellians; though her temple was destroyed in the upheaval he rebuilt a far more splendid one in the Campus Martius when the trouble had subsided. Hadrian worshipped the Egyptian gods in a private temple at his villa. Commodus carried the divine child in his own arms as he walked tonsured in a religious procession. Claudius had banned Jewish and Druidic rituals but had encouraged the Hellenisation and tolerated the Egyptianisation of Rome. It did no good for satirists to scoff at the cult of the dog and the cat. The world would have its way, for the very philosophers were impelled to sublimate their sense of the mystery of life, symbolised by the gods, into cosmic systems while the masses delighted in the frank gratification of their feelings.

Religion thus proved to be the Alpha and the Omega of emotionalism while it colored most of the efforts at transcendentalism. Whether woman fascinated or repelled man, she was the one eternal principle. Even when men tried to extricate themselves from that sex dilemma, as Zeus bore Dionysus in his own thigh, as primitive men took to bed and received medical care when their wives were giving birth to children, or as celibates tried to forget, their very resentment induced a concentration upon the sex phenomenon which over-emphasised rather than relaxed its grip on the body and mind. The consciousness of awe, pain, gratitude, hunger, penitence, hope, love, and mercy could find no satisfactory outlet that did not involve sex.

At one time it seemed that Serapis might become a male god of wrath created out of fear of the elements, a Thor hurling his bolts of lightning and working vengeance on wilful mortals disobedient to his commands. And the father and mother gods ran a lively race for favor — he the principle of power, destructive and born to rule; she the principle of life, constructive and unifying. However, no such division could endure. The father god could not crowd out the mother because even man could not live without mercy. Eventually, according to the Christian faith, God was to send his own dearly-beloved son to earth to display his loving-kindness and he sent the Son in the arms of a Mother.

As Rome grew mature, Isis and Serapis found a more intellectual rival in Mithra, the Sun God — the source of all life, even female. While Mithraism was not so feministic as the cult of Isis, still it had priestesses at its altars. Aurelian's mother was one of these and, trained in its maxims, it was possible for the emperor to dramatise himself as a god — the Light of the World. In the more personified or vulgar brand of sun worship, a second coming of Mithra was promised, for which people were to prepare themselves diligently if they expected favors. The idea was discipline and, as a token of their desire for purification, devotees passed from one to another the sacred cup filled with sacrificial blood. It was thus a more active creed than Buddha devised; fate was to be affected by behaviorism. Yet it had its meditative aspect, representing an astral curiosity and in that relation was a colder proposition among its more philosophic adherents. One of its fine points was its tolerance; since Nature knows no such divisions as race and class, Mithraism took no cognizance of these. And yet even Mithraism which spread to the confines of the Roman

Empire, setting up altars in Britain, for the very reason that it was a religion, in spite of its naturalistic tendency, opened the way for orgiastic license, for crime and political machinations. Nature was non-moral, one could say; why then need mortals be moral ? Inevitably Mithra got confused with Isis and emperors and men. In the sections of the East where he was born, the Sun God was supposed to authorise monarchs and require prostrations and, being gracious enough in Rome to adopt Caligula and Nero as solar deities, the outcome, Dion relates, was an increasing theocratic development at the capital of the empire. The Cæsars did not risk in the West the assumption of the rôle of little brothers of the Sun and the Moon but they went part way. Commodus and his successors used the title "invictus" which was sacred to the Sun and in the third century rulers were calling themselves "eternal" as they continued to do when their political power had become but the shadow of a sun in the fifth century after Christ.

Before the light went out, the imperial crown had acquired the rays of the orb; Gallienus had sprinkled gold dust in his hair and gloried in a statue of himself dressed to symbolise the sun. Aurelian struck coins with the inscription "deo et domino nato" as he returned with the spoils of Palmyra and built a great temple to the Sun. Only two decades before Constantine announced himself a Christian convert, imperial princes had combined their resources to rebuild a temple of Mithra at Carnumtum on the Danube.

Desiring a kingly and military creed, the Roman adherents of Mithraism tried to hold Isis and Serapis at long range. Nevertheless in the "last stone records a votary of Mithra is found combining a devotion to Isis," while a strange goddess named Fortuna, who had earlier been associated with the Sun in the form of a golden image, was enshrined in the imperial bed-chamber.

With the Hebraic influx to Rome a more austere view prevailed. The Apostles, who brought the hope of ultimate salvation to a dying culture, were positive that guidance to the grand haven must be predominantly male. Dr. Elfriede Gottlieb, in *Die Frau im Frühen Christentum,* shows how masculinism subdued feminism but, in her concentration on the one, she misses the permanence of the other. A reviewer succinctly outlines her story of the circumstance: "These great men of God were surrounded by meek women, sisters in the Lord, who were in charge of their physical welfare, and who competed with them in the teaching and dissemination of the gospels in the women's quarters. At the beginning they were esteemed almost as highly as the men. Their help was indispensable; important messages to the most distant communities were intrusted to them. Some of them gradually reached prominence because of their intellect, fervor and energy. In Corinth, where many cultured women of the wealthy free class enthusiastically adopted Christianity, they even wished to teach and preach in public."

Eventually they were rebuffed temporarily by a few evangelists forging ahead with their grand conquest of souls. Dr. Gottlieb is more conscious of the rebuffs than of the ways in which women evaded them by routes straight or devious. Some of the means they employed in outwitting the masters of ceremonies and the part which women's wealth played in shaping theology, practice, and organisation, are as vital a phase of the story of Christendom as the bold assertions of masculine monopolists. Women were even lecturing on theology in the Middle Ages.

The same thing happened in Islamism. Perhaps it was for the very reason that his religious ascendancy rested on the benefactions of a woman that Mohammed so rigorously assailed the sex on which he was dependent. The holy man who lived mainly at the expense of the opposite sex swaggered in this vein: "I have not left any calamity more hurtful to man than woman. O assembly of women, give alms, although it be of your gold and silver ornaments; for verily ye are worthy of Hell on the Day of Resurrection." He gave them Hell. They gave him Funds.

But the fathers of the Christian Church had a Titan to battle against when they tried to suppress the popular Isis. An old Greek tablet carried this description of the Mother Goddess: "I am Isis, the mistress of every land: I laid down laws for mankind, and ordained things that no one may change; I am She who governs Sirius the Dog Star; I am She who is called divine among women; I divided the earth from the heaven; I made manifest the paths of the stars; I prescribed the course of the sun and the moon; I found out the labours of the sea; I made justice mighty; I brought together man and woman; I burdened woman with the newborn babe in the tenth month; I ordained that parents should be loved by their children; I put an end to cannibalism; I overthrew the sovereignty of tyrants; I compelled women to be beloved by men; I made justice more mighty than gold or silver; I made virtue and vice to be distinguished by instinct." Certainly this was an achievement of which any male god might have been proud.

If woman became the symbol of Sin to Christian Fathers, she remained the centre of the people's affections anyway. Our Lady of Mercy is still borne to French fields for aid in the spring planting. Mother Worship among the Christians was a blend of many elements. In writing of the recent suicide of the Russian poet, Mayakovsky, Bolshevist and film-maker, Eugene Lyons thus interprets the fierce conflict which led to his self-annihilation: "Yet subtly, inevitably almost, some basic things older than Marx or Stalin intrude upon the scene. Above the throb of the tractor the camera recorded the beat of life. Better machines, better social forms, more decent human relations — but also juicy apples, luscious females, fertile fields and pregnant women, the terrible urgency of sexual love, the continuity of nature. The elemental personal sentiments, personal yet universal, were caught upon the screen — the timeless ingredients of life." So too monks in their mediæval cloisters, trying to shut out "the timeless ingredients of life," were forced back upon first principles, their little shrines to the Madonna defying every papal ban.

Apples or rice, fields, and women have been inextricably bound up together in all religions. The origin of this bond is now traced by anthropologists through the matriarchate — or primal society ruled by women — to the sources of their early power in their relation to agriculture and the ownership of the land. The Greeks worshipped the goddess Demeter, Mother Earth, the Mother of corn and fruits, evidently a composite of ripe grain, fertile fields and pregnant woman — a type of personification, with attendant rites, surviving in its symbolic form in Japan, where it is a crime to express scepticism about the Sun Goddess ancestor and protector of the race. Among the legends which associate her with agriculture is that set down in the *Nihongi,* written in 720 A.D., which tells of her being teased by her brother who let loose the piebald colt in her rice fields and how, when that failed to distress her to his heart's content, he killed her colt and threw its skin into the room where she sat weaving. Unable to bear such interference with her work in field and shop, Amaterasu Oho-Mi-Kami shut herself up in a cave. The world she controlled then grew dark and vegetation ceased. Every attempt to lure her forth and bring the sun back to the earth was futile until at last a laughing female dancer aroused her interest and she peeped out, agreed to walk out, and soon brought succor and happiness to her race. Demeter, Artemis and Hera similarly reanimated the world long before the Christian goddess came upon the scene.

The identification of women with the fertility of the earth as well as with human reproduction ran everywhere round the globe. Dr. George Grant MacCurdy of Yale, director of the American School of Historic Research, reports idols of the mother goddess, or goddess of fertility, found in such excavations of ancient sites as those on the Bay of Biscay and in Siberia, seven thousand miles apart. He believes that these testify to the intercommunication of ideas no less than to the identity of spiritual thought coursing back at least to the Middle Stone Age. Sun worship he thinks followed mother worship and might be either a continuation of mother worship or a change to male symbolism. It came with the development of agriculture, the success of which depended on the life-giving qualities of heat. The Corn Woman to this day has rites in parts of Europe and like the good god and the bad of ancient legends, the good corn mother has as her counterpart the witch — usually the ear cut after sunset. Frazer sees in "the gruel of oat-meal and ale which the harvesters of Scotland sup with spoons as an indispensable part of the harvest supper, the equivalent of the gruel of barley-meal and water, flavored with pennyroyal which the initiates at Eleusis drank as a solemn form of communion with the Barley Goddess Demeter." Demeter also represented grains of other sorts.

With the worship of Mother Earth went seasonal myths connecting up with the worship of Mother Mary. The Greeks believed that in the autumn Demeter grew old and disappeared to reappear every spring at their calling — an idea which the Romans in turn embodied in their imitative goddess Ceres. Sometimes it was the daughter, Persephone, who rose up from the underworld in the spring.

In Egypt the son of the goddess came to rejuvenate the

world. In Christendom at Easter time the Son of the Virgin Mary came forth from the tomb and said to his mother who stood by: "I am the Resurrection and the Life." As cities arose in the midst of peasant communities the goddess of agriculture usually got a finer altar but Ezekiel relates how the peasants continued to mourn in the temples of Jerusalem with the archaic Mother for the loss of her divine Son. All the new female urban gods were but versions of Mother Earth — Gæa, the Earth; Kore, the Maiden; Despoina, the Mistress; Themis, the Oracle; Thesmophorus, the Law-giver; Karpophourus, the Fruit-Bearer; Pandora, the Giver of All. Davidson says that in Dravidian lands of southern India the village gods were always feminine and in orthodox Hindu circles the Mother is prominent when not predominant. Over all India Buddha and other males have come and gone as deities but the "Mother Goddess still reigns supreme alike among the primitive tribes of the jungle and the civilised and educated thought of Bengal." A modern nationalist slogan is this: "The Mother is calling us; let us go back to the Mother."

In the service of the Mother Goddess, however, men early acquired the right to act as high priests and to administer the land owned by the deity. Often such priestly administrators were eunuchs, for her subjects sometimes thought her as devastating as nature, believing that she could end the fertility of a husband or son as easily as of a field. The legend of Samson and Delilah partakes of this tradition. The Mother Goddess therefore must be prayed to fervently for favor and blessing and adequately propitiated to ward off injury.

In one of her earliest forms the Earth Goddess seems to have been a bisexual serpent deity, says Zimmern in *Tammuz-lieder*. And her original friendship with the serpent not only glows in the tale of Adam and Eve but is so deep-rooted and persistent in the minds of human beings that to this hour it is an awful heresy in certain quarters to read the Book of Genesis in the light of anthropology. When the Roman Christians took up the Old Testament, they solved its puzzles adroitly, determined to master a sex so unequivocally supreme. Had they also examined old Greek texts with similar perspicacity they would have discovered precedents for their Savior's turning water into wine — in the power granted Œnothropæ by Dionysus to change not only water into wine but into corn, olives or anything else she chose. Semitic students have believed until recent years that the Hebrews were unique among races in escaping female deities but that hope of distinction must now be abandoned. Like all the great races, scholars are inclined to believe, the ancient Semites worshipped a goddess prior to the elevation of Jahweh to monotheistic preeminence. Paul tried in vain to uphold male supremacy but the female at last won back in a new form the position she had occupied in the beginning of religious veneration. While the female did not regain a place in the Christian Trinity such as she enjoyed at Delphi where Hestia, who was thought to have invented the art of building houses, was jointly worshipped with Apollo and Poseidon, the Trinity in reality was widely ignored in favor of the traditional goddess.

To Protestant Americans, more accustomed to revering the dynamo than the Virgin, the potency of her sway is more difficult of comprehension than to any other people perhaps who ever lived. Looking backward from 1900 Henry Adams wrote: "In any previous age, sex was strength. Neither art nor beauty was needed. Every one, even among Puritans, knew that neither Diana of the Ephesians nor any of the Oriental goddesses was worshipped for her beauty. She was goddess because of her force; she was the animated dynamo; she was reproduction — the greatest and most mysterious of all energies; all she needed was to be fecund. . . The true

American knew something of the facts but nothing of the feelings; he read the letter, but he never felt the law. Before this historical chasm, a mind like that of Adams felt itself helpless; so he turned from the Virgin to the Dynamo as though he were a Branly coherer. On one side, at the Louvre and at Chartres, as he knew by the record of work actually done and still before his eyes, was the highest energy ever known to man, the creator of four-fifths of his noblest art, exercising vastly more attraction over the human mind than all the steam-engines and dynamos ever dreamed of; and yet this energy was unknown to the American mind. An American Virgin would never dare command; an American Venus would never dare exist."

It was probably to the great Mother, whatever their notions of her personality, that the prayers of European peasants were lifted more often than to the agonising Christ. To her magic powers, her mercy and tenderness, her intercession with the males of the Trinity, the agricultural age turned with renewed loyalty after the collapse of the Roman urban culture. And in the twelfth and thirteenth centuries, Virgin Worship was intrenched beyond repair. Albertus Magnus called Mary the "Great Goddess" on account of her quality of pity. Father God on the other hand was an object of considerable terror while Christ the Son was a stern judge of conduct. The Queen of Heaven would listen to the gentlest plea for intercession with these magnates and, since she could also work miracles, she stood forth as the perfect symbol of divine protection, the mother complex, a "magic-wielding woman" as she had been from the dawn of time. Aurelian had attributed to the intervention of his mother, a priestess of the Sun, his victory over Zenobia. And now among the Christians, praises for multiform services soared from the throats of musicians, dripped from the pens of poets, took shape under the tools of sculptors, and glowed from the brushes of painters as mediævalists took up the adoration of woman where their forebears had left off.

ASPECTS OF CHIVALRY

WHEN the barbarian peoples succumbed to Christian evangel-isation, their legends and lore about the mysteries passed over to Christian management to be remodeled by priests and peda-gogues. That they were not discarded wholesale was due to the circumstance that fundamentally this barbarian back-ground was much like the Christians' own. All the redactors had to do therefore was to give them a Christian slant. What else was possible ? How could a Chinese of today for exam-ple cast out his whole heritage when the truths in Christian teachings become illuminating ? Neither Paul the pioneer nor the sophisticated Augustine and Jerome of a later time could completely shed old ideas for new. Trained in Greek and Latin literature, Jerome continued to believe that the same discipline was important for girls and boys. Augustine was at one period in his life such an admirer of Vergil that he could weep over the tragedy of Dido and when he formed a scheme for Christian education, his training automatically de-termined the result. All the Church Fathers and Mothers reflected inherited moral ideology while they were adding to their stock of ideas.

Notwithstanding the enormous population gathered into ascetic Orders, the Christian directorate had to subdue lords and ladies as well to the new doctrine of sex or they would defeat the progress and unity of the entire religious enterprise. So more or less consciously the Elders of Christendom under-took the task of altering the manners and minds of the tem-poral rulers by revamping their traditions. At all the courts of Europe priests became advisers in matters intellectual. And little by little they imbued the courts with sex ideas running as closely as politics would permit to the ecclesiastical ideal of chastity. In other words they carried over to the State the respect for the Mother and Child which ruled in the monasteries — comprised in the term "Chivalry." Its successful incorporation into the ideology of the West still marks off that hemisphere from the Far East where the courtesan to this hour has dominated literature and court life. If dead barbarians could have heard with their ears and seen with their eyes the results of redaction the very Heaven or Hell to which they had adjourned would surely have been enlivened by an appreciation of the wonderful technique displayed. Literally, symbolically, æsthetically, ethically, devotionally, ecstatically, or grossly, in harmony with their various personalities, Christian writers of both sexes commented upon or remodeled for their barbaric pupils the beliefs in which the latter had been nurtured, in order that they might share in the blessings the new religion had to offer. Through much the same process of reinterpretation Greek myths had passed during the Hellenistic era and again during the early Christian era — now to be altered by the amalgamation of these two heritages with northern archaisms as old as the original Homeric society. And as Bury shows in a recent study of the *Romances of Chivalry on Greek Soil,* there flowed back to the Ægean and Ionian seas, through the intermarriage of Greek women and Western men after the Crusades, when this reinterpretation reached its apogee, a readaptation of newly adopted legends to meet Hellenic traditions and later Greek demands for international culture.

In fact the Romances of Chivalry shaped by the Christian writers were books of etiquette both for grandees and court fools. But in the new code of manners, it was not different food and drink, napery and conduct at the table alone that counted. Primarily another mode for loving was devised. And because books of etiquette must ever be related to the economics of their time, the chivalrous product was a feudal text par excellence. The raw material was rough enough in all conscience and perhaps it is well to consider that for a moment before examining the finished product, whereby "many a knight lived exclusively on the bounties supplied by his lady-love."

Through the monk Gildas, an insight is caught into the original "copy" out of which the poetic Christian, Sir Thomas Malory, finally created the lofty Arthurian knights bent on their quest for the Holy Grail. Gildas pictures these knights in reality as "sanguinary, boastful, murderous, addicted to vice, adulterous, and enemies of God, and their names ought to be forgotten. They are generally engaged in plunder and rapine, and they prey by preference upon the innocent; if they fight in order to avenge or protect anyone, it is sure to be in favor of robbers and criminals. They wage wars, but mostly against their own people and unjustly. They lose no opportunity of exalting and celebrating the most bloody-minded amongst themselves. They are ever ready to take an oath, and as often perjure themselves; they make vows, and immediately act perfidiously and treacherously. Although they keep a large number of wives, they are fornicators and adulterers."

We might be suspicious of his veracity if we had only this Christian view of paganism to rely on but there are other contemporary documents which lend countenance to his claims. "An old gloss in some of the manuscripts of Nennius informs us," according to Briffault, "that Arthur was 'from his boyhood renowned for his cruelty. . . Layamon [author of *Le roman de Brut*] who lived on the Welsh border and inserted many ancient native traditions in his poem, confirms that reputation. . .

Geoffrey of Monmouth [in *Historia Britonum*] says that Arthur tore the Irish 'without pity' and that in the wars with the Scots and Picts 'he indulged in unparalleled ferocity.' " Layamon tells how Arthur treated his own people, threatening to punish disobedience by having the rebel drawn by wild horses or his limbs chopped off. In a drunken bout his knights fought one another with carving knives and Arthur, who appeared on the scene after several had been killed, ordered "the warrior who began the disturbance to be buried alive in a bog: he further orders his knights to strike off the heads of all the male relatives of the culprit and to cut off the noses of all the females."

Henry III, we are told, roared with glee when he heard his cook had been tortured to death because his brother did not like the way a meal had been prepared. With respect to the Frankish wing of the Barbarian world, Gregory of Tours surpasses Gildas in his reports of horror prevalent among high and low. Gregory belonged to an old senatorial family of Rome and had received a classical education. After his father's death, his mother lived on an estate she owned in Burgundy. With that background, he was shocked by raw brutalism. But he makes excuses, Biblical fashion, for the princes such as Clothwig, the founder of the Frankish kingdom and "eldest son of the Church," who are lenient with Christian bishops: "Thus did the Lord fell down each day by his hand some of his enemies and extend his dominions, for he walked before the Lord with an upright heart, and did what was pleasant in His eyes." In juxtaposition to the bishop's Christian praise for the soldier of the Lord, let us place lines from J. C. L. de Sismondi summing up the charms of another of Gregory's favorites, the great king Gontrar: "He is only known to have had two wives and one mistress. His temper was, moreover, reputed to be a kindly one, for, with the exception of his wife's physician, who was hewn to pieces because he was unable to cure her; of his two brothers-in-law, whom he caused to be assassinated; and of his bastard brother, Gondebald, who was slain by treachery, no other act of cruelty is recorded of him than that he razed the town of Cominges to the ground, and massacred all the inhabitants, men, women and children."

Of the true Charlemagne something is gleaned from the *Annales Regni Francorum* edited by F. Kurze: "Having accepted the submission of the Saxons, who delivered to him their arms and the leaders who had resisted his aggressions, he summoned their chief men to Verdun, and after a conference in which they gave him what information they could, he had them beheaded on the same day, to the number of 4500." After which massacre, "the king having satisfied his desire for vengeance, proceeded to his winter quarters at Thionville to celebrate the Nativity of our Blessed Lord. . . As soon as the grass began to sprout again . . . he spread massacre, arson and pillage in every direction." L. Halphen in *Etude critique sur l'histoire de Charlemagne* describes the way Charlemagne and his priestly advisers turned over the administration of the Empire to persons whom Alcuin designates as "rapacious wolves" rather than judges.

Like the vast Mediterranean area which Islam conquered, German Europe seems to have been won to Christianity by terrorism. Tersely for the German Empire, S. A. Dunham, declares: "Those abominable princes generally, such were their premature vices, died of old age before thirty."

As the Crusades swept along, St. Bernard in the same breath recounts the "insensate ferocity, greed and cupidity of the warriors" and how "every blow of whose (the Knights Templars') sword is a victory for Christ." In a similar spirit wrote Peter of Blois.

If such were the men, what were the women ? We must

acknowledge their fitness for their times. The instructions given by his mother to Perceval (Peridur) who became Parsifal in Wagner's opera, were as follows: "If thou see a fair jewel, possess thyself of it." Women were more interested in men's muscles than in their brains and preferred to be the brides of competent fighters even as in ancient Sparta or among the American Indians. At times mediæval women fought well in their own might: a woman slew Simon de Montfort.

But a terrible sex war raged over property. A thirteenth century English petition in the Rolls of Parliament states that "heiresses in every part of the Kingdom were, by guile or force, brought in the power of designing men." Women were often heads of fiefs, their male "protectors" having died of violence as a rule. So other "protectors" sought their land. Besides, kings handed them about ruthlessly and not always to be wives, threatening to throw them to grooms if they resisted, irrespective of their age or marital status. For instance the *Chanson de Doon de Nanteuil* celebrated the glorious fight of a warrior who hit the "enemy in the bowels" that he might seize the court beauty for his bride. In another song by Girbert de Metz, an empress inspired her retainers to deeds of valor by pledging the daughters of her princes and counts as rewards. When the sword was the breadwinner, marriage was made of lust. Ladies were in circulation as well as coin and commodities. Bundling was general and everybody went to bed minus *robes de nuit*. One has only to read Shakespeare in the least expurgated edition to discover how barbarism lingered into the seventeenth century.

Both Baron Bernard de Cahusac and his Baroness "spent their lives robbing and destroying churches, stripping travelers, making widows and paupers, mutilating innocent persons. . . The wife of this tyrant, oblivious of all pity, used to cut off the breasts of poor women or lop off their thumbs." Precedents for the Christian Inquisition were near at hand. There was Adelaide of Soissons, for instance, who deprived a deacon, whom she hated, of his tongue and eyes and poisoned her own brother to get possession of his property. If Queen Elizabeth, delighted by Drake's singeing of the Spanish beard, knighted the pirate, chivalric predecessors had done worse. The Countess of Belesne, we are informed, "rides about the country at the head of a large troop of men-at-arms, quartering herself and her men upon terror-stricken monks, upon whose larder and cellar their invasion descends like a flight of locusts. By guile, craft and treachery, she dispossesses one after another all her neighbours, who are reduced to beggary. One of them, with his two brothers, at last succeeds in gaining access to her bedroom and cuts off her head, an event which 'caused much joy.' "

Many of the prelates of the Middle Ages were survivors of Gallo-Roman families inured to centuries of warlike behavior. Their "sole concession to their sacred calling was to avoid 'the shedding of blood' by using a mace in battle instead of the sword." They blessed battle fields and battle axes. Their concern was primarily with the ruling classes by whom they lived — or died. Accordingly the inner light they brought to bear upon the problems of social order was a weird composite of their own past, their struggle for existence, and their dreams.

In England several of the abbesses ranked with barons. In Germany they were often noble women who owned their monasteries by direct grant from the king. Therefore they could not be controlled against their will by papal legates and bishops. The Abbess of Gandersheim for example was a genuine feudal lord, owning the large estate on which her retreat was located. She was summoned to council whenever her overlord wanted something of his vassal and she arranged by demands on her dependents to supply him with the knights he might require for a war on his neighbors. She held court on her holding and administered local justice in her own right. Under Otto I the Abbess of Gandersheim and the Abbess of Quedlinburg were allowed to strike coins. The second of these abbesses was the aunt of Otto III and during his minority she helped his mother to rule Germany. Indeed she ruled it alone while the emperor was taken on a prolonged visit to Rome in 997. At that time she had the menacing Wends to oppose and succeeded in defending the State against their threatened invasion. In 999 she summoned representatives to appear at Dornburg for a session of the Diet.

That such aggressive men and women should arrive at a stage receptive to the ethereal refinement of Dante whose beloved Virgin, Beatrice, "assimilated to the moon, leads him through the seven spheres of purgatory while she lectures him on theology," is well-nigh incredible. Dante's chaste male lover testifies that "the lady who in my heart awakened love seems like unto the orb that measures time and sheds her splendour in the sky of love." The Virgin was indeed translated. But so were cave men — young ne'er-do-wells, flaming youth, paramours of feudal ladies — and made to behave in their Courts of Love according to the rules of a detailed Christian book of etiquette. In this progression troubadours had played a prominent rôle. Some of these singers merely wandered with their songs and lutes. Others were retainers at the courts. And lest the notion persist that they were all men, it is well to remember Beatrice, Countess of Die. The Paulist doctrine of love as sin made great headway in the northern redactions but in Italy, especially at the Sicilian court of Frederic II and among the chanteurs, older Roman concepts of extra-marital freedom continued to exert an influence.

Amid general European promiscuity and blood-letting, in

which illegitimacy was a mark of distinction, no less a grandee than William the Conqueror being celebrated as William the Bastard, an enormous output of chivalric literature was produced, based on what was believed and admired but carried into realms of an imagination knowing no bounds of mortal limitation. Kings and queens, lords and ladies joined in fiction-making until Charlemagne bloomed forth as a second Moses; one of Arthur's knights as Christ; Alexander of Macedon visits the Garden of Eden; the Celtic fairy queen, etherealised as the Platonic sister of Arthur, attends mass and builds a chapel to Our Lady of the Lake. We have but to compare this human feat with the myth-making of which Napoleon was the center, or watch in our own age the deification of Mussolini as the savior of his people, or saga creation with Alexander of Jugoslavia as its theme, to understand the process by which hero worship is built up whether for religious or political ends.

Gradually women were "purified" in their turn. Aggressive and lustful creatures were made to appear reluctant by the æsthetes of chivalry. Through their decisions in the standardised courts, ladies began to dictate the literary outpourings of their courtiers and instead of resigning themselves to their lovers gladly or being seized by the impatient and bold, they fed out their favors to poor and hungry bachelors, dependent upon them for sustenance, by a rigorous code of love promotion. Thus was dramatised as love the court paid to a lady by her vassals.

Dante sublimated this patrician loving to the highest possible degree. "Never before has it entered the mind of any poet thus to apotheosize the lady of his affections; to contemplate in her eyes the most sublime mysteries of faith; to introduce her among the most exalted spirits of the heavenly host; to make her the symbol of theology and revealed truth and to constitute her for himself the medium of graces and blessings from the Most High. Thus to apotheosize the young maiden who had won his undying love at the threshold of youth, and to make her the symbol of all that is most pure, most holy, most profound, most elevated, presupposed, as has well been said, conditions which were unique in the entire history of literature — a love very intense and very pure, born at a period of lively and simple faith, in a soul profoundly religious, in an intelligence marvelously open to all the knowledge of its time and served by the most powerful and most delicate poetic talent which the world has ever known."

It seems also that German women in the fifteenth century, in their literary efforts, preserved the ideology of courtly loving, after the actual days of chivalry were over and remained as in the Italy of Dante but a memory, when the knightly caste itself was dissolving, and the city and trading classes were rising to assertion. In 1437 a feudal lady, mentioned by Alfred Kleinberg, wrote a novel which was a curious medley of bourgeois practicality and chivalric sentiment. In the feudal palaces of course the courtly tradition lingered but the ladies of the court, its special conservators, also wove it into the folk tales of the people.

More slowly evolved the notion of romantic married love. It was long in fact before the love of husband and wife was considered possible by pious intellectuals. The obeisance of the wife to the husband, rather than affection, was dramatised as religion since husbands were beneath jealousy and wives beyond fidelity. Not until the dominant males at courts, the husbands of the ladies, saw the minor courtiers favored through their precise courtesy, such as is delineated in Spenser's *Faëry Queen,* did they in turn begin to compete with these "superior lackeys" and respond in turn to lyric love.

Moorish contacts affected the French poets and supplied

musical instruments for the accompaniment of their songs. Through Blanche, the daughter of Louis IX, married to a Spaniard, came some of this influence to soften the tenor of trouvères. When Provence then began to exalt love above war, from Provençal Christianity there percolated into other parts of Christendom, especially into Italy as the result of a political hegira, the note of romanticism in the sex relation apart from the court of love, reaching its loftiest range in the poetry of Petrarch and Dante. Formerly it would have been deemed anarchy — at least an indictable offense — for a poet to address sonnets to any female he chose to admire. In an early version of Tristram, the courtier is made to deserve death at the hands of the king for his hymn to Iseult the queen. But after the establishment of the right of courtiers to adore queens, husbands their wives, and any man any woman romantically selected, women themselves dared again to sing of love, Sappho fashion.

When minstrelsy reached the masses, however, the Church with the royal assent called a halt, for no such a rival was wanted. It seemed noble to have Eleanor of Aquitaine, her father and her son advancing literature but ignoble to have poor bards roaming among the people at large with their lyrical entertainment. Alcuin succeeded in getting a ban placed on the common minstrels and they were refused communion, but when the nuns and priests found that censorship was defied they entered into a popular competition with their miracle plays and hymnology.

In such matters the Church and State were one. Thus by representing love "as subject to subtle and esoteric codes unintelligible to the common crowd, as bound up with lofty and heroic principles, and as inspiring elevated sentiments, the customary freedom of sexual relations was dissociated from vulgar licentiousness, the application of Christian standards was eluded, and the charge of immorality parried." One thing, in short, was permissible for the court. Another for the people. This tradition lasted throughout feudal times and colored later history. While Rubens could fill imperial palaces with nudes in the most Christian countries, the humble members of the Church, Catholic and Protestant, had to beware of excursions into the ways of all flesh.

This code of the knights and ladies Don Quixote tried to explain to his lowly squire as follows:

Don Quixote: "Know that in this our style of chivalry it is most honorable for a lady to have a large number of knights in her service, who are devoted to her without venturing farther in their inmost thoughts than a desire to serve her for her own sake, and without expecting other guerdon in return for their many and honorable exploits save that she should deign to acknowledge them for her knights."

Sancho replies that he has heard the same explanation about serving God for His Own Sake without thought of reward but he can't quite understand that and asks whether God won't do something for him.

Don Quixote: "To the devil with thee. . . One would think that thou hast never studied."

In fact Sancho could not read.

CANON LAW AND ITS VIOLATIONS

In such circumstances the nature of the canon law should occasion no surprise. Neither should its violations. But the law is apt to be emphasised in histories to the neglect of its evasions. In spite of the fact that the completed canon law prescribing strict monogamy was the work of some twelve centuries, in contrast with such a restraining measure as a modern prohibition of liquor which in the United States was but the work of half a century or so, each represented an effort to legislate mankind into codes of conduct it could not or would not accept; and no treatment of either phenomenon is adequate that fails to take into account the open defiance or subterfuges by which mankind executes its own will.

Take the canon law. Divorce was rife in Rome during the Christian attempt to frame religious legislation. And among the untutored northern races polygamy or promiscuity was general when the Christians undertook to subdue them to their monogamic and ethical preferences. Compromises were therefore unavoidable from the start. While a celibate clergy took unto itself the sole right to baptise, marry, bury, and administer the estates of the dead, refusing illegitimate children the right to inherit, while it made marriage legally monogamic and indissoluble, it did grant divorce for exceptional reasons and it did allow princes more than one wife when politics seemed to require concession. Although the canon law remained as enduring law, after Frankish dominion gave way to feudalism and civil anarchy, although it announced its divine origin, although it became a highly elaborate system, deriving form and texture from Roman codes and elements from German law, although its interpreters and administrators were often the sole possessors of learning in the various communities and thus were called upon constantly for assistance, it could not completely alter the economics, politics, sex or culture of the races it was designed to dominate.

It could not so much as keep its own clericals in line with its sexual prohibitions. The people, including the monks who were fed by pious endowments, took the matter into their own hands more or less quietly. As early as 324 A.D., the Pope decreed that celibacy was fixed for all ministers of the altar. But in reality chastity was no more fixed than the prescriptions of certain seventeenth-century New England Blue Laws on the statute books are operative in the twentieth century. In 1215 the Fourth Council of Lateran made such a drastic effort to enforce celibacy that disobedient priests had to become more clandestine with their concubines and children. National and local synods, pastoral epistles, statutes of churches, and all the records of ecclesiastical discipline display the determination of the directors of Christendom to master the sex impulse of the clergy. Yet the answer of the clergy, to an astounding degree, was nullification. Even in the case of the faithful celibates, it was hard for them to preach marital happiness and duties to others while they denied themselves the blessings about which they eloquently discoursed. The image of the Virgin and her Son, which they were finally allowed to keep before their eyes on a pledge to concentrate on chastity, seemed to have more compassion for sin than for loneliness.

As a consequence, in times and places, the very monasteries and convents became centers of easy living. Penalties imposed by Charlemagne and Louis the Fair failed to check the propensities of males and females to remain thoroughly mortal. And as the Church made concessions on marriage in cases of political need, so it made concessions to other arrangements for association in times of financial need. The chances to make money by alliances with prostitution were often too appealing for resistance. Consequently the ancient story of temple prostitution was sometimes repeated in Christendom if with a stronger flavor of hypocrisy.

As he was about to leave Lyons in 1251, after an eight-year residence, Cardinal Hugo, speaking for Innocent III, said to the people: "Friends, since our arrival here, we have done much for your city. When we came, we found here three or four brothels. We leave behind us but one. We must own however that it extends without interruption from the eastern to the western gate." Saint Boniface, in his *Epistola* dealing with England, tried to explain the corruption in monasteries and the looseness in convents on the ground that not one monk or nun in a hundred probably chose the religious life through conviction, most of them being primarily interested in economic shelter and similar security, since the retreats were generally far better than their own abodes and in many instances extremely luxurious for the age. Moreover the retreats were seats of privilege.

One of the choice illustrations of the discrepancy between faith and conduct may be taken from the Merovingian age. It concerns the philanderings and pamperings of the poet Fortunatus within the convent of Poitiers founded by a queen of France, Radegund, and managed by the Abbess Agnes. Often their guest, while he dined at the lavish feasts they provided to gratify his gluttony, made especially attractive by dishes of silver and crystal, he fed his hostesses on flattering verses and amusing talk, thus relieving them from the hunger engendered by penance and prayers. Reared in a proud caste, Radegund dared to defy orders prohibiting such mixed assemblies.

Radegund's wilfulness was known to Bishop Maroveus and he was at a loss to know how to deal with it. Pious protestations in her letters did not blind him to her waywardness and he refused to visit her convent for grand religious fêtes or give her his personal protection. A long battle, at one stage, pitched and sanguinary, took place after the death of Radegund between the convent, where she had lived, and the forces of Maroveus. Some of the Sisters declared that sinful practices had been encouraged within the cloister by the abbess and, since one of the accusing nuns was the daughter of the mighty Chlothar, the charges were taken seriously. In the course of the dispute over the administration, several nuns broke out of their cells, rallied noble and commoner bandits to their side, returned to besiege the stronghold, fell upon an attending bishop and other officials who had come to the scene for the purpose of conciliation, beat and injured internes, and threatened to fling the abbess from the walls. Maroveus was brushed aside by the doughty daughters of ruling families who proceeded to go over his authority to that of their regal relatives. Only after two years of such civil war, during which temporal and spiritual rulers of Burgundy and Austrasia exhausted every resource to quell these rebellious and warlike ladies become nuns, prepared to starve, fight, and abuse to win their ends, was order secured and the peace of the Church attained.

This struggle particularly involved a temporal-spiritual controversy with the nun Chrodieldis, the revolt leader, standing between the throne and the altar — a king's daughter protecting her rebellion by the Cross — both crown and tonsure being forced to unite to save their dignities. During the clerical investigation it was disclosed that "men were freely admitted to the baths, that games of hazard were played, that plays of a distinctly satyric type were produced, and that laymen were entertained within the walls." The beautiful chief, Radegund, was then dead but she had admitted before her decease that, during her régime, when her niece was betrothed, she had given her a grand convent celebration and had ordered a bridal gown cut for her from a rich altar cloth. Later commentators had much to say about the troubles which the Evil One had brought to the cloistered saints and saintesses.

Some of the Sisters who thus revolted eventually accepted forgiveness and were content, after the sentence of excommunication had been revoked, to return to the convent and subside. Not so Chrodieldis. Instead, she forced the king to give her an estate in Touraine where she could retire. It mattered neither to her nor to him that the land thus bestowed had already been the prey of outlawed barons, for everyone concerned belonged to the same school of politics.

As we have seen, the much lauded Roman order has been greatly exaggerated and its wide-flung imperial system had long been beset by civil conflicts when final dissolution came. In spite of papal labors for uniformity there was still more disorder under feudalism. Juvenal the pagan was merciless on the Romans and Roman times and half a century after Constantine became a Christian, Marcellinus still found conditions about as bad. A Christian historian in the fifth century is hardly less gloomy. And throughout the Middle Ages priests were continually bursting into protests against the general anarchy and horrors which prevailed. Highway robbery, for instance, was a common occurrence owing to the fact that no one with civil power policed the roads between fortresses. Monsters in human form pillaged and mutilated, raped and burned. The Abbot Joachim of Floris, a nobleman, cried out against the state of affairs in the twelfth century and Arnold of Brescia in 1155 was first hanged and then thrown to the flames for his bitterness. "Black pessimism" filled the soul of a Franciscan father, Adam Marsh. Equally significant was the effect of the harsh military operations on the artists whom we find ceasing to paint Christ as a young shepherd with a lamb gently folded in his arms and now making him "older, sterner, and more melancholy." Wealth and luxury had crept even into Christian leadership just as they had penetrated among the puritanical pagans of Rome. It was charged that at Avignon even "the widow's mite often found its way into the lap of a prostitute." Toward the close of the papal dictatorship in Italy, Machiavelli declared: "To the Church and priests of Rome we Italians owe this obligation — that we have become void of religion — and corrupt."

RELIGIOUS EDUCATION

It was not to preaching missionaries, to books on chivalry, to law or wealth alone that the mediæval Church looked for power and expression. By formal instruction in religious works and selected secular books, it sought to extend and consolidate its dominion. So discipline in religion was grafted upon the methods inherited from Roman and Greek times, all bent to serve orthodox purposes. At the courts of kings, at the seats of bishops, at hundreds of monasteries and convents scattered in busy cities and in mountain fastnesses, religious persons copied old manuscripts, wrote books, discussed abstruse theological points, and taught boys and girls the rudiments of Christian learning. In time colleges and universities sprang up from one end of Christendom to the other, to provide higher training for the clergy in particular.

At nearly every point in this development of religious education, women appeared in forceful rôles. If, for example, we turn to the work of the Venerable Bede, rightly called "the father of English history," we find entries showing the daughters of the ruling class going to the better religious schools of France, like their brothers. There we also learn that Anglo-Saxon women, notably Eanswith, daughter of King Eadbald of Kent, sought to obviate the necessity for going abroad by founding seats of learning at home. Very soon afterward Queen Ethelburg opened a convent at Liming and within a short time Queen Sexburg established one at Sheppey. Between 696 and 716 King Wihtred and Queen Werburg granted charters to at least five abbesses permitting them to administer convents. Noblewomen joined these leaders of their class in taking the veil. Travel however was not denied them and they retained their contact with the court and the higher politics of their age.

From Bede and other sources it is discovered that about the middle of the seventh century the Abbess Hild, a royal princess, niece of Edwin, first Christian king of Northumbria, founded two convents — one at Hartlepool and a still more famous one at Whitby. King Oswiu endowed them and sent his daughter Aelflaed to Hild to be educated. But the great lady who took upon herself educational responsibilities in England did not confine her cares to her own sex. She administered a double, if not strictly coeducational, school. The men and women students lived in adjoining dormitories and met for prayers or other religious purposes. After speaking in highest terms of her qualifications for this position, Bede says of Hild that "her prudence was so great that not only did ordinary persons, but sometimes even kings and princes seek and receive counsel of her in their necessities." She was a great church landlord, could hear confession and even excommunicate. In addition she was an educational and cultural factor of inestimable influence in England, numbering five bishops among her pupils. Her example was so widely imitated that, when the thirteenth century arrived, education in England was considered equal to that on the Continent. Hild was popularly known, not as the "Mother of the Legions" but as the "Mother of her Country" on account of her cultural guardianship of the English people. Bringing the young Cædmon to her abbey, she set for him the task of preparing an Anglo-Saxon version of the Bible in his poetic style — a performance which has made his name immortal but owes its achievement to the perception of its value by the lady head of the retreat at Whitby.

As for Catholic Ireland, even before Charlemagne coöperated with the clergy in devising an educational system for his realm, St. Brigit founded at Kildare a college for noble-women and permitted other students from a wide area to study by their side. Irish educators early moved into England and it was from Irish and English educators that Charlemagne assembled his faculties. The Benedictine Order was similarly recruited both in its masculine and feminine contingents. Pupils of the Sisters, as of the Brothers of England and Ireland, who had worked in the convent libraries, copying texts and writing their own, invigorated the religious societies and internationalised Christian exegesis. From England St. Boniface took a learned nun, St. Lioba, "friend and counselor of spiritual and temporal rulers," across the Channel to start the education of Teutonic women in the doctrines of the faith from a retreat at Bischofsheim. Eventually German nuns were to reach great distinction of their own for their mental accomplishments.

In *Woman under Monasticism,* Lina Eckenstein says, referring to their educational position: "The contributions of nuns to literature, as well as incidental remarks, show that the curriculum of study in the nunnery was as liberal as that accepted by the monks, and embraced all available writing whether by Christian or profane authors. While the Scriptures and the writings of the Fathers of the Church at all times formed the groundwork of monastic studies, Cicero at this period was read by the side of Boëthius, Vergil by the side of Martianus Capella, Terence by the side of Isidore of Seville. From remarks made by Hroswitha we see that the coarseness of the Latin dramatists made no reason for their being forbidden to nuns, though she would have seen it otherwise; and Herrad was so far impressed by the wisdom of the heathen philosophers of antiquity that she pronounced this wisdom to be the 'product of the Holy Spirit also.' Throughout the literary world, as represented by convents, the use of Latin was general, and made possible the even spread of culture in districts that were widely remote from each other and practically without intercourse." And a striking intellectual sympathy with the past sets Herrad off from the early Church Fathers who saw in the resemblance between Mithraic and Christian cults the work of the devil; for she assigned all wisdom, or inspiration, to the work of gods, past and present.

Where the monks were apt to devote their intellectual exercises to speculation, the nuns were inclined to concentrate on love and charity. "Nearly all the great mystics, Eckehart, Susa, Tauler," writes Gabriele Reuter, "formed affectionate spiritual friendships with nuns from whose letters emanate a beautiful, flower-like poetry. These women rose from the mass of the silent — impressive personalities of the highest intellect and spiritual calibre to whom the present age can only look up with admiration."

The Herrad to whom reference has been made was the Abbess of Hohenburg in Alsace who, in one of the most celebrated of illuminated manuscripts called *Hortus Deliciarum,* or "Garden of Delights" as it is translated, attempted to make all life enchanting. In encyclopædic form she tried to assemble all the knowledge of her time and at least transcended the Aristotelian ambition in the matter of illustration. Her text perished in the fire which consumed the library of Strassburg in 1870 — a war hazard — but a collection of about two hundred of her pictures, copied from it, still exists.

Writing of Herrad's achievement, the noted French academician, Charles Jourdain, says that it ranged from divine science to agriculture and meterology and was an amazing product to have come from a convent. In fact it is a challenge to the women of the twentieth century in the sweep of its intellectual range and its erudition.

The Abbess Gertrud of the convent of Helfta in Saxony was an ardent bibliophile and set her nuns to transcribing with vigor. Matilda, her sister, and another nun, called Gertrud the Great to distinguish her from the abbess, followed up the copying apprenticeship with impassioned creation. A critic of Matilda's work now maintains that the Matelda in Dante's *Purgatoria* is the very same nun who lived in the convent of Helfta and expressed her emotions in verse.

In the latter part of the tenth century a German nun of the Benedictine Order, Hroswitha, won fame as a poet and historian. She wrote metrical legends for her Sisters, contemporary history in meter, and seven Latin dramas modeled on the style of Terence. Giesebrecht ranks her with Wittikind and Routger for her historical ability while all students of the Middle Ages agree that she stood in a class by herself as a playwright. She did the unique thing of utilising the theme of music in a play, making a morality plot out of eight spheres revolving about the earth — a musical octave or device later employed by Dante and Shakespeare. Speaking of her in *Allgemeine Geschichte der Litteratur des Abendlandes,* Egbert declares: "This fruitful poetic talent which has the inspiration and the courage of genius necessary to enter upon new ground shows how the Saxon element was chosen to guide the German nation in the domain of art."

Hroswitha was an innovator as well as an artist. She lifted the perspective of classical tragedy, of which she was a close student, beyond its absorption with fatalism and death to an interest in romantic love, handling the Christian view of life with the skilled technique of a pagan. Well aware of the ferocity of the religious clash between paganism and Christianity, she made Christ triumph over destiny on the stage, dramatising his nativity and ascension as the victory of a living God who had brought hope to humanity. Before popu-

lar morality plays were widely adopted as instruments of religious education, Hroswitha had set examples difficult to sur-
pass. If feudal and patriotic, she was also highly imaginative,
as befitted the exciting age in which she lived — when the
Greek Princess Theophano, the wife of Otto II, aspired to
reproduce in her new home the culture of Byzantium. Having in her convent a young niece of Otto and receiving royal
guests from time to time, it was inevitable that she should
eulogise the Ottos, setting beside her artistic and dramatic
defense of the Church a defense of the prevailing political
order.

Of more lowly birth, but belonging to the same religious
Order, was another German political writer of striking power
a century later — Hildegarde of Bingen. She began at the
age of eight to study in a convent presided over by a noble
woman and in her maturity she rendered distinguished service to the State and Church as a dreamer of dreams, a seer,
and teacher. The display of her talents was accompanied by
such magnetism that Bernard of Clairvaux, preparing at Bingen
in 1147 for the Second Crusade, regarded her as divinely inspired and urged the Pope the following year at the synod
of Treves to recognize her as an official prophet of the Church.
It was her custom to preach in the market place and to answer
questions in the manner of the ancient oracles. Whether
inquiries came from Popes, such as Anastasius IX and Adrian
IV, from the Emperors Conrad III or Frederick I, or from
the masterful theologian Guibert of Gembloux, she framed
ingenious replies. Hildegarde's was not a spirit of playfulness
but of grim and commanding obedience to religious law.

Because they disliked the "perfume" with which Christian
theologians disguised evil-smelling economic realism, gentle
humanists in the Church from time to time endeavored to
purify the religious and intellectual atmosphere. For instance

a spiritual revolt against learning and sophistry, resembling the Buddhistic and early Christian movements, led the "Seraphic One," St. Francis of Assisi, and his young disciple, St. Clare, to cast off the higher verbalism and class distinctions and live like Christ nearer to the masses. Pity and the love of the common life more than of manuscripts commanded their minds. And while the mystics of this persuasion served "the people" with kindness, instead of literature, artists also began to think in such terms. Thus Giotto, the friend of the monk Francis, ignored martyrs in order to paint "The Holy Family" in warm human tones, while Cimabue removed the bleeding Christ from the Cross to converse with his neighbors and regain his human rôle as a great teacher and guide. It is true that Francis felt in his own flesh the wounds of the Christ but that identity was remote from anything the scholastics were able to feel.

Of St. Francis everyone knows and, lest he be forgotten in the years to come the Capuchins and the Italian government are now together immortalising him by the erection of a statue on the hillside overlooking Siena, home of many mystics. But the girl Clare, who forsook her knightly caste as he the circle of traders to follow in Christ's footsteps, is apt to drop from memory although the reciprocal inspiration and influence of these two great Italians are really essential parts of an indivisible story.

"Students of Franciscan lore," writes Luzzatti, "judge the conquest of Clare and of her virgins by the ideal of the Poverello as of singular interest, because of the influence which came of it over the order. Francis formed and fortified Clare; Clare sweetened Francis. He infused into her tender twin soul constancy, strength, endurance in their common ideal; he was the pillar upon whom leaned the weak maidens of Clare, the spring which quenched their thirst after the ideal and nourished them in divine wisdom, the honored father, moderator of pains inflicted upon innocent flesh, and the guide who brought to fruit the delicate flowers of San Damiano.

"Clare was to him a faithful sister soul, devoted in the most ineffable veneration, the oil which fed the flame, his counselor in the days of his trial, a hope for the future and for the unity of the rule. Staunch in her gentleness, she never yielded to the current flatteries of innovators, and remained the solid bulwark of his first teaching with a few faithful disciples.

"And Clare was still the inextinguishable lamp which shone over the rule for another twenty-seven years after the passing of the master — shone bright (almost a reproach !) within the always rude walls of San Damiano, even when there rose majestic (discordantly, one might almost say, against the holy, simple background of the hills) the sumptuous church that Friar Elia erected proudly to the glory of the founder. . .

"It was Clare who solidified and strengthened his Order with her fresh youth, her continuous good works, her unshakable faith. That clear and strong virginal mind embraced the whole height of his ideal, but with practical sense rendered it easier, more accessible to all, at the same time protecting it from profane contacts, and spread it beyond little Umbria, beyond great Italy. Perhaps Friar Bernard alone had as much as she of the worship of absolute poverty; perhaps no one after the *Serafico,* not even the gentle Leo, knew as well as she how to include the whole of creation in a great, illimitable love. And when the new currents set to turn the order from its difficult course and to start it along a broader way, when it faced about toward the consolations and distractions of learning, forgetful of the unchanging attitude of the founder toward studies, when it accepted possessions and abandoned the jealous prescription that it keep itself absolutely poor — even then the ideal continued to be followed faithfully and in its entirety by the Spirituals and the Poor Clares."

"It is not generally known," says Mozans, "how she sustained the Poverello during long hours of trial and hardship. It was during those periods of care and struggle that we see how courageous and intrepid was 'this woman who has always been represented as frail, emaciated, blanched like a flower of the cloister.' She defended Francis not only against others but against himself. In those hours of dark discouragement which so often and so profoundly disturb the noblest souls [the Ferrero biography shows how vain and trying Francis could be] and sterilize the grandest efforts, she was beside him to show the way. When he doubted his mission and thought of fleeing to the heights of repose and solitary prayer, it was she who showed him the ripening harvest with the reapers to gather it in, men going astray with no shepherd to herd them, and drew him once again into the train of the Galilean, into the number of those who give their lives as a ransom for many." His finest work, *The Canticle of the Sun,* was composed while Clare took care of him. In the last years of his life, Francis established a third Order — the Brothers and Sisters of Francis — a lay organisation of those who tried to live according to his principles without ascetic retirement.

Commenting on the rise of mysticism in a recent review of L'abbé Bremond's work dealing with the subject, Agnes Mackensie remarks in *The New Statesman:* "It is interesting, at the present time, to notice, as in so much French and so little English history, how far the reform was a movement of both sexes. To read, in fact, is to be slightly puzzled by recent feminist complaints of the Church. Here, as a matter of fact, the women led. M. l'Abbé looking at the whole movement, sets in its forefront the sober little figure of a quiet Dauphiny bourgeoise, not even a nun. Marie Teyssonier (Marie of Valence) was not only a saint, in the unofficial sense, but the acknowledged spiritual mother of men like Père Coton, Henri IV's Confessor, whose noble and attractive personality had an enormous influence. Through the little group whose head was Madame Acarie, the Carmelites of the Teresian Reform, that school of saints, were first brought into France — and the nuns came before the friars. Their quickening contagion spread to the other orders, the Benedictine nuns taking fire early in the person of nearly a score of great abbesses. It was largely the example of the nuns that renewed the life of the monks and of the secular priesthood, and kindled the fire among the laity. That St. François de Sales did no more to make Ste. Chantal than she to make him is merely typical. Yet if the revival was feminine in inception, it was neither feminist nor effeminate. There is no trace of sex-hostility, and it carries the best tradition of French devotion — a high sweet sanity and a noble fervour, transcending reason but never forgetting it. And as always happens with the real mystic, these souls whose life was scarcely of this world had an impact on it like a bursting shell."

Several of these attractive personalities the reverend father fully describes in their social setting, such as Madame Acarie, "mystic, organiser, tackling a difficult husband and six children, recovering the family fortunes from disaster, finding time to found a religious order and to guide them through their initial difficulties, and to become too much the fashion in a country of whose very language she had been ignorant." The Abbé also brings into the story whole groups of mystics, such as the young Benedictine abbesses — courageous girls of the best blood in France, who combined wit with devotion and administrative talent. When someone inquired of Françoise de la Châtre whether her nuns were nobly born, she replied quickly: "Yes, madam. They are all a great King's daughters."

UNDERNEATH the immense development of the Church, accompanied by the fusing of old gods and new, the construction of papal authority, the spread of learning, and the repeated outburst of religious enthusiasms, was a movement of economic and intellectual forces destined to disrupt the ecclesiastical order, introduce Protestantism, and usher in the era of positive knowledge. The Church, defenders claimed, was founded on a rock and had as its supreme master an infallible Pope; but it was also founded on earthly considerations — on vast landed endowments and on fees exacted by the priesthood for every kind of rite or ritual. As landed proprietors, religious persons, whether men or women — popes, abbots, and abbesses — were feudal lords and derived their incomes from the fruits garnered by laborious peasants, serfs bound to the soil of the lords, lay and clerical. To be sure the religious clothed their possessions with divine sanctions and some of them may have been, as alleged, more tender to their tenants, but to the peasant, who had to surrender to his overlord nearly all his returns beyond a bare livelihood, it made little difference whether a clerical bishop or a secular prince presided over his fate. In other words, the Church in its various branches rested mainly on agriculture — on the feudal arrangement with its hierarchy of lords, temporal and spiritual, based on serfdom. Being a landed class, the clergy were linked by economic ties with secular landlords and their fate made common.

Like ruling classes in all times, mediæval theologians worked out a system of ethics which justified and gave a moral tinge to the economic order on which they relied for support. The overlord had certain duties to his underlings, at least the duty of leaving them enough to live on so that they could go on producing. To this extent feudalism was benevolent. Though rightless at law, the serf had rights by custom; he could not be ousted from the soil or sold into bondage. But he also had certain positive duties, especially that of rendering payments and services to his lord, lay or clerical, in return for the privilege of tilling the soil at his feet. According to theological ethics prices and wages were to be just, usury was forbidden although the taking of what amounted to interest appeared in many guises, speculating and profit-making through manipulations were banned, and an order of fixed responsibilities and duties was created for "the best of all possible worlds." While modern writers, engaged in a war on capitalism, are prone to idealise the feudal scheme and its ethics, it must be admitted that there were certain elements of economic security in it, that the mediæval theologians celebrated the dignity of labor with common things, in contradistinction to the Greeks and Romans who poured contempt upon toil, and that the political economy of the scholastics was suffused with a kind of moral ardor which may in some cases have mitigated the harshness of feudal exactions. At least scholastic economy has served as a convenient club in many an assault upon capitalism and its sponsors. And its ideals, if not its authority over practices, may have fertilised that very protest against the system of today. In reviewing this aspect of Christendom, it is important to remember the degree to which women were tilling the soil of Europe throughout the Middle Ages as well as their participation in the handicrafts. Every act of the Church was a direct influence in their lives. Noble nuns and ladies of the manors might dictate to ecclesiastics; peasant women like peasant men and artisans took what they could get.

Whatever may have been the merits of feudalism, it was destined to go and in its passing the economic foundations of the historic Church were shattered. With the rise of commerce, especially after England, France, and Spain became powerful centralised monarchies, the town gained in importance and a rich trading class began to vie with the lay and clerical nobility and resent its pretensions and exactions. Generally speaking, the bourgeoisie was warmly supported at first by kings eager to win backing in their efforts to reduce feudal lords to submission. These ambitious bourgeois and ambitious monarchs were not troubled much, of course, by theological difficulties but there was an inherent antagonism between their economic pretensions and those of the Church and its lay allies in the feudal lords.

Doubtless a hot dispute would have come even if there had been no differences of religious opinion. But other circumstances made for diversity of views and disputes in matters intellectual. The increasing knowledge of pagan learning, which indeed had never been entirely lost to Christendom, kept the theologians at their wits' ends reconciling the richness of Greek thought with the strait and narrow boundaries of the Christian epic. Finally as the Renaissance flowered, with the swift expansion of commerce, many a Christian, lay and clerical, began to occupy himself more with ancient wisdom than with the speculations of the scholastics, and things reached such a pass that Erasmus could burlesque the whole monkish show in his *Praise of Folly* — Erasmus the good Catholic. Evidently the theological monopoly could stand no such strain as this. Something was bound to give way if knowledge of the new learning ever escaped to the lower classes. It so happened that the printing press and cheap paper soon supplied the medium which communicated revolutionary lore to those who had economic reasons for diminishing the income of the clerical estate.

In due time all of northern Christendom, nearly all the segments of Europe which had never been thoroughly subdued to the arms, law and religions of Rome, broke away from the ancient Church, with profound repercussions in thought and government, including the rôle of women in the civilising process. This is no place to attempt even a barest outline of that upheaval, but certain elements of the picture help to explain the transition from the age of the gods to the age of positive knowledge. First of all, ambitious princes, aided by beneficiaries, noble and bourgeois, despoiled the Church of millions of acres of good land and distributed the goods among favorites. In this revolution, the economic support of thousands of women in the convents was destroyed and they were deprived of opportunities to devote themselves to their historic cultural pursuits. For the convent, early Protestantism made no substitute. When it took over monastic colleges, it closed the nunneries. But the overthrow of the celibate clergy and female anchorites had astounding social effects. For instance, the family, which had long furnished rituals and good round fees for the clergy, was secularised. The politics of princes and ruling classes brushed aside the theological speculations that had long monopolised the attention of the clergy, foreshadowing the rise of political economy. Though many Protestants were as pious and zealous as Catholics in their devotions, on the whole the secular area of life was widened immensely and religious interests were destined to be restricted to a small corner — the relative size of which can be determined by comparing the secular and theological works of any modern library, to name a single clue.

Contrary to many traditions, Protestantism was far from tolerant. Some of the later sects within its general fold spoke for liberty but sects in a position of political dominance have rarely in history surrendered their monopoly graciously. And as a matter of fact Protestantism in the beginning marked a reaction with respect to the position of women. In casting off the supremacy of the Pope, it took on the supremacy of a single book, the Bible, and especially its oldest God, Jahweh, harsh and patriarchal. There were fine illustrations of ancient matriarchs in the Old Testament, it is true, but the overweening emphasis was masculine and stern. Popes had always palliated what could not be prevented, and women, from the Mother of God to the lowliest peasant woman, came within the purview of Catholic teaching and practice. But with the triumph of the Old Testament theology among the Protestants, especially of the mercantile groups, there was a recrudescence of Augustinian and other Church-father aversions to sex. All thought of equality and easy relations of men and women in religious activities, such as those once pursued by monks and nuns, became anathema — as Anne Hutchinson found out to her sorrow in early Massachusetts. The Quakers later rectified this to a considerable extent but they were a relatively small offshoot of Puritanism. What is also significant was the decline in the princely leadership of religion with the insurgence of bourgeois control. Thus among the Protestants, there were fewer women of noble families to assume direction of thought even if the convents had been reopened. So in time the thrifty housewife of the bourgeois establishment, competent within her sphere, took the place of the Mother of God or a devout Clare as the ideal intellectual fixation.

In the social revolution that accompanied the religious upheaval, women were of course involved as individuals and as members of families and asserted themselves in every aspect of the fermenting social scene. At the dawn of Protestantism they still remained under the shadow of demonology and the symbolism of wicked temptation. No Church father ever delivered a more sweeping diatribe against the sex than the following explosion by Bishop Aylmer in the presence of Queen Elizabeth: "Women are fond, foolish, wanton flibbergibs . . . evil-tongued, worse-minded, and in every way doltified with the dregs of the devil's dunghill." Yet Elizabeth would have liked to retain a celibate clergy if she could.

But the abolition of clerical celibacy did something to improve the status of women. It relieved society of the necessity of protecting itself against clerical vagaries and removed from intellectual dominance a class of men and women who, by their very vows of chastity, proclaimed as inherently evil all sexual relations. By denying the sacramental character of marriage, Protestantism in due course put that institution on a civil and contractual basis, preparing the way for easy divorce and the settlement of the family relations by the adults involved. Although the Puritans theoretically went back in their severity to something like mediæval asceticism, actually the Protestant revolt set in train a movement which repudiated the historic obsessions with sex, decried hypocritical indulgence and its morbid aftermath, boldly attacked the problems of illegitimacy with which the Middle Ages had dealt furtively and often cruelly, and paved the way for a realisation of the rational, humorous aspects of biology. Yet it is well to be on guard against attempting to delimit too exactly the influence of Protestantism on the sex relations. Many changes came in spite of Protestantism rather than on account of it and practices among Catholics were so often different from official views that precision in generalisation is almost impossible.

Whatever judgment partisans may render, it is well to remember that on both sides of the religious battle women appeared as patrons, advocates, persecutors, and martyrs. In England a woman was one of the chief causes of the breach with Rome; if Henry VIII had married a young wife at first and issue had assured succession, England might have remained indefinitely in communion with the Pope. Mary and Elizabeth, both daughters of Henry, one Catholic and the other Protestant, were persecutors, cruel and vindictive. After he cast off the Pope, Martin Luther married a former nun of the Cistercian order, Catherine von Bora, who combined intellectual skill with practical competence and shared in many of the intense parleys on theological and political strategy held in their home. In a significant letter to his wife, Luther makes one of his clearest statements on the position of Zwingli with respect to the sacrament of the Lord's Supper. For a time Calvin found a patroness in Renée, the duchess of Ferrara, a cousin of Margaret of Navarre, daughter of Louis XII, who made her court a center for men of letters and finally embraced the reformed faith though opposed by a resentful and brutal husband. On her return to France after the death of her husband she transformed her estate into a home of religious propaganda and thus came into violent conflict with Catholic authorities. All this is merely by way of illustrating the truth that, when an objective history of Protestantism is written, it will not be merely a story of theological battles, princely ambitions, or masculine vagaries.

On the other side of the widening chasm stood St. Teresa (1515-1582) of Spain, "the Doctor of the Church," whom Catholics delight to honor as "the greatest intellectual woman of all time." While Catherine de' Medici sought to suppress Protestantism by the sword, Sister Teresa chose the way of penance and mercy, a humane adaptation of political economy. The rich she styled stewards of God employing social responsibility at His behest. If some among their number felt compelled to sell all they had and give it to the poor and to return to labor with their hands, that self-denial was not required by the moral law. Members of the nobility, to which Teresa belonged, were, in her scheme of things, to serve the masses as lords and ladies bountiful; the abuses of wealth were to be lopped off and class antagonisms smoothed away by generosity and piety. Turning to the vast clerical estate, Teresa worked for reform there by a restoration of rigid discipline. Though Teresa scourged herself and wore haircloth, she warned her colleagues against excesses in asceticism. Not by that route lay the way to heaven but through alms-giving and self-sacrifice. For luxurious living she proposed the wearing of straw sandals, sleeping on straw pallets, abstaining from meat, and living on alms. Though Catholic priests opposed her program of discipline, Teresa won over the Pope, founded the Barefoot Carmelite Sisters and a similar Order for men, organized retreats for the faithful, and established convents and monasteries.

In the midst of her busy and sacrificial life, she found time to write religious works of such power that the modern Catholic scholar, Dr. Walsh, has ventured to rank her with Dante. Among many titles three may be especially mentioned: *The Way of Perfection, The Castle of the Soul,* and *The Book of Foundations,* to anglicise their titles. Bossuet and Fénelon proclaimed her their teacher "in the science of the saints." German mystics gave her unfailing reverence. At the portal of the Vatican she stands immortalised in marble and in the libraries of the world great collections of books associated with her name bear witness to a continued intellectual interest in Teresa's life and work.

A BALANCE SHEET

IF A balance sheet is struck at the end of fifteen centuries of Christian development with a view to an analysis of our heritage, many items stand clearly in the ledger. For example Europe has got rid of the legal slavery on which Greece and Rome were founded, has substituted asscription to the soil for chattel bondage, and has in religious theory at least taken the lowest orders of society into the fellowship of the spiritual — whatever that may mean in terms of social practice. But the spirit of acquisition and dominion in which slavery flourished is far from extinct, for both Protestants and Catholics resorted to it with avidity in the exploitation of the New World and its effects linger in this industrial age. The acquisitiveness — the robber psychology — of the pagan Greek and Roman remains in Christendom. Neither the revival of ancient puritan revolts nor the asceticism that came from the Orient have been able to subdue economic power to the ideals of conscious restraint.

In matters pertaining to the care of life there has been no marked gain over Greek and Roman antiquity. The landed proprietor of the feudal age looked down with contempt upon the merchant as did the Roman senator and Greek philosopher. If common labor was dignified in words and often practiced by zealous monks and nuns, it nevertheless remained in fact unhonored drudgery for the mass of laymen at the bottom who performed it. If the serf was better off than the Roman slave, and unquestionably he was, his position was far below that of the free Roman farmer of early republican days. Although the abuses of Roman slavery largely disappeared with the rise of serfdom, due partially perhaps to Christian and Stoic teaching as alleged, serfdom itself was accompanied by abuses glaring enough and on that subject the writings of the mediæval scholastics are singularly restrained. Aquinas himself wrote on slavery with a coldness and precision that would have pleased any slaveowner of Roman days: "Inducing a slave to leave his master is properly an injury against the person . . . and, since the slave is his master's chattel, it is referred to theft." Day laborers were in his eyes simply *pauperes* seeking daily bread and limited to the minimum of existence. Artisans and merchants, to be sure, are entitled to just wages and prices, but it is conservative to assume that they owed as much to the strongly organised gilds of which they were members as to the genial teachers of the Church authorities. With respect to trade in general there was an evolution; St. Augustine thought that it was evil because it turned men from God; Leo the Great thought that it was neither good nor bad in itself and that its merits depended upon the manner in which it was carried on; and as commerce grew, ingenious devices were discovered for covering mercantile practices. In other words, no genuine system of Christian economy can be generalised from the writings of the theologians scattered over fifteen centuries. Efforts in this direction usually spring from modern controversies, not from a wide understanding of the mediæval teachings.

In the matter of economy, fifteen centuries of the Christian era have introduced some humanity but have not carried it far beyond the best teachings of the Greeks and the Romans. After all, the economy of life in the large was not the center of intellectual interest in the Middle Ages any more than in antiquity. The fundamental center of thought was salvation in the next world. Ideologically, this earth was at best a sad and dreary place, full of sin and sorrow, a school of discipline to be endured merely as a kind of gateway to paradise. Many monks and some nuns did study "natural science," such as it was, but their horizon was usually limited to Aristotle and vague speculations, while their religious faith discouraged worry about the manifold manifestations of nature. They made some advances in the Middle Ages along scientific lines, as we shall show in later pages, but their vision was almost

exclusively bounded by Biblical cosmology. For practical purposes the Bible had said all that was necessary to say on the
creation of the world, the ways of animals and humans, the
geography of the earth's surface, astronomy, miracles, signs,
wonders, sex, medicine, hygiene, insanity, witchcraft and opinion. If theology itself had not restrained mentality to narrow
channels of inquiry, the tyranny of sacred books and class
psychology would have prevented the rise and growth of
experimental science or the concentration of ethics on that
essential interest of culture — the care for life. Greek intellectualism, Roman politics, and mediæval theology alike
made scant contribution to the problem of decent and genial
living for society as a whole.

A few citations, chosen from Andrew D. White's compen-
dious treatise on *The Warfare of Science with Theology,* may
serve as illustrations. The ancient nations, even distinguished
thinkers, believed in witchcraft and in diabolical spirits as the
source of insanity and hysteria; a few wise physicians of the
Greek and Roman world held otherwise but made no headway against popular delusions; mediæval theology bore down
heavily on the popular side; and ancient delusions lived on
until the end of the eighteenth century. Socrates had believed
that certain investigations in physical science were impious
intrusions into the realm of the gods; mediæval theologians did
not depart far from that view. Plato thought lightly of
physical science and contributed many elements of magic to
mediæval theology; his speculative successors outdid him in
nearly every magical particular. In medical science the Middle Ages marked a distinct decline from the position attained
by the best thinkers of antiquity and merely continued perhaps
popular customs and beliefs at a low level.

In the history of sanitation the inner nature of mediæval
interest can best be illuminated. As White points out: "Liv-

ing in filth was regarded by great numbers of holy men, who set an example to the Church and to society, as an evidence of sanctity. St. Jerome and the Breviary of the Roman Church dwell with unction on the fact that St. Hilarion lived his whole life long in utter physical uncleanliness; St. Athanasius glorified St. Anthony because he never washed his feet; St. Abraham's most striking evidence of holiness was that for fifty years he washed neither his hands nor his feet; St. Sylvia never washed any part of her body save her fingers; St. Euphraxia belonged to a convent in which the nuns religiously abstained from bathing; St. Mary of Egypt was eminent for filthiness; St. Simon was in this respect unspeakable — the least that can be said is that he lived in ordure and stench intolerable to his visitors." With these examples before them it is not surprising that the mediæval scholastics gave little attention to sanitation, that epidemics raged periodically through the centuries, and that magic, exorcism, and propitiation were the chief weapons employed in combating these dreadful specters, as they were in the last days of Athens. In spite of centuries of Greek intellectualism, Roman enjoyment of power and pomp, and the long battle of the gods, humanity was still far removed from an understanding of the world in which it lived, a knowledge of common things necessary to a good communal life, and a theory of mankind and the world with which to move on to a nobler existence here below.

The compensation was considered to be a spirituality that rose above materialism. But that spirituality did not eliminate the consciousness of earthly possessions whenever they were menaced. Nor has the capacity for persecution disappeared after fifteen centuries of Christian teaching; both Catholics and Protestants could burn heretics at the stake with the same zeal displayed in destroying Christian martyrs. Women as well as men could rejoice in the creak of the rack and the crackle of the faggots as their victims were done to death, and women as well as men continued the cry against heretics. Ladies who professed Christ could be as cruel and vindictive as Roman matrons who cheered with the mob when martyrs were flung to the wild beasts in capacious amphitheaters. The gentle sex seems at times of hysteric outbursts to be very much the same after the lapse of ages, seeing their God on the side of the strongest battalions. If there has been a change in "spirituality," it is a matter of degree rather than of kind.

PART VI

TO THE CONQUEST OF THE EARTH

OUT of the East into the West with the rise cf Empire flowed a taste for power, luxury, pomp and mystical religions, the last of which was Christianity. But out of the East into the West with the movement of Commerce, especially after the Crusades, flowed curiosity and criticism of traditions on the tide of classical manuscripts. And from curiosity and criticism came a wide and varied positive knowledge of this world and the peoples in it — a positive knowledge so extraordinary in its range and so intensively applied that it undermined the whole order inherited from the long centuries of pure speculation.

The so-called "Decline of the West" in fact merely marks the twilight of the era of mother goddesses, god-kings, oracular wisdom, castes, and reliance on force as the prime mode of acquisition. The Rise of the West on the other hand, even now scarcely heralded but none the less emergent, marks the sunlight of searching inquiry, accurate information, secular liberties, sensational tools for the exploitation of nature, labor movements and consideration for the masses, democratic education, universal enfranchisement, racial catholicities, and a humanism related to the care of all life that scientific advances alone could produce. A huge complex moving through primitive struggles for existence, warfare, tyranny, superstition, otherworldliness, commercial expansion, and industrial development now flowers in a culture the like of which the world has never known and to which the entire earth is being tied with ropes literally of steel; for it is the conquest of the earth in the interests of mortal life that constitutes the novel idealism of the new age.

Primitive life was narrow, limited by the immediate horizon, concerned with adaptation to nature more than its exploitation, sacrificial in its burden-bearing, over-worked, and cramped by superstitions. Greek and Roman life was provincial, essentially Mediterranean — a wider horizon to be sure, but restricted in comparison with the vast Occidental-Oriental, two hemispheroid, arctic to antarctic, urban, forest and desert contacts of the present time. Relatively little was known to European antiquity about the Far East and nothing about the Far West. Greek and Roman intellectualism was highly speculative, shot through with archaic fears and fancies peopling an unseen realm with enemies mightier than man; through its aloofness from economic realities, it was unable to avert the doom of thinkers, classes, states and civilisations. Life in mediæval Christendom was still provincial and timid, European, mystical, theological, having to do with gods and devils of an unseen world — a shadow realm — more than with men and women in this world. Furthermore the culture of mediæval Christendom like that of Greece and Rome was stamped with the ineradicable brand of caste despotism mitigated only by gentle speeches about the dignity of labor and an effort to check usury. With this heritage Protestantism as such made no fundamental break; it remained theological; indeed it intensified abstruse debate on the mysteries by returning to the Sacred Word for supreme authority, elbowing aside even more severely the pagan writers whom the Catholic scholastics had revived and studied, and building its culture on unchangeable fiats delivered in the childhood of the race.

With this whole past the world of positive knowledge, turned to the conquest of the earth, is a departure. Its horizon is the globe — traversed and charted by explorers, traders, travelers by land, sea and air, archæologists, anthropologists, and students of comparative religions, literature, and practices. In its outlook the little peninsula of Asia known as Europe is but a sector in a range covering the four quarters of the globe — a range that includes not merely the mud hut or the wigwam, the Acropolis or the Academy, the Forum or Parliaments, St. Peter's, Notre Dame, and Westminster, "tin cathedrals" of the non-conformists and the wooden benches of New World emigrés worshipping according to their consciences, but Broadway in New York, the Shoso-in at Nara in Japan, the Temple of Heaven in China, the Taj Mahal in India, railways, steamships, cables, wireless, aseptic surgery, and international quarantine. This extension of outlook overrides barriers of caste as well as nations and continents. If contemporary democracy is fragmentary, its stoutest foe has no hope of restoring, in its frozen form at least, the system of submerged classes, on which all previous civilisations rested. Intellectualism is now concerned to an ever-increasing degree with the precise knowledge of nature and its application to human labor, including the burden of primitive women — the care of life. Destiny has new connotations since the Rise of the West.

For one thing, and by no means an insignificant aspect of the changed conceptual thought, the sense of tragedy is lightened. The old corn woman of the fields — be she god or be she devil — can no longer determine the happiness or grief of agriculturists equipped with chemical fertilisers and tractors. Perhaps no farmer would return to the primitive romance if he had the choice of ways and means. When a house is on fire, evil spirits may no more postpone relief until propitiatory rites have been performed. Blood transfusion from mortal to mortal supersedes the practice of health infusion by rubbings over the chests of graven images or the touching of eyes and toes. If to this hour Balkan believers in magic come to the Sava River once a year with bottles, kegs, pails and caskets with which to dip up the water made holy by priestly intervention and carry it away for emergencies as a healing gift from Heaven, believers in scientific cures and disease prevention employ matter-of-fact remedies and enjoy the patronage of multitudes among the religious-minded. Fire-engines, water filters, railways, housing laws and serums have reduced the magnetic power of idols beyond the dreams of ancient Ionian well-wishers and divorced the new age from the old with a sharpness almost comparable to the change from pithecanthropus erectus to man. The noise of the motorplow drowns the tones of the Angelus but crops flourish better for the change and the head bowed over the hoe can lift to gaze upon the world at large. When Leonardo da Vinci declared that an insect is as important as a planet on which thought had interminably revolved, the time was approaching for everything on the earth below or in the heavens above to come within the scope of free inquiry and analysis. Even the notion of original sin gave place to the doctrine of evolution. Man, it is now claimed, has not degenerated, as the ancient and mediæval thinkers maintained, but has advanced mentally and spiritually through the ages of his life. Biology and philosophy, history and literature are summoned to court to testify in favor of the new creed.

Perhaps humanity is finding again a lost trail after untold centuries of wandering through blind alleys, following false guides, and experiencing the tragedies of decimation, ruin and death. Possibly it is returning in its advance to the original trail blazed by primitive woman — to prime concern with food, clothing and shelter, health and the arts associated with labor, in short with the care of life, all life — prepared to carry its exploration to romantic lengths and altitudes.

THE SECULAR ORGANISATION OF FEUDAL CHAOS

WOMEN's first help in the new civilising process was rendered in the political field. They were energetic and forceful agents in creating unified States out of feudal vandalism, though historians have favored the deeds of Louis XI, Henry VIII, Louis XIV, Napoleon, or Frederick the Great in their celebration of the rise and development of modern societies. Where they have mentioned women in this connection, they have generally fallen into the habit of ascribing their achievements to ministers and councilors, viewing their strength as evidence of "masculinity" and their weakness as a sign of "femininity," usually without stopping to think that the rule is absurd because it could with equal logic be reversed. A few commentators have referred to the "intrigues" of ladies at courts forgetting to place the same emphasis on the intrigues of men at the same institutions.

It is necessary therefore to call attention to neglected factors in the narrative. First of all the national State, in its making, has been associated with a few powerful families — Tudor, Bourbon, Hapsburg, Hohenzollern and Romanoff. When after a thousand years of bitter rivalry among feudal households, one rose to dominance and ruled a nation, the schemes, negotiations, and intermarriage of men and women marked every step in the story. Was it Spain? Then it is not too much to say that the emergence of that country from the banditry of feudal arrangements and its advance to leadership in exploration and the arts, were due, to a degree immense and beyond calculation, to the clear-headedness, pertinacity, and indomitable character of Isabella of Castile and Leon. By her marriage with Ferdinand of Aragon general unity was at last attained as far as important feudal families were concerned. But she was not a passive member of the union. Both in council and in the field she was continually active. The low and petty basis of Spanish politics she overcame by strong-arm methods inspired by piety, sobriety and devotion to the ideal of order. She made mistakes, such as her massacre and expulsion of Moors and Jews which reduced the industrial and commercial skill of her population, and her religious policy was in line with the harshest traditions of the Catholic Church that claimed her allegiance. Nevertheless a genuine history of the rise of Spain to competence as a nation must take cognizance of Isabella's genius. Had Isabella II, who ruled from 1843 to 1868, some four centuries afterward, had as much character, discernment and capacity, had she been enlightened instead of wholly unscrupulous and reactionary, Spain might have been spared long years of anæmia and folly, might have grown normally into a constitutional régime and escaped the agonies of a second civil conflict precedent to the revolution of yesterday.

If we turn to France rising out of the turmoil of feudal fighting, we find three women standing at the portal of the future and showing that dispirited land her responsibility. These were Christine de Pisan, Jeanne d'Arc, and Agnes Sorel, all of whom contended for the mastery of the timid king, Charles VI, in order that the ground might be cleared of the English invaders and France go about her organising task. As the biographer of Christine suggests, the poet who sang that "men must work and women must weep" overlooked the fact that "men and women alike must needs do both," for Christine felt compelled to throw her extraordinary intellectual vigor into the task of creating a great State capable of restoring a devastated region to healthy conditions. She appealed to the king and the court to gird themselves for a courageous attack on the evils which were eating at the vitals of society, and when they continued to dawdle, she sent to Spain a plea to use its influence in stopping the awful work of the English sword. But she was more sensitive than Isabella to the rôle of a middle class in civilisation and tried to institute a liberal policy toward the French bourgeoisie. Christine's name and fame reached throughout the Western world.

Christine feared that her ardent desire to see France a nation was in vain but she lived until the hour when the Maid of Orleans successfully commanded armies which Frenchmen were loath to lead and her dying word was a tribute to the girl who had given them courage. Then it became the turn of Agnes Sorel to make the enthroned Charles VI every inch a king.

When Louis XI consolidated the realm, he gave attention to marriage jointures as well as to arms and poison and conciliated the middle class as Christine de Pisan had advocated. From that time forward until the Capetian-Bourbon line finally came to an end, women entered into family politics and negotiations at every stage. It was Catherine de' Medici, the wife of one French king and the mother of three more, who as Queen on the death of her husband inspired the murder of Coligny and the massacre of St. Bartholomew. What France lost through the persecution of the Huguenots, the New World gained, for mercantile genius was rich among the sect and many of its most talented men and women migrated to the English colonies in America if they did not settle in Protestant countries such as England. Merciless in her final policy toward religious dissenters, Catherine of the Medicis was a leading spirit in the rise of France as the social dictator of Europe. Her love of art and her passion for sumptuous luxury imparted to France a generous measure of the elegance that clustered round the throne.

The history of the French court during the long reign of Louis XIV is to a high degree the story of a succession of royal mistresses — de la Vallière, de Montespan, de Maintenon who became his unofficial wife when the queen died. If there is any aspect of French policy during this period into which feminine negotiations did not penetrate, it is difficult to discover it. Wars were fought in relation to family interests. The fateful decision to revoke the Edict of Nantes granting toleration to Protestants was made under the pious influence of Madame de Maintenon. Through the wars, diplomacy, ruinous extravagance, and revolutions that accompanied the Bourbons to their tragic finish, feminine operations continued unabated. And when the last of the Napoleonic adventurers was unhorsed, the Empress Eugénie was visible in the spotlight of the manipulations which brought the downfall of the imperial line. Women helped to make France a State and helped to reshape the State once established.

Consider England also. The wars of two families — Lancaster and York — threatened to disrupt that kingdom but the House of Tudor brought unity and strength. Even the Protestant revolt there was facilitated, if not produced, by the domestic difficulties of Henry VIII, growing out of his marriage with Catherine of Aragon against which he entered a protest at the time, with which he could not be reconciled **after it was** found to be a son-less union. Whatever weight may be ascribed to his flirtations as a cause of the religious reformation, his solicitude for the continuance of his line, with all that meant to the peace of the realm, was mainly responsible for his extraordinary career in theology, matrimony and politics. And of the three Tudor successors to this remarkable king, two were daughters, each every inch a sovereign, while the third, Edward VI, proved a weakling in body and mind. Mary, called the "bloody" by Protestants, measured up to the clerical and masculine standards of her age. Of Elizabeth, the cleverness of her administration, and the brilliance of her reign nothing need be said to English-speaking peoples; they bulk large in all histories of England. When every allowance is made for fortune and for the wisdom of her counselors, it is admitted that she was resourceful, dominant and ingenious and that with superb skill she steered the Ship of State through troubled waters to a haven of political security and great economic power. Compared with Elizabeth, the Stuarts, who followed on the throne, seem trivial rulers. One was a wise fool, the other lost his head on a scaffold, a third dallied with mistresses, a fourth was driven into exile. Tried by every test even Queen Anne, belittled by critics, was their superior in statecraft. And did not Victoria, two centuries afterward, set the tone for a whole epoch ? Whether one likes the tone or not is another matter.

In the upbuilding of central and eastern European States women were likewise powers on the throne and not merely behind it. For about a quarter of a century indeed — the third quarter of the eighteenth — they were dictators in Europe. Maria Theresa was one of these. Into the creation of the Austro-Hungarian Empire a combination of family fortunes, intrigues, and negotiations entered and when the signal for its collapse was given, the wife of the heir apparent was murdered with the Archduke at Serajevo — the double tragedy intensifying the sense of horror with which the news was received by the outside world. Of that long political history no sketch can be given in this limited space but a few notes may be injected. When Charles VI died in 1740 and the male line was broken, there came to the throne a woman, Maria Theresa, who was lacking in none of the qualities demanded of a powerful ruler and for forty years she exercised them in war and peace with a skill that none can gainsay. If the story of her theatrical winning of the Hungarians by holding up her infant son in her arms and calling upon them for allegiance is apocryphal, it is true in spirit, for she gained her point.

In military exploits and diplomacy she was so efficient that all Europe had to reckon with her skill. She shared in the partition of Poland with a vigor her tears failed to minimise. Devout Catholic though she remained, Maria Theresa feared the Pope as little as she feared her rival, Frederick the Great, and she suppressed the Jesuits with a severity that brooked no opposition. With an eye to the future she trained her son and successor, Joseph II, in the arts of statecraft, his greater liberalism betokening an advanced era rather than a distinct mental vitality. European relations in mind, she married her daughter, Marie Antoinette, to the dauphin of France, instructing her to be tender to the king's mistresses for the sake of harmony between the two peoples. The monarchical system in mind, she provided her with a counselor whom she might have done well to heed, considering the fact that public approbation was essential to sovereignty. Besides all this, she found time to bear five sons and eleven daughters, so that any danger of failure in the line was obviated. If Austria does not appear in the arena when the world comes to an end, it will be no fault of Maria Theresa.

During her reign, Frederick was seeking slices of her territory to the west and Catherine the Great was keeping the whole Western World in a furor over her operations to the East. Thus we come to the Romanoffs, builders of the Russian State. In the daughter of a Lithuanian peasant, Peter the Great found first a mistress and then a wife, and before his death she was proclaimed his successor. This extraordinary woman, Catherine I, unlearned in Letters but shrewd in judgment, ruled with dignity and caution during the brief span of her remaining years and bequeathed a worthy heritage, according to regal standards. Catherine I however has been completely overshadowed by Catherine II, known as the Great, ruler of Russia from 1762 to 1796, for in the whole history of statecraft there is no more amazing figure. The daughter of a petty German prince, married to the Grandduke Peter who treated her with utter brutality, Catherine II rejoiced when he was removed from the scene shortly after his accession to the throne and immediately took the crown herself. Whether she helped to dispose of him is not certain but she was capable of it.

When once the scepter was firmly in her hand, Catherine ruled with a rod of iron. For more than thirty years as monarch of all the Russias, she was at the very center of European wars, diplomacy and plunder. The Balkan question she lifted to a major issue by her self-appointment as protector of the Near East against the Turk; her destruction of the Turkish squadron in the Ægean Sea and her occupation of the Black Sea, with her threat to expel the invader from the entire Balkan area to the very gates of Vienna, made her even more than the Turk the terror of the European nations; and rulers united against her. But in all the tricks of the political trade, Catherine showed herself strong and versatile and her performances are written so large in the European drama that her name appears in the most conventional histories. Critics are fond of attributing her power to her masculinity and her weakness to her femininity but to this kind of reasoning biology may well be indifferent. Frederick, her neighbor, would have to be brought into the discussion in any case, so parallel ran their personalities.

In religion she was as sceptical as Voltaire, though she knew the advantages of its uses. In benevolent despotism she was, like her Prussian colleague, deeply interested and toyed in a similar fashion with it until it became dangerous. If she did not suggest the partition of Poland, as asserted, she shared in it with joy. In the barbarism of the knout, assassination, and execution, Catherine II was equal to the best Romanoff traditions while in the matter of loose living she was free enough to please either Frederick or Napoleon. When all is said and done, Catherine shared the concern of her predecessors for the greatness and strength of Russia and it seems to have been her historic mission to prepare the way for the autocracy attacked by the Vera Figners and Vera Sassuliches who helped to overthrow Catherine's species of government and bring on the modern age in Russia.

Unlike the law of other families, that of the Hohenzollerns, founders of Prussia and the German Empire, excluded women from the throne, the large supply of eligible sons making such a diversion unnecessary. Yet, as those who have examined court memoirs report, the women of the Hohenzollern household also influenced the course of Prussian politics in ways both direct and subtle. Passing over the earlier period for a survey of our own, fraught with such memorable consequences, we may take as an illustration the Empress Victoria, daughter of Queen Victoria of England and wife of the Emperor Frederick III, ruler for a few months in 1888. Under her advice and that of her father, the Prince Consort of England, Frederick in his young manhood openly espoused the cause of liberalism against the autocratic policy of Bismarck and, had he lived, Germany might gradually have developed a parliamentary system of government, on an English model. What might in that case have resulted with respect to domestic and foreign affairs is a matter for interesting speculation. With the military party weakened through civilian control, would Germany have fallen an earlier victim to France and Russia ? Or would there have been a more rapid orientation in the direction of England which would have kept that power out of the conflict of these recent years and assured German hegemony on the Continent ? This speculation belongs to the mythology of history but it seems significant to note that a contingency of fortune prevented an English empress from driving the Hohenzollerns in the direction of liberalism, with all that was involved in such a reform.

After the great States were erected, they were more or less democratised one by one and the surviving dynasts transformed into ceremonial heads. With that evolution, the rôle of royal women declined in politics, in favor of rule by anonymous masses. Although conspiracies could still affect the selection of ministers here and there, the iron régime of political parties materially reduced the area of such operations. Nevertheless woman suffrage was steadily gaining headway and women were being drawn into the organisations and debates of political parties. If it was no longer possible for an Isabella, an Elizabeth, an Anne, a Maria Theresa, or a Catherine to determine elaborate policies of State; if the curtain had gone down perhaps forever on an old play, the future was lifting the curtain on another perhaps more wonderful.

THE DISCOVERY OF NEW WORLDS

THE Continent of Europe, on which these great States were taking form amid family strife and warfare, much organisation flowing from chaos, was in spite of its area a diminutive stage, the world at large considered. If the men and women who acted according to the rules of a feudal Shakespeare evolved into the creators of strong nations, the battlements of the separated nations and even the walls of Europe were shaken by explorers and traders who finally merged all mankind in a single theater, under a single sky, in a common destiny, world-wide.

Europe conquered by arms a large part of the globe but that does not mean she possessed what she conquered, any more than the nobility of old Rome really possessed the land into which the caste sank down to its political and economic death. Europe spread Christianity far and wide but its religious march was firmly halted by floods of humanity against which it could not prevail. Contacts with Oriental civilisations in turn altered the outlook of Europe as their splendors made the eyes of Marco Polo start in their sockets and fired the imagination of those who listened to his travel tales. Civilisations already seasoned when cocks crowed on the mud and stone huts of Greece and Rome were to rise on the horizon of Occidental thought and affect Occidental enterprise. Contacts with primitive tribes and races, perhaps even more, were to illuminate the darker corners of European mentality as anthropologists shed their light on man, explaining mysteries wholly veiled to the ancient philosophers and the theologians of the Middle Ages.

It was a Spanish Queen who led the advance toward world consciousness — beyond the spectacular to the total actuality. We have already seen her operating on a local stage, unifying and administering a nation, a woman of great energy, moral confidence, and intellectual acumen in spite of many mistaken policies that can be ascribed to her. It was under the patronage of the Spanish monarchy and with the help of its treasury that Columbus sailed on his first voyage of exploration which uncovered the New World and led eventually to the uncovering of the Far East. In vain had this dreamer begged and pleaded with rich merchants and rulers for help when at last, as he was on the verge of despair, the crown of Spain came to his aid — to the help of a forlorn and "foolish" navigator bent on making a quixotic adventure across the high sea.

It would be a mistake to attribute the support for his final victory to Isabella alone. Historical writings inform us that she recalled Columbus to her presence and said: "I will assume the undertaking for my own crown of Castile and am ready to pawn my jewels to defray the expenses, if the funds of the treasury should be found to be inadequate." But modern researches have questioned and perhaps cancelled the letter of that story. Nevertheless some important things are clear. The learned men of Salamanca brought the Scriptures to bear in their anxiety to disprove the theories of Columbus and ridiculed the very idea of this venture. The cause of the navigator seemed lost. Then the Queen's confessor took kindly to his plan, urged her to support it, was summoned to discuss it again with her, and arranged for the interview that set Columbus on his way. In its midst, success was threatened but Isabella saved the day, whatever share of credit may be assigned to the royal finance ministers or any other participants in this fateful affair. Columbus was seeking a route to the Orient and its culture; he discovered America and virgin soil occupied only by a few tribes of primitives.

While Spain led in the exploration which stretched the European horizon and changed European economy through the ensuing flow of gold and silver coin, England successfully colonised the newly discovered continent, women being as active as men in the enterprise, for colonisation required family participation. To make colonisation succeed, the sea power was imperative. And that was Elizabeth's cue. While she was on the throne, her courtier, Sir Walter Raleigh, framed a grand scheme for launching a new England, with which the Queen gladly collaborated. But good fortune withheld its favor for a time. Companies of adventurers were able to accomplish what the noble lord failed to achieve and women were members of the first successful colonising corporation that made Virginia a reality. Women of talent and experience in the industrial arts and management, active in almost every kind of trade, knowing what it was to toil in the field as well as by the fireside, with courage to brave the perils and hardships on land and sea, helped to make secure the foothold money and arms alone could not maintain.

Political and religious émigrées, wives, servants, laborers and capitalists turned to New World exploitation, to the conquest of the earth, gladly, while slaves from Africa, paupers and criminals from "merry England," bent their backs over the toil enforced upon them, bravely, if less enthusiastically. There was no phase of foundation, settlement, expansion, agriculture, commerce and politics which the women did not share. There was no hardship or terror that they missed, from the death-specter of the first New England winter to the scalping knife of the Indian, from the tyranny of government in a wilderness to the promotion of popular education. If colonial colleges shut women out of their precincts, the exclusion bore no relation to their own learning and culture.

Generalities in colonisation may be rendered concrete by a few details. Among the agricultural leaders of Maryland was Margaret Brent, one of thirteen children belonging to a Gloucester nobleman whose wife claimed descent from William the Conqueror. At all events Margaret decided to be a conqueror on her own account by exploiting latent resources in the New World. Bent on economic independence and having the capacity to achieve it, she came to Maryland in 1638 with a sister and brothers. The two girls held letters from Lord Baltimore assigning them areas of land as large and privileges as generous as those awarded to the first male grantees. Having brought with them five men and four maid servants, they were prepared to receive the acreage ordinarily offered to colonists, together with additional holdings, and to develop their estates. With great skill and energy, Margaret cultivated her property and extended it until she became one of the largest landlords in the colony, transporting men and women to work for her as her holdings expanded. As one of the chief landlords, Margaret Brent was deeply concerned in law and order. When the Claiborne rebellion broke out, she raised a band of volunteers to help Governor Calvert and in recognition of her administrative talents he named her as his executrix in official letters of administration. In order that she might take care of his estate, as well as her own, the Provincial Court made her an attorney and in this capacity she brought innumerable suits to collect rents and satisfy claims. Convinced that she needed a voice in the legislature, so that she might more efficiently discharge her obligations, she sought that privilege and, when it was denied, she withdrew to Westmoreland County, Virginia, a change which gave her property in both colonies and enabled her to play the part of manorial lord with the appropriate gusto.

About a hundred years later, in the colony of South Carolina, Eliza Lucas Pinckney, daughter of an English planter and administrator, wife of Charles Pinckney and mother of two "rebels," Charles and Thomas Coatesworth, rivaled Margaret Brent as a manager and went beyond her in agricultural experiments. At the age of seventeen during the absence of her father, Eliza acted as administrator of the plantations, imported special seeds from the East Indies, and took great pains, she said, "to bring the Indigo, Ginger, Cotton, Licern, and the Cassada to perfection." Her success in experimentation made her plantations an exhibit for surrounding planters and the skill with which she kept books gave them lessons in business efficiency. Nor did her managerial responsibilities cease with her marriage. Amid the duties of wife and mother, she carried them forward with unabated interest and indeed increased them during the absence of her husband in public service. After his early death she coupled the direction of his estate with that of her own, meeting the difficult situations that arose at the period of the Indian wars and experiencing the devastations of the Revolution when her property was laid waste. Yet at the close of the conflict, during which her fortune had been wrecked, her sons exiled, their property sequestered, and the blood of those near to her shed in battle, Eliza Pinckney was among the first Americans to counsel moderation and reconciliation. "Let me forget as soon as I can," she wrote in her old age, "their cruelties; I wish to forgive and will say no more on this subject, and hope our joy and gratitude for our great deliverance may equal our former anguish." Thus to economic capacity of the first order, to a talent for thinking and writing clearly, she joined the good sense of that statesmanship which subordinates passions to the great work of healing and construction. Without exaggeration it may be said that Eliza Pinckney was a planter of rare competence, a sensitive mother, an educator, a person of fine intellectual calibre, and a wise counselor.

In the French settlement of Canada, no less than in the English colonies, women helped to guarantee the proper nurture of life and the advancement of the physical frontier. French pioneers, who took up agriculture in the New World and developed industries, had wives and daughters as helpmeets coöperating in every department of economy. French women have been famous for their competence and enthusiasm for business responsibility. Into the making of New France went sturdy peasant girls from the mother country, orphans gathered from asylums, *filles du roi* dispatched to supply eligible mates for the bachelors, some "adventurous damsels of loose character," and fearless, devoted Church workers to lead in education, religion and nursing. The path-breaking priests were very soon followed by nuns equally courageous. As early as 1639 Ursuline Sisters had established schools for Indian children at Quebec and they soon founded a hospital for the sick, French and Indian, at Sillery, opened in December, 1640. Throughout the French régime, Catholic nuns participated in the enterprise of tempering the hard life of the wilderness with the amenities of Old France. No hardship daunted them — whether it was visiting the sick in the dead of bitter winters, living with the savage natives to learn their dialects and instruct them in ideals considered lofty by the Europeans, making lonely journeys to distant outposts, or keeping endless vigils in hospital wards. The name of Madame de la Peltrie, for one, must be entered beside the names of Margaret Brent and Eliza Pinckney in the history which deals with the extension of Europe that started in the sixteenth century and is still in motion.

As the thin frontier of settlements pushed to the west in America, women faced and endured wild beasts, wild men, and merciless nature alike. They were of every kind that humanity provides: the female relatives of sturdy farmers and mechanics, of hunters and trappers, of miners and prospectors; and women without families at hand who went west individually as missionaries, teachers, feminists, or "fast girls of the roaring camp." Some were quick with the rifle and dirk, others strong at the plow and loom, many soft and gentle in the sick-room, and hundreds invaluable as tutors as they pushed to the frontier from the factories of New England when the poor of Europe thronged into that section to work for a lower wage. If a grand debauch at a religious "revival" was the order of the day, women proved as capable of hysteria as anybody. If it was a problem of founding a school for a war on illiteracy and ignorance, their energy and counsel were sought and found helpful. If a long trip had to be made across mountains and the desert to Oregon, Utah, or California in the search for homes and happiness, they could ride and tramp over the interminable trails, perish like the best of pioneers in a Donner expedition, or climb the Rockies with the Lees and Whitmans victoriously. As always and everywhere, life was one.

When the epic is completed, covering the expansion of the Europeans across the North American continent, the development of Latin civilisation to the south, the establishment of New Zealand and Australia, the government of subject races and the explorations of the wilds, women's work will be found woven into the labors of men, and vice versa. A long and important narrative could be written on the single theme of British women's agricultural achievements in Canada.

THE RECOVERY OF SECULAR LEARNING

Excursions on the high seas and the discovery of new worlds furnished a setting for the recovery of ancient wisdom by means of which the cultural abyss was bridged between two ages of rationalisation. It is a mistake to connect the revival of classical, secular learning with the outbreak of Protestantism or to assume that it came suddenly near the close of the so-called Middle Ages. There were times and places in Western Christendom in which the great writers of classical antiquity were unknown, but no one who has tried to follow the history of any ancient idea through the mediæval period will be bold enough to fix dates for the reappearance of Plato or Seneca, for example, after the tide of the barbarian invasions into Rome subsided. Certain it is that Catholic scholars began the restoration of ancient learning and sought in some cases to work it into Christian apologetics. And it is also true that the process of reviving the old learning was long and arduous — a tangled story hard to ravel.

However, the progress and transfusion of this ancient culture, with its attempts at right reason about the universe and life, accorded precisely with the rise of commerce and the sea power. Throughout the early stages of this awakening, Italy led the way. Her geographical position made her the immediate heir of treasure in the matter of texts and scholarship, while her hardy seamen who rose to the opportunities opened by the Crusades paved the way for archæological explorers.

In 1391 a chair of Greek filled by a Greek was established at the University of Florence after tutors of Italian birth had tried to teach the new learning. Its occupant, Emanuel Chrysoloras of Constantinople, prepared a Greek grammar for his pupils. In 1445 some one wrote a work on the Greek syntax for the numerous universities that had arisen in Europe before the Middle Ages were far advanced. In 1448 an edition of Homer appeared. In 1497 came a Greek dictionary. As the Greek manuscripts began to sift into Italy such aids to their understanding were of course imperative. By the sixteenth century Italy had at least five excellent collections of classical literature and institutions for their use had been founded.

In this grand era of classical patronage kings and queens, potentates of the Church, lords and ladies, merchant princes, their wives and daughters, vied with one another in the purchase of superb relics, writings, and works of art. Pope Nicholas V was such a devotee of the fashion that he ran heavily into debt owing to the large sums he paid for treasures. Estimates place his manuscripts at between five and nine thousand and they were the foundation of the magnificent Vatican library which American money and efficient cataloguers have just made available for a selected circle of modern readers. Another classical bibliophile endowed the library in St. Mark's.

The Medicis likewise used their commercial and financial resources in the lavish purchase of museum pieces. When Giovanni Medici became Pope Leo X, he made Rome the great rival of mercantile Florence, where his family reigned, with respect to classical letters and art. He maintained scholars, assembled books, founded libraries in which to house them, established a Greek college and a Greek press in the holiest city of Christendom. Moreover he encouraged the teaching of the classics, Roman and Greek, throughout the schools of the Church, probably unaware of the dynamite in pagan philosophy or else convinced it could be handled with discretion. He set up a Platonist Academy in Florence and caused the Greek philosopher to be regarded as a doctrinally sound Christian. Side by side in the universities the new learning was taught with theology until the innovation crowded aside the clerical learning and secular departments grew in proportion to the spread of theological decay.

Long years before the death of Giovanni Medici most of the great Latin classics were in the possession of Italian bibliophiles and the Greek classics were pouring in steadily. When the equipment for a study of the past reached such proportions, news of its hidden glories induced a pacific crusade — that of Dutch, German, English and French students to the Italian centers of the new learning. They did not advance from their fastnesses this time at the bidding of the Church but on their own initiative to examine the wisdom of the ancients, much as American students of the nineteenth century flocked to German universities and artists to Italy and France. Of course this crusade was also devastating to the childlike innocence of its participants and it reacted on all Western Christendom as returned students brought back to their respective peoples what they had discovered across the Alps.

Suddenly also in the middle of the fifteenth century the printing press reached such a point of development that it could lend its artificial hand to the distribution of ancient learning. When classicism was so democratised the æsthetes and aristo-crats, lay and clerical, originally its sponsors, felt genuinely alarmed. Like many Englishmen who still resist the type-writer, exclusionists denounced the printing press as a speci-men of barbarism and materialism, prophetic of all machine-age attitudes taken by the precious. But there was more involved, of course, than æsthetics or novelty. Gutenberg's first publication was the Vulgate version of the Bible, thus put into wide circulation and serving to undermine authorita-tive interpretation by starting popular debates. Besides there were broad-minded Italians such as Theobaldi Manucci, of the celebrated Aldine publishing house in Venice, a Greek scholar and tutor who was so democratic in his sympathies that, while he invented beautiful type, he sold his out-put cheaply. Manucci himself had to face every sort of labor and copyright difficulty, and war silenced his presses for a time. Yet within twenty-two years his house had issued at least twenty-eight Greek and Latin classics while his estab-lishment had become the intellectual focus of a spirited circle of native and foreign classicists, disciples of rationalism, includ-ing Erasmus, transformed into Hellenists under Manucci's leadership. After his death, his family carried on the publish-ing plant for a century or more.

When Erasmus, Grocyn and Colet went as students to Italy, Italian women were already immersed in the classics. Ladies of the feudal caste had often received a better education than the lords and knights, who were in the field fighting much of the time, and it was now easy for them to turn that apprentice-ship in learning to full account, when a richer diet than the lives of the saints and the writings of the Church fathers was provided for their minds. And in the merchant families which rose to wealth and power in Italy through the Crusades, women gladly turned to the new culture as an occupation for their leisure and energy. The revival of classical wisdom re-quired both freedom and money. Once more therefore fem-inine patronage provided shelter, food and audience to scholars from the East. As Roman matrons had mothered the phi-losophies of their Hellenic age, so Italian matrons now nur-tured the advance from the mysteries to the cult of rationalism.

While the ladies and *jeunes filles* of the courts embroidered or sewed or wove, their instructors read to them from Cicero, Vergil, Sophocles or such other manuscripts as they had at hand. Then native teachers followed with readings in the vernacular from Dante, Petrarch and Ariosto. "Especially the wives and daughters of the condottieri," Burckhardt explains, "that is, of the hired leaders of armies, the self-made men of the time, who were lifting themselves up into positions of prominence, were the most frequent among the educated women of the Renaissance." There were also families of bankers, traders and manufacturers who took up the new cul-ture rendered fashionable at court. Admirals and navigators, able to provide leisure and funds for their women, vied with the glass-makers of Murano or the merchants of Genoa in giving them the opportunity for self-improvement along the new line. It was the daughter of Bartholomew Perestrello, a captain in the service of Prince Henry the Navigator, whom Columbus married. In her home he is thought to have found inspiration for his grand exploration. Schools for the "mod-ern" education were soon established in all the Italian cities and like the Church opened to the ambitious poor as well as the rich of both sexes.

What was *au fait* at Florence, Ferrara or Urbino was not necessarily the fashion at Venice, Genoa or Palermo. Feudalism was strong in one center of classicism, leaving tutoring and studying to the women and girls in the castles while men were away fighting. In other places, mercantile families, or the bourgeoisie, took the lead and the young people of both sexes were longer trained. But both groups produced women of distinction in their classical accomplishments. Fighting fathers and brothers on furloughs from the wars were not a little impressed when their daughters and sisters recited Greek and Latin stories and romances, pointed out the Milky Way to demonstrate their familiarity with astronomy, read verses of their own composition, and chatted with their tutors and courtiers about secular affairs. Composing Beautiful Letters, ladies inspired their admirers to excel them.

All the women of the Gonzaga family were celebrated for their culture of the new mode. At one time the daughter of the king of Naples was a noted scholar and philanthropist and her daughters, brought up in such an atmosphere, were regarded as grand prizes to be won in marriage by the sons of feudal lords. French and Spanish ambassadors and military officers were excited by the accomplishments of Italian women in the ducal palaces. Scholars, poets and philosophers were their guests and over assemblies of warriors, writers and savants they presided with such skill that a novel civilisation sprang up in Italy, news of which the foreigners bore home to their countryfolk, inspiring emulation by the local bourgeoisie.

Over the salon at Urbino in the heyday of the Italian classical revival, that is in the sixteenth century, reigned Elizabeth of Gonzaga whose "quick intelligence and ready sympathy" drew to the "Italian Athens" scholars, artists, and poets of the highest renown on the Continent. One of her courtiers, Castiglione, while he had a forum in his own palace where dialogues in the Greek style were the vogue, wrote an account of Elizabeth's in which he said: "Man has for his portion physical strength and external activities; all doing must be his, all inspiration must come from women." Among the gifted members of Elizabeth's coterie was Raphael who was helped at every stage of his career by imaginative women.

At Ferrara "there were as many poets as there were frogs in the country round about" and the most talented competed before the Duchesse Renée for honors. Here Clement Marot, the precursor of modern French poetry, helped to transfuse the Christian heritage with Hellenic romanticism, in rivalry with Ariosto, the Italian poet, diplomat, official, satirist and lover of liberty, and with Torquato Tasso who composed lyrics in praise of the young daughter of the house. Titian and Leonardo painted the regal intellectuals while the poets recited for them and the scholars discussed with them philosophical concepts. Again patrons were determining the drift of thought and culture. Women and monarchs, women and monks, were now being succeeded by women and secularisers. Peculiar emphasis was placed on the companionship of the sexes in things of the imagination, Italian in its source, and inspired by the freedom, wealth and eager curiosity of wives. The family was beginning to assert new prerogatives as against asceticism and, if the courtesan was not lacking in the picture, she was no longer supreme. As Hanns Floerke shows in *Das Weib in der Renaissance,* the power of love was injected into religion and the result was a great resurgence of creative genius. The formal chivalric court of love however was taking on intelligence.

Since Christianity provided no common meeting-place for the sexes and the Italian cities boasted no Pericles to act as dictator, the distribution and application of classical learning were largely in the hands of the circles gathered about the salonières. Assuming their responsibility in keen response to the charms of free thinking, clever hostesses checked license on the one hand in their experiment with easy associative privilege and stimulated wit and talent on the other. They erected the first great competitor of the Papacy out of their new enthusiasms. Art no less than Letters reflected their influence and, also by direct action, the ladies contributed to the cultural wares. Van Dyck declared he learned more from Sophonisba Anguissola, an Italian portrait painter, who lived in the late sixteenth and early seventeenth centuries, even in her blind old age than from many seeing men.

Some of the women were genuine scholars, though these were usually of the middle class. Through the fragmentary records we see Olympia Morata lecturing at the University of Ferrara on the Ciceronian paradoxes; Elena Cornaro Piscopia answering questions for her degree "in the presence of thousands of learned men and applauding students from all over Europe"; and Clotilda Tambroni, a professor of the Greek language and literature at Bologna, delivering an oration when Maria dalle Donne was granted her degree in medicine and surgery, being chosen for the honor in view of the fact that there were very few Europeans who equalled her in her mastery of the ancient tongue. In nearly every great intellectual center of Italy women were lecturing on literature, philosophy and theology, for religious faith could not escape the impacts of the new learning. They were studying medicine and natural science in the light of pagan revelations of wisdom. Great Italian women teachers of the awakening "sent forth such students as Moritz von Spiegelberg and Rudolph Agricola to reform the instruction of Deventer and Zwoll and prepare the way for Erasmus and Reuchlin." Some of the women crossed the Alps themselves, as the ancient learning was said to do when Erasmus and other returned students bore back to outlying countries the knowledge gleaned in Italy. Olympia Morata, for example, meeting difficulties at Renée's court where the duchess and all her friends were persecuted by the duke for their intellectual forthrightness, fled to Germany with a young Bavarian student of medicine and philosophy, and was planning to continue her teaching in Heidelberg, to which she had been invited, when an untimely death closed her career.

It was no accident then that Isabella of Spain should be the agent for the Spanish classical enlightenment as well as a State-maker and the patron of Columbus. The closure of Constantinople to western commerce in 1453 was Italy's loss and Spain's gain. The discovery of the New World and the new wealth that poured into Spanish coffers from the rich societies of Mexico and Peru, looted by her conquistadores, made Spain the financial successor to Italy and with the transfer in material leadership went some of the cultural accomplishments of the proud Italian cities. Isabella studied the classics herself. She established a classical school within her palace, her faculty including women. She attended examinations and watched closely the progress of instruction, eager to prevent the enervation of idleness among her courtiers. She collected texts for them to read and helped the Spanish universities to take up their cultural lag as well. Other women assisted her in all this enterprise. One lectured on the classics at Salamanca and another on rhetoric at Alcalá. Afterwards Philip II added women artists to the courtly entourage. He invited Sophonisba Anguissola to exhibit her portraits in Madrid, encouraging Spanish women to take up the brush as well as Letters. And the daughters of Jean de Juanes,

Dorothea and Marguerita, did so with marked success, giving lustre to the Spanish Renaissance.

A similar story is that of the French enlightenment. It was none other than Christine de Pisan, with her flair for political progress and her consciousness of the rôle of the bourgeoisie, who acclimatised the classics in France in the late fourteenth century. During the years when the Maid of Orleans was dreaming grand national dreams, Christine, a widow, was earning a living for herself and three children with her pen. Venice was her birthplace and Italian was her cultural inspiration.

But she had grown to maturity in France where her father was a retainer at the court — an astrologer — making it possible for her to gratify her love of reading in the splendid library of Greek and Latin authors purchased by the king, perhaps at the suggestion of Petrarch, who in 1333 visited the French court during his quest for classical manuscripts lying idle in monasteries. Those authors she supplemented by readings in the science of the Arabs and, when the task of bread-winning was suddenly thrust upon her, she had a novel and important way of meeting the situation. In Boëthius, Dante and Aristotle she found both consolation and copy for her vocation as a writer. It is possible that she knew Dante personally; at all events she shared his interest in the State and believed with him that woman was a proper companion for man either in Paradise or on earth. As between Plato and Aristotle she preferred the latter and in all she wrote emphasized the peril inherent in tyranny, as the master had done. In generous measure she drew from the classics the nutriment of her vigorous mentality. Her spirit, her wide range of knowledge, her call to the French to advance intellectually as well as politically led Henry IV, desiring to "uplift" England to invite Christine to visit his court but, when she decided that was impossible, she found her way across the Channel through her books.

An exceptionally learned woman, Christine de Pisan was in all this effort applying a rationalism gleaned from pagan writing to a frightfully chaotic scene. She was a student of the Hebrew, Assyrian, Roman, French and Breton histories among others. In her "leisure" hours, she studied science. When she addressed herself to the public she thus had ideas to deliver. For women she wrote *Le Livre des trois vertus,* designed to inculcate political consciousness. *Le Livre de la paix* was an attempt to show princes their obligations of mercy, toleration, and justice.

Other women also helped France to become civilised. In the fifteenth century Queen Anne of Bretagne undertook to educate the women of the court, giving them instruction both in their native French and in the classics, importing Italian tutors for the latter. But Marguerite d'Angoulême, or Margaret of Navarre as she is generally called, the sister of Francis I, was the first indigenous genius of the French Renaissance. Her inspiration it seems came through a correspondence with Vittoria Colonna and led her to induce her brother, the King, to found the College of France. Erasmus suggested that bona fide teachers of the classics be installed.

Margaret was brilliantly qualified to be the patron of a critical régime, though a literary dispute continues to rage over her purpose in writing the *Heptameron.* Was she an heir to Juvenal, some ask ? Or was she the original Rabelais, we may inquire ? Obviously she did not share the clerical attitude toward Sin. In fact she was fascinated by the phenomenon of love in all its manifestations. But her age was rough and she was of her age. Still she was more than her age, for she had poetic genius and dared to indulge it in a vivid caricature of the society in which she moved and had her being. Though not a heretic, she was tolerant of free thought and as long as she enjoyed the protection of her brother, the King, she befriended those who differed from her in their views of life, notably Lefévre d'Etaples, Budé, Marot, Rabelais, Des Periers, and Dolet. In keeping with her generosity toward the opinions of others, in harmony with her willingness to listen to new ideas, was her belief in the fundamental virtue of humanity — a belief that Rousseau was to elaborate in after years.

Margaret's spirit was more sensitive than that of Rabelais whose relish for every animal function, if concealed in a wild jargon of words, even made him unique among men. Yet her poem entitled *The Mirror of the Soul,* censored by the Sorbonne, was sufficiently strong to grip the hardy Queen Elizabeth across the Channel, who was capable of laughing and responding with a witty repartee to any jest, however Rabelaisian, and she translated it into English. To the right wing of the Church Margaret was even more abhorrent than Rabelais because it could understand her better and besides she was a woman — of the sex it relied on particularly for stability. She would doubtless have been burned as a heretic if her royal brother had not intervened, for she gave shelter to many religious reformers.

Plato was her own master and his ideal of happiness her own dream. Until Calvin took charge of the religious revolt, Margaret of Navarre and her court, says Taylor, "were the refuge and center of the better scholarship and fuller humanism and far-seeing piety which characterised advancing thought in France." It was the free Platonism nourished by Margaret that Calvin set out to destroy like a god of wrath. Temporarily Calvin and the Catholic theologians of the same disposition succeeded but only temporarily, for after more than a century of suppression it again broke forth in the humanistic philosophy that prepared the way for the French Revolution.

In England, queens, noblewomen and rich bourgeois aided in the spread of the new learning. As the result of an appeal for financial patronage made by his friend, Blount, Erasmus, justly called "the Voltaire of the Renaissance," was enabled to give England some of the benefit of his scholarship and spirit. That he could be a "good European," equally at home in Rotterdam, Paris, Turin, Basle, London and Oxford, where he appealed with wit for the use of reason, was in no small measure due to the support of women from his early to his latest years. To his publishing ventures no less than his teaching, they rendered assistance. Princess Mary translated his *Paraphrase of the Gospel according to St. John* into English when Edward VI decided to place this version in the churches of the realm. Explaining his concern for the democratisation of the Scriptures, Erasmus said he thought "the weakest woman should be able to read the Gospels and the Epistles of St. Paul." As events turned out, permission for the weakest to read the Bible opened the way for the strongest to upset the intended allegiance to authority; and in due time the question of who was strong or weak ceased to be a matter of sex.

Off on her own classical tack, ran the young Lady Jane Grey whose pathetic sixteenth-century story is one of the world's great caste tragedies. She was exotic enough to prefer Plato to the hounds and voluntarily stayed with the thinker and dreamer while the rest of the court rode away to the chase. Political machinations however tore her from her beloved books and the result was her martyrdom at the age of sixteen, a victim to the plots of her family.

Mary, Queen of Scots, likewise a tragic sacrifice to fate, was also in a measure a classicist. When she was but thirteen, she delivered a Latin oration at the court of France, having received the preparatory training in a French convent. She was commended for a Latin poem and her letters are among the English treasure trove.

Like Isabella of Spain, Queen Elizabeth encouraged her nation in active over-seas and cultural development at one and the same time. Elizabeth knew six languages "better than her own," she said, when she ascended the throne. And she was familiar not only with their mechanics but with their philosophic contents. Her vigorous prose and witty speech were an inspiration to her friends and a foil in dealing with opponents. "Compared with this most brilliant woman of her generation, Queen Victoria was a mere schoolgirl. . . If Elizabeth Tudor were here and now to walk into a woman's college, there would be no office therein commensurate with her attainments except the Presidency," an admirer has remarked and we might question the presidency. She was equally competent as the Queen of sea rovers and pirates and as the Queen of literary innovators. To Sir Walter Raleigh, she was the political leader and symbol of the State. To the "English Castiglione," Edmund Spenser, she was "The Faëry Queen."

Scholars from the universities of Oxford and Cambridge who returned from the grand tour, full of Italian enthusiasms and equipped with literary models and cues, under her approving ægis made of her reign a golden age of English Letters. If the immortal Shakespeare did not travel in person to the shrine of classicists, the air in which he composed was charged with Italian influences. To Elizabeth in 1565 was dedicated the fine treatise on rationality written by an Italian religious refugee, Giacomo Aconcio, pioneer of toleration. He paid for his daily bread by engineering, having obtained a commission to drain the English swamps, but the Queen and the Earl of Leicester protected him from angry Churchmen while he worked out a common denominator for all religions by means of which they might obtain peace.

Thus from the Continent there blew through England a current of opinion and pagan rationalisation to fortify the State separated by Henry VIII from Papal control over thought. Interest in classical learning and manuscripts led to more concern in England with the vernacular, as it had in Italy, Spain and France — embracing within its range of mentality phases of life neglected by the Latin-speaking clergy — an agency of inter-communication beyond their authority. Latin had unified religions and social opinion, symbolising the infallibility of the Papacy. Until the age of Elizabeth, the educated English classes had read the Church Fathers and other Continentals and very little else. Henceforward they were to face their own people, their problems, and their interests, as they independently conceived them.

Meanwhile the classical revival was swinging along in the Germanic world though it had a different effect there on account of the persistence of the feudal system. As early as 1424 the Brethren of the Common Life had founded a school at Herzogenbusch with Greek as one of its departments and on this foundation the master humanists, Agricola and Melancthon, erected their classical programs. By 1600 approximately two thousand Teutons were studying the old writings with renewed inspiration and making themselves such effective protagonists of rationalism that the French Church began to think in terms of a race war. Melanchthon advocated the opening of equal educational opportunities to women.

He had before him in that advocacy the precedent of learned abbesses who had long enjoyed access to convent manuscripts of ancient composition and used them to advantage. When the poet Celtes gave a copy of his verse to the Abbess Charity

Pirkheimer of Nürnberg with words of praise to her as an ornament of his race, she replied to his eulogy that his effusion was an illustration of the lowest taste of the ancients instead of the highest. Many books were dedicated to her and Dürer was among the artists who moved in her circle of friends. German women participated with ardor and conviction in the political and religious upheaval for which the revival of learning was a herald, and from the naturalist classical philosophy, they drew inspiration for the contributions they made in generous proportions to the positive knowledge of the modern age.

THE DEVELOPMENT OF MODERN SCIENCE

ILLUMINATING as was the discovery of ancient learning and opinion, it ceased to satisfy students of the past and a veritable "battle of the books" occurred between the ranks of classicists and modernists during the eighteenth century. In this dispute natural science was a major factor. It had been making startling headway in spite of clerical proscriptions and in fact within holy orders themselves.

While the naturalist approach to wisdom derived from the ancients was an influence in freedom of thought, the Greeks and Romans actually knew very little about nature and much that they thought they knew was now found to be wrong and misleading. Catholic as well as Protestant scholars discovered errors and became more critical about habits of thinking and observing. Thus the monk Roger Bacon, like the nun Hildegard, departed from the straight and narrow scholastic codes of the Church in his interests and discoveries. The compass, the printing press, and gunpowder, all of which had direct and potent effects on the course of civilisation, even antedated the furor over secular learning at the opening of the sixteenth century. They belonged to the age of Columbus, a pious believer in the Pope, untrained in the mood of the Greeks and the Romans.

In other words, though it was associated with the revival of the classics, the development of natural science, pure and applied, owed little to any precise lore in the works of the ancients. By the time of Francis Bacon the opening of ocean highways had cut athwart provincial moods and doubtless inspired him to set notable examples in experimentation, and to preach the gospel of research into common things instead of complete reliance on books as a means of finding the Truth. He framed a utopia for a land across the sea, "The New *Atlantis,* in which the lot of mankind was to be improved by science, at the same time that he clung to a belief in magic and mysteries.

A far more powerful thinker than Bacon, at least on the side of mathematics and method, was René Descartes, a French scholar and investigator, who literally founded a new school of thought disruptive both of classical and theological tradition — a school so radical that in France its teachers were at first more eagerly received by women, such as Madame de Sévigné and her daughter, Madame de Grignan, than by professors in the universities familiar with the classics.

In his *Principia Philosophiæ,* published in 1644 at Amsterdam, Descartes declared: "Undoubtedly the world was in the beginning created in all its perfection. But yet as it is best, if we wish to understand the nature of plants or of men, to consider how they may by degrees proceed from seeds, rather than how they were created by God in the beginning, so, if we can excogitate some extremely simple and comprehensible principles, out of which, as if they were seeds, we can prove that stars, and earth, and all this visible scene could have originated, although we know full well that they never did originate in such a way, we shall in that way expound their nature far better than if we merely described them as they exist at present."

In debt to the Renaissance, Italian, French and English, familiar with the discoveries of scientists — Galileo, Torricelli, Harvey and others — drawing his inspiration from mathematical and physical science for his speculation in the realm of morals, Descartes like his Greek predecessors promulgated the doctrine of ethical rationality. He was a psychologist in his approach to the science of society and man. Neither economics nor religion nor politics was the substance of his thinking but his emphasis on freedom from presuppositions and his call for experimental rather than apocryphal knowledge was so popular that he was the center of a new university, salon, and clerical movement toward general scepticism. Courtiers of both sexes met for readings in Cartesian logic in such French drawing-rooms as Mme. de Sévigné's, Mme. de Grignan's, and the Duchess de Maine's. These may have been the *femmes savantes* ridiculed by Molière, no sponsor of scientific interests or yearnings. But such homes were the nursery of Fontenelle and as a few monks fell into line, the Abbé de Saint-Pierre led their advance. If Voltaire and his colleagues on the Encyclopædia thought Descartes a "trimmer," Pascal was well aware of the peril to theological dogma.

Owing to the fact that his scientific morality was such a menace to the Church, Descartes had to spend most of his maturity in exile. It was mainly in Holland during the golden age of Dutch commercial prowess when traditional concepts of values were yielding, as they had in Italy, to the spirit of adventure and inquiry, that Descartes made his home. There he met the daughter of the King of Bohemia, likewise an exile, under whom he had served as a soldier. Since it is the habit of émigrés to herd together, Descartes and the king's daughter saw much of each other and to her, the Princess Elizabeth, he dedicated his *Principles of Philosophy*. But he did not do this merely to be ingratiating, for he declared that in Elizabeth alone were combined those "generally separated talents for metaphysics and mathematics" he sought to bring together into moral thinking.

His second royal intellectual companion was Christina, the daughter of King Gustavus Adolphus of Sweden, who like Descartes cared so little for economics and politics that she eventually abdicated to escape marrying and holding the crown, with its obligation to study finance and budgeting. She was a reckless spendthrift and not a little mad but she stimulated trade, manufacture, and mining, issued the first national school ordinance, sent a vessel in her royal navy to fetch Descartes to her court, and there discussed with him, as the Princess Elizabeth had done, the refinements of a rationalist philosophy. But Christina closed her restive career within the fold of the Catholic Church.

Descartes had no quarrel with the creed of self-perfectibility. Some critics said he was denying God, and Cartesianism was banned in certain universities; others declared he was simply trying to prove the existence of God by higher mathematics and drew from that experiment their metaphysics. Freedom to think and to live by rules of reason induced a greater scepticism with respect to theology which brought as its collateral the Positivist creed of freedom to think for secular ends. The correspondence of Descartes with his noblewomen friends is saturated with moral considerations relative to the senses and the passions, in the manner of the idealistic Greeks. The Positivists who followed him filled their writings with science, nation planning, economics, politics and worldly pursuits beyond the dreams of any civilised person in the early days of intellectualism. For as positive knowledge enlarged, social consciousness expanded. With alterations in the quality and range of economics and politics, the middle classes and then democracy substituted the realities of political economy for the esoteric flights of caste speculations involving a mere awareness of impending intellectual changes.

When Newton, an English professor at Cambridge, followed Descartes with a mechanistic view of planetary action and gave the "formula of the proportions according to which they act," this great controversy between the occultists and the naturalists was launched in earnest. In spite of his rationalisation, Descartes was the exponent of the near-occult philosophy, to be likewise found on many pages of old pagan manuscripts. With the appearance of Newtonism the thinkers of the West were arrayed against one another on the issue of naturalism. The fact that Newton was intensely interested in the application of science to the problems of navigation made his position doubly significant to Voltaire, a member of the French bourgeoisie who, during his stay in England, was impressed by the way she was building up her political power through the agency of science.

Newton was familiar with the Descartian philosophy. He lectured on the Frenchman's Geometry and, through the Royal Society to which he belonged, contacts were made with French intellectual developments as well as with a home growth displayed by such reasoners as Sir Christopher Wren, Halley and Hooke, discussing the laws of gravity. Upon the German Kepler's measurements, Newton based some of his researches. And yet with all his forward-looking work, he remained an alchemist searching in his own furnace fire for the magic way to transmute baser metals into gold, and a loyal member of the Anglican Church, interested in its history and in the Scriptural arguments for deity. That Newton became such a pivot of French scepticism was largely accidental for the French debate on mechanism versus occultism preceded Voltaire's entry into the fray.

Newton reached France in a curious way. He was popular at the court of George I where the Princess of Wales, afterwards Queen Caroline, particularly, tried to keep pace with his investigations. So in one of their conversations he told her that he had composed a new system of chronology and she asked to see the papers on which it was set down. For her private use he prepared an abstract, pledging her to secrecy. Though she kept her pledge, the Abbé Conti, to whom he gave a second copy and from whom he exacted a similar promise, told the story in France and therewith the grand argument was begun on the eve of Voltaire's return full of fight.

Once in action and determined to overthrow Descartian "timidity," Voltaire turned to a learned woman for main assistance. This was the mathematician, linguist and metaphysician, his patron and companion, the Marquise du Châtelet who, at his urging, translated Newton's *Principia* into French and, what is more, elucidated the English work for the benefit of French Descartians.

Novel as this English-French exploration into the universe seemed to be, in truth a nun in a cloister had, in important respects, anticipated Newton centuries before. Her theories simply did not get into circulation in such a crucial intellectual age. The list of modern astronomers should really be headed by Hildegard, a German Benedictine, who somewhat redeemed mediæval narrowness by bridging the cultural abyss between the pagan astronomer, Hypatia, and the twelfth century. Perhaps she carried the science further afield from astrology. We shall rely on Mozans for our information about Hildegard: "When the earth was by everyone considered as the center of the firmament, while universal gravitation — the sublime discovery of Newton — had not as yet entered into the scientific theories of that epoch," Hildegard asserted that the sun is the "center of the firmament and holds in place the stars that gravitate around it, as the earth attracts the creatures which inhabit it. . . . She anticipated subsequent discoveries regarding the alternation of the seasons . . . before navigators had visited the southern hemisphere." Her theory of universal gravitation was prophetic of the sensational doctrine to come, for she declared: "The stars have neither the same brightness nor the same size. They are kept in their course by a superior body." Try as they might to hold women to responsibility for original sin, the mediæval theologians could not prevent their sharing in responsibility for scientific virtues.

Returning to the century which Newton so brilliantly opened and du Châtelet illuminated, we meet Maria Agnesi, an Italian mathematician and philosopher, arguing in 1758, through one hundred and one *Propositiones Philosophicæ* that it was contrary to public weal to deprive Italian or any other women of the opportunity to exercise their intellectual powers. Her championship of her sex was particularly meaningful because few, if any, men of her age excelled Agnesi in training and scope of interests. She had begun when she was only nine years old to defend women, writing in Latin on the subject. With a discipline acquired through the study of Greek, Hebrew, French, Spanish and German, she was able to mingle with the scholars who were guests in her father's home, conversing with them in their own tongues, and as she became a mathematical genius, abstruse questions in that field were both argued in her presence and submitted to her for comment. In differential and integral calculus she did distinguished work. When her *Istituzioni Analitiche ad uso della gioventù italiana* appeared in 1748, experts immediately ranked her with Cardan, Leibnitz and Euler for her talent in analysing infinitesimals. Her treatise was so well written besides that it was used as one of the models in the preparation of the great dictionary of the Italian language issued by the Della Crusca Society. Antelomy translated the second half of this work, dealing with infinitesimals, into French in 1775, Bossut of the Academy making annotations for the version. It was translated into English by John Colson, professor of mathematics at Cambridge in 1801 and he was so enthusiastic over her perfection in the long series of mathematical demonstrations that late in life he undertook the study of Italian to master her methods.

Deeply impressed by Agnesi's work, the French Academy of Sciences appointed a committee to report on it, and the representative of this agency wrote to her in the following terms: "Permit me, Mademoiselle, to unite my personal homage to the plaudits of the entire Academy. I have the pleasure of making known to my country an extremely useful work which has long been desired, and which has hitherto existed (in England and France) only in outline. I do not know of any work of this kind which is clearer, more methodic or more comprehensive than your Analytical Institutions. There is none in any language which can guide more surely, lead more quickly, and conduct further those who wish to advance in the mathematical sciences. I admire particularly the art with which you bring under uniform methods the divers conclusions scattered among the works of geometers and reached by methods entirely different." But according to its constitution, the Academy was prevented from admitting Agnesi to membership, while it was able to receive with applause Benjamin Franklin, who decried his own mathematical shortcomings and the lack of facilities for its study in the New World. Even the fact that Agnesi was professor in the University of Bologna could not overcome the barrier. Therein lies irony. The very idea of the Academy came to its founder, Richelieu, from the academy-like salon of Madame de Rambouillet.

Agnesi died a good Catholic and her English admirer, Colson, a good Protestant, each having contributed to the development of secular interests. Some of her writings were circulated privately, unpublished, such for example as her commentary on the *Traité analytique des sections coniques* of the Marquis de l'Hôpital — which his wife had helped him to prepare. The "witch of Agnesi" is still the name of the curve that she invented and discussed.

Among the contemporaries of Maria Agnesi was another Italian woman, Laura Bassi, distinguished for learning, who, it might seem, in view of the fact that she had twelve children, needed only the consolations of religion to carry her through life. But she was profoundly interested in Newton's mathematico-physical theories. Like Agnesi and Newton she was a university professor — in experimental philosophy or physics — her chair being secured for her by the Pope. Previous to her appointment, however, she proceeded to the doctor's degree, passing a rigorous examination conducted by five inquisitors chosen by lot from among men, whose names, Fantuzzi remarked, "will always be held by our university in glorious remembrance." In the end there was no question of the candidate's equipment and she was offered the chair proposed by the Pope with unanimous acclamation. Then as Romans had flocked to Alexandria in earlier times to study with Hypatia, now students came from the four quarters of Europe to work with the learned Bassi. Until her death she was engaged in delivering public lectures on experimental philosophy. She was elected to the Academy of Bologna, if denied admittance like Agnesi to the French Academy. Her correspondence with the eminent scientists of Europe was voluminous and continuous and one of the amusing letters in the list came from Voltaire in 1774 asking her to wedge him into the Academy of Bologna after he was rejected by the French Academy: "There is not a Bassi in London, and I should be more happy to be a member of the Academy of Bologna than of that of the English, although it has produced a Newton. If your protection should obtain for me this title, of which I am so ambitious, the gratitude of my heart will be equal to my admiration of yourself. I beg you to excuse the style of a foreigner who presumes to write you in Italian, but who is as great an admirer of yours as if he were born in Bologna." Bassi had him taken into the Academy and an appreciative letter follows. So thorough was Bassi's knowledge of Greek that only three Europeans in her day were said to equal her mastery of that tongue.

If we trace the records of the other sciences up to the era of the French Revolution, we find women working competently and often brilliantly in every field. Sometimes the women labored independently of other members of their family. Often the household was the workshop in which husband and wife, brother and sister, or father and mother and children coöperated in scientific pursuits, testing, observing, recording, discovering, criticising, weighing, generalising, and encouraging. Whether it was Johann Müller, sometimes known as "Regiomontanus," a German astronomer of the fifteenth century who in his Nuremberg study had the assistance of a scientific wife; Tycho Brahe of the sixteenth century, the Danish astronomer at Prague stimulated by and stimulating his sister to become a noted worker in that field; Helvilius in the seventeenth century at Dantzig enjoying for twenty-seven years the zealous collaboration of his wife who edited and published their joint findings after his death; Gottfried Kirch of the same cycle at Leipzig whose wife ignored anthropomorphic traditions and, at a time when planet positions were treated as omens for conduct, wrote a book, in 1714, dealing naturalistically with the conjunction of Jupiter and Saturn, discovered a comet and trained her daughters for accurate calculations in the service of the Berlin Academy of Sciences, adding a famous son to the calendar of astronomers; or the celebrated Herschels, brother and sister, he a delicate and sensitive thinker helped practically and intellectually by a girl who was able to discover eight comets by her own observations while she "minded the heavens" for the man — the modern age of science was promoted by men and women working together amid the rigors the discipline required. Writing to the son of Frau Kirch, a professor of astronomy at Upsala genially confessed: "I begin to believe that it is the destiny of all the astronomers whom I have had the honor of becoming acquainted with during my journey to have learned sisters. I have also a sister, although not a very learned one. To preserve the harmony, we must make an astronomer of her." Galileo maintained his courage only with the sympathy of a daughter, a Franciscan nun, who kept in close touch with his researches, theories and political difficulties. When she died, he could work no more, and his life also ended.

Lalande makes Madame du Pierry, the first woman professor of astronomy in Paris, of consequence to his thinking, in the late eighteenth century. Many of her notes he utilised — notes made in calculating eclipses "with a view to determining accurately the motion of the moon." She was the author of numerous astronomical tables exhibiting patient research and unquestioned skill. Lalande was Director of the Paris Observatory and even before Mme. du Pierry crossed his scientific horizon, he had chosen Mme. Lapaute, wife of the royal clockmaker, to aid the noted mathematician, Clairaut, in working out a complicated problem connected with estimating the amount of attraction which Jupiter and Saturn exercise on Halley's comet, whose approaching appearance had been forecast. She had already made difficult computations relative to the oscillations of pendulums of various lengths and Clairaut was happy to have the help of "the learned computer" of Paris.

Her energy was also an asset. "It would be difficult," wrote Lalande, "to realise the courage which this enterprise required, if one did not know that for more than six months we calculated from morning until night, sometimes even at meals, and that at the end of this enforced labor I was stricken by a malady which affected me during the rest of my life." Without the help of Mme. Lapaute, he went on to say, he could not have undertaken the publication of the *Connaissance des Temps* which the Academy of Sciences issued for the use of astronomers and navigators; the calculations would have been too laborious and difficult to put through. In the years that followed, Mme. Lapaute worked out herself for the whole of Europe the calculations for the eclipses of 1762 and 1764 with the charts and tables of parallactic angles, one of them being published by the French government. In 1774, when Lalande was succeeded as editor by another Academician, she began work on the Epheméris, the seventh volume of which came down to 1784 and the eighth to 1792. Unaided she made for the last volume all the computations for the sun, the moon and the planets.

Nor does Lalande forget to record the skill of his niece-in-law, Mme. Lefrançais Lalande: "She is one of the rare women who have written scientific books. She has published tables for finding the time at sea by the altitude of the sun and stars. These tables were printed in 1791 by the order of the National Assembly. . . In 1799 she published a catalogue of ten thousand stars, reduced and calculated."

Sometimes it is the master-pupil relation which brings results. The mother of Catharine de Parthenay sought for her daughter, who later became the celebrated Princess de Rohan, the finest teachers of Europe among whom was François Viète, called the father of modern algebra. For her education he prepared an elaborate work on Astronomy and to her he dedicated his mathematical analysis, *In Artem Analyticam Isagoge,* in these terms: "It is to you especially . . . that I am indebted for my proficiency in mathematics, to attain which I was encouraged by your love for this science as well as your great knowledge of it, and by your mastery of all other sciences."

An interest in geology led the Baroness de Beausoleil as early as the first half of the seventeenth century, when the American colonies were just being founded, to develop to more significant proportions the sciences of mineralogy and metallurgy. She spent thirty years studying the French mineral resources and published reports addressed to Richelieu in an effort to persuade him to exploit French subsoil wealth and thus become the richest ruler of the happiest subjects in Christendom, as she argued. She prescribed the discipline for mining engineers — the training in chemistry, mineralogy, geometry, mechanics that was needed. Her significance lies also in the fact that she was a rebel against the superstitions of her age which taught that "gnomes and kobolds" existed under the earth or at least that magic of some form must be employed in the location of deposits.

Also from the realm of medicine, first in the convents, then in the medical schools and hospitals and finally in the laboratory, came new knowledge to push aside demonology, and liberate man from his fears. One dramatic incident supplies a background for the new attack on disease. In the seventeenth century women were still handling the old herb woman's lore and keeping their contacts with healing, but herbs were different in different localities of course and so they did not all know the same things. With the opening of the Atlantic, the exchange of knowledge was extended. In 1640 for instance the Countess of Chinchon, wife of the Governor of Peru, introduced into the Old World what accordingly became known as Cinchona bark — a remedy for malaria. Millions of Europeans had been killed by the ravages of this disease and the decline of Greece and other political powers have even been traced to its influence. "The main obstacle in the way of the conquest of the Papacy by the Holy Roman Empire," one charge runs, "was malarial fever; had a Frederick I or a Frederick II possessed a remedy, how the course of the world's history would have been deflected!" By 1700 at any rate Cinchona bark was in wide use for the treatment of the disease.

The story of women's relation to medicine runs throughout the records of mankind. Centuries before the eighteenth, the Benedictine physician, Hildegard, had quickened the search for medical certainties in Europe. Before Rabelais, a doctor and monk of that Order, lectured realistically on medicine and anatomy in France, Hildegard, of the twelfth century, not so harsh a satirist, was yet enough of a naturalist and sceptical enough about magic to write works strikingly free from demonology on the causes, symptoms and treatment of diseases. In a study of Hildegard published in France in 1882 assurance was expressed that the nun knew many things that the doctors of the Middle Ages, so-called, did not know and "which the investigators of our own age, after rediscovering them, have announced as something entirely new." She wrote treatises on what were styled "simples," that is, the plants and herbs used for healing, and gave their value in therapeutics. By the sixteenth century her nine volume medical work had gone through several editions and the great Rudolph Virchow, originator of cellular pathology, in a book on pathological anatomy and physiology, paid his respects to this complete and skillfully prepared materia medica. Discussing its place in the history of medicine, Haeser described it as "an independent German treatise based chiefly on popular experience."

But Hildegard went beyond the populace. Long before

Cesalpine or Harvey described the coursing of blood through veins minutely and before Descartes made blood the center of life, Hildegard compared its movement to that of the stars through the heavens. At the same time she was a noted practitioner among many famous nuns celebrated for their skill in the convent hospitals. According to the monk Theodoric, who was an eye witness, "she had to so high a degree the gift of healing that no sick person had recourse to her without being restored to health." If the Sister herself believed that help came to her from Heaven through prayer and if the public ascribed to supernatural causes the healing derived through practical arts, Hildegard did not attribute to magic her success.

Wherever there had been a priesthood in the past, one of its functions had been healing and the Egyptian pharaohs as they became god-kings adopted the art as one of their perquisites; thus Imhotep figured long after his death in tradition as a great god of medicine. Twenty-five hundred years after his death the Greeks were calling him Imouthes and identifying him with their divine healer, Æsculapius. The magical heritage still held the Roman physician Galen in its clutches notwithstanding his private practice, his realistic knowledge and extended worldly experience. He traveled to Alexandria and to Smyrna and was deeply influenced by magic medicine when he became official physician to Marcus Aurelius and Commodus. Though he was a fine surgeon, the first great authority on the pulse, and an important writer on medicine, he was inclined to believe more in amulets than in prescriptions, famous as he was for some of these. That Hildegard should still be clinging to the mysteries was natural but there was also in her case a reaching out for practical cures in a natural way. She sighed for the Arab wisdom which, she understood, was obtained through practices derived from the Jews, the Greeks and the Indians.

In the development of healing, the rôle of hospitals is clear. So if the nuns had not carried nursing along as they did and served so gallantly in the care of the sick, the men who came after could not have gained their clinical data. When Italy or Leyden acquired superior facilities — and that too by women's money to a remarkable degree — only those students could travel there to observe who had unusual means and hence the element of wealth entered into the extension of scholarship. Free secular orders of nurses arose among men in the field during the Crusades and topping them came clerical organisations of nursing women prepared to serve during epidemics and disasters or to go on to the ends of the earth to care for the sick poor. The suppression of the monasteries and convents was at first a terrible hardship on the sick poor. Nor were the first secular hospitals much of a gain. In fact, from the modern point of view, they were horrible affairs which Mme. Necker in France, Florence Nightingale in England, and Clara Barton in the United States criticised and helped to reform.

Many of the Church prelates realised that they did not possess the magic of Christ, whatever his powers may have been, and were tolerant of the medical center established in the eleventh century at Salerno where scientific strides of undoubted value were made.

Owing to the casual and debatable character of the documents that have come down to us, the exact status of women in medicine at Salerno may never be determined. Mozans, citing original sources, makes wide claims for them. He insists that the school at Salerno threw open its doors to women and that they demonstrated their prowess as physicians and as professors of medicine, accepting the theory that "Trotula" was the wife of a distinguished physician and herself the author of learned works on medicine. But it is claimed from the Latin texts which he quotes that his interpretation is too generous and two German scholars have been sceptical, if not destructive, in their criticism of this view. Meyer-Steinegg and Sudhoff, in their *Geschichte der Medizin im Uberblick* (1928) declare flatly that "Trotula is certainly not the name of a female doctor but a gynæcological work bearing the title Trotula." Yet the lady is not without recent champions and the cautious student will not regard the issue as entirely closed.

In the midst of many traditions and myths, however, some things seem to be certain. The official document permitting Francesca, wife of Matteo de Romana, of Salerno, to practice medicine, at least in a limited fashion, shows clearly that she was examined in the art by learned doctors and surgeons of Salerno and received her license from them. That document also states definitely that "the law permits women to practice medicine" and that "from the standpoint of good morals women are better adapted to the treatment of their own sex." Meyer-Steinegg and Sudhoff, who traverse the Trotula tradition, add that "the fact that Salerno was a layman's school and not clerical, though clerics were not excluded, established from the beginning the possibility of teaching gynæcology and obstetrics. In the beginning midwives alone were called in, except in extreme cases requiring the attendance of surgeons. Those summoned in cases above the lowest and most common forms of midwifery were, one should suppose, wives and daughters of medical teachers in Salerno." It appears to be established also that the women of Salerno had developed a number of rules and practices with which the doctors of the city were familiar, though sometimes dissenting from the views expressed. Sudhoff is positive on a few points. He says: "That women played an important part in the history of the medical school at Salerno is indisputable. . . As a laymen's school, the members of which were married, it imposed no restrictions on its members as far as obstetrics was concerned. Here the influence of women on medical practice may have got its start. When it came to the examination and selection of midwives, matrons from the families of the town councillors in other towns of the middle ages were active. . . It may be taken for granted that in Salerno the wives of professors participated [in developing the art of midwifery] and perhaps even held teaching-chairs for midwifery pupils." Whether their activities in the school went beyond that is open to question. It may be added with safety that girls in convents during the Middle Ages were often taught the rudiments of medicine, including the care of the sick and wounded. This is not saying that the medicine as practiced by women was not crude beyond modern imagination, as indeed was that of the men, but it establishes the fact that the slow development of positive knowledge in this field had its beginning long before the Renaissance and the Protestant upheaval and that women had an important part in it.

Whatever progress was made in medicine in the later Middle Ages, which rested mainly on the teachings of the ancients, it certainly had not reached the high level of antiquity by the opening of the sixteenth century when Paracelsus started a revolution with the introduction of clinical methods. This great German genius, for such he undoubtedly was, came by his inspiration honestly. Not only was his father a physician but his mother previous to her marriage had been superintendent of a hospital at Einsiedeln and continued to maintain her keen interest in the practical aspects of medicine — aspects which her son made the basis of amazing achievements. Yet, in spite of his labors and the steady recovery of ancient learning, medicine remained at the opening of the seventeenth century at about the same stage of backwardness in which he had found it. But one significant change had taken place. With the growth of instruction in the subject at the universities, professional tendencies set in, restraining the activities of women in this field and emphasizing book-learning as distinguished from the use of herbs and experience in the sick room.

As medicine and all care of the sick became professionalised, the status of women in the science of medicine altered. Men even assumed priority in obstetrics over the women whose experience had long been placed without pay at the service of the poor. The consequence was that for a long time the poor were more neglected while the rich who accepted the new fad of men nurses were often rewarded for their love of novelty with especially inadequate care. A noted English oculist, summoned to the court of Denmark to treat the Queen in the seventeenth century, was struck by the change apparent there and its baleful outcome; he declared he knew several women whose advice was better and safer than that of the court physicians he encountered. Hugh Chamberlen in a work on midwifery admits that the rivalry of doctors not only in England but throughout Europe "hath very much caused the report, that where a man come, one or both (mother or child) must necessarily dye; and makes many for that reason forbear sending, until either be dead or dying." Against this menace Ralph Verney cautioned his wife by letter in 1647, advising her not to trust unduly to male physicians in the care of her infant but still to respect experienced women and midwives. Hobbes is said by the author of his sketch in the *Dictionary of National Biography* to have preferred "an experienced old woman" to the "most learned and inexperienced physician."

It grew harder to care for the sick but, in spite of prohibitive legislation and the establishment of medical schools and licenses for practitioners, women continued to help the poor in emergencies and to advise the prosperous on demand. A French midwife of the aforesaid century, Madame Louise Bour geois, was called by Pechey the most famous woman in the world, so much in demand was she at courts and castles on account of her skill and lore. When competent and distinguished midwives in London saw their hold weakening in the sickroom, one of them, Mrs. Celleor, petitioned the King and got his consent to found a midwife corporation by Royal Charter with a view to better training, more extended scientific research and study, following an example set in France at the Hôtel Dieu where a school of midwifery had already been founded. Jane Sharp, who had practiced midwifery for thirty years, declared in a volume which went through many editions, giving specific directions for such assistance, that her sisters in the art must be both speculative and realistic because "She that wants the knowledge of Speculation is like one that is blind and wants her sight: she that wants the Practice, is like one that is lame and wants her legs. . . Some perhaps may think, that then it is not proper for women to be of this profession, because they cannot attain so rarely to the knowledge of things as men may, who are bred up in universities, Schools of Learning, or serve their Apprenticeship for that end and purpose, where anatomy Lectures being frequently read the situation of the parts both of men and women . . . are often made plain to them. . . But that objection is easily answered." Here she cites by way of illustration the freedom of the Israelitish women, adding: "It is not hard words that perform the work, as if none understood the Art that cannot understand Greek. Words are but shell."

A fine picture of a Continental midwife of that age is given in the modern novel, *Ambition,* by Guttman, evidently based on careful historical researches: "It was old Frederic William, desiring to possess the best of everything, who had brought Frau Siegemund to Berlin from Silesia and formally appointed her Electoral court midwife. Frau Siegemund, a majestic lady of fifty, had enemies in plenty. But her reputation as the best midwife in Germany and the adjacent countries did not decline. She was summoned to the childbed of exalted ladies in both Holland and Denmark. Two reproaches were addressed to her. She had herself never borne a child. How was she to know the feelings of a woman in labor? Her second offense was literary ... Justine, the daughter of a parson in Jauer, knew how to handle a pen and recorded her obstetrical experiences for the use of humanity. She intended to make a book thereof. It was reasoned that a blue-stocking could be of no good at the bedside of an expectant mother. Far to be preferred were the honest old midwives who could neither read nor write, who had no trained head but an experienced womb. Justine Siegemund had her answer ready. She asserted that in these enlightened times obstetrical science had attained fixed principles and that under the rough and ready empirical fumbling of your ordinary midwife both mothers and babies died like flies. If the midwives did not learn their business better, the time would come when people would summon academically trained physicians to women in childbirth, as was even now unluckily being done in France. And 'twas a swinish and unChristian thing to have men put their hands on pregnant women."

Everything worked against the practicing midwife, with her ancient lore, good, bad, and indifferent. There was money in the profession and men sometimes more interested in profits than in science pushed into the field. Religion also entered into calculations. In England, where there was fear of secret baptism by Catholics, midwives were licensed by the bishops and gradually the privilege was restricted to those who had received a specific training. This was followed by a growing control on the part of male physicians and the prosecution of unlicensed women who took cases of childbirth. Thus the old woman doctor was left behind in "progress," and many years were to pass before a rebound came which opened medical education to women, tardily, with reservations and limitations even in the most favorable circumstances.

Yet this restoration of women to medicine is not as recent as modern feminists sometimes imagine; nor was the original thread ever broken entirely. That American women in the early nineteenth century should have considered themselves original or have been attacked by the critical public for attempting to teach anatomy, with the aid of beautiful manikins designed by a French woman, seems incredible when one remembers that Maria dalle Donne, a doctor of philosophy and medicine, occupied at Bologna a chair in medicine and surgery established for her by Napoleon in 1802; that Anna Morandi-Manzolini was a professor of anatomy in the same university; that Maria Petraccini-Terretti taught the subject in the University of Ferrara; that Italian culture permitted Dorotea Bocchi to hold a chair in medicine at the University of Bologna and to teach students who came to her from the four corners of the earth.

Touching physics on one side and medicine on the other was the realm of chemistry. With the modern founder of that science was intimately associated his talented wife. The daughter of Jacques Paulze, a savant guillotined at the same time as her husband, Madame Lavoisier inherited intellectual interests and then especially prepared herself for work with her husband. She studied English and Latin to help him acquire foreign learning and put into French the chemical memoirs of Cavendish, Henry, Kirwan, Priestley, and other scientists. Like all good interpreters she knew what she was translating. In his notes about his French travels in 1787, Arthur Young refers admiringly to her conversations on Kirwan's essay on phlogiston and other materials in that field.

Having gifts in drawing, engraving, and painting which the great David disciplined, she was able, in recording experiments and illustrating Lavoisier's great treatise on chemistry, to help immensely in making effective the presentation of contributions in the science of chemistry. Her correspondence with famous scientists indicates her warm championship of the Lavoisier theories. One of her notable converts, for instance, was the Swiss chemist, de Saussure, who wrote back: "You have, Madame, triumphed over my doubts, at least in the matter of phlogiston, which is the principal subject of the interesting work of which you have done me the honor of sending me a copy." After the death of her husband at the hands of the revolutionists, Madame Lavoisier kept up her association with the great scientists of her day, many of whom had been guests in her house, such as Cuvier, Laplace, Lagrange, Arago, Prony, Berthollet, Delambre, and Humboldt. When, nearly a hundred years later, the Massachusetts Institute of Technology opened its chemistry courses to women, it did but tardily recognise a creditable tradition of women in that field.

In entomology in the middle of the nineteenth century Eleanor Omerod was a true pioneer. Before the English Board of Agriculture was ready to appoint a government entomologist, she was consulting expert to the Royal Agricultural Society, examiner in agricultural entomology in the University of Edinburgh, a member of European and American learned societies, the holder of medals two of which were Russian, the scientist who saved England and her colonies vast sums in insect damage prevention. Her specialty was the pests that injure trees, shrubs, cereals, vegetables, flocks and herds, if so broad a field could be called a specialty. Her initial interest was awakened by the observation of conditions on her father's large estate.

Pasteur is the name that springs to mind when silkworm

diseases are mentioned. But more than a hundred years before his researches in that direction a German woman, Maria Sibylla Merian, and her two daughters had gone to the equatorial regions of South America to study, collect, describe, sketch and paint the insects of Surinam, after familiarising themselves with the collections of fauna and flora in Europe. Their first publication dealt with the life-history of silkworms and their various reports appeared in several languages, including French, receiving the highest praise for their scope and accuracy.

In the early nineteenth century an interesting pair of Bohemians, Herr and Frau Kablick, were plunging through jungles and climbing lofty mountains to advance natural science. The former specialised in zoölogy and mineralogy; the latter in botany and paleontology. Fossil animals and plants named for the wife bear witness to the success of her labors and through her coöperation museums were expanded to include the more elaborate knowledge she had helped to create.

And when we come to Pasteur we find that by the skill and devotion of his wife and daughter his great researches into the diseases of silkworms were rendered possible. "Mme. Pasteur and her daughter constituted themselves veritable silkworm rearers. . . And not only in the silk-producing districts of southern France were they thus occupied, collecting and sorting mulberry leaves, but also in a special laboratory in Ecole Normale after their return to Paris. And when in the midst of these researches, on the successful outcome of which hinged one of the greatest sources of national wealth, the indefatigable savant was stricken with paralysis and his life was for a while despaired of, it was again his devoted helpmate that afforded him solace in suffering and exercised a supervision over those experiments which the great man was still conducting almost in the presence of death."

And so we could go on indefinitely backwards and forwards linking up the personalities and the means by which positive knowledge was increased. It is hard to pass over briefly such couples as the François Hubers — the Swiss naturalist blind from the age of seventeen, given hands and eyes for forty years by his wife Marie who had such skill that his printed work on the subject of bees made him noted for sure insight; or the Charles Lyells constantly pursuing geology together. One can only mention hurriedly Janet Taylor, granted a pension by the British government and honored in many ways for her writings on nautical astronomy and navigation, of such assistance to seamen who ruled the waves; Mrs. Ayrton "whose investigations on the electric arc and on the sand ripples of the seashore won for her the first medal ever awarded to a woman by the Royal Society," not because she was the first to deserve it but because the Society was becoming a little more liberal; the devoted mother and wife of Charles Darwin who shielded him from every other strain that he might get through the terrific labor involved in his researches; Mary Somerville connecting the physical sciences when they were comparatively new and going off at tangents, writing abstruse monographs on Curves and Surfaces of Higher Orders, on Molecular and Microscopic Science, and on the Theory of Differences, translating and criticising the *Mecanique Céleste* of Laplace so well that her book was a compulsory text at Cambridge for the most advanced students; and the women who in every country diffused the work of such scientists as Newton, Laplace, and Charles Darwin by their translations and interpretations.

Clemence Royer in introducing Darwin to the French pointed out the political and social implications, as did Herbert Spencer in England, carrying the battle over his evolutionary doctrine into the learned, scientific, and religious societies of her land. In 1870 the uproar over the theory of evolution led her to enlarge and elaborate her summary and evaluation under the title *Origine de l'Homme et des Sociétés*. So radical was her position that she was joined with such scientific heretics of distinction as Vogt, Büchner and Hackel by conservative French contemporaries. "After the appearance of this production, she wrote numerous other works, several of them on subjects relating to natural science, especially in its connection with anthropology and prehistoric archæology. And so great was her breadth of view and so exceptional was her grasp of all subjects discussed by her that Renan declared of her: 'Elle est presque un homme de génie.'" No woman could, of course, be a genuine genius. Perhaps she was less or more than a man of genius in her refusal to seek admittance to the French Institute where politics and small prejudices so often determined membership.

There is no room for mention of the armies of women who have explored in all the fields — anthropological, archæological, botanical, geological. But their effort has been a very positive factor in lifting science above the level it occupied in Fontenelle's day to a place where it now stands as the supreme agent of human welfare, ready for utilisation if the will of society is equal to its opportunities. From the mass of data relative to women's scientific coöperation, four cases must, it would seem, be cited, at all events for the light they shed on incentives.

In the case of Sophie Germain, as of Newton, the offer of a prize was stimulating. Lagrange, her teacher, declared insoluble the problem for which the Academy of Sciences on the order of Napoleon proposed to reward anyone who could illuminate it, who could "give the mathematical theory of the vibration of elastic surfaces and compare it with the results of experiments." Lagrange said it would first necessitate a new system of analysis. But Sophie Germain accomplished the task and in 1816 at a public session of the Institut de France she was honored and admitted to further sessions — the first of her sex to be accepted by the male savants who managed that assembly. Of one of her memoirs on vibrating surfaces M. Navier remarked: "It is a work which few men are able to read and which only one woman was able to write." De Prony hailed her as the "Hypatia of the nineteenth century." With intense specialisation she united a broad philosophy. One of her books is entitled *Considérations Générales sur l'Etat des Sciences et des Lettres aux Différentes Epoques de Leur Culture.*

The fact that Russian universities were closed to women and that to attend German universities they had to go through the formality of a student marriage handicapped Sonya Kovalévsky in the second half of the nineteenth century. Even Heidelberg was closed to her sex but she managed to get private instruction in her beloved mathematics from such experts as von Helmholtz. In 1874 the University of Göttingen was however so impressed by the quality of her work, particularly a dissertation on the theory of partial differential equations that it excused her from the regular oral examination and granted her a degree *in absentia*. Her speculations on the fourth dimension received wide acclaim. Her memoir solved a problem that had long eluded scientists and Kroneker stated that "the history of mathematics will speak of her as one of the rarest of investigators." Biographers declare that she could "with the greatest ease turn from a lecture in Abel's Functions or a research on Saturn's rings to the writing of verse in French or of a novel in Russian or to collaborating with her friend, the Duchess of Cajanello, on a drama in Swedish, or to making a lace collar for her little daughter to whom she was most tenderly attached." After completing her German studies she was given a chair in the University of Stockholm where she became a full professor in 1884. Four years later she carried away a French prize offered by the Academy of Sciences. Before she died the Academy of Science of St. Petersburg elected her to membership.

Neither prizes nor universities were however the background for Mme. Marie Curie who in collaboration with her husband, Pierre, made the discovery of a new element, radium, which was such a sensation in 1898 and was fraught with such meaning in the realm of radio activity. In a shed at the rear of their modest home they experimented and there they made their find. Her husband received the greater credit, as far as academies were concerned; and, although her own initiative is known to those familiar with the actual development leading to this discovery, in her biography of Pierre nothing so petty as credit is discussed; nor is there any trace of a whimpering claim to devotion, taken for granted. Her spirit is that of the true scientist and personally she needs none of the palliatives of little minds. Yet to the study of scientific progress the true leadership is pertinent.

In the modern age of splendid and elaborate equipment, it shocked the scientific world to learn how great a contribution could come from meager physical resources. On the other hand, laboratory equipment is unquestionably essential for certain kinds of work.

Dr. Rhoda Erdmann has convincing evidence to offer on this point. On the eve of the World War, she was engaged in researches at the Friedrich-Wilhelm University of Berlin. In her own country the competition between the sexes was so severe and women were so often confined as a consequence to the status of mere helpers that when an opportunity was given her in 1913 to carry on her studies of cellular parthenogenesis in the Ozborn Zoölogical Laboratory at Yale University in the United States, she went to work with keen joy. At the end of ten months, the duration of her privilege, she sailed for

Germany — the last of July, 1914. While she was on the high seas, the War broke and she was held in England as she reached the first port. Scientific colleagues there invited her to remain and work in the English Institute but when her Yale friends sent for her, she again took up her residence in New Haven and went on with her researches. She was in the midst of important advances when the United States entered the War against her own people and, in the hysteria engendered by battle fever, suspicion of hostile purposes even fell upon the learned alien at Yale. Nervous citizens accused her of seeking secretly to poison the chickens of the town, saying that her laboratory enterprise was only a cover for evil designs. So she was removed to a home for wayward girls in New York City where she was incarcerated during the hot summer months without exercise except in a tiny prison courtyard and enjoyed no freedom beyond its gates other than that which a doctor finally insisted upon under the guise of a visit to him once a week. In a small room with seven women of the streets, she spent four and a half months guarded. Returning to Germany in February, 1919, she found research conditions worse for men and therefore gloomier for women. In Berlin she was then presumed to be exceedingly fortunate to attain the heights of a secretaryship to some man with research enterprises on hand — in marked contrast with the advantages Dr. Florence Sabin, for example, of the Rockefeller Institute of New York has enjoyed — enabling her to make contributions to science leading to high recognition, such as admission to membership in the American Academy of Sciences and her recent appointment as head of the Anatomical Institute at Johns Hopkins.

If Dr. Erdmann's case illustrates in an extreme form the difficulties which women can encounter in their efforts to add to positive knowledge now that science has gone so far beyond the amateur stage, requiring for the prosecution of research expensive equipment and opportunities for a life-time devotion to specialties, it makes the problem striking. Undoubtedly the facilities open to women are multiplying — in universities, government establishments, and private industrial laboratories in the United States particularly; and the reports of such institutions indicate that women are making significant contributions in every field. Yet it must be confessed that the way is not smooth for them. Naturally no men in power welcome competition that endangers bread and butter — to which the best of them are sensitive, and there are matters of sex that disturb the profoundest of academic calms. Relations established in the laboratory have disrupted many a scientific family, leading to dismissals from universities and to divorce courts.

THE IDEA OF PROGRESS AND CRITICAL HUMANISM

NATURAL science — the study of and experimentation with common things — had not advanced very far when it became associated with a revolutionary concept, that of Progress. In the minds of the ancients, mankind revolved in a vicious circle, without hope of infinite improvement through the use of reason coupled with the conquest of nature. The best that the mortal mind could achieve was a simple adaptation to simple resources and self-restraint — the good life on a humble scale. Theologians of the Middle Ages hardened the doctrine of self-discipline by concentration on the glories of a life after death, regarding mortal existence as a vale of tears to be passed through like a purgatory. Then came natural science offering to help humanity during its earthly career, taking on the warmth of the original researches into nature lore for the purpose of caring for life. Though supposed to be coldly neutral in its operation, it was capable of dazzling applications to the benefit of the people at large and therefore introduced a new social psychology. Certainly Lord Bacon conceived science in human terms and a hundred years after his death the faith he had dimly foreseen took definite shape among French thinkers.

According to the historian of *The Idea of Progress,* J. B. Bury, "between 1690 and 1741 the conception of an indefinite progress of enlightenment had been making its way in French intellectual circles and must often have been a topic of discussion in the salons, for instance of Madame de Lambert, Madame de Tencin, and Madame Dupin where Fontenelle was one of the most conspicuous guests. To the same circle belonged his friend, the Abbé de Saint-Pierre, and it is in his writings that we first find the theory widened in its compass to embrace progress toward social perfection." And why in those particular salons was it probably a topic? Because they were the foyers to the Academy of Sciences which Fontenelle served as secretary and in them natural science was the favorite theme. Though Saint-Pierre was a son of the Church, trained by the Jesuits, his scientific interests qualified him to mingle in the group among whom Fontenelle moved with ease and doubtless he received as well as imparted philosophy.

No understanding of the evolution of thought for a full century is possible in fact without reference to the French salons, those peculiarly feminine institutions, where the wit, intelligence, and imagination of the day, emancipated from the damp of the cloister and the smell of the lamp, found full play. Here all the "new ideas," literary, political, scientific, and social were discussed, expanded, encouraged and put into general circulation. If the salon was more "superficial" than the university or the academy, which is doubtful, it was at least more human, more in touch with the world of fermenting reality, less precious, more powerful in the making of great history —

often tragic for the makers. In the eighteenth century all social life "falling back upon itself, flows into Paris, branches and spreads, throbs and flowers in a thousand drawing-rooms. Only then do we see it in its full splendor and style, at the apogee of its power and charm, teeming and full-blown, that great influence of the day, which was to end by annihilating Versailles — the salon," declares a French student of the subject.

For a country that had no Parliament providing for the discussion of public affairs, the salon furnished a favorite and excellent forum, giving place to wit and grace no less than opinion. Here the court could be criticised, religion freely examined, manners and morals turned over as personality dictated, only excess anger being debarred. Not a single thinker who led in the overthrow of the old régime of regal and clerical dictation seemed to have escaped its influence.

If one salon was closed, another was always open for a trial of theory. For example, after the death of Mme. de Lambert, the intelligentsia who had been her especial friends, moved over to the salon of Mme. de Tencin, the "bonne amie" of Fontenelle who said to him one day as she placed her hand on his heart: "Vous n'avez là que du cerveau." At Mme. de Tencin's "the man of letters found a welcome, liberty and advice, applause to give him confidence, a smile to encourage him, inspiration and emulation to quicken his imagination and conversation in the charming audience of a mistress of the house who listens and hears, who seizes main features and *nuances,* who feels as a woman and judges as a man. . . In this salon, the first in France to receive a man at his intellectual value, the littérateur began the great rôle he was destined to play in the society of that age; it was from here, from the salon of Mme. de Tencin, that he made his way to other salons and rose step by step to dominate a society which at the close of a century was to grant him so large a place in the state. . . This woman hastened to the amusements of the mind, enjoyed comedy, novel or witticism, with a heart, a passion and a soul that seemed to escape from her life and abandon themselves utterly to the joys of her mind. What intellectual life, what movement, what vivacity of idea and idiom in the salon this woman collected exhaustively from among men of letters and quickened for her pleasure! Here Marivaux brought depth to subtlety; here Montesquieu awaited the passage of an argument to return it with swift or powerful hand. Here Mairan uttered an idea in a word, and Fontenelle commanded silence with one of the delicate stories he seemed to have found halfway between heaven and earth, between Paris and Badinopolis !"

Mme. de Tencin herself left a pen portrait of Louis XV which, admirers have declared, no historian will ever equal. And she was capable of criticism and fire of her own. Like Mirabeau she had a fierce combat with her father to escape burial in a convent all her life. And like him she was always at the center of strife. She played politics, she wrote, she served a term in jail. A product of conflict, both her turbulence and her intellect were of the French quality which was to bear the thinkers into revolutionary battles.

"Because they were continually occupied; because they were forced by the exigencies of their domination, by their place in society, by the interest of their sex and by their very inaction to carry on an incessant and almost unconscious work of judgment, comparison, and analysis, the women of that age attained a sagacity that gave them the government of the world. It permitted them to strike straight at the heart of the passions, interests, and weaknesses of everyone. The women of the day acquired this prodigious tact so speedily and at such slight cost that it appeared almost as a natural sense in them. It might well be said that there was intuition in the experience of so many young women with this admirable contemporary gift of knowledge without study, of that knowledge which caused the *savantes* to know a great deal without being erudite, of that knowledge which made women of Society know everything without having learned anything. 'Young intelligences divined far more than they learned,' said Sénac de Meilhan, in a profound epigram.

"This genius, this habit of perception and penetration, this rapidity and sureness of vision instilled in woman a rationale of conduct, a quality frequently hidden by the outward aspect of the eighteenth century, yet easily discernible in all the expressions that escaped it. This quality was the personality and property of judgment brought back to the reality of life: the practical spirit.

"What lessons this positivism of appreciation and observation, this imperturbable and apparently natural scepticism taught; how subtle it was, what terrifying depths and lengths it went to! It was this wisdom, without the illusion of God, of society, of man, of faith in anything whatever, builded of every mistrust and every disenchantment, clear and absolute as the proof of a mathematical operation, having only one principle, the recognition of fact, that placed this maxim in the mouth of a young woman: 'It is to your lover you must never say you disbelieve in God; but to your husband it does not matter at all, because with your lover you must leave yourself a way of exit. Religious scruples and devotion cut everything short.'" Of all this the Goncourt brothers have written well.

The salonières lived vividly. They had convictions and they had courage. If they made their contacts with thinkers of the opposite sex through the agency of patronage as Roman ladies did first with Greek philosophers and second with monks, they likewise suffered a great deal and the heavy burden of experience deepened their vivid living. Several of the leading personalities were frank courtesans but brilliant free lovers. The fact that Julie de Lespinasse could hold a salon every night for twelve years attended by some of the greatest men in France proves the power of her own intellect. Mme. de Maintenon, the king's mistress, urged reason upon the court. Respectable mothers emphasized education. In the presence of Ninon de Lenclos wit flashed. She had no delusions. She was as serene in her naturalism as Montaigne, declaring: "The joy of a soul is the measure of its force."

Besides, there was old Mme. du Deffand, three years the senior of Voltaire, who promoted vigor of style by her own elasticity of thought and range of expression when she burst into criticism of her own sex or the other at will. She could even be objective about her own country — rarest of all gifts — thinking it "gay, bright, and shallow." But she liked gayety and seemed its very embodiment. Thus she found Rousseau's *Emile* ridiculous, his *Héloïse* boorish, his *Contrat Social* dull and obscure; Buffon monotonous; she hated to be bored and Milton was one of the writers who had that effect upon her. Democracy she feared might only substitute a thousand tyrants for one. With all her devotion to wit and pleasure, she had a penchant for truth if she was not always its practitioner. One of her shafts was directed at Mme. du Châtelet, the learned scientific patron and intimate friend of Voltaire. But the criticised struck back. And social life sparkled with intellectual fire. Mme. du Deffand held bi-weekly financial, political, literary and art assemblies in her home which were attended by the "most brilliant talker of his age," d'Alembert, whom she helped in his leisure to be handsomely articulate by her monetary assistance, and all the other famous French savants, besides distinguished foreigners coming to chatter and to listen.

Educated by the Jesuits like Voltaire and many of her other

friends, from her early years Mme. du Deffand had an instinctively infidel mind. She once said: "I was hardly ten years old when I began to understand nothing." That was the beginning of wisdom of course. But she did not try to wade into metaphysics, morals or formal philosophy. She jumped at conclusions. As for history, "Well, one is obliged to read a little history," she said, "because it helps one to know men, the only science that excites my curiosity." Concerning Helvetius' writings on the spirit, she said that he raised a tempest simply by expressing in public what everyone was thinking in private. Incidentally Mme. de Graffigny added that all the fine points he made had been gleaned from her salon. In Mme. du Deffand's creed that "to despise the world to the full one must be a worldling," the completely rationalist mind of the influential salonière is sharply revealed — a foil for creative inspiration and a foe to sophistry. At a time when its popularity was sweeping all critics aside, she did not hesitate to pronounce Richardson's *Clarissa Harlowe* utterly arid. If in applying her mental talent to the management of her forum for debate, she found her personal pleasure in idle curiosity about the ideas and personalities of others, in her sceptical presence they produced their best and were put on their p's and q's to be worthy of the attention they received. She was no sycophant of the authoritative.

Her business and theirs was not obsession with commercial responsibility such as prevailed in England, ruler of the sea. Instead it was the flow of wit and humor, essentials of great thinking, and the circulation of criticism. The "world" did not exist for these talkers except in so far as they represented it, but they did represent the French world of State and Church whose privileges and perils they discussed in every detail. The "arch sceptic of her day," apprenticed to debates by Jesuit logicians, was so independent in her mature freedom and so forthright in her judgments on the opinions and faiths of her associates, male and female, that she charged the very air with rationalism.

That the intellectual French woman of the eighteenth century was humanistic in her outlook is fully demonstrated by her love of Letters, to which Christine de Pisan and Mme. de Rambouillet had early directed the energies of the sex. The salonière "lived in familiar communion, in a daily intimacy with letters; boasted always a literary basis, foundation and refuge. In this world preoccupied with thought and wit, in mansions and châteaux, each of which had its library, the woman of the age, who in the boredom of the convent had already acquired a great taste for reading, fortified herself in pen and print. She lived in an atmosphere of books, sustained by them; at every turn, her correspondence proves what earnest entertainment she sought in them, what nourishment she drew from the gravest of tomes, from philosophical works or historical narratives, after the day's libel or the current novelty. From this rose a literary culture, developed by the fashions of the salon, by the pastime of translation, by the popular amusements of certain tests of wit demanded of woman, which so often placed a pen in her hand. . . Besides the professional authoresses, who tried their hand at every genre, from epic poetry to the strolling theatre, an almost endless list might be drawn up of women of society, who turned author unassumingly, on occasion by example, almost by mistake. . . Political economy itself assumed the wit of Morellet and the verve of Galiani to recommend itself to the mind of woman. Thought knew no manifestation, intelligence assumed no form, wit imagined no tome, boredom itself put on no disguise, that was not an homage to an all-powerful mistress, who governed the value of a work and the reputation of an author." The "Journal Politique," discussing science, poetry, art, domestic economy, agriculture, navigation, naval architecture and what not, was edited largely with a view to catching women's patronage.

They presided over the fate of authors, at least for the day. "Every mode of literature, every sort of writer, every pamphlet, every volume, even a masterpiece, required that the woman sign its passport and open it a way to publicity. The book she adopted sold; she herself placed an edition in a few days, whether it were by Rousseau or by La Blatterie. The man that she sponsored was a success; he grew famous like La Harpe or Marmontel. Every favor a minister could bestow upon letters in the way of money, privilege, pensions, the support of newspapers and the championship of the *Mercure* passed through her hands and went exclusively to her clients. The fortune of men like Suard was purely her work. She spelled success, she was favor; and what a crowd stood under obligations to her! There was Robé, protected by the Duchess d'Olonne; Roucher, protected by the Comtesse de Bussy; Rousseau, protected by the Maréchale de Luxembourg; Voltaire, protected by Madame de Richelieu, who obtained from the Keeper of the Seals that nothing be done against him without forewarning her; the Abbé Barthélemy, protected by Madame de Choiseul. . . The Academy, in this age, withstood woman no better than the public or public opinion. Throughout the entire century was it not woman who drew up its lists of candidates ?"

This is by way of prelude — this woman's world, the salon — to an understanding of the new conceptual thought thrown out upon the waters by Fontenelle and Saint-Pierre. In this atmosphere, the latter formulated the notion that mankind had not fallen after all from a high estate of bliss nor was it chained to a revolving wheel of dire fate but could by taking responsibility refashion the world to human and humane ends.

He ventured also to make some specifications — a plan for universal peace, the subdivision of great landholdings, the suppression of royal and clerical privileges, provisions for the reform of prisons, and the care of the dependent, the sick, the aged, and the insane. While many of his ideas were vague and illusive, Rousseau found in them inspiration and fruit, carrying forward with terrific effect their revolutionary implications.

Among the contemporaries of Saint-Pierre, one who outlived him, was another man of the salon and the same spirit, Fontenelle, a populariser of science, a critic of manners and morals, a defender of modernism, convinced that history was a romance of progress rather than a sad tale of decay. And it is symptomatic of the age that, besides circulating among the salons, he addressed himself in the preface to his *Conversations on the Plurality of the World,* to the ladies especially and that, according to Thorold, "all women devoured it eagerly." His treatise on astronomy he framed for a charmingly curious marquise. It may be said that all this is superficial, but, in the field of manners, morals, and opinion where so much of history is made, is profundity always more illuminating than wit, or logic more enlightening than intuition ? Did Mommsen, for example, who knew all that could be known about Rome, have any deeper insight into the course of the German Empire in which he lived than the sadlers, tailors, and brewers who made up the Social Democratic Party ?

At all events Fontenelle, as has been said, prophesied to the seventeenth century what was to come and stood to the eighteenth as a fine reminder of its origin. "He was a characteristic and magnificent man of letters, being, indeed, the first specimen of that type which was to play so important a part throughout the eighteenth century. Now the man of letters as such does not need to be an original thinker. Still less need he be a creative artist. On the other hand, he requires, in order to fulfill his functions in the republic of the mind, a quick and facile intelligence, apt to seize the finer shades of opinion, all of which he should be ready to welcome in turn. For he must be without prejudices of any kind, which, in the average state of human nature, is tantamount to saying that he must eschew personal convictions. He is skilled to detect the real trend of ideas; among contemporary notions he readily, and as it were instinctively, distinguishes those that are pregnant with the future from merely associational survivals. He is to the thinkers who are the creative forces of the time, what the Pensée-writer is to the moral philosopher; he circulates the small change of their ideas. He can only permit himself one passion, curiosity."

When Voltaire, the intellectual heir of Saint-Pierre and Fontenelle no less than of English writers, turned to the new humanism associated with the revolutionary creed of progress for all mankind and undertook to rewrite history in terms of the common life rather than of kings, he responded to an inspiration derived from the Marquise de Châtelet, the translator of Newton's *Principia,* an accomplished mathematician, linguist and philosopher on her own account. Of this motive we learn through Tallentyre: "The most ambitious, the most voluminous, the most characteristic, and the most daring of his works," the *Essai sur les mœurs et l'ésprit des nations et sur les principaux faits de l'histoire depuis Charlemagne jusqu'à Louis XIII,* was begun at the home of this young mistress at Cirey in response to her brusque denunciation of history as it had hitherto been treated. She pronounced it 'all an old almanac. What does it matter to me, a Frenchwoman living on my estate, to know that Egil succeeded Haquin in Sweden, and that Ottoman was the son of Ortogrul ? I have read with pleasure the history of the Greeks and the Romans; they offered

me certain pictures which attracted me. But I have never yet
been able to finish any long history of our modern nations. I
can see scarcely anything in them but confusion; a host of
minute events without connection or sequence, a thousand
battles which settled nothing. I renounced a study which
overwhelms the mind without illuminating it.' "

Voltaire came to the same conclusion: "History is nothing
more than a picture of crimes and misfortunes." He wrote to
Walpole, likewise a habitué of the French salons: "Truly the
history of the Yorkists and Lancastrians and many others is
much like the history of highway robbers." With that perspective he entered upon the task of tracing the record of the
human mind. And as it unfolded in his research, he declared:
"Only philosophers should write history. In all nations history
is disfigured by fable till at last philosophy comes to enlighten
man; and when it does finally arrive in the midst of this
darkness, it finds the human mind so blinded by centuries of
error that it can hardly undeceive it; it finds ceremonies, facts
and monuments heaped up to prove lies. . . History is after
all nothing but a pack of tricks which we play upon the
dead. . . History proves that anything can be proved by history." Doubtless social history would have come in time but
it is not without significance that what seems to have been the
earliest grand protest against the customary tale of "begetting,"
war and politics was made by a French marquise. If Voltaire
did the work, she supplied the germinating idea.

Feminine interest and promotion marked the course of criticism and liberalism across the Rhine in Germany, land of
Frederick the Great and military heroes, disintegrating the
synthesis of the landed aristocracy and its peculiar attachments.
No small part of the modernist movement there was due to
the versatility and ingenuity of the Jews who in a country
primarily feudal were leaders in commerce, a bond which

united them with the liberalism of England and France while it threw them athwart the Germanic tradition. Conventional history having neglected their share in the transformation of Germany from a rigid to an elastic society, it may be emphasized here for the sake of redressing the balance.

This peculiar character of the German enlightenment may be explained partly in economic terms. Hargrave in *Some German Women and Their Salons* outlines their position in the eighteenth century: "The Jews lived in a luxury and refinement unknown to the proud but poor Gentile aristocracy. Jewish women enjoyed leisure and opportunity for culture in a measure undreamed of by their German contemporaries. Henriette Herz describes how Jewish women lived whilst their men-folk were busy in shop and counting house, how they formed circles for reading, for languages, for philosophy. They read Racine and Voltaire in French, Shakespeare in English [the Schlegels translated him into German]; they learnt Italian in order to read Dante in his own tongue. Such women with their quick Oriental minds, cultured and refined, were the modern women of their day, certainly the most charming and accomplished. Their drawing-rooms attracted the more liberal men of note, who rose above the prejudices of the day — the artists, musicians, travelers from foreign lands, the intellectual among the young aristocrats [for instance Prince Ferdinand, the nephew of Frederick, who was distressed by the weakness of the court as were many young Frenchmen in the neighboring realm]. . . Small wonder that the more intellectual Germans were attracted, for such pleasant freedom of intercourse was unknown in their circles. There one was bored by stiff etiquette and general dullness (*Schloss Langeweile,* 'Castle Ennui') and the women had lost the art of frank, unaffected intercourse with men, whilst the Court was so often plunged into mourning that some one dubbed the Courtiers *Pleuresenmenschen."*

For the purpose of holding what Carlyle would call a "small rushlight" over this phase of neglected history, a single person may be chosen to illustrate a movement. She is Rahel Varnhagen who presided over a salon of her own and set the pace for her contemporaries outside. A professed Christian, she cherished no dogma, her adoption of the dominant religion being rather a testimonial to her sympathy with national ideals than a display of evangelical fervor. With an emancipated mind, she was prepared for the kind of inquiry and debate which filled France with intellectual ferment. In a single sentence she analysed her spirit and that of her friends: "What is man but a question ? He is here for that, for asking honest, bold questions, and humbly waiting for answers. Not asking boldly enough and giving one's self flattering answers, that is the deep source of all error."

Rahel Varnhagen, whom Brandes ranked as "the first great and modern woman in Germany," was born in 1771 into an orthodox Jewish circle where her father, a wealthy jeweler and banker, held fast to the ways of his fathers. But his child was "a winged one," to use the language of Jean Paul Richter, often a guest in her home after she fled from her backward looking family to become the center of a forward-looking group of individualists. Richter declared that she was the only humorous woman he ever met, her philosophy of free will and personal courage being enlivened by exceeding grace and wit. This was a delight and refreshment to Richter, generous as he was to progressive women devoid of humor. Keenly appreciative of individuality, he set forth in 1807 a doctrine of education, *Levana,* in which the program of producing classical parrots is attacked as unworthy of higher possibilities. And as for *Emile,* he held that, while Rousseau's humanism was commendable, under his pattern of woman in a state of nature a negative product would result.

While German intellectuals were discriminating among women, Rahel was selecting favored thinkers among the men. Thus she called Fichte and Goethe Germany's two eyes. In the opinion of Heine she was its spirit: "The most spirituelle woman in the universe." He regarded his acquaintance with her as "the beginning of a new period of life." Countless witticisms and epigrams that fell from her lips became national currency and exercised a wide influence upon the life and art of her country. She touched everything with a light but sure hand. And she was always at the front, in the vanguard of progress, ever echoing Goethe's cry for "Light, more Light," whether it was in her youth among the Romantics or in her mature years turning heart and soul to "Young Germany."

Her closing comments dealt with the transformation in interests. "How could people go on discussing things which 'we' left off discussing ten years ago?" she asked and in the same breath added: "How very few people have ideas!" meaning new ones. Yet she was always glad to be alive "because the world is really progressing, because ideas, dreams are becoming alive, because industries, inventions, associations realise these dreams. . . The Present is the Future, and the world is moving (*Sie geht, die Welt*)." Her sympathies extended to the working classes "because they are the most and the poorest." Hence she was akin in humanistic temper to Saint-Pierre and understood his disciples. But whereas the Abbé across the border had looked to monarchs to inaugurate the new day of humanism, she was sensitive to the limits of centralised authority. A feminist of fearless daring, she yet supported universal education and framed burning words on motherhood amid her plea for sex equality. Her personality was so aflame that Beethoven, meeting Rahel by chance when he was strolling, sought an introduction and composed in her presence.

But of course the impression must not be given that German Romantic leadership was Jewish. The movement had a universality of interest and aspiration which it would otherwise have lacked. Caroline Schlegel, to whom the German enlightenment is deeply indebted, was a Teuton of the Teutons but her French sympathies at the time of the revolution brought her imprisonment; her share in translating Shakespeare into German must never be overlooked. Jews and Teutons alike, believing that the past had been tragic with its broken cultures, its bigotries and its conflicts, sought to unify all knowledge, to familiarise themselves with the history and literature of all peoples, and draw into a single perspective arts, religion and philosophy. They considered Kant's categories as a relic of provincialism. They were cosmopolites. Every new work of Goethe, Schiller, Fichte, or Schelling was a sensation and so were foreign works. They formed circles of intelligentsia in the leading German cities and within them debated sex no less than national controversies, their tendency being toward the synthesis of life as all one. Thus they paved the way for Hegel and laid the basis for a new history such as Ranke attempted, rising above the dead classification of meaningless facts in an effort to indicate the spirit that animates society. They were dreamers rather than rationalists. But speculators on the "Ifs" of history suggest that the revolution of 1848 might have been prevented had Bettina von Arnim's open letter to the king, containing a program for reform, been heeded.

Through Mme. de Staël, German Romanticism was borne to France. After visiting Rahel and studying the German society, the French woman wrote an interpretation of German culture which, Carlyle said, inaugurated a new mode of thinking about the Teutons in foreign circles. Mme. de Staël was the first of the French to grasp the import of the German form of modernism — that totality of the universe, of nature and life, which it comprised — and though her book on the subject was ordered burned by Napoleon, its effect was stupendous none the less.   From France the interpretation reached England affecting even "the schoolmistress heroines of Charlotte Brontë who are proud of being themselves, portionless and plain, yet fitting soul-mates for their heroes."   Across the wide sea, Emerson, in an air of Puritanism, also felt refreshed by the German "over-soul."

Russia meanwhile was establishing contact with the French critical movement through the efforts of Catherine the Great at the same time that Frederick the Great was taking on the modern spirit with flourishes.

So the whole Western world stirred with new emotions and faced a new direction.   The humanism which the Renaissance mothered had been transformed in the French alembic, reflected and modified in Germany, merged in the democratic process, and was giving inspiration to a reasoning method which was to mark the maturity and independence of the West from its long tutelage to the East.

UNIVERSAL DEMOCRACY

THE widening of the intellectual horizon through the discovery of new worlds — ancient, Oriental, and American — the making of order out of feudal chaos, adventures on the high seas culminating in bourgeois power and aggression, the advance of positive knowledge and its flowering in the idea of progress led to the democratisation of intelligence and brought hitherto inarticulate masses into the historical arena.

The preciosity of antique intellectualism and the other-worldliness of mediævalism were now outmoded not only for the classes but to an astonishing degree for the masses. On the one side the tendency toward the democratisation of the positive knowledge recently accumulated is political, reflected in the transfer of governments from monarchs and aristocracies to all the people without distinction of rank or property, men and women alike. Under this head the constitutional history of three hundred years can be mainly written.* On the other side it is educational, the ladder to learning now extending from the kindergarten to the university; careers in research are open to talents irrespective of birth; a war has been started on illiteracy from the steppes of Siberia to the desert villages of Mexico; the press has battered down the walls of institutionalised wisdom; the electric fluid of thought may start anywhere and flow in every direction. Equally fundamental — indeed but a part of the same tendency — has been the drift toward economic democracy, toward the production and distribution of goods by and for the masses, setting up minimum standards of living for everyone. The *laissez faire* school collapsed with caste economy and socialism carried the reasoning a step further until capitalism is beginning to see that its only hope of salvation lies in the enlarged and secure buying power and desires of the multitudes.

It is easy to laugh at democratic pretensions, to point out reactions against them in Italy and Russia, for instance, and

* In exploring the origins of representative government students of history encounter queens at the very outset. According to Stubbs (Constitutional History of England, 4th ed., II, p. 167) "the first recorded appearance of town representatives in the Cortes of Aragon is placed in 1162" and "in that year queen Petronilla summoned to the Cortes at Huesca 'prelados, ricos hombres, caballeros y procuradores.'" By the same authority (II, p. 232) we are told that "the year 1254 then is the first date at which the royal writs direct the election and attendance in parliament of two knights from each shire (in England), the occasion being the granting of an aid in money to be sent to the king in Gascony, and the parliament being called by the queen and the earl of Cornwall." Henry's unfortunate excursions into Gascony were encouraged by his queen, Eleanor, daughter of the Count of Provence, and she was eager to wring money from the county gentry to help pay the bills incurred in the attempts to execute the designs which she had at heart. Love of money was the root of representative government and Eleanor had her full share of it.

to discant on its "failures." It is also easy to draw consolation from contrasting the follies of democracy with those of aristocracies, monarchies, and despotisms, most of which have succeeded in destroying themselves, and to indicate by historical parallels that great reactions in the past have been mere preludes to new advances. But the game is scarcely worth the candle for those who are seeking to understand the course of human affairs and men and women, rather than to exercise their wits for the pleasurable frictions it gives. We are in the presence of realities. Governments may change radically, economic representation may be substituted for the representation of free and equal heads, and as yet undreamed alterations may be made in the structure of States, but there is nothing in the present scene which indicates the remotest possibility of restoring the chattel slavery of antiquity or the soil-bound servitude of mediæval times. Nor is it possible to conceive of a return to the old conditions in which perhaps ninety per cent of the people of all classes could neither read nor write, and were without books, newspapers, and magazines. Equally unthinkable is a restoration of a purely class economy in which the masses contentedly produce wealth to sustain ruling orders and remain satisfied with the barest minimum of subsistence. Capitalism does not require it in fact and would come to an almost dead stop if it tried to proceed on that assumption; and certainly none of the substitutes offered for capitalism contemplate a return to production mainly for upper class privileges and enjoyments. Both fascism and communism are governments *for* crowds if not *by* them. Indeed the guess might well be risked that, while science and machinery last, mass production for the masses will increase rather than diminish.

When the unfolding drama of political democracy is viewed broadly, it will be found to divide into several great acts and many minor scenes. It opens with the so-called Puritan revolution in England in the seventeenth century, runs through the American and French revolutions of the eighteenth century, and after a ' ıg period quieter evolution breaks out in the storms following the crash of the World War. In cursory and popular histories this story is usually told in terms of a few heroic figures thrown up in crises, and in terms of stirring, even thrilling, episodes. But scholars, who have gone behind the stage set for infantile minds, who have with minute care examined changes in economic life and the movements of opinion that have preceded and accompanied this amazing transformation of the Western world, relate a story in many volumes never reaching the popular counters; have in fact destroyed for those that care to know the catastrophic and great-man myth of history. Carlyle and his hero worship are buried forever beneath a mountain of sources and documents of which he never heard. Beyond the circle of materials used in constructing his gigantic Cromwell, for example, are multitudes of prosaic records telling of great shifts in economic arrangements, of sectarian experiments with self-government in matters ecclesiastical, of obscure figures whose varied activities and ideas made possible the reduction of the English monarchy and aristocracy. Had Carlyle even read his contemporary, Buckle, he could have discovered how shallow was his theory of history.

When the history of democracy is expanded to take in all the factors that may be reckoned as efficient causes, then at every stage women must figure in our calculations, in ways prosaic, strange, illuminating, and, to soft minds, often shocking. For example if we step behind the scenes where Charles I, Charles II, Cromwell, Pym and Hampden are playing their acts in the popular spotlight, we encounter women helping aggressively to shape their play. For the social historian there are the women merchants, artisans, proprietors, and managers who participated in the economic movements that transformed English society, created the class basis for Cromwellian politics, and supplied carpenters, brewers, cobblers and tinkers for his pious army. But if individuals are taken into account, women stand forth as genuine personalities. Do we seek for types of the Puritan mind furnishing the stern faith and discipline for the popular uprising ? It is perfectly represented in the seventeenth-century mother of Nehemiah Wellington, a turner of Eastcheap, who has left an etching of her character in a few words: "She was very loving and obedient to her parents, loving and kind to her husband, very tender-hearted to her children, loving all that were godly, much misliking the wicked and profane. She was a pattern of sobriety unto many, very seldom seen abroad except at church. . . God had given her a pregnant wit and an excellent memory. She was very ripe and perfect in all stories of the Bible, likewise in all the stories of the martyrs, and could readily turn to them; she was also perfect and well seen in the English chronicles, and in the descents of the Kings of England. She lived in holy wedlock with her husband twenty years, wanting but four days." Here was typified, as John Richard Green has pointed out, the dignity, self-respect, and consciousness of calling and responsibility which invested the "lower classes" of England with the power of resistance to tyranny.

Ascending in the social scale we come to better known women on both sides. In the Cromwellian party stands the heroic figure of Colonel Hutchinson, one of the men who put Charles I to death at the risk of their own lives and, standing beside him, Lucy Hutchinson, author of a memoir which, for clearness of portraiture and purity of style, deservedly ranks among the classics of the period. In all the political controversies of that stormy time she took the keenest interest; she appeared in the lobby of Parliament to oppose objectionable legislation; and with due managerial skill she looked after the estate while her husband was absent in the forum and the field. In the royalist camp women were equally staunch and some were given to the kind of living that helped to undo the royal court. It is with full justification that Hallam, in explaining the triumph of constitutional government over harsh and arbitrary rule, exclaims: England is "much indebted to the memory of Barbara duchess of Cleveland, Louisa duchess of Portsmouth, and Mrs. Eleanor Gwyn." Of such curious stuff was the fabric woven in the first great revolution which started democracy on its modern course.

Long afterward when the English principles of the seventeenth century were being elaborated and preparations were being made for the English democracy of the twentieth century, it was a woman, Mary Wollstonecraft, who made the first stinging reply to Edmund Burke's defense of government by great property. A modern student of the age, Walter Phelps Hall, renders a judgment to the effect that her *Vindication of the Rights of Man,* the first of at least thirty-eight replies to Burke, has "in thought if not in diction no superior." With vigor and prophetic insight she attacks Burke's argument all along the line. She accuses him of undue reverence for "the rust of antiquity and those unnatural customs which ignorance and self-interest have consolidated into the sage fruit of experience." She asks him why progress should be retarded by the worship of the mouldy past, why the life of an honest mechanic should often be sacrificed to secure the property of the rich, why men should be kidnapped for the navy, why land should lie waste in huge estates while labor starves for the want of land, how he could defend the political system that he himself had shown to be inept and corrupt, how he could praise the English clergy while "it is a well-known fact that when we the people of England have a son whom we scarcely know what to do with — we make a clergyman of him," and how he could defend the right of birth to rule in the face of knowledge that talents were not a class possession and that education was a powerful element in the formation of character. As arguments went on both sides in those days, Mary Wollstonecraft's displayed learning and acumen and had the merit of discerning the future more clearly than all Burke's labored and turgid rhetoric, whatever its intellectual merits. It is also worthy of note that her plea for men preceded her more celebrated defense of the rights of women, published as the eighteenth century drew to a close.

In that other chapter of the development of Anglo-Saxon democracy, the American Revolution, which had tremendous repercussions in Europe, alike on Burke and Wollstonecraft, "Daughters of Liberty" vied in energy with "Sons of Liberty," boycotted English goods, spun and wove to supplant English textiles, stirred up "patriotism," and cheered the bold boys who rioted and overturned statues. There were women among the editors and publishers whose little sheets spread revolutionary propaganda and revolutionary news throughout the colonies. Women wrote plays and satires to ridicule and answer Tory pamphleteers, adding fuel to the fire fed by Tom Paine's celebrated tracts. Among the prominent revolutionary families women carried burdens of agitation and of war. Abigail Adams, wife of John, urged her timid husband to strong action, demanded consideration for the rights of her sex while those of men were being debated, and looked after property and children when he was absent on difficult undertakings. In Virginia Martha Washington took charge of the plantation while her revolutionary husband was for nearly seven years in the field, shrinking from no discomfort or trial as long as the fortunes of America were at stake. If money was to be raised by the sale of bonds or melted plate, women were enlisted in the operation. Since thought, labors, devotion, and sacrifices are indispensable to any historic movement, no picture of the American Revolution that approximates reality can fail to consider women's participation. Among the residents of England who defended the American cause, while John Wesley and Edward Gibbon attacked it, was Catherine Macaulay, a writer of no particular brilliance but great vogue, sensitive to the futility of the English policy and openly encouraging the "rebels" across the water. Some of her historical writing bordered on the absurd but her political judgment was superior to that of the gentlemen who governed the country.

The American Revolution had scarcely closed successfully when another scene in the development of democracy opened in France. That revolution, too, had been long in preparation, and whether attention is given to the movement in mercantile economy which preceded it, to the extravagances of the royal court which made it inevitable, to the agitations which prepared the way, to the follies of the aristocracy which precipitated it, to the vacillations of the monarch which led to republican experiments, to the course of political discussions which accompanied every major step in the drama, women appear in the foreground or the controlling background. Of the rise of the French bourgeoisie who made the revolution and finally dominated its system of public and domestic economy, space forbids us to speak. Nor is it necessary to comment again on the feminine leaders of salons who patronized the philosophical forerunners, stimulated debate on dangerous issues, asked pertinent questions, disseminated revolutionary ideas, and carried the spirit of revolt into the very ballrooms of Versailles. Love of scandal and gossip has perpetuated their names, chatter about their doings, and their memoirs, although academic history as written and circulated has given scant notice to their main acts in the play. It is hardly thinkable that an old society can dissolve as long as women adhere tenaciously to its conditions of survival or that a new one can arise unless women have shared in the economic and intellectual transformation behind it and in the fashioning of the new moral synthesis upon which it is to rest. Everything in the history of the French revolution warrants emphasis on their importance as molders of opinion and fomenters of deeds.

Between the years 1791 and 1793 when the fateful and tragic course of the upheaval was being determined, Madame Roland lived and operated at the very center of the fray. It is true that her husband was more visible in the scrutiny of the forum but, as Danton said, he was always guided by his wife. For this counsel she was prepared through ardent study in her youth, mastering the works of Plutarch, Bossuet, Montesquieu, Voltaire and Rousseau and pondering on life and destiny in the light that came from them and from her own spirit. Shortly after her marriage, she began to assist her husband in writing for the New Encyclopædia; she also wrote a series of political articles for a Lyons newspaper which he signed, articles that immediately caught the attention of the early revolutionists at Paris and drew her husband into their circle. This development was followed by their removal to the capital, his appointment to high office, and their participation in all the scenes of desperate days until Madame Roland was taken to the guillotine and Monsieur put an end to his own life with the sword.

During these brief but momentous times her salon was the headquarters of the revolutionary leaders and there important operations in the strategy of revolt were discussed and settled before they came out into the open of the forum. Until her death, the wife wrote letters and speeches for her husband and affected manœuvers. Besides that, she was in constant touch with other revolutionists, aiding, advising, and urging them to

action. Of the important decisions of the time, the most vital
— that of appealing to the provinces against the Paris dictatorship — may be laid directly on Madame Roland. And she
fought to the last ditch when the radicals became more extreme
than she and her husband, defying them as she mounted the
scaffold with her famous apostrophe: "O Liberty! What
crimes are committed in thy name!" If masculine historians
are wont to speak of her "masculine" intelligence and courage,
the balance may be redressed by citing her feminine predecessors all the way back through the desperate and sanguinary
scenes of imperial Rome.

From top to bottom the French Revolution is shot through
with feminine thinking, action, and intrigue, paralleling the
course of masculine operations and sometimes directing them.
Historians may well dispute whether, in developing the policies and determinations of the court party, Marie Antoinette
was more or less powerful than Louis XVI, more or less inept,
and forced conclusions more or less fatal. Those who think
they know cause and effect may undertake a decision but, however it may run, in every phase of the French Revolution from
the opening of the Estates General until Marie Antoinette was
sent to the scaffold (and in fact after her death), her whims,
conceptions, and resolutions were matters to be considered in
all seriousness. Was it the encouragement of foreign armed
intervention to save the monarchy? Was it negotiating to divide the forces of moderation and defeat every salutary reform? Was it temporising to gain time for vain hopes?
Was it revealing French military plans to foreign foes? Marie
Antoinette was more than equal to all these lines of action.
Yet inept as she may have been in politics, she was more dignified, courageous and consistently alive than Louis.

If we turn from the women at the top who took part in the
Revolution as thinkers, negotiators, and manipulators to the

writers who sought to direct its course and to gauge its tendencies in the very midst of the storm, cognizance must be taken of Madame de Staël. Though a child of the salon, as the daughter of the Neckers, and mistress of a salon of her own in later days, she really made "the world her salon instead of the salon her world," for she was in fact a "new woman," running to and fro across the Continent, as much at home in Germany or Italy as in England or Russia. At the time of her marriage with the Swiss diplomat, Germaine Necker was the richest heiress in France; and thus she had the means with which to gratify her activist impulses when Napoleon drove her from pillar to post with his decrees of banishment. What a span and what a life! When her father and mother left the red stews of the capital, she remained at her point of observation. She saw members of the Estates General file past her window and she lived to see her *bête noire,* Napoleon, go down to defeat at Waterloo. Driven to England as an émigrée for a time, she returned to Paris to hold a salon to which came the brothers of Napoleon on expeditions of negotiation. Meanwhile she captivated the French with her *Essays on Literature* and *Daphine,* the first novel of feminism. When Napoleon drove her from the city she replied with *Ten Years of Exile* in which she "debunked" the Emperor to the delight of his enemies — an excoriation that seemed even wittier after the great master of Europe had bitten the dust. While in Germany she met the first thinkers of that country, including Goethe, exchanged parries and thrusts with them, and wrote a noteworthy treatise on that land. It was daring of a supreme order to visit the enemy, study his good points as well as his bad, draw analogies for the provincials and the haters, and offer the product to a conquering people blindly following the Corsican. Of course Napoleon ordered her book burned in the public square.

From start to finish, Madame de Staël was also a critic and

defender of her sex. She objected to the assumption that women could only be educated by men and proved her point as she handed them viands in her drawing-room. Her views on marriage were obnoxious to clericalism but were symbolic of the rising bourgeoisie. Her conduct was a pledge that women might henceforth travel where they please, observe what they will, and express their conclusions freely. It may be admitted that the extravagant praise accorded her as a writer is extreme; it is possible that her essays on Rousseau display rhetoric and not reason; it is likely that she borrowed heavily from others, a failing, if such it be, not limited to de Staël. But the very title of one of her books, *Literature in Relation to Social Institutions,* as it is translated, displays a penetration that characterises few of the greatest literary critics to this day. And the magnetism of her daring and her manifestoes has extended to the four corners of the intellectual world. She was one of the rare individuals whom Napoleon could not subdue, while Margaret Fuller declared, somewhat flamboyantly, that the beams of her intellect "make the obscurest school-house in New England warmer and lighter to the little ragged girls who are gathered together on its wooden bench. They may never through life hear her name; but she is none the less their benefactress."

At the bottom of the social scale where violence took the place of negotiation and oratory, women often led in demonstrations of mass power, in conflicts on barricades, in bread riots, and in ominous manifestations of will driving constituent and legislative assembles to extremes. In *The Women of the French Revolution,* Michelet says: "Men were the heroes of July 14, women of the 5th of October. Men stormed the royal Bastille, women overcame the monarchy itself, brought it into the hands of Paris, that is, of the Revolution." After all, the taking of the Bastille was an empty gesture, a mere symbol of protest — a threat to the monarchy but intrinsically unimportant. The October march to Versailles on the contrary was a signal for the terror; it was made by hungry and desperate women; while the hungry men of Paris grumbled in angry groups, women took courage by the forelock and besieged the seat of power at Versailles — the center of the monarchy, the aristocracy, the Estates General, and the clergy.

Among these women were wood carvers, shopkeepers, housewives, market tenders, and prostitutes. At their head was Rosa Lacombe, absent from the proud tomes of "regular" history, but dominant in action as she seized a trumpet and struck up the battle notes. "The rats are on the march !" ran the cry along the streets. At first the women attacked the City Hall. Soon their ranks were swollen to seven or eight thousand, mostly armed with weapons of some variety. From the City Hall they started on the long tramp to Versailles, the procession growing in numbers as it approached the citadel of the monarchy. One committee entered the National Assembly. Another forced its way into the King's apartments demanding "Bread," and wrung from him a decree ordering the victuallers of Paris to feed the starving multitude.

To have them nearer the hungry, the mob then insisted that the king, queen, and dauphin return with it to Paris and take up their residence in the Palace of the Tuileries, virtual prisoners of the radicals. The National Assembly followed the royal family to the city and henceforward all proceedings were carried on under the pressure of the irreconcilable revolutionists. It was starved, determined women assisted by a few straggling men who gave a fateful turn to the course of French history, unwittingly no doubt, without program beyond the immediate need, but significantly and dramatically.

This stroke of state marked a great awakening among women. Pamphlets on the rights and problems of female citizens rolled from the presses and were widely circulated. Working women, who had lately been driven out of the gilds and therewith shunted to a life of prostitution — the historic alternative to security — now demanded the dissolution of these ancient bodies, thus incidentally helping the bourgeoisie in its war on unions of artisans. Associations of women were formed for various purposes and coöperated with different factions of the revolution until they were dissolved by force. Rosa Lacombe, chieftain of the tramp to Versailles, challenged the dictatorship of Robespierre in the name of popular rights and called for a social no less than a political revolution. In brief, women were at the heart of the French Revolution helping to start and direct the avalanche which swept democracy into Europe.

There is no room here to establish their connection with the ferments and revolutions of 1830 and 1848 so fruitful in the extension of manhood suffrage throughout the Western world. Some day when the narrative of history is properly enlarged that integral chapter will be told. It is important for the moment, however, to draw attention to the part played by women in the agitations culminating in the overthrow of the Russian autocracy, in view of the place Russia now holds in the political spectrum. Were there space something could be said of the Empress Catherine II toying with the dangerous ideas of the French Revolution, of Madame Kruedener, adviser of Alexander I, a source of inspiration for the Holy Alliance, and of Polish women participants in the fight for freedom. Other times and pages may take care of that. But we cannot overlook the vast popular movement in manifold forms which finally defeated the Tsarist autocracy nor miss in the observation the vigorous women agitators and doers of the deed.

While Herzen and Bakunin labored over Hegelian dialectics and conceived of the revolution in grandiose phrases, others "went to the people" in a heroic effort to raise them out of the slough of suffering, stolidity, ignorance and illiteracy. Among the leaders in this attack on tyranny was the extraordinary Vera Figner, first a humanist and at last a revolutionist. In a remarkable passage in his work, called *Sixteen Years in Siberia,* Leo Deutsch has given a living portrait of this champion of revolt: "I had come to know Vera Figner in St. Petersburg during the year 1877, at a time when she had already adopted the idea of going 'among the people.' Twenty-two years of age, slender and of striking beauty, she was even then a note-worthy figure among the other prominent women socialists. Like so many other girls, she had thrown her heart and soul into the cause of the Russian peasants, and was ready and willing to sacrifice everything to serve the people. . .

"I remember well, how once, when our whole circle had met together at Lesnoye, a summer resort near St. Petersburg, we were arguing hotly with her as to how propaganda among the peasantry might be made to yield the most fruitful results. She had just returned from a small village on the Volga, where she had been living as a peasant for purposes of propaganda. The impressions she had received there had stirred her deeply, and she described in graphic language the fathomless misery and poverty, the hopeless ignorance of the provincial working classes. The conclusion she drew from it all was that under existing conditions there was no way of helping these people.

" 'Show me any such way; show me how, under present circumstances, I can serve the peasants, and I am ready to go back to the villages at once,' she said. And her whole manner left no doubt of her absolute sincerity and readiness to keep her word. But her experience had been that of many others who had idealised 'the people' and also their own power of stirring them; and we were none of us prepared with any definite counsel that could deter her from the new path she had determined to tread — simply because she could see no other leading to the desired end."

Discouraged by the results of "peaceful penetration," Vera Figner turned to the terrorism of the ruling caste and took part in the plot to assassinate Alexander II. Dynamite was stored in her house and violence became her gospel of salvation for the people. Although the task of giving the signal for flinging a bomb at the Tsar was assigned to another woman, Sophia Perov, Vera was finally caught in the police net and condemned to death. By executive "clemency," her sentence was commuted to penal servitude for life. Masculine historians with an affection for blood and iron might do well in passing to give a page, at least, to this astounding personality in the Russian upheaval even though the Eleventh Edition of the Encyclopædia Britannica, that compendium of all important knowledge, is silent with respect to Vera Figner, while it finds space for commentators on the Old Testament.

Still it is not to this woman that terrorism owed its origin. Nor to any man in the revolutionary movement. But to another woman, Vera Sassulich. When the "go to the people" expedition of the early seventies proved inadequate, radical leaders decided to organise open demonstrations against the government of a peaceful, if positive, character. Vera Sassulich however was not content with such tactics. So one day in 1878, after a band of propagandists among the people had been rounded up, tried, and condemned, she went to see General Trepoff, head of the police in St. Petersburg, ostensibly to present some business of her own, and while he was looking over her papers she drew a revolver, shot him, and flung the weapon on the ground, calmly awaiting her fate. At her trial, she offered as her defense the fact that Trepoff had caused a young medical student, in prison for a political offense, to be brutally flogged and on this plea she was acquitted by the court. Her liberty only fomented terrorism and Vera Sassulich became the teacher of the violent wing of the revolution, arguing for the payment of autocrats in their own coin.

From rich data revealing women's relations to the rise of democracy everywhere, at least one more paragraph must be constructed, dealing with the movement which overthrew the monarchical system of Germany and established the republic at the close of the late World War. A full chapter would contain entries on the connection of women with the rise of Marxism, on the first German unions of working women, on protective legislation, on the activities of women during the existence of the law against socialists, on August Bebel's treatment of the thesis of woman and socialism, on the punishment of women for slandering the army and the flag, on their participation in national and international conferences, and on the organisation of special conferences for women. If the bulk of German women clung to the fixed order, a dynamic minority helped to push it over and, in any balanced account of its downfall, Clara Zetkin and Rosa Luxembourg must find places beside Bebel and Karl Kautsky. Rosa indeed paid the extreme penalty with Liebknecht. In the elections for the national assembly at Weimar to draft a new constitution, for a republic, all the parties offered women candidates and many were victorious at the polls, including twenty-two Social Democrats, three Independent Socialists, six Democrats, six members of the Catholic Center, and three Nationalists. During the proceedings, women served on committees, shared in debates, and joined in negotiations. The final document establishing a democratic republic bore the impress of their demands, notably the section abolishing legal sex discriminations. Thus far had Germany traveled, women aiding, since the days of Frederick the Great who had flirted a little with the American Republic beyond the sea and asked Voltaire to his court.

The World War, destined to produce a new Germany, also brought new electorates to other countries. By this time woman suffrage was well on the path to victory in nearly every part of the Western world. The struggle for that form of political democracy had almost paralleled the agitations and revolutions of three centuries. In the Cromwellian age, rumblings had been heard among the humblest of the "levellers" who are themselves almost unknown to reputable written history. At the close of that revolutionary seventeenth century, Mary Astell began to write on the theme of feminine prerogatives, for it seemed impossible to separate a discussion of these from the debate on masculine rights. If the *Tatler* ridiculed her notions expressed in *A Serious Proposal to Ladies,* Defoe frankly stated that she had anticipated him in certain ways with her observations on the cultural changes taking place in England. Mary Astell was the daughter of a Newcastle merchant; she was well educated, and brought to bear on the political, industrial, ecclesiastical and educational issues of her time both learning and satire. If contemporary critics regarded her as "eccentric" or rejoiced when she assailed the foibles of her own sex, her insight into what was occurring as a prophecy of what was to come in England qualifies her for a permanent place in the history of modern democracy.

In the next century the rights of women were taken up with more precision by Mary Wollstonecraft who followed her reply to Burke with her *Vindication of the Rights of Women.* In this work she argued that such inferiority in physical strength as woman suffered ought not to count against her in a civilised society that had renounced brute force as its supreme god and turned to the arts of decent living. Furthermore she held that if in many ways women were legally subject to men, this was a matter of custom and law open to alteration by intelligence. Then she came to education and the feminine mind. Men, ran her plea, are trained for the serious business of living, for trade, the professions, and public life, while women are largely denied equal opportunity to come to grips with reality. Their education is superficial and designed to encourage listless inactivity and stupid acquiescence in social tabus. "We might as well never have been born, unless it were necessary that we should be created to enable man to acquire the noble privilege of reason, the power for discerning good from evil, whilst we lie down in the dust from whence we were taken, never to rise again." The upshot of her contention was equal opportunity and equal privileges. Though the clever Horace Walpole and the gentle Hannah More laughed at this "hyena in politics," her electric words had gone forth, to be read in America, in France, and Germany, as well as England, forming the basis of a hundred books and a thousand pamphlets that gave literary expression to a vast aspiration and movement. All that was said later on this subject was mainly in the nature of a comment on her argument and all the activities of women and men (not forgetting John Stuart Mill or Emmeline Pankhurst) which established woman suffrage in law and widened the rights of women in education, property relations, and personal independence did but fulfill Mary Wollstonecraft's prophecy, forlorn, foolish, and hopeless as it seemed to the "wise" men and women of the eighteenth century.

THE INDUSTRIAL REVOLUTION

THAT the religious, intellectual, scientific and political revolutions could swing forward so victoriously was due in large measure to the strength that came to the bourgeoisie through new industrial methods. The invention of power-driven machinery opened a novel age of mankind, transferring family industries to factories, producing en masse the food, clothing and shelter which sustain life, ending the exchange of commodities by barter, and distributing the money obtained through sales in accordance with middle class standards. Books in common circulation tell the story of the spinning jenney, the loom, the steam engine, and the locomotive and give the names of Cartwright, Arkwright, Crompton, Watt, Stephenson, now supplemented by Edison and Ford, as household words. Such men were the agents, guileless about ultimate consequences, of a radical change in the modes of caring for life which removed them further from feminine control than had ever been the case before and in fact made man director of physical comfort for the first time. The consequences of this strange economic adventure Esmé Wingfield-Stratford calls the great Victorian tragedy, though he is thinking of men and women alike in that designation.

If the history of modern invention is in the main an account of men's devices, when the whole case is examined up-to-date the descendants of primitive women again come into the picture. Some of the evidence that women have inventive genius of the new type is indisputable and some is a matter more or less of rumor. Whether Mrs. Nathanael Greene actually did think out the cotton gin herself before she introduced Eli Whitney, a clever artisan in her household, to fellow-planters interested in a quicker process of cleansing the fibre, and set him on his task of constructing the instrument, those who have inside information alone can say. But the records of the Patent Office of the United States are precise. During the period from 1790 to 1888 women are there seen making fruit presses and corn huskers, street car rails, conveyors for coke crushers, and refinements in elevator operation, among other things. As soon as their interest was aroused, women put their wits to work and likewise turned out inventions covering almost every field of industry. A between-cover examination of the United States patent record, for instance, merely for the years from 1892 to 1895, when the separate initiative of women was listed, reveals the share they had in devising agricultural implements, art appliances such as the method of decorating pottery, baby carriages, barrel attachments, motor vehicles, building appurtenances, culinary utensils, educational equipment, conveniences in the way of furniture and furnishings such as cutting-tables, invalid chairs, convertible beds and wardrobes, kitchen cabinets, and curtain fixtures, together with heating apparatus, plumbing fixtures, preserving and disinfecting schemes. They also improved printing and binding tools, railway cars, couplings and spikes, screens and awnings, sewing and spinning machines, toys and toilet articles, theatrical aids, trunks and bags and typewriters. They offered new washing and cleaning affairs.

Because she "detested the tiresome work of stripping sugar cane to make molasses, a Texas farm woman invented a device which did the work better, and stripped in an hour as much cane as could be stripped by hand by four persons." The skill of the women in the line of invention has up-to-date run throughout the range of fifty industries — from coal mining to submarine explosives, chemicals and artificial fuels, agricultural machinery and hospital supplies, to mention but phases of ingenuity. With increasing frequency women's inventions appear in the records of the Patent Office and they now take out on the average about five hundred patents a year. Owing to this rapidly enlarging output, the Women's Bureau of the Federal Government calls for better laboratory facilities for women because they lack the opportunities to develop the devices in which they are interested.

New inventions and the infinite subdivision of manufacturing processes had deep-running social effects. Among them was the luring of male peasants from the fields to tend huge engines in the cities and the transfer of many noblewomen from palaces to mills and offices. Machine industry has been the great leveller. Feudal lords and planters, the power of land reduced by the power of trade, itself driven by mass production, have become subjects of business men or, in one instance, slaves of a technological government — the present Russian republic. Ladies and servants have been more and more drawn into the machine culture and forced to make adjustments other than those resting on caste.

If one concentrates on the consequences to women of the machine age, no better guide to understanding is available than the background limned by Alice Clark's study of *The Working Life of Women in the Seventeenth Century*. At the time there were few productive enterprises in which English women were not active. Poll tax returns show that they were still engaged in the varied occupations they had pursued throughout the Middle Ages, some running back to the dawn of human society. In the fourteenth century, for instance, we find women of Oxford in the trades of butcher, brewer, chandler, ironmonger, netmaker and wool comber, while in the sixteenth in the town of Chester they are working at the trade of smith. In the century of Mary Astell, the seventeenth, they were mistresses of gold wire drawing. They were prominent among the petitioners of the Court for grants of wardships and monopolies or patents. They asked to be allowed, among other things, to dig coal upon a royal manor, keep a tennis court, utilise waste land, make and sell silk stockings. Names of women often appeared in connection with the shipping trade and with contracts, one person being granted the permission to buy imported wheat in order that she might supply the East India Company with biscuits. They were Army and Navy contractors. They managed insurance businesses. They joined the Companies of Adventurers in financing and controlling some of the American colonisation and the Indian trade — cultural heirs of the Rosa de Burford who in 1318 lent money to her bishop and sold him a cope embroidered with coral besides.

Alice Clark is also authority for the statement that "able business women might be found in every class of English society throughout the seventeenth century." Yet their national rivals, the Dutch, excelled them in energy and competence; indeed a visiting Spaniard thought that among the Dutch the sexes had got irretrievably mixed. Because the male of the Dutch species made too many contracts over his cups for the good of the trade, contractors learned to have a greater confidence in his more sober mate. For such reasons both English and Dutch men regarded marriage as an advantageous economic arrangement. The coöperation of wives, whether they were gentlewomen or workers in the crafts, was accepted as a matter of course when not discussed enthusiastically. The home was the center of manufacturing and of commercial transactions. There was no need of a Business and Professional Woman's League to uphold privileges and push advantages because business and professional work was done by the men and women together.

Contemporary writings testify to the stability which this joint labor and joint management of physical comfort and commodity exchange provided. A man knew that after his death, if there was a large business involved, it would not go to smash through the inability of his widow to carry it on and that, if any misfortune overtook him while he lived, the "rational faculties" of his wife would be applied to solve the problem thus created. Men expected their widows to be executors of their estates though the duty often required business enterprise. Names of wives accompanied names of husbands on commercial papers, and accounts, which either husband or wife could settle, were paid to the partnership.

Membership in the gilds was a correspondingly joint affair. The woman's equal responsibility for the craft which gave representation, and particularly her duties connected with the apprentices, made a sex distinction out of the question. If a trade was thriving, the wife hired a servant to do the housework and devoted her energies entirely to the business. When she became a widow, she inherited the shop, the apprentices and the good will essential to trade. In the gild of her craft, she retained her membership therefore and drew into it her second husband by virtue of her direct business connection, provided the two continued to work in the aforesaid craft. Otherwise, if she followed her new husband to his trade, a different craft, she became a member of his different gild. Craft sisterhoods, possibly made up in the main of women who remained widows, also were on the list of gilds; but they were not confined to widows for, irrespective of marriage, many women managed trades and industries.

In such circumstances the notion did not exist that man was the superior and woman the inferior citizen. Each was dependent on the other if married. The man, that is, did not "support" his wife. Together they supported themselves and their small children, their servants and apprentices. There was no question of his wage and hers. The only question was the size of the family income jointly produced.

Sometimes the man signed petitions for the common business and again the signature was the woman's. When the Queen once proposed to change her regal residence from London, it was the women who protested lustily on the ground that their businesses would be injured. However, when machine industry rose on their horizon, a joint union of men and women tried to check its threatened mastery of the cotton trade. Defoe begins to note with astonishment that the servant had begun to desert the kitchen for the factory, compelling the business woman to bear the double burden of housework and craftsmanship or else to forsake the latter for the former, with all that the change implied in the way of economic dependence.

On the distributive as well as the productive side of early industry women had been active in all lines. In the seventeenth century they were prominent in the retail market and as cities grew in size the woman shopkeeper became a distinct figure in English society. Buying and selling had long been considered women's natural function; they stopped at no article of commerce from books to beer. Women were also peddlers. Like the Indian squaw, often pitied by the "civilised," the great Nordic female was wont to lift her pack of merchandise on her back and tramp great distances through the countryside, in all kinds of weather, to sell goods to housekeepers at their doors. Quaker women particularly figured in this form of itinerant retail business.

Now this whole scheme into which woman's life in town and country had been so long articulated was broken up by the industrial revolution. Henceforward manufacturing of nearly every kind, even if light, was based upon heavy industries better adapted to masculine muscles. From the home, in which woman had been an equal worker and producer, industry was transferred to the giant factory, filled with expensive machinery, and managed by men with whom her only connection was that of an impersonal wage worker. It is not necessary to dwell upon facts so often emphasized in modern works on economics. As immense department stores, built upon huge capital, crowded in upon the small shops, women did not surrender entirely their ancient function as individual purveyors, but by the thousands they found themselves "clerks" where they once had been partners if not mistresses. In other words in the initial stages of the industrial revolution, at least, women lost heavily in economic independence and prestige. Workers were transformed into hands or idle wives clinging to capitalistic oaks.

From that point the story of industrial change is in part the individualist account of wives and daughters struggling to regain what they had lost in the form of economic independence. On one side it is a battle for business and professional opportunities on the new level, for control over property, for the possession of wages, and for political rights essential for the protection of economic interest. Their advances have been steady. Women now operate in nearly every branch of industry and transportation, in almost every one of the bewildering list of occupations created by modern technology — chemical, metallurgical, textile, construction and on through the catalogue. In the retail trade of the United States they manage approximately 80,000 stores. They furnish thousands of traveling salesmen, though they ride in Pullmans, motors or airplanes, no longer carrying packs upon their backs. They are found in engineering and aviation. On the railways they serve as switchmen, flagmen and manual laborers. They toil in every division of agriculture from wheat raising to dairying, often on a grand scale. In all, about ten million women in the United States are classed as gainfully employed and their legal privileges have been raised with respect to their business enterprise. Through associational effort women have improved their standing and training in the professions no less than in the business field and wherever the machine age spreads, the same result follows.

Among the proletariat at the bottom as well as among the bourgeois at the top of the new economic system a lively spirit is manifest. Working women are a factor in the labor movement in every land. They strike against harsh conditions just like the men. They likewise demand shorter hours, higher pay, and better sanitary facilities within the industrial plants. By the formation of women's unions they have created a labor movement within the labor movement of which they are a part. To escape their competition, the men's organisations have been forced to admit them to membership wherever the craft contains large numbers of both sexes. Women continue to carry on their historic character as organisers, agitators and victims of law and the police. They are arrested and imprisoned. If their criticism of the American government renders them "undesirable" to the powers that be, they suffer deportation beside their brothers and often get in their homelands the punishment they thus evade in the land of their adoption. During the tempestuous career of the Knights of Labor, when no distinction was made of sex, race, or craft within its membership, women shared in its mass revolt. Later they worked with the Industrial Workers of the World which strove to level craft aristocracies in much the same manner and effect labor solidarity on a single plane. After the crash of the World War, they were active among the Communists giving their strength to a globe-shaking movement for the abolition of classes.

Throughout the years of the Russian adventure into a single-level society women have been ardent among its supporters as well as among its foes. The Russian government relies upon them for a vast amount of the actual labor in the mills and the fields, partly because it needs the time of men for the army more, and partly, it reports, because the women are strong and capable. In its central directorate they also have some share.

When the future of human society as a totality comes into purview in connection with the industrial revolution, aspects of life more important than the individual struggles and triumphs of men and women arise. One involves a romantic ideal —

the emancipation of mankind from the narrow limitations of its own muscular energy. Perhaps invention can supply us with unlimited mechanical power and lift the major burdens, at least, from weary backs and exhausted nerves to arms of steel and the drive of motors. At the same time mechanical energy by speeding up production and distribution may keep pace with or even outrun population with its flood of food, clothing and other supplies humanity requires. For humanity in the large modern inventions may thus be esteemed as the greatest discovery of all time — the supreme achievement of mankind.

There is likewise a romance in the rise of the masses to philosophic consideration. No longer can societies equipped with machines think in terms of petty, tedious production, caste privileges of exploitation, and illiterate laborers unorganised and servile. The masses must be taken into account in any serious consideration of the good life. The good life for whom ? That becomes the foremost issue of the modern age.

Then there is the new idea of progress which neither the ancient nor the mediæval worlds knew. The elasticity it brings to thinking and the experimentation it injects into action create a novel setting for moral teachings and provide fresh connotations for the word, "responsibility." There must be progress in public as well as private obligations.

Side by side with the romantic view. however, courses the "practical" use to which the new tools have been put. In the dull pages of English parliamentary inquiries, the story is told of the first heedless plunge into machine industry, with a crushing realism that transcends Russian fiction at its lurid best. There are drawn the pictures of the early factories, old barns and cart-houses transformed into loom houses, new buildings low-ceilinged rushed up with little or no regard for light, health, or sanitation, crowded with dangerous machinery; of the young children snatched from poorhouses or gathered from selfish or impoverished homes, enslaved to the tools for interminable hours, and paid a pittance for their toil; women, old and young, working in mines and mills for wages that scarcely sustain them from day to day; men and boys, if sometimes rewarded according to a somewhat higher scale, working under conditions no less injurious to body and mind; hideous tenements rising around hideous plants, dark, congested, disease-breeding quarters for the "hands" that tend the machines. The injured seldom receive any compensation. Long periods of unemployment in times of depression spread misery, sickness and death like plagues.

To summarise in the terms of parliamentary reports, we see practical economics producing starvation wages; slavery for children and little more, if that, for adults; perilous machinery without safeguards; slums for homes; dire poverty for the sick and unemployed; menaces to health unheeded; poorhouses for old age; illiteracy for the masses ignored; accidents in mines and factories; lads five years old working underground twelve hours a day; girls no older working as long in the fetid air of spinning mills; suffering common and appalling ! And on top a smug, self-righteous bourgeoisie, preaching a convenient *laissez faire* philosophy of "rugged individualism," which absolved them from all responsibility for the laboring multitudes that created its wealth and privileges.

Against practical business the romanticists of an economic bent have battled as strenuously as political idealists fought against regal prerogatives. The bourgeoisie itself, relieved of feudal pressure, was called to terms by many of its own members for its inhumanity to man. First among the social attacks on the industrial slavery of the machine age was utopian socialism, stemming from the teachings of Saint Simon, Fourier, Robert Owen and their women associates. Among its writers, propagandists and social experimenters from Brook Farm to Oneida, from Icaria to New Harmony were forceful personalities of both sexes.   And for the women of this direction Frances Wright may well be the chosen representative.

After receiving a thorough education in the land of her birth, Scotland, Frances Wright crossed to France and lived for several years in the household of Lafayette, where she absorbed the ideas of the French Revolution.   In 1818 she visited the United States and on her return published a survey called *Views of Society and Manners in America.*   Later she came back to America and embarked on a career of writing and agitating against chattel slavery and the evils of industrialism alike.   For a time she was associated with Robert Dale Owen, son of Robert Owen, in editing the New Harmony Gazette which was finally transferred to New York and made the organ of radical thought in every department — economic, religious, political, and sex.   With her editorial work she combined lecturing, taking the platform boldly in defiance of the tradition that it was a masculine monopoly, and until her death kept up a propaganda for the rights of men and women, contributing powerfully to the intellectual ferment that filled the land in the tempestuous days of Jacksonian democracy.

The second general reaction to early capitalism took a form known as "scientific socialism," with which the names of Karl Marx and Friedrich Engels are associated.   Yet it would be a distortion of history to treat scientific socialism as the original creation of Marx, struck off by him in the realm of his capacious, if bitter, imagination.   While he was yet a child, a French woman, Flora Tristan, was working in that field and, long before the appearance of the Communist Manifesto, had proclaimed many of its fundamental ideas, crystallising conceptions already in the air and giving them appealing form.   It is fitting, therefore, to suggest for her a place in the history of the remarkable movement known as modern socialism. Flora Tristan was born in Paris in 1803, fifteen years before the birth of Marx — a child of proletarian poverty brought up in the darkest quarters of her native city. For a time she worked in a lithographic establishment in Paris, then as a "serving person" in England, Switzerland, and Italy. This experience she enlarged by a journey to Peru to visit some relatives of her father, making the perilous journey on an unseaworthy vessel, as the only woman among nineteen men. Her journeys awakened in her the conviction that, despite the differences in religion, patriotism, family, and morals among the various countries, those who labored with their hands were "an oppressed class." Fired by this belief she took up the pen and toiled as a champion of the workers.

Turning from utopian socialism before Marx discovered its limitations, Flora Tristan declared in the true Marxian spirit: "The workingclass must help itself. The international union of all workers is an imperative demand. This must be preached everywhere and the way to it demonstrated." At a later time she declared for "a strong, lasting union of the workers of all lands, a recognition of their equality with other classes, and a representation of their interests through delegates elected by them." Then she demanded an abolition of all aristocratic privileges, public housing of the workingclasses, schools and educational institutions for all workers, and institutions of care for the aged. "Union is power," she insisted; "if we unite in the social and political field, on the ground of equal rights for the sexes, if we organize labor, we shall win welfare for all." With this for her creed, she carried on a propaganda amid poverty and sickness in spite of hatred and contempt — writing, organising women, and speaking, with the flaming zeal of a missionary until death early cut short her career. And in 1848, the year that the Communist

Manifesto was written, a committee of grateful followers erected in her honor a memorial in the city of Bordeaux. With justification have socialist women of Germany written: "It may well fill women with pride that it was a woman who expressed the great ideas of a Marx and an Engels before these leaders had spoken, and that this woman was a working woman, who by her own force had reached the conclusion that union in the social and political field, demanding equal rights for both sexes and the organization of labor, must lead to the well-being of all." While Marx knew labor through books and observation, Flora Tristan knew it through toil and suffering. It could not be said, of course, that she was "a powerful and logical thinker," whatever that may mean, but she certainly anticipated Marx in many fundamental particulars and was a forerunner in the vast social movement that bears his name.

It is not possible even to outline here the varied and complex movement of opinion, agitation, legislation, and administration by which the evils of early industrialism were attacked in general and in detail — to sketch the history of factory legislation, prison reform, the advance in sanitation, housing, city planning, sickness and accident insurance, workers' compensation, and that wide field of ameliorative activity known as "social work." Yet it is this immense popular movement, this heroic, if often misguided, effort to provide a standard of security and decency for all, to apply science to the welfare of the multitudes at the bottom, that marks off the age of the rising West from the servitude of the Middle Ages with its artistic and architectural glories, from the slavery and degradation of Rome with all her pomp and power, and from the bondage and slums of Athens with her towering intellectualism. When the balanced narrative is written it will not be built around the names of a few figures — Carlyle's heroes —

but will take into account the work of thousands of men and women, mostly unknown to traditional history, who have built up the structure of modern welfare and are still laboring to carry it higher while making its foundations deeper and firmer.

This mechanical and economic revolution, accompanied by the accumulation of new positive knowledge respecting anthropological origins and by corresponding speculations on its practical upshot, ran deeply into the historic family as it had evolved from primitive time through the culture of antiquity and the Middle Ages. Irrespective of theory, the industrial revolution individualised all the component parts of the family to the very baby in arms. Women now worked outside the home by the millions. Daughters could find innumerable ways of earning a living besides the ancient one of marrying an eligible mate or becoming a public woman. Women could command wages and stand on their own economic feet. Moreover the family, transferred from the country to the city, encountered rival interests to the association of the hearth and was pulled apart — a movement involving a disruption of the man and wife relation and the parent-child authority. And in all the problems that arose from the new situation the State steadily intervened, assuming through political institutions many historic functions of the family, such as education, the care of health, and corrections. Hence monogamy and the care of all life, including physical comfort and culture, were to proceed under novel conditions. What can happen under a severely technical régime is illustrated in Soviet Russia where the State invades the traditional family, assumes heavy responsibilities for the protection of life, and seeks to draw women all the way into the operations of the mechanised system of economy. What is happening elsewhere is compromise — some family care, some public care —

with women more or less responsible for the nature and degree of that arrangement, according to their incomes and intelligence.

SUMMARY AND EPILOGUE

LOOKING backward toward the horizon of dawning society, what do we see standing clearly against the sky ? Woman —assuming chief responsibility for the continuance and care of life. We are in the presence of a force so vital and so powerful that anthropologists can devise no meter to register it and the legislator no rein strong enough to defeat it. Whether woman possesses sex or is possessed by it may be left to masculine metaphysicians for debate. Its reality however cannot be escaped. To an extent not yet gauged by historians, hunting, wars, states and institutions have been shaped to meet the supreme exigency of continuing life and must be if mankind is to go on living at all. Whether it is the primitive woman bringing a mate to her house, Henry VIII breaking with the Pope, or Napoleon rearranging the alliances of Europe with reference to his dynasty, the final necessity is always present.' Otherwise human life and everything built upon it would perish from the earth. Church fathers may curse it, woman brought to death's door in childbirth may wonder with Erasmus at her "folly," and man caught in the institutions of support may rage at his "chains," but while life remains it must be continually recreated, nourished and esteemed. From this elemental force in the rise and development of civilisation there is no escape and more of human history can be written in its terms than any of Clio's disciples have yet imagined. If the whole story is ever told, it will probably be necessary to bring in a new Doctor Bowdler to get it past the censor.

But sex itself has been only one segment of woman's life, far less important than the collaterals issuing from it in connection with the care of life once created. Thus we see primitive women as the inventors of the domestic arts — cooking, spinning, weaving, garnering, guarding, doctoring, providing comforts and conveniences, and making beginnings in the decorative arts. They are launching civilisation. Other animals have sex and continue life but none surround it with such artificial supports which, examined closely, are found to form the prime substance of culture. Woman, by means of these domestic innovations, lifted her low-browed male companion above the wild beasts that he hunted with stone and club and devoured in the raw. Under all the social forms and transformations that have existed since primitive times, activities connected with food, clothing and shelter, woman's first interest, have continued, setting commerce in train, spurring invention, establishing systems of economy more amazing. When men acquired responsibility for weaving garments, the manufacture of soap, and the confection of lingerie, women remained workers, designers, arbiters of taste, and beneficiaries of profits. Amusing as it may seem, it is primitive woman's interest that is now the prime concern of the civilised men. War for war's sake is no longer openly celebrated by the male, however zealously he cherishes in secret his passion for battle. Modern societies — bourgeois, democratic, fascist and communist — all agree in declaring that their fundamental end is the manufacture and wide distribution of those commodities which the old Romans of the republican era declared tend to effeminacy — the conveniences and luxuries that give ease and satisfaction in the continuance and care of life — primitive woman's burden and one that will abide while mankind endures.

After the great State was founded on primitive societies by

the sword, when kings, priests and noble classes were established to engage the attention of historians, women merely
dropped out of the pen portraits. They remained in the
actuality. They were members of all the castes from the slave
stratum at the bottom to the ruling families at the top and,
even where restrictions were the tightest, took part in nearly
everything that went on in the world. Whether it is Aspasia
talking to Pericles and friends, Diotima "teaching" Socrates,
Roman women participating in senatorial conflicts and battles
over the succession to the imperial throne, queens contending
for their patrimonies, the daughters of the rich setting fleets
and caravans in motion to bring them the luxuries of the
East, or the wife of Pythagoras interpreting and spreading a
faith, the truth that women have always been in or near the
center of things is illustrated. They have shared in the burdens and privileges of their respective classes, have joined in
wars, have owned and managed vast estates, have insisted on
dominance in disputes among ruling families, have displayed
the lusts of men, have served the temples, and have been
deified as gods. If the formalities, such as exclusion from
public gatherings in Athens and from the senate in Rome, are
penetrated and realities are kept in mind, the energies and
influence of women are easily discerned. There was no great
historical contest in politics in which they did not appear
somewhere. There was no religious cult which they did not
affect. There were no exercises in intellectualism which they
did not practice. If poets from Ovid to Molière made fun
of learned women, these women were no funnier than most
of the men who crowded the salons, as the court jester was
fair enough to indicate, and some of them spoke with authority
on poetry, mathematics, science, philosophy and ethics.

For a time after the dissolution of the Roman Empire, if
most of the histories ring true, women retired in favor of the

sword, but the retirement was certainly temporary if not illusory. They early appeared in the Middle Ages as managers in the families of barbarian conquerors and their princely retainers, as heads of convents and schools, as restorers of the arts, as manipulators in the papal politics of Italy, as theologians and saints, as the symbol of virtue divinely typified in Mary the Mother of God. They labored with men in the fields providing the economic goods on which the upper structure of mediæval civilisation rested. They worked in the crafts around which were built the gilds and urban liberties. They suffered as witches, died as heretics, and furnished a military leader in Jeanne d'Arc. The whole art of chivalry, whatever may have been its civilising influence, developed around woman. The writers of canon law and its administrators were endlessly harassed by her conduct. Again and again women of the upper classes shone as the literate wives of illiterate lords and knights, thus sharing with the clergy the world of written wisdom. Exclusion from Oxford and Cambridge did not condemn English ladies to total ignorance; what a complete survey would reveal no one knows but the guess may be hazarded that the women of the upper classes, in fact of all classes, were about as well educated as the men of their circles. Even the famous abstract speculator, Abelard, had to have an intellectual companion, Heloïse, as a foil; and Francis of Assisi, critic of scholasticism and learning, the girl Clare as counselor and friend. Although the law of property ran inevitably in favor of the fighter, so constantly exigent was defense, it did not run against woman as such nor did it in practice prevent thousands of women from holding and controlling property, from devoting it to the patronage of religion and the arts as well as to the intrigues and uses of their class.

In the modern age there have been changes in form rather

than in substance. Women patronised and assisted directly in the development of the new learning — the recovery and enlargement of ancient secular wisdom. It was a woman, Queen Isabella of Spain, who was chiefly responsible for the underwriting that sent Columbus forth on the voyage of discovery destined to open a new epoch in the history of Europe and reveal to it the smallness of its empire; after a Queen had dared, kings were prepared to support other voyages. When secular learning widened out into natural science, women acted as promoters, critics, and creative thinkers and workers. They faced all the hardships involved in the conquest and settlement of the New World, standing steadfastly beside the men under the wintry clouds at Plymouth and beneath the sunny skies of Virginia. The Catholic fathers had scarcely reached the frontiers of Quebec when dauntless nuns appeared to carry forward the task of evangelisation. When natural science was touched with humanism and became an instrument in formulating the concept of Progress, it was mainly by the salons of French women that ideas were patronised, tried out, and set in circulation. In this age, no more than in mediæval times, did a general exclusion from universities mean ignorance among women; the very notion is based upon an exaggerated view of the rôle of institutions in the origin and diffusion of learning. It is yet to be known whether institutions help rather than hinder thought.

With the rise of machine industry and the multiplication of occupations, the restrictions of all inherited law were found irksome, attacked and broken down, after many a stubborn battle to be sure but with surprising speed considering the herd capacities of the human race. In the rise of political democracy, women were belligerent — Mary Wollstonecraft joining Tom Paine in vindicating the rights of man — a favor reciprocated when the rights of woman were also to be vindicated. Finally, women have been identified with the ideas and movements of social amelioration from the sixteenth century to the latest hour, as thinkers, experimenters, propagandists and administrators.

And now that the long trail has been trod to this point, what of the life ahead of us ? What are its possibilities and probabilities ? There exists the assumption that what is called the bourgeois, or capitalist, order of things, lately acquired, will endure, if not forever, at least indefinitely. At the present moment it seems to be shaky in France, bewildered in England, disturbed in the United States, questioned in Spain, and distressed in Japan. But its current troubles may pass. If the established economic mill keeps running, then the future before various women is clear. They will acquire through inheritance, transfer, or their own efforts more property with all the rights and privileges thereunto attached. The number of professions and employments open to women will increase. The thousands of workers engaged in supplying luxuries to the plutocracy will grow and the gainful occupations of women will become more gainful. Into the great games of business, advertising, selling and speculating, they will enter with expanding zest, with profit to themselves and economic security. Hundreds of callings, though bearing a dubious relation to the care of life in the large, will give them personal independence. The learning of the schools and the facilities of the laboratories will be placed at their disposal in enlarging measure. The parasitic women of the bourgeois circle will spend, patronise, dabble and entertain and occasionally, very occasionally, play with fire like Marie Antoinette. In other words, those who sit at the feast will continue to enjoy themselves even though the veil that separates them from the world of toiling reality below has been lifted by mass revolts and critics. While this state of affairs lasts, no great thought will be imperative, on the part of women or of men within the prosperous circle, and the repetition of conventional formulas about the Kingdom, the Reich, the Republic, or Democracy, will suffice as in Cicero's day for wisdom and for statecraft.

But other contingencies enter into speculations. The free and easy political democracy of early capitalism may be turned into a middle class dictatorship, as in Italy, managed by men who naturally will look out for themselves in the distribution of economic plums. Supported by arms, dominated by a small self-appointed clique, and bent on the perpetuation of its power, the fascist régime is a menace to the liberties of women. And yet fascism is in the process of evolution. So far it has been able to steer a zig-zag course between capital and labor, closer to the interests of the former than the latter but not completed by any means. In Russia another type of dictatorship is in vogue, autocratic in its form of government but communist in economic theory and to some degree in practice. There the privileges and luxuries of the bourgeois are materially curtailed, if not extirpated, with corresponding effects upon the position of the women formerly belonging to the upper classes or serving them as caterers and retainers. Hence in Russia the bourgeois form of marriage is in process of dissolution, if marriages and families remain. The emphasis in communism, if its ideal is realised, will be on woman as a worker, and the opportunities for a life of leisure, patronage, noblesse oblige, religious service, and idle curiosity will vanish. What that will produce in terms of culture, the future alone can say. After traveling a long and strange road, women of the upper orders in Russia are back where all women began in primitive days, to the prime concern with labor and the care of life, where the vast majority of women in all times and places have stayed through the changing fortunes of politics.

Amid the hopes for bourgeois endurance and the contingences of change, the eternal battle between the State and the Family promises to continue. The State, originally built on the family, is confronted as of old with family loyalties inimical to the public service and to the common life and the common good. In a sense it is true, as political and social critics of the family have long contended, that men and women struggling to advance the family in status and satisfactions often act as enemies of the State, willing to resort to chicanery in economics and corruption in politics in order to augment the property of their group. Thus Ritchie insists that "no real or positive equality in social conditions can be secured so long as individuals are looked at in any respect as members of families and not in every respect as members of the State alone. Suppose two workmen receive equal wages but the one has no children and the other has six, all too young to earn anything, where is the equality in the social condition of the individuals supported out of these wages ? Even under the system of a compulsory minimum of education, has the child of incapable or vicious parents — quite apart from his hereditary disadvantages — an equal opportunity given him, in any true sense, with the child who has grown up in a careful and regular household ?" To the problem of equality, political dictatorship may provide a better answer perhaps than individualist economics and family politics. The State may try to iron out handicaps of birth and domestic neglect. Even in an individualist nation like the United States, the family is invaded from two directions — one political and the other economic. The State insists upon domestic changes favorable to civic stability, and bourgeois marriage dissolves with amazing swiftness owing to the shift in forms of property and the individualisation of women in the arena where goods are produced.

If the State, bourgeois or communist, continues to apply to

family property and nurture strong astringents in the interests of individualism or equality, what then ? There seem to be two possibilities, judging by the experience at hand. The family may resist invasion, as it did in Rome, may withdraw more loyalty from the State, disintegrate its authority by opposition and by the refusal of public service, preferring ease and luxury to the severe régime of sacrifice, and dissolving order again into the chaos of family feudalism — for that was the essence of feudalism. On the other hand, the State may defeat this antagonism and press deeper and deeper into the family association, reducing its advantages of property and nurture.

What would be the outcome of State supremacy it may be impossible for any one to forecast though there have been in the past a few brilliant cases of insight into the future. Some speculators see the end of monogamy. But this is an assumption. Monogamy has always been one form of sex relations, surrounded by many others. It is conceivable that the aggression of the State upon the family may mean that monogamy will at last be tried on its merits, certainly with less and possibly with no economic incidence, surviving the storm for reasons deeply fixed in human nature and experience. Though the State may take over more of the education and nurture of children, it will still find that women must be employed in the operation of caring for life. Perhaps by the route of trial and error along new lines, with birth control, humanity will decide that amenities of the home are more conducive to the fundamental mores upon which civilisation depends in final analysis than any abstract loyalties that it can generate through politics and economics alone.

If this analysis of history is approximately sound and if the future like the past is to be crowded with changes and exigencies, then it is difficult to believe that the feminism of the passing generation, already hardened into dogma and tradition, represents the completed form of woman's relations to work, interests and society. In so far as it is a sex antagonism, even though based on legitimate grievances against exclusions or discriminations in employment, it is and has been partial and one-phased, not fundamental. The converse is true with respect to man's hostility to the presence of women at the center of every sort of activity. Women have always been alive to everything that was going on in the world. They always will be. If, as our engineering writers are constantly telling us, society is to be increasingly technical in nature, then competence, not sex, will be the basis of selection and women will have to stand that test with men. Feminism as sex antagonism bearing the wounds of many honorable battles may then drop out of sight. Masculinism as sex monopoly may then yield to concepts of expertness.

The ordinary woman who has functioned in accordance with nature's laws does not hate man or exaggerate his importance; most of the time she is as indifferent to him as he is to her; but with respect to the amenities and enjoyments of life the sexes are one. Love, joy, and beauty are bound up in their relations. As Aristophanes could say twenty-three centuries ago, "there is no pleasure for a man unless the woman shares it," so the modern feminist will soon discover, if she has not already, that there is no pleasure for a woman unless the man shares it. Yet if the feminism of the older generation passes, the eternal feminine will be here at the center of all things — that is, the care of life — and, unless the growth of positive knowledge and the humane applications of science during the past three hundred years are a delusion and a mistake, governments and economic institutions, all the arts of comfort and delight, will revolve around the care of life, renewing themselves at that fountain of eternal youth whence come healing waters for despair and cynicism — the enduring belief that it is good to live, to love, to suffer and to labor.

BIBLIOGRAPHY

NEEDLESS to say, this bibliography is not exhaustive. The writings of the persons who figure in the story have been omitted; they are invaluable source material but are well catalogued and largely accessible, in the great libraries at least. The diaries, letters, journals, and memoirs of women, particularly of French women, are still unmined treasure. Rich data and new interpretations come almost daily from the press in the form of biographies of queens and forceful social leaders; the list of biographical works would itself be mammoth. Some of the best biographical studies are found in series, such as *Women of Colonial and Revolutionary Times* (in America) published by Scribner's in 1896. Dictionaries of biography, ancient, mediaeval and modern, pagan and Christian, supply both important source clues and sketches of personalities. Unfortunately it is impossible to recommend many general histories, for the reasons given in the text.

Abbot, Edith, *Women in Industry*. Appleton 1915.

Abbott, Evelyn (editor), *Hellenica:* a collection of essays on Greek poetry, philosophy, history and religion. One of these is on oracles. London 1880.

Abrams, Annie, *English Life and Manners in the Later Middle Ages*. Dutton 1913.

Adam, H. L., *Woman and Crime*. London 1914.

Adams, Henry, The Education of. Houghton Mifflin 1918.

Addams, Jane, *Women at The Hague*, Macmillan 1915; *The Long Road of Woman's Memory*, 1916; *Newer Ideals of Peace*, 1911; *Woman and the Larger Citizenship*, 1913.

Allen, Grant, *Evolution of the Idea of God*. London 1901.

Angus, S., *The Religious Guests of the Graeco-Roman World*. Scribner 1930.

Anzoletti, Luisa, *Agnesi*. Milan 1900.

Atkeson, Mary Meek, *The Woman on the Farm*. Century 1924.

Bader, Clarisse, *Woman in Ancient India,* London 1925; *La femme romaine,* Paris 1877; *La femme grecque,* Paris 1872.

Baker, G. F., *Constantine the Great and the Christian Revolution.* Dodd, Mead 1931.

Balmforth, R., *Some Social and Political Pioneers of the Nineteenth Century.* London 1900.

Barnes, H. M., *The Twilight of Christianity.* The Vanguard Press 1929.

Batty, J., *The Spirit and Influence of Chivalry.* London 1890.

Bauer, Dr. Bernhard A., *Wie Bist Du, Weib.* Vienna 1923.

Baumer, Gertrud, *Die Frau in der Krisis der Kultur.* Vienna.

Beard, Miriam, *Realism in Romantic Japan.* Macmillan 1930.

Bennett, Helen C., *American Women in Civic Work.* Dodd, Mead 1915.

Bercovici, Konrad, *Alexander.* Cosmopolitan 1928.

Biederman, K. F., *Deutschland im achtzehnten Jahrhundert.* Leipzig 1854.

Bloomfield, Maurice, *The Religion of the Vedas.* Putnams 1908.

Blos, Anna (editor), *Die Frauenfrage im Lichte des Sozialismus.* Dresden 1930.

Bolitho, W., *Twelve against the Gods.* Simon and Shuster 1929.

Botsford and Sihler (editors), *Hellenic Civilisation.* Columbia University Press 1915.

Bradbury, Harriet B., *Civilisation and Womanhood.* Richard Badger 1916.

Bradford, Gamaliel, *Daughters of Eve.* Houghton Mifflin 1930.

Breasted, J. H., *A History of Egypt.* Scribner 1905.

Briffault, Robert, *The Mothers.* Macmillan 1927. Contains an extraordinary bibliography on the subject of women.

Brinton, D. G., *Religions of Primitive Peoples.* Putnam 1897.

Bury, Blaze de, *Les salons de Vienne et de Berlin.* Paris 1861.

Bury, J. B., *The Idea of Progress,* Macmillan 1920; *History of the Papacy in the Nineteenth Century,* 1930; *Romances of Chivalry on Greek Soil,* Clarendon Press 1911; *Selected Essays,* Cambridge University Press 1930.

Buxhoeveden, Sophie, *The Life and Tragedy of Alexandra Feodorovna, Empress of Russia.* Longmans 1928.

Candolle, M. Alphonse de, *Histoire des sciences et des savants depuis deux siècles.* Geneva 1873.

Cannon, Mary A., *Education of Women during the Renaissance.* National Capital Press, Washington, D. C. 1916.

Cartwright, Julia, A. (Mrs. Ady), *Isabella d'Este,* London 1903; *Beatrice d'Este,* 1912; *Baldassare Castiglione,* 1908; *Christine of Denmark,* 1913. Other works.

Cheyne, T. K., *Jewish Religious Life after the Exile.* Putnam 1898. Other works.

Chivalry. See bibliography in Briffault, *The Mothers.*

Clark, Alice, *The Working Life of Women in the Seventeenth Century.* Harcourt, Brace 1920.

Collison-Morley, L., *Italy after the Renaissance.* London 1930.

Colum, Padraic, *Orpheus, Myths of the World.* Macmillan 1930.

Croce, Benedetto, *History, its Theory and Practice.* Harcourt, Brace 1923.

Cronau, R., *Woman Triumphant.* R. Cronau 1919.

Dantzig, T., *Number: the Language of Science.* Macmillan 1931.

Davids, T. W. Rhys, *Buddhism, its History and Literature.* Putnam 1896.

Dawson, C., *The Age of the Gods,* London 1928; *Christianity and Sex,* 1930.

Denio, Francis, *The Literatures of Greece and Israel in the Renaissance.* The Stratford Company 1925.

Earp, F. E., *The Way of the Greeks.* Oxford University Press.

Eberhard, Dr. E. F. W., *Feminismus und Kultur Untergang.* Vienna 1927.

Eckenstein, Lina, *Woman under Monasticism.* Cambridge University Press 1896.

Elnett, Elaine Pasvolsky, *Historic Origin and Social Development of Family Life in Russia.* Columbia University Press 1926.

Ellet, Elizabeth F., *Domestic History of the American Revolution.* Baker and Scribner, 1850; *Court Circles of the Republic,* Hartford, Conn. 1869.

Frazer, James, *The Golden Bough.* Contains data on kings as gods. Macmillan 1926; *Myths of the Origin of Fire,* 1930; *Lectures on the Early History of the Kingship,* 1905; *The Magic Art and the Evolution of Kings,* 1911.

Ferrero, G., *Women of the Cæsars.* Century 1911. Other works.

Flick, A. C., *The Decline of the Mediaeval Church.* Knopf 1930.

Floerke, Hanns, *Das Weib in der Renaissance.* Munich 1928.

Führende Frauen Europas. Autobiographical Sketches. Munich 1928.

Fuller, Margaret, *Woman in the Nineteenth Century.* London 1845.

Gamble, Eliza B., *The Sexes in Science and History.* Putnam 1916.

Gardner, E. G., *The Arthurian Legend in Italian Literature.* London 1930.

Geyer, Anna, *Die Frauenerwerbsarbeit im Deutschland.* Jena 1924.

Gibbon, E., *The History of the Decline and Fall of the Roman Empire.*

Gilman, Charlotte P., *Women and Economics,* Small, Maynard 1898. Other works.

Goncourt, E. and J. de, *The Woman of the Eighteenth Century.* Minton Balch 1927.

Gottlieb, Elfriede, *Die Frau im frühen Christentum.* Leipzig 1930.

Greece, The Legacy of. Essays by Gilbert Murray, W. B. Inge, J. Burnet, Sir T. L. Heath, D'Arcy W. Thompson, Charles Singer, R. W. Livingstone, Arnold Toynbee, A. E. Zimmern, Percy Gardner, and Sir Reginald Blomfield. Oxford University Press 1928.

Gribble, F., *Women in War.* London 1916.

Grote, G., *History of Greece.* London 1846.

Gulick, C. B., *Life of the Ancient Greeks.* Appleton 1902.

Hall, E. B., *Women of the Salons.* Putnam 1926.

Hamel, F., *An Eighteenth Century Marquise: a study of Emilie du Châtelet and her time.* London 1910.

Hamilton, Edith, *The Greek Way.* W. W. Norton 1930.

Hanscom, Elizabeth D., *The Heart of a Puritan.* Macmillan 1917.

Hargrace, Mary, *Some German Women and their Salons.* London 1912.

Harrison, Jane E., *Prolegomena to the Study of the Greek Religion.* London 1903. Other works.

Hartland, E. S., *Primitive Paternity,* London 1910; *Primitive Society,* 1921.

Hegemann, W., *Frederick the Great.* London 1929.

Henderson, B. W., *Life and Principate of the Emperor Nero.* London 1903. Other works.

Henry, Alice, *Women and the Labor Movement.* Doran 1923.

Hersch. Virginia, *Woman under Glass.* The romance of St. Teresa. Harper 1930.

Higgins, G., *Anacalypsis: an attempt to draw aside the veil of the Saitic Isis and inquire into the origin of languages, nations, and religions.* Macy-Mazius, N. Y. 1927.

Hill, J. J., *Highways of Progress.* Doubleday, Page 1910.

History of Woman Suffrage in four volumes, edited by Ida Husted Harper, Elizabeth Cady Stanton, Susan B. Anthony, and Matilda J. Gage. For the American story. Fowler and Wells 1881.

Hidgkin, L. V., *A Quaker Saint of Cornwall.* Longmans 1931.

Hoggan, Frances, *American Negro Women during their first fifty years of freedom.* London 1913

Hoover, C., *The Economic Life of Soviet Russia.* Macmillan 1931.

Hourgronje, C. Snouck, *Mohammedanism.* 1916.

Humphrey, E. F., *An Economic History of the United States.* Century 1931.

Irvine, Helen D., *The Making of Rural Europe.* Dutton 1923.

Jellinek, Camilla, *Die Frau im neuen Deutschland,* Stuttgart 1920.

Johnston, H. W., *The Private Life of the Romans.* Scott, Foresman, Chicago 1903.

Jones, W. H. S., *Malaria and Greek History,* to which is added *History of Greek Therapeutics* and the *Malaria Theory* by E. T. Withington. London.

Jones, H. S., *The Roman Empire.* Putnam 1908.

Kalckreuth, Dunbar von, *Three Thousand Years of Rome.* Knopf 1930.

Kallinikov, J., *Women and Monks.* Harcourt, Brace 1930.

Kemp-Welch, Alice, *Of Six Mediaeval Women* (Christine de Pisan, Roswitha, Marie de France, Mechthild of Magdeburg, Mahaut, Countess of Artois, and Agnes Sorel). Macmillan 1913.

Key, Ellen K., *The Century of the Child*, Putnam 1908; *Love and Marriage*, Putnam 1911. Other works.

Kollontay, Alexandra, *A Great Love*. The Vanguard Press 1929.

Lacroix, P., *Histoire de la Prostitution*, Paris 1851; *Military and Religious Life in the Middle Ages*, London 1874.

Laidler, H. W., *A History of Socialist Thought*. Thomas Crowell 1927.

Langdon-Davies, J., *A Short History of Woman*. The Viking Press 1927.

Lange, F. A., *History of Materialism*. London 1877.

Lea, H. C., *An Historical Sketch of Sacerdotal Celibacy*, Lippincott 1867; *A History of the Inquisition of the Middle Ages*, Macmillan 1902.

Leach, A. F., *The Schools of Mediaeval England*. Macmillan 1915.

Legge, F., *Forerunners and Rivals of Christianity*. Cambridge University Press 1915.

Levine, L., *The Women's Garment Workers*. B. W. Huebsch 1924.

Lion, Hilda, *Zur Soziologie der Frauenbewegung*. Berlin 1926.

Livingstone, R. W., *The Mission of Greece; the Pageant of Greece*. Oxford University Press 1928.

Luzzatti, Luigi, *God in Freedom*. Macmillan 1930.

Macchioro, V., *From Orpheus to Paul*. H. Holt 1930.

Magre, M., *Messalina*. Louis Carrier 1931.

Mahaffy, J. P., *Greek Life and Thought*, Macmillan 1887; *Social Life in Greece*, 1877.

Maine, H., *Early Law and Custom*. London 1890.

Marrett, R. R. (editor), *Anthropology and the Classics*, Oxford Lectures by Arthur J. Evans, Andrew Lang, Gilbert Murray, F. B. Jevons, J. L. Myres, and W. Ward Fowler.

Marti, O. A., *Economic Causes of the Reformation in England*. Macmillan 1930.

Marvin, F. S., *Science and Civilisation*. London 1923.

Mason, O. T., *Woman's Share in Primitive Culture*, Appleton 1904; *The Influence of Environment upon Human Industries or Arts*, Smithsonian Institution, Washington, D. C. 1896; *The Birth of Invention*, Smithsonian 1893.

Maspero, G., *Life in Ancient Egypt and Assyria*, Appleton 1892; *Les chants d'amour du papyrus de Turin et du papyrus Harris*, in the Journal Asiatique I, 35.

McGee, W. J., *The Seri Indians*, in the Seventeenth Annual Report of the Bureau of Ethnology, Part I.

Meyer, J. J., *Sexual Life in Ancient India*. Dutton 1931.

Michlet, J., *Les Femmes de la Révolution*. Paris 1855.

Misciattelli, P., *The Mystics of Siena*. Appleton 1931.

Mommsen, T., *History of Rome*. London 1864.

Mozans, H. J., *Woman in Science*. Appleton 1913.

Muir, W., *The Life of Mahomet*. London 1858.

Mukerji, D. G., *The Face of Silence*. Dutton 1926.

Müller, F. M., *The History of Ancient Sanskrit Literatur(, Selected Essays* on language, mythology and religion, Longmans 1881. Other works.

Murray, G., *Aristophanes and the War Party,* London 1919; *Euripides and His Age*. Other works.

Mythology of all Races edited by L. H. Gray. 13 vols. Marshall Jones 1916.

Nash, R., *The Conquest of Brazil*. Harcourt, Brace 1926.

Neff, Wanda F., *Victorian Working Women*. London 1929.

Nevinson, Margaret, *Ancient Suffragettes*. London 1911.

Nutting, M. Adelaide, and Dock, Lavinia, *History of Nursing*. Putnam 1907.

O'Brien, G., *An Essay on Mediaeval Economic Teaching*. Longmans 1920.

Ornstein, M., *The Rôle of Scientific Societies in the Seventeenth Century*. University of Chicago Press 1928.

Osborn, H. F., *From the Greeks to Darwin*. Scribner 1929.

Ozanam, A. P., *Dante et le philosophie catholique du troisième siècle* (especially Part IV, Chapter II).

Palewski, J. P., *Histoire des Chefs d'Enterprise*. Paris 1928.

Park, Maud W., *Organised Women and their Legislative Progress*.

Parsons, Elsie C., *The Family*. Putnam 1906.

Paturet, G., *La condition juridique de la femme dans l'ancienne Egypte*. Paris 1886.

Peake, H., *The Origins of Agriculture*.

Perceval, A. P. C. de, *Essai sur l'histoire des Arabes avant l'Islamisme,* Vol. II.

Petrie, W. F., *Social Life in Ancient Egypt*. London 1923.

Playne, Caroline E., *Society at War*. Houghton, Mifflin 1931.

Plutarch, *Lives*.

Poestion, J. C., *Griechische Dichterinnen; Griechische Philosophinnen*.

Putnam, Emily J., *The Lady*. Putnam 1910.

Radin, P., *The Story of the American Indian,* Boni and Liveright 1927; *Primitive Man as Philosopher,* Appleton 1927.

Ragg, Laura, *The Women Artists of Bologna*. London 1907.

Ravenel, Florence L., *Women and the French Tradition*. Macmillan 1918.

Ravenel, Harriot H., *Eliza Pinckney,* Scribner 1896.

Reade, W., *The Martyrdom of Man*. The Truth Seeker Company, N. Y. 1887.

Reich, E., *Woman through the Ages*. London 1909.

Repplier, Agnes, *Mere Marie of the Ursulines*.

Rice, Clara C., *Persian Women and their Ways*. London 1923.

Richards, S. H., *Feminist Writers of the Seventeenth Century*. London 1914.

Rigault, R., *La querelle des anciens et des modernes en France.* Paris 1914.

Robinson, J. H., *The Mind in the Making.* Harper 1921.

Robinson, W. H., *Under Turquoise Skies.* Macmillan 1928.

Rodgers, W. C., *A Treatise on the Law of Domestic Relations.* Flood, Chicago 1899.

Rome, the Legacy of. Essays by C. Foligno, Ernest Barker, H. Stuart Jones, G. H. Stevenson, F. De Zulueta, H. Last, Cyril Bailey, Charles Singer, J. W. Mackail, Henry Bradley, G. McN. Rushforth, G. Giovannoni, and W. E. Heitland. Oxford University Press 1928.

Rome, The Mind of. Cyril Bailey (editor). Essays by Cyril Bailey, J. Bell, J. G. Barrington-Ward, T. F. Higham, A. N. Bryan-Brown, H. E. Butler, Maurice Platnauer, and Charles Singer. Oxford University Press 1928.

Rostovtzeff, M., *A History of the Ancient World.* Oxford University Press 1928.

Ruhle, O., *Karl Marx.* Viking Press 1929.

Salons, The Great Literary. Lectures delivered at the Musée Carnavalet. London 1930.

Sayce, A. H., *Lectures on the Origin and Growth of Religion.* Scribner 1887.

Schreiner, Olive, *Women and Labor.* Stokes 1911.

Shotwell, J. T., *An Introduction to the History of History.* Columbia University Press 1922.

Sichel, Edith, *The Renaissance.* Holt 1914.

Sihler, E. G., *From Augustus to Augustine.* Macmillan 1923.

Sismondi, J. C. L. de, *Histoire des Français,* Paris 1821; *History of the Fall of the Roman Empire,* Longmans 1834.

Spencer, Anna G., *Woman's Share in Social Culture.* Lippincott 1925.

Spengler, O., *The Decline of the West,* 2 vols. Knopf 1928.

Suttner, Berta von, *Die Waffen Nieder,* or *Ground Arms.* McClurg, Chicago 1906.

Takekoshi, Y., *Economic Aspects of the History of Civilisation of Japan.* Macmillan 1930.

Tallentyre, S. G. (pseud. for Evelyn Hall), *The Women of the Salons.* Putnam 1926.

Tarbell, Ida, *The Busines of Being a Woman.* Macmillan 1912.

Taylor, H. O., *The Classical Heritage of the Middle Ages,* Macmillan 1911; *Thought and Expression in the Sixteenth Century,* 1920.

Taylor, Rachel A., *Invitation to Renaissance Italy,* Harper 1930; *Aspects of the Italian Renaissance,* Houghton Mifflin 1923; *Leonardo the Florentine,* London 1927.

Thomson, J. A. K., *The Greek Tradition.* London 1915.

Thompson, J. W., *The Middle Ages, 300-1500.* Knopf 1931.

Thorold, A., *Six Masters in Disillusion.* London 1909.

Ticknor, F. W., *Women in English Economic History.* Dutton 1923.

Tinker, C. B., *The Salon and English Letters.* Macmillan 1915.

Trevelyan, E. J., *Hindu Family Law.* London 1908.

Van Buskirk, W. R., *The Saviors of Mankind.* Macmillan 1929.

Varney, Mecca M., *L'influence des femmes sur Auguste Comte.* Presse universitaire de France.

Vinogradov, P. G., *Custom and Right,* Oslo, 1925; *English Society in the Eleventh Century,* The Clarendon Press 1908. Other works.

Walsh, J. J., *The Century of Columbus.* Catholic Summer School Press, N. Y. 1914. Other works.

Walsh, W. T., *Isabella of Spain, the Last Crusader.* McBride 1930.

Ward, May, *The Influence of Women's Clubs.* Philadelphia 1906.

Warmington, E. H., *Commerce between the Roman Empire and India.* Cambridge University Press 1928.

Waterman, P. F., *The Story of Superstition.* Knopf 1929.

Weinberg, Margarete, *Die Hausfrau im der deutschen Vergangenheit und Gegenwart.* Berlin 1920.

Weinhold, K., *Altnordisches Leben.* Berlin 1856.

Wendland, P., *Die Hellenistische-Römische Kultur in ihren Beziehungen zu Judentum und Christentum.* Tübingen 1907.

Westermarck, E., *The Origin and Development of Moral Ideas.* Macmillan 1917.

Weston, J. L., *The Legend of Sir Perceval.* London 1906. Other works.

Wharton, A. H., *Salons Colonial and Republican.* Lippincott 1900.

White, A. D., *The Warfare of Science with Theology in Christendom.* 2 vols. Appleton 1896.

Wilkins, Louisa, *The Work of Educated Women in Horticulture and Agriculture.* London 1915.

Wilson, H. W., *Sacred Books of the East.*

Wingfield-Stratford, E., *The History of British Civilisation,* 2 vols. Harcourt, Brace 1928; *The Victorian Tragedy,* London 1930.

Winter, Alice A., *The Heritage of Women.* Minton, Balch 1927.

Wolseley, Frances G., *Women and the Land.* London 1916.

Woodward, Helen, *Through Many Windows.* Harper 1926.

Woody, T., *A History of Women's Education in the United States.* The Science Press 1931.

Wright, F. A., *Feminism in Greek Literature.* Dutton 1923.

Wright, T., *Womankind in Western Europe.* London 1869.

Young, E., *The Anglo-Saxon Family Law.* London 1876.

Zahm, J. A., *Great Inspirers.* Appleton 1917.

INDEX